Ontologies of English

In applied linguistics, being explicit about ontologies of English, and how they underpin educational ideologies and professional practices, is essential. For the first time, this volume presents a critical examination of the ways in which English is conceptualised for learning, teaching, and assessment, from both social and cognitive perspectives. Written by a team of leading scholars, it considers the language in a range of contexts and domains, including: models and targets for EFL, ESL, and EAL teaching and testing, and the contested dominance of native-speaker 'standard' varieties; English as a school subject, using England's educational system as an example; English as a lingua franca, where typically several languages and cultures are in contact; and English as broader social practice in a world characterised by unprecedented mobility and destabilisation. Readers are provided with a balanced set of perspectives on ontologies of English and a valuable resource for educational research and practice.

Christopher J. Hall is Professor of Applied Linguistics in the School of Languages and Linguistics at York St John University, UK. He is the author of *Morphology and Mind* (1992) and *An Introduction to Language and Linguistics* (2005), as well as co-author of *Introducing Language in Use* (2nd edition, 2014) and *Mapping Applied Linguistics: A Guide for Students and Practitioners* (2nd edition, 2017).

Rachel Wicaksono is an associate professor and head of the School of Languages and Linguistics at York St John University, UK. She is co-author of *Mapping Applied Linguistics: A Guide for Students and Practitioners* (2nd edition, 2017).

THE CAMBRIDGE APPLIED LINGUISTICS SERIES

The authority on cutting-edge Applied Linguistics research

Series Editors   2007–present: Carol A. Chapelle and Susan Hunston
1988–2007: Michael H. Long and Jack C. Richards

For a complete list of titles please visit: www.cambridge.org

Recent titles in this series:

Task-Based Language Teaching: Theory and Practice
Rod Ellis, Peter Skehan, Shaofeng Li, Natsuko Shintani *and* Craig Lambert

Ontologies of English: Conceptualising the Language for Learning, Teaching, and Assessment
Edited by Christopher J. Hall and Rachel Wicaksono

Feedback in Second Language Writing: Contexts and Issues
Edited by Ken Hyland and Fiona Hyland

Language and Television Series: A Linguistic Approach to TV Dialogue
Monika Bednarek

Intelligibility, Oral Communication, and the Teaching of Pronunciation
John M. Levis

Multilingual Education: Between Language Learning and Translanguaging
Edited by Jasone Cenoz and Durk Gorter

Learning Vocabulary in Another Language, 2nd Edition I. S. P. Nation

Narrative Research in Applied Linguistics
Edited by Gary Barkhuizen

Teacher Research in Language Teaching: A Critical Analysis
Simon Borg

Figurative Language, Genre and Register
Alice Deignan, Jeannette Littlemore and Elena Semino

Exploring ELF: Academic English Shaped by Non-native Speakers
Anna Mauranen

Genres across the Disciplines: Student Writing in Higher Education
Hilary Nesi and Sheena Gardner

Disciplinary Identities: Individuality and Community in Academic Discourse
Ken Hyland

Replication Research in Applied Linguistics
Edited by Graeme Porte

The Language of Business Meetings
Michael Handford

Reading in a Second Language: Moving from Theory to Practice
William Grabe

Modelling and Assessing Vocabulary Knowledge
Edited by Helmut Daller, James Milton and Jeanine Treffers-Daller

Practice in a Second Language: Perspectives from Applied Linguistics and Cognitive Psychology
Edited by Robert M. DeKeyser

Task-Based Language Education: From Theory to Practice
Edited by Kris van den Branden

Second Language Needs Analysis
Edited by Michael H. Long

Insights into Second Language Reading: A Cross-Linguistic Approach
Keiko Koda

Research Genres: Exploration and Applications
John M. Swales

Critical Pedagogies and Language Learning
Edited by Bonny Norton and Kelleen Toohey

Exploring the Dynamics of Second Language Writing
Edited by Barbara Kroll

Understanding Expertise in Teaching: Case Studies of Second Language Teachers
Amy B. M. Tsui

Criterion-Referenced Language Testing
James Dean Brown and Thom Hudson

Corpora in Applied Linguistics
Susan Hunston

Pragmatics in Language Teaching
Edited by Kenneth R. Rose and Gabriele Kasper

Cognition and Second Language Instruction
Edited by Peter Robinson

Research Perspectives on English for Academic Purposes
Edited by John Flowerdew and Matthew Peacock

Computer Applications in Second Language Acquisition: Foundations for Teaching, Testing and Research
Carol A. Chapelle

Ontologies of English
Conceptualising the Language for Learning, Teaching, and Assessment

Edited by

Christopher J. Hall
York St John University

Rachel Wicaksono
York St John University

CAMBRIDGE
UNIVERSITY PRESS

University Printing House, Cambridge CB2 8BS, United Kingdom

One Liberty Plaza, 20th Floor, New York, NY 10006, USA

477 Williamstown Road, Port Melbourne, VIC 3207, Australia

314-321, 3rd Floor, Plot 3, Splendor Forum, Jasola District Centre, New Delhi - 110025, India

103 Penang Road, #05-06/07, Visioncrest Commercial, Singapore 238467

Cambridge University Press is part of the University of Cambridge.

It furthers the University's mission by disseminating knowledge in the pursuit of education, learning and research at the highest international levels of excellence.

www.cambridge.org
Information on this title: www.cambridge.org/9781108710633
DOI: 10.1017/9781108685153

© Cambridge University Press 2020

This publication is in copyright. Subject to statutory exception and to the provisions of relevant collective licensing agreements, no reproduction of any part may take place without the written permission of Cambridge University Press.

First published 2020
First paperback edition 2022

A catalogue record for this publication is available from the British Library

Library of Congress Cataloging in Publication data
Names: Hall, Christopher J., 1961– editor. | Wicaksono, Rachel, editor.
Title: Ontologies of English : conceptualising the language for learning, teaching, and assessment / Christopher J. Hall, Rachel Wicaksono.
Description: 1. | New York : Cambridge University Press, 2019. | Series: Cambridge applied linguistics | Includes bibliographical references and index.
Identifiers: LCCN 2019037005 (print) | LCCN 2019037006 (ebook) | ISBN 9781108482530 (hardback) | ISBN 9781108710633 (paperback) | ISBN 9781108685153 (epub)
Subjects: LCSH: English language–Study and teaching. | Ontology.
Classification: LCC PE1066 .O58 2019 (print) | LCC PE1066 (ebook) | DDC 428.0071–dc23
LC record available at https://lccn.loc.gov/2019037005
LC ebook record available at https://lccn.loc.gov/2019037006

ISBN 978-1-108-48253-0 Hardback
ISBN 978-1-108-71063-3 Paperback

Cambridge University Press has no responsibility for the persistence or accuracy of URLs for external or third-party internet websites referred to in this publication, and does not guarantee that any content on such websites is, or will remain, accurate or appropriate.

For Juan (CJH)

For Rian and Clara (RW)

Contents

List of Figures	x
List of Tables	xi
List of Contributors	xii
Series Editors' Preface	xvii
Acknowledgements	xix
Transcription Conventions	xx

PART I INTRODUCTION — 1

1 *Approaching Ontologies of English* — 3
   Christopher J. Hall and Rachel Wicaksono

2 *An Ontological Framework for English* — 13
   Christopher J. Hall

PART II ENGLISH IN/FOR L2 LEARNING AND TEACHING — 37

3 *English in the Real World: Norms and the Ontology of English(es)* — 39
   Peter Harder

4 *From Constructions to Social Action: The Substance of English and Its Learning from an Interactional Usage-Based Perspective* — 59
   Søren Wind Eskildsen

5 *Native and Non-native Speakers of English in TESOL* — 80
   Rachel Wicaksono

PART III ENGLISH IN SCHOOLS — 99

6 *The Origins and Adaptations of English as a School Subject* — 101
   Andy Goodwyn

7	*A 'Godlike Science': English Teaching in Secondary Schools* Rachel Roberts	122
8	*Beliefs about 'Good English' in Schools* Clare Cunningham	142

PART IV ASSESSING ENGLISH   163

9	*English Varieties and Targets for L2 Assessment* Claudia Harsch	165
10	*The Role of the L1 in Testing L2 English* Fumiyo Nakatsuhara, Lynda Taylor, and Suwimol Jaiyote	187
11	*Mind the Gap: Dis/Continuities in the UK Assessment of L1 English Language* Angela Goddard	209

PART V ENGLISH IN LINGUA FRANCA CONTEXTS   231

12	*What Is English in the Light of Lingua Franca Usage?* Iris Schaller-Schwaner and Andy Kirkpatrick	233
13	*English as a Lingua Franca and Transcultural Communication: Rethinking Competences and Pedagogy for ELT* Will Baker	253
14	*Exploring Standards-Based, Intelligibility-Based, and Complex Conceptions of English in a Lingua Franca Context* Nathan Page	273

PART VI ENGLISH AND SOCIAL PRACTICE   293

15	*English as a Resource in a Communicative Assemblage: A Perspective from Flat Ontology* Suresh Canagarajah	295
16	*Mobile Learners and 'English as an Additional Language'* Robert Sharples	315
17	*Mobility and English Language Education: How Does Mobility in Study Abroad Settings Produce New Conceptualisations of English?* Khawla Badwan	335

PART VII	COMMENTARY AND CONCLUSIONS	353
18	*Pushing the Ontological Boundaries of English* Alastair Pennycook	355
19	*Using Ontologies of English* Rachel Wicaksono and Christopher J. Hall	368
	Index	377

Figures

2.1	An ontological framework for language	16
2.2	From L-ENGLISH to English as subject	30
7.1	A conceptualisation of SSE	137
9.1	CEFR-CV scale *Overall Phonological Control*	170
9.2	CEFR-CV scale *Sociolinguistic Appropriateness*	171
9.3	CEFR-CV scale *Acting as Intermediary*	175
10.1	Weir's socio-cognitive framework for validating speaking tests	189
11.1	An extract from the Reading Comprehension Test	216
11.2	Another extract from the Reading Comprehension Test	217
14.1	Three related binaries for depicting conceptualizations of English	276
15.1	Jihun's social networks	302

Tables

2.1	English as L-ENGLISH, instantiations of the LANGUAGE CAPACITY	21
2.2	English as linguistic manifestations of ENGLISHRY	22
4.1	"What do you say" by action and chronology	70
9.1	L2-reference in the CEFR-CV listening and interaction scales	170
10.1	Comparison of paired speaking-test scores between the shared and non-shared L1 pairs (N = 40)	195
10.2	Correlations between listening and speaking scores (N = 40)	195
10.3	Correlations between listening and paired speaking scores for shared and non-shared L1 pairs (N = 40)	197
10.4	Pronunciation descriptors in the *TEAP* holistic scale	200
10.5	Pronunciation features in two proficiency levels (%)	203
10.6	Rating category measurement report	203

Contributors

Khawla Badwan is a senior lecturer in TESOL and applied linguistics at Manchester Metropolitan University. Her research is on language and culture in contexts of mobility and contact. She writes about scalar approaches to language, learners' perceptions of language, international students in UK higher education, multilingualism and identity, and language in a globalised world.

Will Baker is an associate professor of applied linguistics and deputy director of the Centre for Global Englishes, University of Southampton, where he supervises doctoral students and convenes the MA programme in Global Englishes. His research interests include English as a lingua franca, intercultural and transcultural communication and education, English medium instruction, and ELT. Recent publications are as co-editor of the *Routledge Handbook of English as a Lingua Franca* (2018), author of the monograph *Culture and Identity through English as a Lingua Franca* (2015), and co-editor of the book series Developments in English as Lingua Franca.

Suresh Canagarajah is Edwin Erle Sparks Professor and Director of the Migration Studies Project at Pennsylvania State University. He teaches World Englishes, Second Language Writing, and Postcolonial Studies in the departments of English and Applied Linguistics. He taught earlier in the University of Jaffna, Sri Lanka, and the City University of New York. His most recent publication is *Translingual Practice: Global Englishes and Cosmopolitan Relations* (2013), which won the best book award from AAAL, BAAL, and MLA. He was formerly the editor of *TESOL Quarterly* and president of the American Association of Applied Linguistics.

Clare Cunningham is a senior lecturer in English language and linguistics at York St John University, where she teaches on modules related to multilingualism and language attitudes. Her current research interests are principally related to exploring and understanding mainstream teachers' attitudes, beliefs, and knowledge about multilingualism, including working on an international collaborative project with the AILA Research Network *Social and Affective Factors in Home Language Maintenance*. She has published papers in the *ELT Journal, Power and Education,* and *Education 3-13.* She is also currently working on pedagogical research concerning the benefits of structured writing retreats for undergraduate students.

Søren Wind Eskildsen is an associate professor in second language learning at the University of Southern Denmark in Sønderborg. His primary research interest concerns the usage-based processes and practices in second language learning over time as seen through the lenses of usage-based models of language and conversation analysis. Other interests include the role of gestures and other embodied conduct in L2 learning. He works with second language data in English, Danish, and Icelandic and from a variety of contexts in educational environments and 'in the wild'.

Angela Goddard is Professor of English Language and a UK Higher Education Academy National Teaching Fellow. She has taught English in schools and universities both in the United Kingdom and abroad. Professor Goddard is Chair of Examiners for English Language A Level at a major UK exam board; she also chairs an international equivalent. She has written many books and articles on language, particularly with an interdisciplinary focus. Her most recent publication is *Discourse: The Basics* (2017).

Andy Goodwyn is Professor and Head of the School of Education and English Language at the University of Bedfordshire, UK. He is also a professor emeritus at the University of Reading, UK, and the president of the International Federation for the Teaching of English. His most recent books are *Expert Teaching: An International Perspective* (2016) and *International Perspectives on the Teaching of Literature in Schools: Global Principles and Practices* (2017). He taught English in secondary schools for ten years, including one year in the United States.

Christopher J. Hall is Professor of Applied Linguistics in the School of Languages and Linguistics at York St John University, UK. He is the author of *Morphology and Mind* (1992) and *An Introduction to Language and Linguistics* (2005), as well as co-author of *Introducing Language and Use* (2nd edition, 2014) and *Mapping Applied Linguistics: A Guide for Students and Practitioners* (2nd edition, 2017).

Peter Harder is Professor of English Linguistics at the University of Copenhagen. His major publications include *Functional Semantics* (1996) and *Meaning in Mind and Society* (2010). His research revolves around relations between language, mind, and social practice, and one of his key interests is the contested role of norms in language and linguistics, e.g. the article 'Variation, Structure and Norms'

(*Review of Cognitive Linguistics*, 2012). He has also written on grammaticalization, e.g. 'A Functional Theory of Grammatical Status and Grammaticalization' (*Language*, 2012).

Claudia Harsch is a professor at the University of Bremen, specialising in language learning, teaching, and assessment. She has worked in Germany and in the United Kingdom, and is active in teacher training worldwide. Her interests focus on language assessment, educational measurement, intercultural communication, research methods, and the implementation of the Common European Framework of Reference (CEFR). She explores aspects like aligning rating scales and tests to the CEFR, using mixed-methods approaches to construct valid language tests and teaching materials, or examining the predictive validity of language tests. Claudia is the current president of the European Association of Language Testing and Assessment.

Suwimol Jaiyote is a lecturer in the Department of English at Naresuan University, Thailand. She holds a PhD in language testing from the University of Bedfordshire, UK. Suwimol's research interests lie in language learning and assessment, and her PhD dissertation was on the relationship between test-takers' L1, listening proficiency, and their performance on a paired speaking test. She received an assessment research award from the British Council in 2014.

Andy Kirkpatrick is Professor in Linguistics in the Department of Humanities, Languages and Social Sciences at Griffith University and Fellow of the Australian Academy of the Humanities. His research interests include the development of new varieties of English and the roles of English as a lingua franca in Asia, language education policy in Asia, and Chinese rhetoric. He has authored some 150 publications. He is currently co-editing two new handbooks namely, *Asian Englishes* (with Kingsley Bolton as co-editor) and *Language Education Policy in Asia* (with Tony Liddicoat as co-editor).

Fumiyo Nakatsuhara is Reader in Language Assessment at CRELLA (Centre for Research in English Language Learning and Assessment), University of Bedfordshire, UK. Her research interests include the nature of co-constructed interaction in various speaking test formats (e.g. interview, paired and group formats), task design, and rating scale development. Her recent publications include the book *The Discourse of the IELTS Speaking Test* (co-authored with P. Seedhouse, Cambridge University Press, 2018) and articles in *Language Testing* (2014) and *Language Assessment Quarterly* (2017). She has carried out a number of international testing projects, working with ministries, universities, and examination boards.

Nathan Page is an educational adviser in the Programme Design and Learning Technology team at the University of York. He previously worked as an English teacher in Japan and as a lecturer in applied linguistics at Aston University, either side of a PhD in Applied Linguistics at York St John University. His key research interest is global diversity in English and its implications for language pedagogy. This interest developed through his substantive teaching role in Japan, which involved training Japanese volunteers as they prepared to work in various Anglophone developing countries.

Alastair Pennycook is Distinguished Professor of Language, Society and Education at the University of Technology Sydney and Adjunct Professor at the MultiLing Centre at the University of Oslo. He is the author of numerous books, four of which have won the BAAL Book Prize: *The Cultural Politics of English as an International Language*, *Global Englishes and Transcultural Flows*, *Language and Mobility: Unexpected Places*, and *Posthumanist Applied Linguistics*.

Rachel Roberts taught English, Media and Film Studies for ten years in secondary schools. She was Lead English Teacher for a local educational authority and has led numerous training courses on English teaching and written a number of study guides. She is currently Lecturer in Secondary English Education, as subject lead for the English PGCE, at the Institute of Education, University of Reading. Her research interests include the use of evaluative language in educational discourse, mentoring, and the teaching of writing.

Iris Schaller-Schwaner is a lecturer in English as a Foreign Language at the University of Fribourg/Freiburg in Switzerland and Head of English at its Language Centre. Her PhD looked at the development of English as a lingua franca in a multilingual university. Her research has focused on ELF in multilingual contexts. Her recent publications include 'ELF as Multilingual "Edulect" in a Bilingual University' (*Journal of English as a Lingua Franca*, 2018) and 'The Habitat Factor in ELF(A) – English as a Lingua Franca (in Academic Settings) – and English for Plurilingual Academic Purposes' (*Language Learning in Higher Education*, 2015).

Robert Sharples is a lecturer in language and education at the University of Bristol. His research focuses on migration, language, and education, with a particular focus on English as an Additional Language. His most recent project investigated the transition programme offered to young migrants in a South London secondary school, using a linguistic ethnographic approach to examine micro-scale classroom interactions in the context of the young people's broader migration trajectories and policy framings of the pupils and school.

Lynda Taylor is Visiting Professor in Language Assessment at CRELLA (Centre for Research in English Language Learning and Assessment), University of Bedfordshire, UK. Her research interests include issues in speaking assessment, the use of qualitative research methodology and ethical issues, such as assessment literacy and testing accommodations. She has provided expert assistance for language test design, development, and revision projects in the United Kingdom and overseas. Key publications include edited volumes *Examining Speaking* (2011) and *Examining Listening* (2013) as well as contributions to peer-reviewed handbooks and journals, e.g. *Handbook of Second Language Assessment* (2016) and *Language Assessment Quarterly* (2018).

Rachel Wicaksono is an associate professor and head of the School of Languages and Linguistics at York St John University, UK. She is co-author of *Mapping Applied Linguistics: A Guide for Students and Practitioners* (2nd edition, 2017). She has taught English, trained teachers, and managed schools in many countries, including a fifteen-year period in Indonesia, and is a Higher Education Academy National Teaching Fellow.

Series Editors' Preface

Almost all applied linguists have some relationship to the English language. For many it is both the object of their research and the medium of expression for their scholarship. It is a global tool for participation in academic communities. But it is also taught as a school subject. For some learners it is a tool for survival or a vehicle for mobility; others have significant personal interest in perfecting their ability to communicate in English and their knowledge of the English-speaking world. It is tested and assessed to inform teaching, to control entry into the increasing numbers of English medium systems of higher education, as part of certification for employment, and as a qualification for immigration in some countries. It is analysed as idealised mental or neurolinguistic systems; as collections of empirical data containing constructions, patterns, or linguistic structures; as instances of a functional meaning-making system; and as a tool for social interaction, an engine for the global political economy, and an instrument of hegemony.

How can a single entity, the English language, have so many meanings? This is the question that Christopher J. Hall and Rachel Wicaksono address in this collection entitled *Ontologies of English: Conceptualising the Language for Learning, Teaching, and Assessment*. They approach the meanings of English by examining, as the title indicates, ontology. Ontology is the metaphysical study of the nature of existence through the use of categories and their relations. The study of ontology is inevitably tied to language because the units of language express categories and syntax expresses relations. For example, the plural morpheme in 'Englishes' signals an ontological question: Is English one or many? This is one of the questions about English(es) tackled in this volume. The book contains chapters exploring ontologies that underpin the normal activities of applied linguists: learning and teaching English as a second language, teaching English as a school subject, assessing English language ability, studying the use of English in lingua franca contexts, and investigating English as a social practice.

With applied linguists so gainfully employed in their respective activities, does recognition of underlying ontologies really matter? Through the many pages of this volume, the contributors help to demonstrate that it does indeed matter. Hall and Wicaksono argue that implicit assumptions about what English is affect ideological positions, and these in turn affect educational and social policy decisions. Insofar as applied linguists' various ontologies of English remain concealed, they are blind to the possibilities for transformative practices in their own teaching, teacher education, assessment, and language analysis. Readers will find that what may at first appear to be an obscure philosophical topic is revealed to be a foundational issue in the field. With this volume, Hall and Wicaksono open a discussion about the elephant in the room for all applied linguists who have a relationship to 'English'. We welcome it to the Cambridge Series in Applied Linguistics.

Acknowledgements

This volume has its roots in a seminar held at York St John University in 2015. We are grateful to the British Association for Applied Linguistics and Cambridge University Press for helping to fund that event, and to the delegates who attended for their stimulating ideas and diverse perspectives. We also thank our students for their feedback on our ontological musings and our colleagues for their intellectual and practical support while we oversaw this project. Special thanks to Clara Jean Wicaksono for her help with the index to this book.

Transcription Conventions

?	Rising intonation on previous syllable
.	Falling intonation on previous syllable
=	Latching
.hh	In–breath
hh	Hearable aspiration (e.g. exhale, laughter token). The more 'h's, the longer the aspiration.
[	Top begin overlap
]	Top end overlap (when relevant)
[	Bottom begin overlap
]	Bottom end overlap (when relevant)
£word£	Marked voice
wo-	Cut-off
:(:::)	Stretching of previous sound (the more colons, the longer the stretching)
(0.2)	Length of pauses in seconds
(.)	Micropause (less than 0.2 sec)
( )	Unintelligible talk
(word)	Uncertain transcription
((*word*))	Transcriber's comments

Part I
Introduction

1 Approaching Ontologies of English

Christopher J. Hall and Rachel Wicaksono

1 Introduction

This book is about the ways in which English is conceptualised in and for the domains of language learning, teaching, and assessment. Examining and being explicit about what we, as applied linguists, think English is – our *ontologies of English* – and how these ontologies underpin our educational ideologies and professional practices, should be an essential component of research in the discipline. Yet the nature of the 'EL' in ELT does not feature anywhere nearly as much as the 'T', and how English is conceptualised in schools tends to be debated more by educationalists than applied linguists. Teachers, learners, policy makers, and other stakeholders do have strong beliefs about what counts as English, who it belongs to, and how it should be taught, learned, and tested. In research we conducted with colleagues at a university in China (Hall et al., 2017), English teachers told us about the ways they conceptualised English as a global language and, more narrowly, as the subject they taught to undergraduate students. This is what one teacher said about the idea that English exists in a 'standardised' form (translated here from the original Mandarin):

Ms F: I believe in the existence of Standard English, perhaps it's some idealistic existence ... Maybe it doesn't really exist in reality. When we speak, the language is never standard ... Even native speakers can't speak Standard English – the idealistic, perfect, Standard English.

The teacher makes an explicit affirmation of her ontological commitment to a conceptualisation of English as an abstract entity. But she also subscribes to the existence of 'the language' in non-standard form, as used by native (and presumably non-native) speakers. Ontological commitments such as these are rarely examined inside or outside academia, yet the inconsistencies they often involve can have profound implications. (The obvious but far from trivial one here being: if

'Standard English' only exists as an ideal, which not even native speakers can know and use, then why teach and test it as 'the language' in both L1 and L2 classrooms?)

We contend that the applied linguistic study of ontologies of English is necessary for two main reasons. First, it can help advance mutual understanding in both academic and professional domains. Leaving our conceptualisations unexamined and unacknowledged creates the potential for flawed reasoning, missed opportunities to recognise (in)compatibilities between different positions, and the perpetuation of ill-considered recommendations for policy and practice. Second, it can lead to better informed educational policy and practice, potentially leading to broader social change. Helping teachers (and ultimately students and other stakeholders) to critically examine the ontological commitments underpinning their own ideologies and practices will enable them to more clearly define relevant learning goals. It will also inform efforts to expose and contest the social injustices currently faced by many English students, learners, and users.

The book has been written primarily for scholars in applied linguistics and education, although from the outset we have asked contributors to try to make it as accessible as possible to external stakeholders. We are not assuming that all readers will be aware of the issues raised or familiar with the constructs discussed, and far less that they will be well versed in the arcane ontological debates of philosophers. But inevitably the topic invites degrees of abstraction and theorisation which necessarily require technical terms (indeed, one of the editors is guilty of inventing several new ones). This chapter is intended to help readers from diverse backgrounds understand what the book is about and how to approach the chapters which follow. Section 2 situates this volume within broader ontological work outside and inside applied (and general) linguistics. Section 3 provides an overview of the individual chapters and the domains they address.

2 What Do We Mean by 'Ontologies of English'?

Ontology is the metaphysical study of the nature of existence, addressing the superficially simple question of "What *is* there?" (Quine, 1980/1953, p. 1; our emphasis). It is concerned with (disputing) what kinds of things (entities, processes, properties, etc.) can be said to exist, what material or immaterial categories they belong to, whether they exist independently of human minds (and language), and the relationships between them (whether, for example, they are part of, instantiate, cause, or emerge from, other things). Since Quine (1980/1953), philosophers have also been interested in what ontological 'commitments' are articulated or presupposed by different theories and belief systems – i.e. what they assume, assert, or reject the existence of. Language has played a central role in ontological investigation, not so much with respect to its own status (although this does of course figure in the literature: cf., for example, Smith, 1987), but because ontological analysis inevitably involves issues of semantics and naming, and more specifically also because language is the principal medium through which immaterial entities (including named languages) are socially constructed. Indeed, in Searle's (1995) model of social ontology, all social institutions owe their existence to linguistic representation and expression.

Within contemporary linguistics, the ontological status of language and languages tends to be taken for granted, although there is extensive discussion of the issue in several key works of the late twentieth century (e.g. Harris, 1981; Katz, 1981; Chomsky, 1986; cf. Seargeant, 2010 for discussion of language ontology from a critical, historical perspective). Regarding English, linguists and applied linguists from very different orientations have expressly denied its existence, or questioned its ontological status. The generativists Isac and Reiss (2008, p. 15), for example, state: 'If we take the mentalistic approach seriously, then we have to admit that there is no entity in the world that we can characterize as "English"'. From the diametrically opposed perspective of critical applied linguistics, Pennycook (2007, p. 94), in a chapter entitled 'The Myth of English as an International Language', asserts that 'languages are political rather than ontological categories'. The ontological status of English has become more prominent in applied linguistics as the effects of globalisation have drawn TESOL scholars to the World Englishes literature and the conceptual pluralisation this affords (cf. Kachru, 1992). More recently, research on English as an International Language (EIL; cf. Sharifian, 2009) and English as a Lingua Franca (ELF; cf. Seidlhofer, 2011) has prompted a shift in emphasis away from conceptualising English in terms of (non-native) varieties, and towards a view of the language as constitutive of (multilingual) practice.

Inevitably, ontological issues spill over into questions of *epistemology* (concerned with the status of knowledge, its sources, and validity) and *ideology* (the sets of beliefs and behaviours which develop in individuals through socialisation into different cultural groups – the result of different epistemic traditions and dispositions). Different epistemologies lead to different ontological commitments, and different ontological commitments underpin different ideologies. Take, for example, the nature and status of what is known as 'Standard

English', a concept thoroughly interrogated in this volume. Its ontological existence is presupposed by most citizens of the so-called Anglophone countries (and by teachers like Ms F) not because they have direct sensory data which attest to it but because it is asserted in the national discourses of education, government, and the media. Knowledge of 'Standard English' is thus validated by an epistemology based on authority rather than evidence. And the ontological commitment to the existence of 'Standard English' is accompanied by the attribution of value to it, thus constituting an ideology in which it is accorded a superior status to other forms of English and a privileged place in broader ideologies of national identity. The relationship is, of course, not unidirectional: the ideology and the epistemological tradition it is associated with also contribute to (arguably *cause*) the ontological commitment to its existence.

Likewise, ideological beliefs based on different epistemological practices can *become* ontologies. Van Dijk (2013, 177) writes: "As soon as ideological beliefs are accepted and taken for granted by all members of a community, by definition they are no longer ideologies but will count as knowledge *in that community*". The stakeholder communities we are concerned with here (linguists, applied linguists, learners and users, teachers, testers, policy makers, politicians, etc.) have beliefs about English which they take as facts, although these facts are not always consistent with each other, and context often dictates which fact will be invoked when. This leads inevitably to the realisation that ontologies are as relative and diverse as ideologies and epistemologies, at least in the case of mental/social entities like languages. Accordingly, then, the title of this volume refers to *ontologies of English* in the plural.

In a related sense, the word *ontology* is used as a count noun to refer to taxonomies of entities which are designated as existing in a particular domain or for a particular purpose, often organised hierarchically. In artificial intelligence, for example, ontologies specify what entities are symbolically represented in information systems and how they are related (for example, in the Semantic Web; cf. Horrocks, 2008). The goal is to achieve maximal explicitness and also standardisation, so as to enable interoperability. In linguistics, in a new specialisation called *ontolinguistics*, there are similar efforts to standardise the set of concepts used in language description (Farrar, 2007). Our project is different. It is not the goal of this volume to agree (or seek agreement) on the ontological status or statuses of English, but rather to help make existing conceptualisations visible, exposing their commonalities and differences, destabilising some of them, and inviting readers to conceptualise anew.

In the sense entertained here, then, ontologies are cultural, susceptible to anthropological investigation. Indeed, there has been debate in anthropology recently about whether cultural differences are intrinsically ontological differences: the so-called ontological turn (cf. Heywood, 2017). In a live debate on the motion 'Ontology is just another word for culture' held at the University of Manchester in 2008 (Carrithers et al., 2010), Martin Holbraad argued that "[t]he anthropological task ... is not to account for why ethnographic data are as they are, but rather to understand *what* they are – instead of explanation or interpretation, what is called for is conceptualization" (Carrithers et al., 2010, 184). Accordingly, the reference in this volume's subtitle to 'conceptualising the language' is both a description of what the chapters are trying to do, and also an invitation to readers.

The idea for this book arose from a BAAL/CUP Seminar held in 2015 at York St John University. One of the outcomes of that meeting was a call to "take a more activist stance to challenge dominant monolithic conceptualisations of English, chiefly by promoting awareness of users' actual knowledge and practices and the alternative ontologies that these imply" (Hall, 2017, p. 137). Lawson (2014, p. 22) states that the value of ontology "lies in bringing clarity and directionality, thereby facilitating action that is appropriate to context". The contexts of applied linguistics are diverse and uncountable, so the actions, like the conceptualisations, must be ongoing and permanent. If we think we can ever finish the ontological project, then we have not understood.

3 How Is the Book Organised?

Following this introductory chapter and completing Part I, **Hall** proposes a framework which situates what we call English within two separate ontological categories: as a subset of the social and cognitive resources, processes, and products which instantiate the broader human language capacity and as a series of reflexes of English national identity. His analysis pays particular attention to conceptualisations of the language as 'Standard English' and shows how this has had deleterious impacts which persist in both linguistics and educational practice. The main body of the book is divided into five main parts. These move from conceptualisations of English as a jointly social and cognitive phenomenon in and for L2 learning and teaching in Part II to those which situate it as part of social practice in lingua franca settings and 'super-diverse' contexts in Parts V and VI. The central chapters, in Parts III and IV, examine the status and role of English in educational settings, as a school subject and medium, and as an object for L1 and L2 testing.

The chapters in Part II are united in conceptualising English in/for L2 learning and teaching as both cognitive and social in nature. **Harder** defines English in terms of the 'operational norms' which hold in social structures and to which community members' cognitive resources optimally adapt. He argues that 'Global English', as the union of all the existing operational norms, cannot constitute a learning goal, and that the 'practical reality' of 'Standard English' may make it the only viable learning target at a collective level. While Harder is ultimately concerned with the implications of ontologies of English for *teaching*, **Eskildsen** focuses on what is actually *learned*, and how it is learned. He conceptualises English as inventories of constructions which underpin individual (cognitive) repertoires of resources for social action. He demonstrates how a combination of usage-based linguistics and conversation analysis can trace learners' development of English constructions through socially situated, co-ordinated interaction, illustrated with data extracts from two classroom learners. In her chapter, **Wicaksono** reviews the social and cognitive arguments that have been advanced to categorise users of English as either 'native' or 'non-native' (primarily place and age). She points out that 'what counts as English' is taken as a given, in both the scholarly literature and in TESOL professional practice, and argues that the 'native'/'non-native' distinction is untenable once the monolithic conceptualisations underpinning it are exposed. Her chapter is also a call to action, suggesting ways in which raising ontological awareness can be embedded in teacher training and hiring practices.

The chapters in Part III consider the ontological status of English as it is understood in schools. In a review of the ways in which school subject English (SSE) has evolved over the past 150 years or so in England, **Goodwyn** highlights the tensions between state conceptualisations, in which English (predominantly English literature) is an aspect of cultural heritage existing primarily in the textual domain, and the conviction of teachers that English should constitute a resource for individual student growth. Goodwyn identifies the practical reality of teaching as a third ontological plane, where both conceptualisations of SSE are tempered by increasing external control and consequent self-regulation. In the following chapter, **Roberts** picks up the baton from Goodwyn to provide a critical analysis of the conceptualisation of English underpinning England's national curriculum for SSE. She interprets the ontological status of English in the curriculum as knowledge (which students must *have*), contrasting this with English as learning (which students can *do*). She argues for a conceptualisation of SSE closer to the 'god-like science' of Frankenstein's creature, characterised by interpretation, creation, and emotion. **Cunningham's** chapter extends the ontological critique of educational conceptualisations of English beyond the literary focus of SSE to the broader notion of 'good English' in schools, as held by teachers of all subjects. She calls attention to the way in which ontologies of English which privilege the 'standard variety' marginalise both pupils with unstandardised Englishes and those with languages beyond English ('EAL' students), with the former (conceived as 'users') often constructed more negatively than the latter (conceived as 'learners').

Part IV addresses how English is (or should be) conceptualised for assessment. **Harsch's** chapter departs from the key recognition that learning targets tend to be based on norms which differ from those governing most international communication in English. Like Harder, she adopts a pragmatic stance with respect to the value of 'Standard English' for some learning contexts and needs, advocating the revised scales of the Common European Framework (CEFR) as a basis for developing appropriate tasks and goals, and the use of corpora and discourse analysis to identify what to assess. **Nakatsuhara, Taylor,** and **Jaiyote** are concerned with the effects on test validity of the porous nature of English as a testable object. They present data from studies of the role of L1 influence in an international test of general English and a national EAP test to demonstrate how conceptualisations of English in/for global and local contexts can or should be relevant to test-taker needs and, once again, argue for a pragmatic approach. **Goddard**'s chapter takes a more critical perspective on English assessment, returning to issues raised in Part III to examine how the SSE curriculum (in England) is being increasingly dominated by a culture of testing which conceptualises English as either a decontextualised linguistic system or as a set of texts which reflect national cultural heritage. Goddard shows how politically driven reforms have led to pupils encountering ontologies of English which lack consistency and relevance for their future needs.

The contributors to Part V examine how global lingua franca usage has led to reconceptualisations of English which present new challenges for educational contexts. The first chapter, by **Schaller-Schwaner** and **Kirkpatrick**, conceptualises English as a lingua franca (ELF) as an aspect of multilingual practice, in which speakers make linguistic choices contingent on a series of contextual factors. This contingency is illustrated in two contrasting multilingual settings, one where English became the lingua franca by official mandate and the other where it emerged 'bottom-up' in opposition to official policy.

Baker's chapter reaffirms the multilingual nature of lingua franca English but argues that more attention should be paid to its multicultural dimension, especially in global ELT. He argues that communicative competence in ELF usage not only blurs the differences between named languages, but also constitutes 'transcultural' practice which, equally, 'transgresses and transcends' pre-assumed cultural boundaries. In the following chapter, **Page** presents data from Japanese volunteers working in international development projects which shed light on the complex ontologies of English that can be inferred from their learning/use of the language for/in global lingua franca contexts. He observes how contextual factors can cause their conceptualisations of English to move along a 'standards-based' to 'intelligibility based' continuum, and advocates that teachers need to be aware of, and be able to respond to, this ontological incongruity.

The final set of contributions in Part VI all pursue the view, anticipated in several previous chapters, that English for learning and teaching is now most usefully conceptualised as social practice. **Canagarajah** looks outside linguistics and applied linguistics for a conceptualisation of language in communication informed by 'flat ontology', a 'new materialist' orientation which stresses the emergence of meaning and structure from collaborative, distributed social practices. Using processual and spatial metaphors (the functional assemblage of *bricolage*; the non-linear, decentring networks of *rhizomes*), he sets out an approach in which English is an ideology, thus undermining traditional pedagogical preoccupations with 'representational' competence. Consistent with Canagarajah's charge, **Sharples** argues that the dominant ('settled') ontologies of English contribute to educational policy and pedagogical practice which are effectively failing the growing populations of young migrants ('EAL students') in the global North. He calls instead for a 'mobile orientation' in which course structures and curricula become more flexible, and classrooms become places where individual trajectories intersect and prior experiences are valued, so that pupils can work towards mainstream discourse norms without being marginalised and having their own linguistic repertoires delegitimised. In her chapter, **Badwan** shows how the 'standard ontology' of monolithic English serves the commercial interests of the publishing houses (who purvey it in textbooks, tests, and access to global academic content), but does a disservice to mobile students in study abroad contexts (who encounter a sociolinguistic reality for which the myths they have been sold ill prepare them). She advocates a more honest pedagogy involving 'conscious learning' to expose the myths and allow learners to adopt appropriate English resources into their communicative repertoires.

Finally, in Part VII, **Pennycook** provides critical commentary on the issues raised in the volume. He highlights the fact that most chapters seek to understand prevailing conceptualisations of English and to advocate a 'plurilithic' stance in the different domains they address. A more radical step, he suggests, is to question the ontological status of language itself and therefore of English, which he casts as a 'second-order' curricular, cultural, and political convenience. In the last chapter, **Wicaksono** and **Hall** take stock and consider the uses of the project.

References

Carrithers, M., Candea, M., Sykes, K., Holbraad, M., and Venkatesan, S. (2010). Ontology is just another word for culture: Motion tabled at the 2008 meeting of the Group for Debates in Anthropological Theory, University of Manchester. *Critique of Anthropology*, *30*(2), 152–200.

Chomsky, N. (1986). *Knowledge of Language*. New York: Praeger.

Farrar, S. (2007). Using 'Ontolinguistics' for language description. In A. C. Schalley and D. Zaefferer, eds. *Ontolinguistics: How Ontological Status Shapes the Linguistic Coding of Concepts* (pp. 175–191). Berlin: Walter de Gruyter.

Hall, C. J. (2017). BAAL/CUP Seminar 2015. (De)Constructing Englishes: Exploring the implications of ontologies of the language for learning, teaching and assessment. *Language Teaching*, *50*(1), 135–137.

Hall, C. J., Wicaksono, R., Liu, S., Qian, Y., and Xu, X. (2017). Exploring teachers' ontologies of English. Monolithic conceptions of grammar in a group of Chinese teachers. *International Journal of Applied Linguistics*, *27*(1), 87–109.

Harris, R. (1981). *The Language Myth*. London: Duckworth.

Heywood, P. (2017). The ontological turn. In F. Stein, S. Lazar, M. Candea et al., eds. *The Cambridge Encyclopedia of Anthropology*. http://doi.org/10.29164/17ontology

Horrocks, I. (2008). Ontologies and the semantic web. *Communications of the ACM*, *51*(12), 58–67.

Isac, D. and Reiss, C. (2008). *I-Language. An Introduction to Linguistics as Cognitive Science*. Oxford: Oxford University Press.

Kachru, B. B., ed. (1992) *The Other Tongue. English across Cultures*, 2nd ed. Urbana: University of Illinois Press.

Katz, J. (1981). *Language and Other Abstract Objects*. Totowa, NJ: Rowman and Littlefield.

Lawson, T. (2014). A conception of social ontology. In S. Pratten, ed. *Social Ontology and Modern Economics* (pp. 19–52). London: Routledge.

Pennycook, A. (2007). The myth of English as an International Language. In S. Makoni and A. Pennycook, eds. *Disinventing and Reconstituting Languages* (pp. 90–115). Clevedon: Multilingual Matters.

Quine, W. (1980/1953). *From a Logical Point of View*, 2nd ed. Cambridge, MA: Harvard University Press.
Seargeant, P. (2010). The historical ontology of language. *Language Sciences*, 32 (1), 1–13.
Searle, J. R. (1995). *The Construction of Social Reality*. New York: Simon and Schuster.
Seidlhofer, B. (2011). *Understanding English as a Lingua Franca*. Oxford: Oxford University Press.
Sharifian, F., ed. (2009). *English as an International Language. Perspectives and Pedagogical Issues*. Bristol: Multilingual Matters.
Smith, B. (1987). Husserl, language and the ontology of the act. In D. Buzzetti and M. Ferriani, eds. *Speculative Grammar, Universal Grammar, and Philosophical Analysis of Language* (pp. 205–227). Amsterdam: John Benjamins.
Van Dijk, T. A. (2013). Ideology and discourse. In M. Freeden, L. Tower Sargent and M. Stears, eds. *The Oxford Handbook of Political Ideologies* (pp. 175–196). Oxford: Oxford University Press.

2 An Ontological Framework for English

Christopher J. Hall

1 Introduction

What is there in the world that we refer to as 'the English language'? Is it more than one thing? If so, how many? And what is their ontological status? For those of us engaged in researching and teaching what we call English, these are fundamental questions, yet they are seldom posed. In addressing them explicitly here, I aim to provide academics, teachers, and policy makers with some conceptual tools and arguments for a deeper reflection on the nature of English, with a view to ultimately benefiting learners and users.

In this chapter, I propose that 'English' corresponds to a series of ontological categories and types, pertaining to different but related (sometimes coordinated) entities, which are significant for language learning, teaching, and assessment in different ways and to different degrees. I don't claim that the framework is exhaustive or the only one possible; instead, I adopt the non-essentialist position that conceptualizations of things are useful only in certain contexts and for certain purposes (Janicki, 2006). Furthermore, my approach is that of an applied linguist, not a philosopher of language, and accordingly I draw only sporadically and superficially on the extensive philosophical body of work on the topic (cf. Santana, 2016, for a recent example). I am interested in how English is conceived by linguists, language educators, and laypeople, not by metaphysicians. So although I appropriate ideas and terminology from this scholarship, I have in mind the 'ordinary understandings' of English that underpin the research agendas, educational practices, and public discourses associated with English learning, teaching, assessment, and use. Although my proposals are theory engaged, they are not here theory committed. Several of the conceptualizations of English I address derive from or are consistent with (often competing) orientations in twentieth and twenty-first century linguistics and applied linguistics, but it is not my intention to advocate one over another, even though I am sometimes critical in my assessment of their claims.

My point of departure is the polysemy of the word *English*. The noun refers to both the people of England ('the English') and a language that was originally used only by these people, but is now used by many more ('English' and 'Englishes'). It is a nominalization of the adjective *English*, derived from *England*, 'the land of the Angles'. Taking this polysemy as the key premise, I will be claiming that *English*, when used in relation to language, labels types of entities associated with two ontological categories, both of which are social institutions (Searle, 1995). One set of types sits within the ontological category of the 'LANGUAGE CAPACITY', the species property for linguistic representation and communication. Within this ontological category (henceforth indicated in SMALL CAPITALS), English is a set of instantiations of the broader capacity. Understood thus, English is something we need not be aware of: it is a set of cognitive and social resources, processes, and products that would exist even if we had no name for it, and that in practice mixes freely in multilingual users with other linguistic (and non-linguistic) resources, processes, and products in the construction and communication of meaning.

The second set of ontological types is socially constructed on the basis of the contemplation of the first set and corresponds to the conceptualizations underpinning value-laden ideologies of English (cf. Sharpe, 1974; Canagarajah, this volume, Section 4). I contend that the construals of English in this set are all directly or indirectly derived from the process of collective identification (Jenkins, 2004) holding at the level of NATION. Very recently in the evolution of the species, consciousness of particular instantiations of the LANGUAGE CAPACITY (languages in the plural) contributed to the social construction of nations, and this consciousness was in turn recruited as a constitutive element of them, to the extent that several specific instantiations of the LANGUAGE CAPACITY so recruited came to share the name of the nations they were associated with. In this sense, 'English' (the language) is something instantiating Englishness, a monolithic property of the NATION England, rather than a 'plurilithic' manifestation of the LANGUAGE CAPACITY. This conceptualization was accompanied by the social construction of a fixed code, 'Standard English', leading to dichotomies of correctness and accuracy.

In line with ideas propounded by Integrational Linguists (e.g. Harris, 1981) and critical applied linguists (e.g. Makoni and Pennycook, 2007), I will suggest that understandings of English provided within linguistics and purveyed in schools are derived from, conditioned by, or defined with reference to, this second ontological category, rather than directly from the first. Such understandings are now, more than ever, open to critique. The times and spaces we live in are radically different from those of the period of several centuries over which English as a national fixed code emerged (cf. Wright, 2015). The unique identification of the English language with the English nation has long since disappeared, and English is a global phenomenon. But the association lives on in our ontological commitments. For the benefit of L1 and L2 learners and users, these commitments need to be explicitly recognised and critically assessed.

The chapter is organized as follows. In Section 2, I develop the ontological taxonomy I have previously used to tease apart the concepts expressed by the word *language*, in applied linguistics (Hall, 2013), in TESOL (Hall, 2017), and in non-native usage (Hall et al., 2017; Hall, 2018). The following two sections map the entity types identified in the taxonomy onto English as constituted by the two sets of resources, processes, and products identified above. Thus, Section 3 deals with English as instantiations of the LANGUAGE CAPACITY and Section 4 with these instantiations contemplated as direct or indirect manifestations of collective identification with the English NATION. In Section 5, I use the entities mapped in the framework to critically assess how English is treated as a subject in educational contexts. Section 6 provides a brief conclusion.

2 An Ontological Taxonomy for Language

The taxonomy for language that I have been developing, only briefly sketched in the publications cited above, comprises eight ontological types. In Hall et al. (2017), these eight types were grouped into four domains: *cognitive*, *notional*, *expressive*, and *social* (see Figure 2.1). These domains should not be taken as constructs of a rigorous ontological theory, but rather as suggestive markers of where language can be construed as existing, in ways that together permeate the human condition. The four domains are intended to mark out aspects of human experience in the following ways. The cognitive domain captures entities and processes that are understood to exist by virtue of their development and operation in the human mind (e.g. visual processing and episodic memory). The expressive domain embraces those physically manifested products of intentional mental processes, which may be understood as signifying or indexing meanings in more or less highly structured ways (e.g. gestures and non-verbal interjections). The notional domain contains entities that exist as theoretical constructs, models, taxonomies, and the like, often elaborated in formal systems, consciously devised to describe and/or explain entities

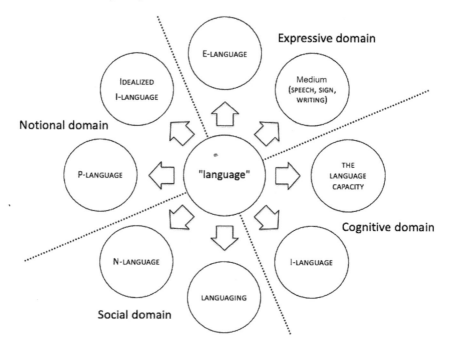

Figure 2.1 An ontological framework for language
(Hall, 2013; Hall et al., 2017)

in other ontological domains (e.g. calculus and Linnaean taxonomy). Finally, the social domain includes all those entities, properties, relations, and processes that are understood to exist at the level of groups of individuals and the relations between them (e.g. trade and choral singing).

In this chapter, I introduce a further parameter of ontological categorization, which distinguishes between English as *resource*, *process*, and *product*. First, though, I describe each conceptualization of language in turn.

2.1 The Cognitive Domain

In the **cognitive domain**, the general species capacity (the 'LANGUAGE CAPACITY') is distinguished from its instantiation in individual minds ('I-LANGUAGE'). This distinction is a useful starting point for understanding how *English* language is conceptualized, since it captures two poles of a continuum on which English is commonly understood to be situated: somewhere between language as a general phenomenon and as individual linguistic resources.

THE LANGUAGE CAPACITY

One way of conceptualizing language is as the species property for linguistic representation and communication that develops naturally in humans but not in other animals, even if exposed to similar environments and experiences. I call this entity 'the LANGUAGE CAPACITY'. Whether the capacity is innate and specifically linguistic (Chomsky, 1986) or emerges from more general predispositions (Tomasello, 2003), it is clearly heritable and is physically located in the mind/brain, rather than the vocal tract or hands, for example. Because it holds at the level of the species, it is universal, so corresponds to the non-count noun *language*.

I-LANGUAGE

According to another common understanding, language is the actual grammar, lexis, phonology, etc., that we each carry around in our heads. Despite disagreement about innateness, linguists agree that the capacity is realised in individual cognitive resources, ultimately represented in neural circuits, which develop through experience (cf. Wicaksono and Hall, this volume, for further discussion). Without sharing his specific ontological commitments, I have adopted Chomsky's (1986, pp. 21–46) term 'I-LANGUAGE' (internalized language) to refer to these instantiations of the LANGUAGE CAPACITY. This conceptualization matches the notion of 'idiolect', and for some linguists it is the only way to understand how language exists. Hall Jr (1985, p. 353), for example, asserted that "all phenomena of language exist only in the 'know-how'... of individual speakers, i.e., in their idiolects ... Each idiolect exists only in the brain of the speaker who uses it". English as a property of individual minds is addressed in Section 3.1.

2.2 *The Expressive Domain*

Beyond biology and cognition, language can be understood as utterances and texts, in what I call the **expressive domain**. Here we can distinguish between (a) linguistic expression, i.e. meaningful words, often in grammatically organized sequences, for which I again adopt a term introduced by Chomsky (1986, pp. 19–21): 'E-LANGUAGE' (externalized language) and (b) physical expression in one of three *mediums*: acoustically in SPEECH, or visually in SIGN and WRITING.

E-LANGUAGE

I-LANGUAGE is concerned with the *potential* in the brain for assembling utterances and texts. But we can also conceptualize language as the *linguistic actualizations* of this cognitive potential, as products of the social processes people engage in: the phonological and lexicogrammatical structures activated and articulated in language production. Hence, language can be conceived in terms of linguistic expressions, the products of I-LANGUAGES, in *use* as tokens (specific instances) or in *usage* as types (across a genre, for example). These products, for which I use the term E-LANGUAGE, may be potential or real, and if the latter, recorded (in the form of transcriptions, documents, corpora, etc.) or unrecorded.

MEDIUM

Language as the *physical* tokens of E-LANGUAGE (i.e. as acoustic or visual signals) is a matter of the *medium* that linguistic expressions take (as SPEECH, SIGN, or WRITING). So when someone's language is described as slow or high pitched, what is being referred to is the physical expression, independent of its linguistic properties. SPEECH, SIGN, or WRITING have no intrinsic meaning; they are physical entities that enable meaning only when processed as E-LANGUAGE using I-LANGUAGE resources.

2.3 The Notional Domain

For theorists concerned with describing the structural patterns they observe in samples of E-LANGUAGE that are derived from similar I-LANGUAGES, languages can be conceived as abstract *systems* of meaning-bearing units and the regularities according to which they are combined and interpreted. As such, they exist as theoretical constructs in what I call the **notional domain**, independent of actual instantiations in minds and events. This scholarly understanding of language has dominated education since classical times, and is the one with which mainstream linguistics has, in practice, been most concerned. A distinction can be made between language as an abstraction from I-LANGUAGE, and language as an abstraction from E-LANGUAGE. I call the former 'IDEALIZED I-LANGUAGE' and adopt Chomsky's term 'P-LANGUAGE' (1986, p. 33) for the latter.

IDEALIZED I-LANGUAGE

Although Chomsky (1986) stresses the cognitive nature of language as an individual mental property, actual accounts of I-LANGUAGE within generative linguistics are based on intuitions of 'grammaticality' that are assumed to hold *across* speakers. A working assumption is that there are separate language systems (grammars) that distinguish groups of I-LANGUAGEs (and therefore groups of people). Chomsky (1986, p. 27), for example, refers to "a system of rules, English, an I-language". A similar assumption holds in other cognitively oriented theoretical frameworks such as usage-based linguistics (cf. Eskildsen, this volume). I use the term IDEALIZED I-LANGUAGE to refer to any abstraction from a set of similar I-LANGUAGEs to a language system assumed to be shared by a specific group of speakers.

P-LANGUAGE

In one ordinary conceptualization, languages exist as abstract entities, independent of individual minds or behaviours, but inferable from the products of those behaviours. This is P-LANGUAGE, where the 'P' refers to the Platonic notion of abstract entities like numbers, not locatable in space and time. Just as numbers can be related in systems that are independent of actual things or events in the world (e.g. 2 + 2 = 4), so language(s) can be seen as abstract systems that exist apart from specific mental states of individuals (I-LANGUAGE) and the products of their behaviours (E-LANGUAGE). This ontological status is apparent in Saussure's assertion that "[a] language [*langue*] is not complete in any speaker; it exists perfectly only within a collectivity" (1916, pp. 13–14). I argue in Section 4.2 that most linguistic descriptions of 'the English language' are (inevitably) describing a P-LANGUAGE abstraction, rather than I-LANGUAGE or its actualization E-LANGUAGE.

2.4 *The Social Domain*

Perhaps most commonly, people conceptualize language as an inherently social phenomenon, pertaining to group identity and activity. This is particularly so when ways of using language are associated with social groups perceived as unified at the level of nation, a conceptualization I call 'N-LANGUAGE'. More broadly, language exists to serve social functions, and so can be conceptualized (but less commonly so) as itself a social process or practice, rather than a national attribute or a cognitive/biological phenomenon (cf. Pennycook, 2010).

I use the term 'LANGUAGING' for this sense. These are both ways of construing language in the **social domain**, as a constitutive element of group beliefs and behaviours.

N-LANGUAGE

Perhaps the most widely held 'folk' understanding of language is in the sense of named languages, monolithic linguistic systems, typically thought of as being used (more or less well) by monolingual citizens of a nation from which the language name often derives. This is what I have called N-LANGUAGE (Hall, 2013), where the 'N' suggests *national*, *named*, *native*, and *normed*. The key role of language in the emergence of modern conceptions of the nation has been noted by political scientists (e.g. Anderson, 1983; Hobsbawm, 1992) and critically discussed by linguists and applied linguists (e.g. Haugen, 1966; Harris, 1981; Joseph, 2004; Makoni and Pennycook, 2007).

N-LANGUAGE is governed by norms at the level of linguistic form (pronunciation, spelling/punctuation, lexis, and grammar), such that certain forms are prescribed as correct (part of 'the language') and others not. The norms are *regulative* rather than *constitutive* (Searle, 1969, pp. 33–37), with social sanctions attached for non-compliance (e.g. stigmatization for unstandardized language use). Haugen (1966, p. 928) argued that this relatively recent conceptualization of language was a natural consequence of the national ideal that "demands that there be a single linguistic code by means of which [communication within the nation] can take place". This 'single linguistic code' is the so-called Standard Variety, which comes to be understood as 'the language' itself, excluding other varieties such as regional or social dialects. With a single code comes the possibility of accuracy judgements (correct/incorrect, compliance/non-compliance). The consequences of this for the ontology of English is discussed in Section 4.1 and, for English as a subject in education, in Section 5.

LANGUAGING

At a more fundamental social level, language can be understood not in terms of abstract symbolic systems construed as components of group identity (N-LANGUAGE), but as socially embedded *processes* (actual communication). Language doesn't just encode referential meanings, but actually *does* things – it has performative and indexical functions, changing social reality through speech acts (Searle, 1969), and signalling social solidarity or difference through "*acts* of identity" (Le Page and Tabouret-Keller, 1985; my emphasis). According to Searle (2010, p. 85), "[l]anguage doesn't just describe; it creates, and partly constitutes, what it both describes and creates". In this sense, then, language is constitutive of social events and the practices that underpin them. For this ontological type I have adopted the term LANGUAGING, as used, for example, by Lado (1979), Halliday (1985), Joseph (2002), Swain (2006), and Jørgensen (2008). Some scholars imply that language only exists as LANGUAGING. Johnstone (2002, p. 235), for example, argued that "[t]o think of discourse as 'language use' means imagining that 'language' could exist prior to being 'used'". I discuss the notion of English as an instantiation of LANGUAGING in Section 3.2.

3 English as Instantiations of the Language Capacity

We are now ready to use the ontological categories and types identified for language in general to try to unpick the multiple ways in which English is understood to exist. To ensure maximal precision, I will introduce a new set of terms for entities within the general taxonomy labelled by the noun *English* (see Tables 2.1 and 2.2 for summaries). In this section, I address English as instantiations of the LANGUAGE CAPACITY. In the following section, I describe how these have been transformed by the conflation of language and identity into another

Table 2.1 English as L-ENGLISH, *instantiations of the* LANGUAGE CAPACITY

L-ENGLISH (a set of instantiations of the LANGUAGE CAPACITY)			
Resource	Process		Product
Cognitive domain	*Social domain*		*Expressive domain*
I-ENGLISHES (instantiations of I-LANGUAGE): Individual phonological, orthographic, and lexico-grammatical resources	ENGLISHING (instantiations of LANGUAGING): Social acts using I-ENGLISHES	ENENGLISHMENTS (instantiations of E-LANGUAGE): Linguistic forms produced using I-ENGLISHES in ENGLISHING	ENENGLISHINGS (instantiations of SPEECH, SIGN, or WRITING): Physical forms produced using I-ENGLISHES in ENGLISHING

22 Christopher J. Hall

Table 2.2 *English as linguistic manifestations of* ENGLISHRY

ENGLISHRY (socially constructed components of English national identity)		
	Resource	
Social domain	*Notional domain*	
N-ENGLISH (a social construction of L-ENGLISH): essentially, the named, national system of regulative norms known as 'Standard English'	IDEALIZED I-ENGLISH (an instantiation of IDEALIZED I-LANGUAGE): theorized constitutive norms for a linguistic system abstracted from I-ENGLISHES, but implicitly conditioned by N-ENGLISH	P-ENGLISH (instantiations of P-LANGUAGE): theorized constitutive norms for a linguistic system abstracted from ENENGLISHMENTS, and sometimes correlated with types of ENGLISHING, but implicitly conditioned by N-ENGLISH

set of senses that co-evolved with the social construction of the English nation.

Although all human beings share language in the sense of the LANGUAGE CAPACITY, it is variably rather than universally instantiated, developing different features under different local conditions. LANGUAGING works only to the extent that the I-LANGUAGES deployed in the process share features. It is only thus that English can be understood to exist independently of the national concept: as a set of instantiations of the LANGUAGE CAPACITY. In this sense, its relation to a specific territorial area, its association with a specific cultural–political group, its name, its integrity as a single system, and the degree to which it can become available to consciousness for contemplation, are irrelevant to its ontological status. The types of entity I identify in this section exist independently of what people think English is, of the existence of the word *English*, and indeed, of whether people are aware that English exists. The fact that two randomly selected language users may not be able to effectively engage in LANGUAGING unless they have some common I-LANGUAGE resources, demonstrates that sets of I-LANGUAGES, what people do with them (LANGUAGING), and the products they leave (E-LANGUAGE in their three *mediums*), can be grouped together into ontological categories of their own. These categories will embrace indeterminate sets of resources, processes, and products, involving prototypical, rather than essential, features. One of these sets is, in this sense, English, an instantiation (or more accurately a group of instantiations) of the LANGUAGE CAPACITY. I will call this ontological category 'L-ENGLISH' and in the following subsections I describe the four types of entity that comprise it.

3.1 English as Cognitive Resource

In one sense, English is a set of resources represented in the minds of individuals, in different quantities and degrees of entrenchment, which allows them to use certain linguistic features and constructions meaningfully with individuals who have sufficiently similar sets of resources. English in this sense includes the set of I-LANGUAGE resources that I deployed to write these sentences and a reader to interpret them, and both of us to produce similar ones. I will call these resources 'I-ENGLISHES'. They are plural because no two people will have identical resources (they are *idiolects*), and also because individuals will have multiple I-ENGLISH resources for different purposes and contexts of use. In Hall (2013) I called these 'I-REGISTERS'. Although uncommon as an object of research, aspects of English I-REGISTERS are inferred in corpus studies by Mollin (2009) and Barlow (2013) for L1 users, and Hall et al. (2017) for an L2 user. Eskildsen (this volume) reports on his own research tracing changes in L2 I-ENGLISHES through time. In LANGUAGING, these resources will be drawn on alongside others, both linguistic (e.g. in Jørgensen's [2008] 'polylingual languaging') and non-linguistic (cf. Canagarajah, this volume). I-ENGLISHES will constantly be refashioned through usage in these LANGUAGING events.

3.2 English as Social Process

In the LANGUAGING sense, English is also a set of social practices, contextualized acts or events, through which speakers realise their communicative intentions, bring states of affairs into existence, and signal social identities and relationships. I call this 'ENGLISHING' (Hall, 2014; cf. Pennycook, 2007, p. 111). In L2 learning and multilingual use, this understanding of English is especially pertinent. More people are now learning English as L2 than as L1, and increasingly are languaging with other L2 learners and users, who regularly have different L1s. Such lingua franca uses of English show considerable diversity in the depth and breadth of the I-ENGLISH resources deployed, in the degree of overlap between them (resulting mostly from L1 influence – cf. Nakatsuhara, Taylor, and Jaiyote, this volume), and in users' ability to deploy them automatically, without conscious effort (their degree of entrenchment; cf. Mauranen, 2012; Hall, 2018). So with fewer reliably shared conventions governing language resources, communicative strategies for L2 ENGLISHING take on particular significance. Empirical studies suggest that miscommunication is less frequent than one might expect (cf. Seidlhofer, 2011, chapter 5). Some who research and write about English in lingua franca mode have argued that the unstable linguistic forms involved imply that this kind of English only exists in LANGUAGING. Canagarajah (2007, p. 928), for example, claims that "L[ingua] F[ranca] E[nglish] is not a product located in the mind of the speaker; it is a form of social action". As such, he argues, it is inseparable from the deployment of other semiotic resources (including other languages). See Schaller-Schwaner and Kirkpatrick (this volume) and Baker (this volume) for more on the multilingual and transcultural nature of ENGLISHING in lingua franca contexts.

3.3 English as Expressive Process and Product

Another way in which English can be understood to exist as an instantiation of the LANGUAGE CAPACITY is as the set of utterances or sentences that have actually been produced in ENGLISHING events, as actualizations of I-ENGLISHES. This is English as E-LANGUAGE, covering both tokens of use (e.g. Theresa May's ten uses of the adjective phrase 'strong and stable' at Prime Minister's Questions on 26 April 2017) and patterns of usage ('strong and stable' as a relatively common ADJ-CONJ-ADJ collocation type). When specific utterances and texts have been (or might be) produced as part of ENGLISHING, I call these (actual or potential) 'ENENGLISHMENTS'. And ENENGLISHMENTS are, of course, physically enacted through expressive processes in two *mediums* (SPEECH and WRITING), which leave acoustic and visible products. Such 'ENENGLISHINGS' will include May's phonetic tokens [strɒŋŋstebl̩] and the corresponding orthographic tokens in written records.

Table 2.1 summarizes this first set of conceptualizations of English.

4 English as Instantiations of Englishness

The types of entity identified in the preceding section capture the ontological status of the linguistic resources, processes, and products that have developed in the minds and behaviours of a set of people that started with groups living in the British Isles around one and a half millennia ago. When these entities, which collectively I am calling L-ENGLISH, became subject to contemplation, and the word *English* was appropriated to name the result of this contemplation, then another set of entity types was created. I claim that the defining characteristic of this set is, explicitly or implicitly, *identity*, at the level of NATION. On analogy with forms like *wizardry* and *devilry*, I propose to call this ontological category 'ENGLISHRY': the (contemplated) practices, products, or perceived characteristics of 'the English' or, in other words, the components of English identity. It is the linguistic reflexes of ENGLISHRY that are the topic of this section. Once more, we can identify subcategories, but in a reduced set of types, namely *resources* in the *social* and *notional* domains.

4.1 English as Prescribed Object: N-English

Probably the most widely accepted conceptualization of English (the 'folk ontology') is that it is the language of England, or that language as adopted/inherited by another nation, or learnt as a 'foreign language'. It has a single, standard form, prescribed through usage guides, 'the dictionary', grammar books, and – above all – educational systems (this is what Badwan, this volume, calls the 'standard' ontology). Although English is no longer uniquely tied to 'the English', the assumption of 'one language, one nation' is deeply embedded. It tends to be forgotten that English people have always spoken other languages in addition to, or instead of, English (e.g. Cornish, French, British Sign Language; cf. Barbour, 2000). And of course there have always been citizens and residents of England and other 'Anglophone' nations whose native languages are conventionally viewed as 'foreign'. The serious consequences of this conflation of language and nation are lived by many people on a daily basis. The 'English Only' movement in the USA, for example, has long been recognised as a socially divisive and psychologically harmful reflex of this ideological/ontological stance (Padilla et al., 1991). See Fortier (2017) for a critique of the language/nation conflation in contemporary Britain.

N-ENGLISH AS 'STANDARD ENGLISH'

There is general agreement that a major factor in how English (later British) national identity was able to be consolidated was through recognition of a unified linguistic code, spread through what Anderson (1983) called 'print capitalism'. The unified code for England (and by extension Britain and the UK) was 'Standard English', with other national varieties subsequently also being socially constructed into existence. Its formulation required codification and then prescription, as the endpoint of a process through which value is transferred from high status user groups to an autonomous linguistic system derived from their usage (cf. Le Page and Tabouret-Keller, 1985). Crowley (1991) chronicled how the endpoint was reached for English. The texts he cites, from the eighteenth to the twentieth centuries, demonstrate how English became conceived as a single monolithic system, used correctly or incorrectly, and how the educational system became the principal mechanism for developing and perpetuating this conceptualization. Noting the polysemy of the word *English*, he identifies the issue of "what is to count as 'proper English' in the realm of language" with "more significant social questions, such as, 'who are the proper English?'" (p. 2). The texts show how the use of 'proper English' has come to serve as a proxy for its users' good morals and good citizenship, as exemplified by socioeconomic elites. For most users, English in this sense is something they may aspire to, but do not fully possess. This is particularly the case for non-native learners and users. One telling reference in Crowley's collection (p. 183), which resonates especially in the current political climate, is to Henry James' assertion that immigrants are particularly guilty of 'corrupting' the language. English in this sense is 'N-ENGLISH', a named monolithic system, normed for the correct *forms* of ENENGLISH-MENTS rather than the effective enactment of *functions* through ENGLISHING.

N-ENGLISH IN EDUCATION

In the early stages of its development, consciousness and contemplation of N-ENGLISH were confined to privileged elites. It was only with the introduction of generalized public education, and with it widespread literacy, that an N-LANGUAGE understanding of English became dominant (cf. Hobsbawm, 1992). In public education, it has always been a central policy that pupils who have acquired L1 I-ENGLISHES need to be further socialized into knowledge and behaviour that reflects N-ENGLISH. Most such children start schooling with I-ENGLISHES that would be described in terms of unstandardized P-LANGUAGES, i.e. resources that don't conform to N-ENGLISH norms and would be grouped together as regional or social dialects. Currently, educational authorities in England stipulate that teachers must "take responsibility for promoting ... the correct use of standard English, whatever the teacher's specialist subject" (Department for

Education, 2011, p. 11). Similar mandates exist in the USA and other 'Anglophone' nations.

When teachers sanction (e.g. correct) L1 users because their ENENGL-ISHMENTS don't correspond to N-ENGLISH norms, the goal is to modify their I-ENGLISH resources. But this educational practice is based on a confusion between ontological types. N-ENGLISH is a component of identity (ENGLISHRY), a matter of social conformity, rather than effective communication (part of L-ENGLISH). By casting English in terms of correctness, rather than social conformity, teachers automatically delegitimize (as incorrect) their pupils' own I-LANGUAGE resources and LANGUAGING practices (cf. Cunningham, this volume), whether these are mono- or multilingual (regrettably, linguists' use of the term *non-standard*, as opposed to *unstandardized*, reinforces this for the former; cf. Sharples, this volume, on the latter). If conformity with 'Standard English' is to be on the curriculum, then, my ontological analysis suggests that it should be presented not in terms of accuracy, but as an (arguably desirable, perhaps necessary) attribute for socialization into broader (national) identity structures. See Section 5.1 for more on this, and Harder, this volume, for an alternative perspective.

4.2 English as Described Object

I pointed out in Sections 2.3 and 2.4 that in describing languages, linguists abstract away from I-LANGUAGES and E-LANGUAGE to systems assumed to hold at the level of unified communities of users, usually with the ontological status of P-LANGUAGE. I would now like to argue that, after the ontological onion skins have been stripped away, linguists' descriptions of 'the English language' are manifestations of ENGLISHRY, conditioned by the N-LANGUAGE notion of 'Standard English' and only indirectly reflecting aspects of L-ENGLISH (cf. Milroy, 2001; Armstrong and Mackenzie, 2013, chapter 2). Conceptualizations of English within linguistics are not themselves instances of N-LANGUAGE, because they involve what are assumed to be the constitutive norms of I-ENGLISH or the regularities holding across ENENGLISHMENTS, rather than regulative norms imposed on the basis of preconceived notions of correctness. But, as the next section shows, linguistic descriptions of English can reinforce the ordinary belief that unstandardized varieties may not be part of 'the language' (Haugen, 1966, p. 924). I will call such conceptualizations of English 'P-ENGLISH' (cf. Chomsky, 1986, p. 33) when viewed as abstractions from ENENGLISHMENTS, and 'IDEALIZED I-ENGLISH' when viewed as abstractions from I-ENGLISHES.

P-ENGLISH AND IDEALIZED I-ENGLISH

A typical P-ENGLISH conceptualization can be found in Huddleston and Pullum's (2002) *The Cambridge Grammar of the English Language*, which sets out to describe "the linguistic system itself" (p. 2), taken to be "modern Standard English". Data for the description come from the authors' intuitions and those of native-speaker consultants, corpora, dictionaries, and other grammars. There is no claim to psychological reality, but there is an assumption that a single system exists, for which constitutive rules are provided. Equally, generativists have sought to describe 'the grammar of English', and again their accounts are clearly filtered through assumptions about grammaticality in a monolithic system, this time as IDEALIZED I-ENGLISH. One such account is Haegeman and Guéron's (1999) *English Grammar: A Generative Perspective*, based on native-speaker grammaticality judgements and using data only from "formal English". The authors' stated intention is "to formulate part of *the grammar of English*" (p. 17, my emphasis).

Another kind of linguistic description conditioned by N-ENGLISH is that based exclusively on samples of ENENGLISHMENT data, represented in corpora, typically from thousands of different writers and speakers. One well-known example is Biber et al. (1999) *Grammar of Spoken and Written English*, the result of an analysis of over 40 million words drawn from several registers (types of ENGLISHING). The authors state that one of their major goals is "to describe the patterns of variation that exist within standard English" (p. 18). The "brief survey of non-standard features" they refer to (p. 20) takes up 4 of the 1,125 pages of the volume. Although differing from traditional and generativist linguistics in terms of methodology and evidence, the conceptualization of English appears to be comparable, limited to what is taken a priori to be 'Standard English', rather than sampling across the much broader range of actual ENENGLISHMENTS. Such descriptions represent P-ENGLISH abstractions conditioned by N-ENGLISH, and therefore again as instantiations of ENGLISHRY.

L2 ENGLISHES

Across the approaches and practices discussed so far, it is tacitly assumed that English 'belongs' to native speakers alone (cf. Wicaksono, this volume). When construed to include those who use English as an L2, most notably in the World Englishes framework, the 'native-speaker' element of N-ENGLISH is discarded. Yet the other elements of N-ENGLISH are preserved: Pennycook (2007, p. 107), for example, suggests that 'the concept of World Englishes does little more than pluralise monolithic English'. So-called 'Outer Circle' Englishes are viewed as named, national systems that follow their own norms, such as Indian English, Kenyan English, etc. (cf. Davis, 2006). Many 'Expanding Circle' Englishes (e.g. China English, Mexican English) are treated similarly. Investigation into English(es) used in lingua franca contexts has exposed many of the 'hidden' ontological commitments to N-ENGLISH in mainstream linguistics. But even in English as a Lingua Franca (ELF) studies, there is evidence of an underlying P-ENGLISH interpretation of the phenomenon. Initial presentations of ELF implied its existence as a variety of English, a "language system" (Seidlhofer, 2001, p. 146). And even after moves to reconceptualize it as a kind of ENGLISHING, in line with Canagarajah's (2007) arguments, there is still a tendency to present ELF in ways that invite reified P-LANGUAGE conceptualizations (cf. Mortensen, 2013; Harder, this volume). Section 5.2 discusses the practical implications for L2 learning and use of the ontological confusion underlying monolithic views of English.

Table 2.2 summarizes the ontological categories of English identified in this section.

5 English as Subject

The emergence of English as a manifestation of ENGLISHRY gave rise to, and subsequently has been sustained by, a set of subjects studied in educational institutions, also called *English* (the topic of Part C and Chapter 11, this volume). These subjects involve the study of N-ENGLISH and P-ENGLISH as L1 resources (Section 5.1) and as L2 resources (Section 5.2), and the study of literature written using I-ENGLISHES (Section 5.3). Figure 2.2 shows their relationship with the ontological types described in Sections 3 and 4. In this final section, I suggest that educational objectives and practices regarding English might be usefully critiqued by applying the framework presented here.

5.1 English as Subject for L1 Users

When children acquiring and using English as L1s are required to study the regularities of 'Standard English' deliberately, as part of a school subject, there is once again an ontological conflict. Educational policy, assuming N-ENGLISH, fails to appreciate that the P-LANGUAGE descriptions of 'Standard English' taught in schools can be deliberately *learned*, but not, like I-LANGUAGE, naturally *acquired*. Instruction, as opposed to ENGLISHING experience, will result in conscious metalinguistic knowledge of a set of P-ENGLISH

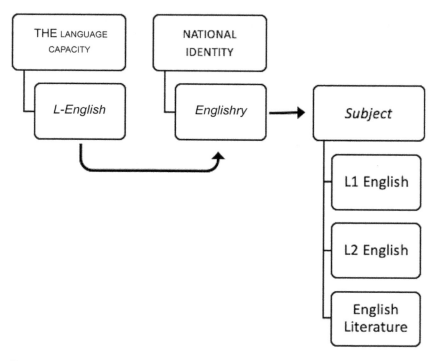

Figure 2.2 From L-ENGLISH to English as subject

facts. In the brain, the unconscious I-LANGUAGE resources drawn upon during LANGUAGING are associated with two kinds of memory systems: declarative and procedural (cf. Ullman, 2014). Declarative systems store arbitrary facts, including vocabulary. Procedural systems store automatized (entrenched) patterns, including grammatical constructions, which are used effortlessly for fluent communication. All consciously learned and deliberately accessed knowledge, however, whether lexical or syntactic, is controlled by declarative memory. Knowledge *about* English (e.g. about P-ENGLISH) is stored there. So for most pupils who have limited previous experience of ENENGLISHMENTS that accord with N-ENGLISH norms, the English they study at school will not become the entrenched procedural I-REGISTER they need for national contexts of ENGLISHING. What they learn as declarative knowledge will be deployed deliberately, and in many cases only laboriously. Of course, extensive involvement in ENGLISHING in appropriate contexts can result in I-REGISTERS that correspond to N-ENGLISH norms, but this cannot be guaranteed. And it makes little sense to expect, as England's current national curriculum does, that young children should deliberately study P-ENGLISH descriptions of 'Standard English' before actually *acquiring* the I-LANGUAGE features corresponding to it through ENGLISHING (cf. UKLA and Owen Education, 2016; Goddard, this volume).

5.2 English as Subject for L2 Learners and Users

For L2 English, ontological confusion also stymies effective educational practice. In L2 English classrooms, the target for learning and the model for teaching are almost always 'Standard English', and accuracy (the extent to which learners' ENENGLISHMENTS follow P-ENGLISH rules derived from N-ENGLISH regulative norms) is still the main parameter of assessment (although see Harsch; Nakatsuhara, Taylor, and Jaiyote, both this volume). The desired *outcome* of L2 English study is, however, normally professed to be communicative competence, i.e. fluent and effective ENGLISHING, but this requires I-ENGLISH resources in procedural memory (Hall, 2014). As a subject, therefore, L2 English is the converse of L1 English: children in L1 environments first acquire a dispreferred (unstandardized) I-ENGLISH at home and are expected to replace it at school with learned N-ENGLISH; L2 learners first learn about 'correct' N-ENGLISH and are then expected to acquire a usable I-ENGLISH. As with L1, it is possible, under the right circumstances (exposure, motivation, etc.), for learners to achieve sufficient conscious control of N-ENGLISH facts in declarative memory to be able to deploy them effectively in interaction, and perhaps to develop an unconscious I-ENGLISH in procedural memory that matches the norms of N-ENGLISH (and many learners may want or need this: see Kohn, 2011; Harder, this volume). But for most L2 learners, the I-ENGLISH they develop will inevitably be influenced by their own L1, by the learning processes they engage in, and by the uses to which they put their resources. This I-ENGLISH is English, but just like most L1 I-ENGLISHES, obeys its own regularities rather than being governed by N-ENGLISH norms (cf. Lemhöfer et al., 2014 for neuropsychological evidence supporting this view). It thus makes little sense to insist on accuracy in those norms (Page, this volume), unless 'Standard English' ENENGLISHMENTS are required or desired for social conformity, e.g. for study in English-medium higher education institutions (Swan, 2017).

5.3 English as Literature

Finally, the term *English* is used to refer not to the study of any of the ontological types described here, but to the study of literary texts, examples of ENENGLISHMENTS produced deliberately as creative/

artistic products using I-ENGLISHES. Here the role and status of N-LANGUAGE is perhaps most palpable, because the 'canon' is viewed as a source and model of its legitimacy, as observed, for example, in dictionary citations and good usage guides. I won't say more about this issue here, except to suggest that maybe it's time to rename the subject, in order to avoid the implication that the essence of L-ENGLISH, or of ENGLISHRY, is to be found in literary form. *English Music* or *English Art* doesn't appear on any school curriculum I am aware of, so perhaps it's time for just *Literature*? See Goodwyn and Roberts (both this volume) for extended discussion of English (literature) as a school subject.

6 Conclusion

My aim in this chapter has been to highlight the ways in which the fundamental elements of human language(s) as instantiations of the LANGUAGE CAPACITY have been reinterpreted through the lens of collective identification with NATION, to give rise to the 'folk ontology' of English as a manifestation of ENGLISHRY. Ordinary uses of the word *English* reflect deep-seated beliefs about the nature of language and its relationship with national identity. These beliefs have been embedded through the operation of hegemonic cultural forces, acting especially through education systems, to maximize "internal cohesion [and] external distinction" (Haugen, 1966, p. 928). The N-LANGUAGE manifestation of this deliberate contemplation and construction of 'the language of the English' is the monolithic social construct 'Standard English'. This construct is inevitably accompanied by notions of correctness and accuracy (and therefore error and failure) in schooling and society at large. I argued in this chapter that it has also influenced linguistic understandings of the notions of 'grammaticality' and 'non-standardness', in that 'the English language' is typically presented in terms of P-LANGUAGE (or IDEALIZED I-LANGUAGE) descriptions of the 'standard variety'. It is, then, unsurprising that for many teachers of English, both as L1 and L2, the subject they teach is understood in terms of P-ENGLISH, and this is what learners expect. The fact that learners can and will only acquire I-ENGLISHES, and that only I-ENGLISHES can be used effortlessly and effectively in ENGLISHING, is mostly unappreciated.

Readers may not be persuaded by my interpretation of how the ontological categories and types I propose underpin beliefs and practices in English teaching and assessment. But the framework should at least provide some points of reference for examining their own ontological commitments regarding English and, particularly, for teasing apart the following:

- effective use of linguistic resources for social practices (I-English in Englishing) versus performance of 'proper' Anglophone identities (conformity with N-English norms)
- actual language functions and usage (Englishing and enenglishments) versus knowledge of idealized language descriptions (P-English and Idealized I-English)
- acquirable cognitive resources (I-Englishes) versus learnable metalinguistic knowledge (P-English, N-English)
- communicative potential and creativity (entrenched I-Englishes and fluent Englishing) versus social conformity (N-English accuracy in enenglishments)
- what *is* out there (I-English and Englishing) versus what one feels *should be* out there (N-English)

I hope that the detailed anatomy of the senses of *English* provided here will help with this ongoing critical process.

References

Anderson, B. (1983). *Imagined Communities: Reflections on the Origin and Spread of Nationalism*. London: Verso.

Armstrong, N. and Mackenzie, I. E. (2013). *Standardization, Ideology and Linguistics*. Basingstoke: Palgrave Macmillan.

Barbour, S. (2000). Britain and Ireland: The varying significance of language for nationalism. In S. Barbour and C. Carmichael, eds., *Language and Nationalism in Europe* (pp. 18–43). Oxford: Oxford University Press.

Barlow, M. (2013). Individual differences and usage-based grammar. *International Journal of Corpus Linguistics, 18*(4), 443–478.

Biber, D., Johansson, S., Leech, G., Conrad, S., and Finegan, E. (1999). *Longman Grammar of Spoken and Written English*. London: Longman.

Canagarajah, S. (2007). Lingua franca English, multilingual communities, and language acquisition. *The Modern Language Journal, 91*, 923–939.

Chomsky, N. (1986). *Knowledge of Language*. New York: Praeger.

Crowley, T. (1991). *Proper English? Readings in Language, History and Cultural Identity*. London: Routledge.

Davis, D. R. (2006). World Englishes and descriptive grammars. In B. B. Kachru, Y. Kachru, and C. L. Nelson, eds., *The Handbook of World Englishes* (pp. 509–525). Oxford: Blackwell.

Department for Education (2011). Teachers' standards: Guidance for school leaders, school staff and governing bodies. Online. Retrieved 27 July 2017 from www.gov.uk/government/publications/teachers-standards

Fortier, A. M. (2017). On (not) speaking English: Colonial legacies in language requirements for British citizenship. *Sociology*. doi: 10.1177/0038038517742854

Haegeman, L. and Guéron, J. (1999). *English Grammar: A Generative Perspective*. Oxford: Blackwell.

Hall, C. J. (2013). Cognitive contributions to plurilithic views of English and other languages. *Applied Linguistics, 34*, 211–231.

Hall, C. J. (2014). Moving beyond accuracy: From tests of English to tests of 'Englishing'. *ELT Journal, 68*(4), 376–385.

Hall, C. J. (2018). Cognitive perspectives on English as a Lingua Franca. In J. Jenkins, W. Baker, and M. Dewey, eds. *Routledge Handbook of English as a Lingua Franca* (pp. 74–84). London: Routledge.

Hall, C. J., Joyce, J., and Robson, C. (2017). Investigating the lexico-grammatical resources of a non-native user of English: The case of *can* and *could* in email requests. *Applied Linguistics Review, 8*(1), 35–59.

Hall, C. J., Wicaksono, R., Liu, S., Qian, Y., and Xu, X. (2017). Exploring teachers' ontologies of English: Monolithic conceptions of grammar in a group of Chinese teachers. *International Journal of Applied Linguistics, 27*(1), 87–109.

Hall Jr, R. A. (1985). Meaning and the idiolect: The idioseme. In K. R. Jankowsky, ed., *Scientific and Humanistic Dimensions of Language: Festschrift for Robert Lado. On the Occasion of His 70th Birthday* (pp. 353–359). Amsterdam: John Benjamins.

Halliday, M. A. K. (1985). Systemic background. In J. D. Benson, ed., *Systemic Perspectives on Discourse: 1. Selected Theoretical Papers from the 9th International Systemic Workshop* (pp. 1–15). New York: Ablex.

Harris, R. (1981). *The Language Myth.* London: Duckworth.

Haugen, I. (1966). Dialect, language, nation. *American Anthropologist, 68*, 922–935.

Hobsbawm, E. J. (1992). *Nations and Nationalism since 1780: Programme, Myth, Reality,* 2nd ed. Cambridge: Cambridge University Press.

Huddleston, R. and Pullum, G. K. (2002). *The Cambridge Grammar of the English Language.* Cambridge: Cambridge University Press.

Janicki, K. (2006). *Language Misconceived: Arguing for Applied Cognitive Sociolinguistics.* Mahwah, NJ: Lawrence Erlbaum.

Jenkins, R. (2004). *Social Identity,* 3rd ed. London: Routledge.

Johnstone, B. (2002). *Discourse Analysis.* Oxford: Blackwell.

Jørgensen, J. N. (2008). Polylingual languaging around and among children and adolescents. *International Journal of Multilingualism, 5*(3), 161–176.

Joseph, J. E. (2002). Is language a verb? Conceptual change in linguistics and language teaching. In H. R. Trappes-Lomax and G. Ferguson, eds., *Language in Language Teacher Education* (pp. 29–47). Amsterdam: John Benjamins.

Joseph, J. E. (2004). *Language and Identity. National, Ethnic, Religious.* Basingstoke: Palgrave Macmillan.

Kohn, K. (2011). English as a *lingua franca* and the Standard English misunderstanding. In A. de Hower and A. Wilton, eds., *English in Europe Today: Sociocultural and Educational Perspectives* (pp. 71–94). Amsterdam: Benjamins.

Lado, R. (1979). Thinking and "languaging": A psycholinguistic model of performance and learning. *Sophia Linguistica, 12,* 3–24.

Lemhöfer, K., Schriefers, H., and Indefrey, P. (2014). Idiosyncratic grammars: Syntactic processing in second language comprehension uses subjective feature representations. *Journal of Cognitive Neuroscience*, 26(7), 1428–1444.

Le Page, R. B. and Tabouret-Keller, A. (1985). *Acts of Identity. Creole-Based Approaches to Language and Ethnicity*. Cambridge: Cambridge University Press.

Makoni, S. and Pennycook, A., eds. (2007). *Disinventing and Reconstituting Languages*. Clevedon, UK: Multilingual Matters.

Mauranen, A. (2012). *Exploring ELF. Academic English Shaped by Non-native Speakers*. Cambridge: Cambridge University Press.

Milroy, J. (2001). Language ideologies and the consequences of standardization. *Journal of Sociolinguistics*, 5(4), 530–555.

Mollin, S. (2009). "I entirely understand" is a Blairism: The methodology of identifying idiolectal collocations. *International Journal of Corpus Linguistics*, 14(3), 367–392.

Mortensen, J. (2013). Notes on English used as a lingua franca as an object of study. *Journal of English as a Lingua Franca*, 2(1), 25–46.

Padilla, A. M., Lindholm, K. J., Chen, A. et al. (1991). The English-only movement: Myths, reality, and implications for psychology. *American Psychologist*, 46(2), 120–130.

Pennycook, A. (2007). The myth of English as an international language. In S. Makoni and A. Pennycook, eds., *Disinventing and Reconstituting Languages* (pp. 90–115). Clevedon, UK: Multilingual Matters.

Pennycook, A. (2010). *Language as a Local Practice*. London: Routledge.

Santana, C. (2016). What is language? *Ergo*, 3(19), 501–523.

Saussure, F. de. (1916/1966). *Course in General Linguistics*. New York: McGraw-Hill.

Searle, J. R. (1969). *Speech Acts: An Essay in the Philosophy of Language*. Cambridge, UK: Cambridge University Press.

Searle, J. R. (1995). *The Construction of Social Reality*. New York: Simon and Schuster.

Searle, J. R. (2010). *Making the Social World: The Structure of Human Civilization*. Oxford: Oxford University Press.

Seidlhofer, B. (2001). Closing a conceptual gap: The case for a description of English as a lingua franca. *International Journal of Applied Linguistics*, 11(2), 133–158.

Seidlhofer, B. (2011). *Understanding English as a Lingua Franca*. Oxford: Oxford University Press.

Sharpe, R. A. (1974). Ideology and ontology. *Philosophy of the Social Sciences*, 4, 55–64.

Swain, M. (2006). Languaging, agency and collaboration in advanced second language learning. In H. Byrnes, ed., *Advanced Language Learning: The Contributions of Halliday and Vygotsky* (pp. 95–108). London: Continuum.

Swan, M. (2017). EFL, ELF, and the question of accuracy. *ELT Journal*. doi: 10.1093/elt/ccx031

Tomasello, M. (2003). *Constructing a Language. A Usage-Based Theory of Language Acquisition*. Cambridge, MA: Harvard University Press.

UKLA and Owen Education (2016). *Curriculum and Assessment in English 3 to 19: A Better Plan*. Leicester: UKLA Publications. Online. www.nate.org.uk/file/2016/04/The-National-Curriculum-for-English-from-2015.pdf

Ullman, M. T. (2014). The declarative/procedural model: A neurobiologically motivated theory of first and second language. In B. VanPatten and J. Williams, eds., *Theories in Second Language Acquisition: An Introduction*, 2nd ed. (pp. 135–158). London: Routledge.

Wright, S. (2015). What is language? A response to Philippe van Parijs. *Critical Review of International Social and Political Philosophy*, 18(2), 113–130.

Part II
English in/for L2 Learning and Teaching

3 *English in the Real World*

Norms and the Ontology of English(es)

Peter Harder

1 Introduction

Ontological inquiry into the nature of language has been somewhat marginal since the "linguistic turn" in philosophy (cf. Rorty, 1967), i.e. for about seventy-five years. Although the shift of emphasis from the more concrete objects of investigation to their formal properties has since been reversed, this change in zeitgeist did not give rise to a new wave of ontological rethinking. That was perhaps mainly due to the impact of social constructionism, which was just as sceptical of ontology as logical positivism, albeit from a different perspective: Rather than looking for 'hard' properties of true reality in formal structure, social constructionists basically aimed at deconstructing all descriptions that claimed to represent true reality. This book is a welcome sign that things may be changing.

To address the specific challenge of the complicated nature of English, it is necessary to have an idea of the more general question of what a language really is (without the scare quotes that have been obligatory around words like 'real' and 'truth'). The present chapter is based on assumptions about the ontological foundations of language discussed in depth in Harder (2010). The key issue in this chapter is the role of norms. In much of the linguistic literature, norms have been viewed chiefly as an undesirable, potentially oppressive factor. I argue that norms also have an essential role in the way the world (really) is, and that this in turn is essential to understanding what English (really) is.

In that process, I argue that a pervasive theoretical conflation bears a major responsibility for the lack of clarity. I am thinking of the conflation between the conceptual content of social practices and the practices themselves as parts of operational social reality, as 'going concerns'. The key difference is that languages as operational practices are causally relevant. They exert 'selection pressures': Children growing up in a community adapt to the language just as they adapt to other features of the social reality they grow up in, such as law enforcement. In contrast, a language viewed purely as a set of conceptual mappings between expressions and meanings (as described in a textbook) has no causal power on its own. A salient context for the purely conceptual view is when a language is viewed as a potential learning target for language classes in a school context. This view will be referred to here under the label 'language-as-code'. (Language-as-code corresponds roughly to what Hall, this volume, terms P-language.)

This distinction is a variant of the oldest distinction in the history of ontology as a philosophical topic, between 'general terms' (aka 'universals') and 'particulars'. Without going into a discussion of this inexhaustible issue, I base my arguments on the assumption that universals exist as properties that characterize classes of particulars, and hence must be understood in relation to such particulars. In the philosophical terminology, languages-as-codes are universals, while operational community languages are particulars.

The structure of this chapter is as follows: I begin by outlining an ontology of language focusing on the under-emphasized role of languages as parts of social structures based on inherently normative foundations. I then give a general overview of different types of norms in relation to language, showing what is missing in the understanding of norms as manifestations of (mostly undesirable) language ideologies, ending up by arguing that norms and variation are mutually dependent (rather than being in conflict). I go on to sketch the inherent difference between two central perspectives on native and standard language norms: the academic perspective and the perspective of teachers. I then discuss the global role of English, with the nature of ELF (English as a Lingua Franca) as the centrepiece. Finally, I bring the threads together and try to conclude about what this entails for the ontology of English, focusing on the ontology of 'global English'.

2 Languages as Parts of Social Structures

Even in the simplest textbook cases, the ontology of languages as objects of description is a complex and contested issue (cf. Hall, this volume). There is no consensus about the relationships between aspects of language such as usage, structure, community, and identity (and the list could be continued). The uncertainty about the ontology of languages is partly due to the fact that one form of conventional wisdom – the structural dichotomy between *langue* and *parole* and its successors – has lost its hegemonic status without leaving an heir apparent.

This section argues that a crucial component is the status of language as part of the social fabric. There has been no lack of interest in the social aspect of language as such; in recent decades, developments like pragmatics, sociolinguistics, conversation analysis, and corpus linguistics have gradually eroded faith in pure structure as the true site of language. However, the discussion has tended to retain the structural dichotomies (*langue/parole*, competence/performance, system/use) as points of departure for the argument, even while arguing against the importance attached to the *langue* side. This in effect amounts to transferring allegiance from the first to the second member of the dichotomies – to the flow of usage – without fundamentally rethinking the basis of the distinction.

The picture I offer instead argues that when a language is a 'going concern' in a community, usage must be understood as standing in a relation of mutual dependency with this social 'system'. This mutual dependency arose out of a co-evolutionary spiral between brain and language (cf. Deacon, 1997): Because situated communicative ability acquired increasing fitness value, it favoured the evolution of a cognitive infrastructure that would enhance this ability, and that in turn enhanced the fitness value of communicative prowess. What came first was usage or 'flow' in the broad sense of communicative interaction; that was the necessary context for the start of the spiral development. But once certain aspects of 'communicative usage' began to gain the status of conventions to be stored for future use, the two sides are mutually dependent. And it is only when this process has got under way that is makes sense to talk about *linguistic* communication, or *language* use.

Thus, when people speak, their *usage* reflects the way their *language* works. Concrete linguistically articulated utterances depend on the existence of a language in terms of which utterances can be formulated. One consequence is that if you do not know a language, you cannot use it or understand other peoples' utterances when they use it. I believe there is no way round some version of this assumption. Even if we assume that there is a strong genetic component to the language ability, the first individual with the right genetic endowment ('African Eve') did not have the option of saying, e.g. *How about making a trip down to the bottom of Olduvai Gorge today?* – to her mates. This means that I take issue with the formulation by Johnstone quoted by Hall (this volume). Johnstone (2002, p. 235) argues that "[t]o think of discourse as 'language use' means imagining that 'language' could exist prior to being 'used'". Although phylogenetically actual communication came first (as pointed out earlier), the co-evolutionary process assumed here entails precisely that in the present evolved state, it is possible, as well as practical, for speakers to have languages available prior to actually using them.

Because of the lack of a consensual format for describing social reality, I am going to give a brief sketch of the assumptions that my argument is based on. It would take us beyond the scope of this chapter to go into a detailed discussion, so I shall just state the centrepieces without attempting to justify them here.

Following Tomasello (2008), I assume that the basic evolutionary event that made language possible was the rise of the capacity for joint attention. Joint attention (as part of joint activity) means that mental properties of others acquire a status as parts of the world I live in. When two people attend to the same object – such as two parents looking at their child together – this is not a simple product of two individual experiences of each parent looking at the child. The ability to 'be on the same page', i.e. to share mental states, is a basic prerequisite of having a language, because language understanding presupposes the ability to home in on shared meanings.

As pointed out by Tomasello (2008, p. 6), the capacity for joint attention also underlies the construction of a social world based on "collective intentionality" as described by Searle (1995). A shared understanding may be used to collectively assign 'status' to things in the world and thus endow them with new causal powers: A river acquires new properties by getting the status of *border* between two communities; paper notes acquire exchange value by getting the status of *money*. The linguistic side of this is that word expressions acquire new powers by being assigned the status of bearers of collectively shared *meanings*. All these properties are grounded in the way individual humans are genetically constructed; but when individuals interact, they may together generate collective entities whose existence requires more than one individual at a time.

Collective processes like these gave rise to the process of cultural evolution (Hull, 1988; Tomasello, 1999; Croft, 2000; Richerson and Boyd, 2005), changing the human 'niche'. Although without a physical substratum in the form of genes, cultural evolution shares with biological evolution the key dynamics of evolutionary processes: the interplay between reproduction and selection. In order for cultural features to stay around, they have to be reproduced from one generation to the next, and for this to happen, they have to survive selection pressures (just as biological species do). Business companies like Enron and words such as the German word *englisch* meaning 'angelic' may fail this test (cf. Keller, 1990) and hence cease to be part of the social world in the next round. This causal interplay between the collective level and the individual level underlies key characteristics of all evolutionary phenomena, biological as well as cultural. One example is the fact that babies *adapt* to language in the community into which they are born (as part of the general dynamics of adaptation and selection).

This is the key motivation for according language-in-society, as a property of the way the world works, a distinct ontological role, rather than just understanding languages as parts of cognitive infrastructure. In order for linguistic adaptation to be causally feasible, there must be an account of the way language is present in the community, so that we have an account of the source of selection pressures; cf. Labov (2014), for example, on the role of the community as opposed to individual factors for predicting language change and development.

Based on these premises, I argue (cf. Harder, 2010, p. 173) that languages, understood as fully operational parts of the way the world works, have a tripartite ontology. They minimally exist in *two* ontological sites that go beyond actual usage events: as an aspect of infrastructure (1) in individual cognitive systems and (2) in societies (communities). Language use, again understood as fully operational language use, depends on both. For language as part of a speaker's cognitive systems, I use the term 'competency' with a $-y$ (drawing on, but marking the difference from, the generative term 'competence' [cf. Harder, 2010, p. 174]). For language as part of society, I use the term 'system', in analogy with other features of societies such as education systems, legal systems, and systems of governance. The classic 'langue-parole' bipartition obscures the distinction between the 'system' and 'competency' aspects, which I believe is particularly crucial for understanding the ontology of English.

3 Norms and the Language System

In academic linguistic discussion, norms are typically understood roughly as 'judgements about what is good or correct' and, as such, are inherently contested and ideologically imbued. However, that type of normativity is only one aspect of a much more complex field. In this section, I am going to discuss four different aspects of the issue of norms in linguistics. The first of these is the most ontologically fundamental: the role of norms as *constitutive* parts of social structure. I then discuss the ideologically central issue of *prestige* norms. This leads up to the issue of *prescriptive* versus *operational* norms. In relation to prescriptive norms, I discuss the contrast between *correctness* and *comprehensibility* as norms for language performance.

The constitutive role of norms in society is not a new insight. The foundational role of norms was a centrepiece in the thinking of Durkheim, one of the founders of sociology; in his theory, norms constitute the basic fabric of social structures (cf. Durkheim, 1996/1893). The reason why this normative status is more than just a subjective preference is that it is a condition of existence for social structures. Consider an elementary social structure such as an agreement to play badminton every Wednesday at 4:00 PM. Such a thing could not exist unless the two people who made the agreement felt a normative obligation to actually turn up on Wednesdays at 4:00. We have all met people who have trouble living up to such obligations. This has two results, of which the second is crucial here: first of all we get annoyed, but secondly we avoid entering into agreements with such people. As a result, this kind of social structure ceases to exist.

Constitutive norms are not what most linguists would think of first when the issue of norms in language is taken up. Instead, what comes to mind is what can be called 'prestige norms': the difference between the symbolic capital associated with different varieties of the language, cf. Bourdieu (1984) on 'distinction'. This is familiar from sociolinguistics and forms the basis of the Labovian mechanisms of change and variation: Some varieties have high social status and form the targets of 'upwardly mobile' social adaptation; other varieties are associated with values belonging lower on the social ladder, but in compensation are the focus of community solidarity and identity in defiance of pressures from above. In modern societies, the centrepiece of this issue is the distinction between standard and nonstandard varieties.

Such prestige norms are not *constitutive* of language: it is perfectly conceivable to have a language community with no such differences in terms of 'distinction'; it is a value almost universally shared among sociolinguists to strive towards such a situation. A sobering thought, however, is that 'distinction' is a linguistic manifestation of a pervasive phenomenon in community life, manifested also in, for example, choice of clothing. Ultimately, as pointed out by Bourdieu, this is a generalization of class distinctions from strictly economic relations to all areas of human life.

Prestige norms are central also in the discussion about language norms in educational contexts. The standard understanding in terms of 'correctness' involves the *prescriptive* role of norms. In that role, norms stand outside the activities themselves and assign an evaluation to concrete instances of them, based on a comparison with the presupposed evaluative standard, like dogs at an exhibition. The second role, which I call the *operational* role of norms, involves situations where norms are causally involved in upholding the practices in question. Operational norms are part of the way the world works (like it or not!).

The distinction is akin to the distinction between explicit and implicit norms (cf. Kristiansen, 2009, for example). This distinction is usually understood in psychological rather than sociological terms, as conscious vs. unconscious or subconscious norms (cf. Labov, 1972); explicit norms are those that people profess when they are asked what they consciously think, while implicit norms are those that are inferred from behavioural evidence of various kinds. Kristiansen's findings include examples in which informants are asked to respond to two varieties of Danish, a locally coloured and a more standardlike form. In some cases there is a double dissociation between their evaluations so that their explicitly stated evaluation may show a preference for the local variety, while their implicit responses show an orientation towards the standard norm.

This dissociation is crucial for my point. The reason for preferring a terminological distinction between 'prescriptive' vs. 'operational' is that the point is the *social* function, not whether the speaker is aware of the norms or not. It is in principle possible that people can be explicitly aware of the operational norms they follow, in which case the term 'implicit' would be misleading.

The 'canonical' language community can thus be described as a speech community with a system of operational linguistic norms, to which members' linguistic competencies are adapted, so that they can achieve their communicative and community-identity-constructional purposes in actual language use. 'Language as code' is the sense in which a language can be either living or dead; an 'operational' language cannot be understood apart from its anchoring in community life.

4 Standard English and Variation: The Academic vs. the Teaching Perspective

From the point of view where norms are understood as monolithic and prescriptive dogma, it may seem absurd to invoke the foundational role of the language system and a set of system-upholding norms to account for what a language 'really' is, especially in an age where variation is the dominant theme in linguistics. But rather than being antithetical to a system, variation can only exist in a universe characterized by a presupposed, structured order (cf. Harder, 2014). In relation to language, this links up with the fact, discussed earlier, that linguistic communication requires a state of co-ordination, as reflected in Bloomfield's (1933, p. 78) "fundamental assumption of linguistics" that "in every speech-community some utterances are alike in form and meaning". There cannot be a language at all, unless there are usage events in which instances of the same linguistic categories are used.

In a diachronic perspective, the built-in role of variation means that evolutionary change results in a 'bush' of related variants (as emphasized by Gould, 1977). It does not result in an apostolic succession whereby one new version replaces one earlier version.

In stressing the importance of variation, it has often been claimed that there is really no such thing as 'a language' as an identifiable social entity (the sceptics include Chomsky, 1986, who illustrates this with the blurry distinction between German and Dutch). This is true if by language one understands a monolithic set of norms that is entirely separate from other equally monolithic entities. But as pointed out by Putnam (2001, p. 38, following Wittgenstein, 1953, par. 88), for example, the existence of grey zones does not entail that entities with grey zones between them drop out of existence. The problem of exactly how to individuate languages, therefore, is a different problem from describing what a really existing language is.

This has implications for the ontology of English(es) as an increasingly variational spectrum of languages. There may be a point at which it becomes problematic to see usage instances representing different varieties of a language as instances of the same category. The precise cutoff point, however, is irrelevant at this stage: one can either choose to see two usage instances as variants (in which case there is a shared superordinate category that both instantiate), or one can choose to see them as separate forms (with no superordinate category that both instantiate). In the second case, the concept of variation ceases to be applicable in analysing the relationship between the two varieties: they are separate entities.

This raises the issue of the role of 'Standard English' in this picture. In the (socio)linguistic mainstream, in the version that is influenced by critical theory, Standard English is typically viewed as the antithesis to variation, and as the embodiment of oppressive, prescriptive normativity. This perspective is to some extent built into a descriptive perspective that takes variation as its key concept, but is motivated by social practices in which tyrannical governments enforce uniformity of social behaviours (in addition to linguistic, religious, ethnic, political, etc.) on an oppressed population. With this pattern goes a scale of values according to which the standard language is the only 'right' one and all other varieties are inherently inferior, as are, by metonymic inference, the people who speak them. For an account of the status of Standard English and its problems, see Hall (this volume).

In such a perspective, it makes sense to operate with a polar opposition between (monolithic) norms and variation, and an associated polar opposition between the system and the rights of the individual. In the academic community, such a polar opposition motivates an ideological struggle against the whole ideological setup in which the standard language, especially Standard English, is the centrepiece. A couple of generations ago, most European school systems would be instances of this: mother tongue teachers served as a form of language police that made children ashamed of their native varieties and imposed an alien standard on them. Few language professionals feel comfortable in this role (cf. Cunningham, this volume).

The question, however, is what exactly follows from the scepticism towards standard English motivated by such scenarios when it comes to the teaching of English today (L1 as well as L2). This has been the subject of a persistent and sometimes acerbic debate. I think it is important to understand this disagreement as motivated by perspectives determined by differences in the way academics and teachers are situated in the real world.

The mainstream academic perspective predicates its position on both the general ideological/intellectual movement away from fixed orders and established power structures towards situated practice and variation, and also on actual changes in the world that motivate such changes. Insight, rather than specific practical purposes, are in focus. Language teaching, in contrast, is a practical activity whose goal is (simply put) to enable individuals to achieve goals that were previously beyond them because of lacking language competencies. The fact that the world is changing and old certainties are under pressure does not tell teachers what they most need to know: what precisely do I want my students to learn?

The issue of Standard English in that perspective can be elucidated by viewing it in the light of the ontology proposed earlier. Standard English does not live up to the specifications for a language with 'canonical' community anchoring: First of all because it represents only part of the variational system as defined earlier: non-standard forms are part of the community resources ('if it ain't broke, don't fix it!'). Secondly, because Standard English is defined irrespectively of 'accent', meaning that it represents only a partial mapping between expressions and meanings. And finally also it is a globally recognized norm, applicable in English-speaking communities across the world, with a status as the appropriate variety for official purposes, especially in written communication, hence without a well-defined community anchoring. Standard Languages are often defined precisely as forms with no localizable features.

As assumed in mainstream sociolinguistics, Standard English thus has a secondary status in relation to the full reality of a canonical operational language: a standard is defined in contrast to other forms of language in the community. The limitations include the 'superimposed' status, which motivates the distinction between 'standard norms' and 'community norms', where the community norm is associated with the local variety, not with the prestige form. So if you speak only Standard English, you exclude yourself from the 'solidarity' end of the scale of community anchoring.

However, in spite of all these limitations, the ontology posited here, with language as an aspect of the social fabric, also shows why mainstream sociolinguistics may underestimate Standard English. An example is when Milroy and Milroy (1991, pp. 22–23) claim that it is "an idea in the mind rather than a reality". It is true that it is an idea in the mind, but from that it does not follow that it is without status in the reality outside the mind. The quoted passage continues: "[it is] a set of abstract norms to which actual usage may conform to a greater or lesser extent". As factors in an operational language, such norms, as argued here, are part of the social environment, not figments of imagination. Linguistic selection pressures are real (cf. Kristiansen, 2009).

To this may be added that it is a bit of a stretch to claim that Standard English exists only as norms, not as actual usage events. Even if we allow that in most spoken English there will be telltale non-standard features, in evolutionary terms the criterion is 'satisficing' (cf. Simon, 1956), rather than perfect adaptation: in contrast to Spencer's (1864) "survival of the fittest", evolutionary processes select for the ability to stay above the cutoff point, not for optimal performance (by any conceivable standard). It would be hard to deny that the amount of English produced with 'satisficing' adaptation to standard norms is enough to grant existence to Standard English also at the level of usage.

The global reach of this form of usage also entails that the empowerment that goes with teaching standard English includes not only the (ideologically suspect) prestige accorded to it in comparison with non-standard varieties – it also extends to the more acceptable property of being widely comprehensible. I return to this issue in relation to the question of the reality of 'global English'.

My take on this issue reflects my experience as a Danish teacher of English at upper secondary as well as university levels. What we as theorists and academics have to say about the nature of English has to stand the test of whether it enables teachers to address the choice of language target intelligently. An unwillingness to tackle the issue of what form of English constitutes the model that teaching is aimed at is dead in the water from a teaching perspective. This puts the teacher in a different position from the expert who is concerned to update the old world order. This issue is nowhere clearer than in relation to English as a Lingua Franca (i.e. ELF).

5 English as a Lingua Franca: The Centrepiece of the New Ontology of 'Global English'?

ELF is a new stage in the development away from understanding English in terms of nation-based norms, going beyond the "post-colonial stage" described by Pennycook (1999, p. 153, quoted here from Seidlhofer, 2011, p. 55): "Thus the postcolonial performative position is one that sees English language teaching as part of a battle over forms of culture and knowledge ... an attempt to challenge central norms of language, culture and knowledge, and to seek ways of appropriating English to serve alternative ends". ELF is by definition the property of all speakers who are engaged in making themselves understood across language barriers, rather than being a variety such as 'Singapore English'. However, as pointed out by Mortensen (2013), the issue is to what extent one can understand ELF as being a variety of English at all – in Mortensen's terms (p. 26) whether one can understand ELF as a "reified" variety in its own right (cf. also Hall, 2018 and Baker, this volume). Mortensen takes his point of departure in a definition that was at the time posted in a key site, namely the website of the VOICE project:

English as a lingua franca (ELF) constitutes an additionally acquired language system which serves as a common means of communication for speakers of different first languages. ELF is currently the most common use of English world-wide. Millions of speakers from diverse cultural and linguistic backgrounds use ELF on a daily basis, routinely and successfully, in their professional, academic and personal lives.

(VOICE, 2011)

Mortensen shows, by reference to a range of ELF cases discussed in the literature, that there is no basis for assuming that ELF constitutes a 'language system' or 'variety' with properties distinct from but comparable to the properties of other varieties of English (like British or American English). Instead, Mortensen argues (VOICE, 2013) that ELF must be defined as "the use of English in a lingua franca language scenario". The website has since changed the definition to the one suggested in Seidlhofer (2011, p. 7), which is more in tune with Mortensen's proposal: "English as a lingua franca (ELF) can be thought of as 'any use of English among speakers of different first languages for whom English is the communicative medium of choice, and often the only option'" (VOICE, 2013).

In the tripartite ontology assumed here, this means that ELF is neither a language competency nor a language system. It fails to be a competency because there are no speakers about whom we could say that they represent perfect mastery of ELF. It cannot be a system because there is no set of community norms in which ELF (as language use) is anchored. ELF is a usage category that subsumes a certain type of language events, when certain conditions are fulfilled. We must therefore look elsewhere to capture the full mode of existence of Global English. The discussion in this section will at the same time be an attempt to sum up the ontology of English as a whole, reflecting the view that any attempt to describe what English is must necessarily capture what Global English is, understood as English in the sense where it is the possession of speakers in all Kachru's (1982) three circles. I begin by discussing the ontological underpinnings of this somewhat intangible object and then discuss what this entails for English as a target of teaching and learning.

As in the case of Standard English, there is a position according to which Global English does not exist: cf. the title of Pennycook's (2007) chapter "The Myth of English as an International Language". Pennycook's position chimes in with the general pattern of deconstruction that is a major feature of critical theory, including critical linguistics. The successful practice of deconstructive analysis has caused social structures once viewed as monolithic wholes to crumble in the face of critical analysis, revealing the myriad processes and counter-processes that are at work under these (at first glance) impregnable edifices, and revealed the interests and ideologies at work behind the scenes.

What this critical endeavour tends to ignore is the question of what remains after the deconstruction. Even if all arguments against widely shared views of English as a global language are true, we still have to account for the fact that people actually use forms of English (rather than forms of Danish or Latin, for example) for cross-cultural communication. As the expanding occurrence of ELF demonstrates, an analysis that concludes that English as an international language does not really exist does not tell us everything we would like to know.

In pursuing what English is, let us go back to the canonical case: an 'operational' language that is embedded in a community system to which its members are adapted, giving rise to usage events with 'satisficing' communicative success, and with an identity that is associated with membership of the community. It may appear as if I am invoking the outdated stereotype of the nation state as the prototype here. But what I have in mind is much more general, applying also to the situation in Papua New Guinea (PNG), for example, about as far from the nation–state stereotype as possible. In PNG, special obligations may be due to *wantoks* ('one talk', e.g. people who speak the same language as you do). As anecdotal illustration, I remember from my visit in PNG a gated company building with a notice saying that at a company festivity, it was not allowed to let in outsiders, "not even if they are wantoks".

Like Standard English, Global English differs in several respects from this situation. Most basically, there is no global community of speakers with a shared set of norms. This in turn entails that there are no speakers with competencies that reflect full adaptation to such a language system. We can therefore abstract no well-defined 'language-as-code' out of the operational practices that one can point to as grounds for assuming the existence of something like global English.

The question is, then, what we have instead. First of all, in terms of the evolutionary analogy, we have an untidy bush of operational varieties rather than a single, well-defined successor species that continues the lineage. It might be argued that there are no absolute criteria for deciding what constitutes 'one' language and so have to say that English is simply a rather big language, with a rather larger variational spread than ordinary native languages – just not a community language.

However, this is again a case where grey zones do not rule out the existence of entities that have grey zones between them. There are uncontroversial cases of entities that are too small to be a complete language (the canonical case is a pidgin language, and its incompleteness is one of the criteria whereby pidgins are distinguished from creoles), and similarly uncontroversial cases of phenomena that are too big to be one language (like the Indo-European language family). In between these two extremes we find a type of situation that arguably captures the ontological status of global English. I am thinking of the phenomenon that occurs when speakers of Danish, Swedish, and Norwegian communicate (although English is invading this usage domain, too).

In such cases each speaker uses his or her own language, while trying to accommodate (cf. Jenkins, 2009, p. 14) by introducing selected features of the other languages – a practice known as 'speaking Scandinavian'. The term 'Scandinavian' here has exactly the status that I am advocating for Global English – it is a superordinate term for the union of the sets of norms that can be invoked (Danish, Swedish, and Norwegian), but there is no single language that can appropriately be called 'Scandinavian'. What makes the two cases analogous is that the sets of norms included are close enough that comprehension can be achieved. We may use the term 'language clusters' about related languages that give affordances for such intercommunication.

Another feature that separates Global English from a canonical operational language is that there is no community identity associated with speaking Global English. While recognizable local variants of English are associated with a sense of group membership, and speakers can be assessed as to whether they qualify as full members of the community, such an assessment is not applicable with global English.

It is a basic assumption of this account that a language cannot exist without drawing on a set of norms, and this applies also to a variational cluster of languages. The norms that underpin Global English can be understood as the union of all existing 'canonical' operational norms in English, anywhere in the world. This would be a rival conception to what Seidlhofer calls 'virtual English', as a view of "what its realizations across the globe, despite all their diversity have in common: the underlying coding possibilities" (cf. Seidlhofer, 2011, p. 111; Hall, 2018). This characterization suggests (1) that it belongs at the abstract level of a 'language-as-code', while the definition I suggest is in terms of norm-driven operational languages and (2) it would constitute an intersection, while the characterization described earlier is the union of all operational norms for English. Such a set of operational languages, anchored in communities, may be said to be 'something we have in common' in the sense that they are part of the shared world that we all have in common, but not in the sense that they are available to all of us as an abstract coding potential.

We can now use this 'norm cluster' to be more precise about the ontological anchoring of ELF in social structures, understood as a form of language use, rather than a system or code. In Mortensen's terms, ELF is the type of language use that occurs between speakers that do not have a shared L1, and speakers instead draw on the 'norm cluster' of Englishes in their language use. This is something narrower than the use of Global English, because Global English (like 'Scandinavian') would also occur between speakers all of whom were native speakers of one of the varieties, albeit different varieties, while ELF by definition occurs only when at least some speakers are not native speakers of any variety of English.

This ontological model can be used to throw light on the dilemma that arises from the teaching perspective. Basically, the change from English to Englishes calls for what Kachru (1983; cf. Baumgardner, 2006, p. 667) calls a 'polymodel' instead of the traditional 'monomodel'. As pointed out by Jenkins (2009, p. 14) "it is not viable to present learners with a single all-purpose model", because learners need to develop their accommodation skills. Although this might suggest teaching Global English as described earlier, this would require teaching not one language, but a whole plethora of different varieties. No obvious all-purpose solution can bridge this gap – and this is one reason why the choice of a native learning target may remain attractive – in spite of the developments that have undermined it. The term 'native' at the same time offers something by which to define the ultimate goal of 'full mastery', while full mastery of a *non-native* variety in practice is not easy to imagine as a teaching target (cf. Wicaksono, this volume, for an alternative perspective).

The role of this dimension comes out in relation to the position of Medgyes (2017), when he expresses his scepticism towards the dethronement of English as a Native Language in favour of ELF. A key point he raises is the difference between having the confident, successful, and effortless mastery of the language that (sometimes) characterizes a native speaker vs. the potentially more patchy resources of speakers engaging in communication by means of a language that is not their first. When it comes to selecting a target of teaching and learning, there is something rather counterintuitive about switching from the first to the second, as Medgyes argues.

What I am arguing is not that native targets remain superior, as Medgyes suggests. I am merely saying that the reorientation away from native forms of English, including the rise of ELF as a key role for English, has not provided any obvious alternative target of learning. The key reason for this is not ideology or political oppression (although these obviously remain important factors), but hard facts about (the ontology of) English. Chief among them is the coexistence of two opposite driving forces: the centrifugal force away from the old monolithic view of English, and the unifying force that drives the global expansion of the use and teaching of English, namely that it offers an internationally shared medium of communication.

In relation to learning targets, the variational approach is clearly superior to the old native-based approach as long as the question can be addressed at the micro-level of individual learner needs: pointing to anything like the Queen's English as the one-size-fits-all solution would be obviously untenable in this perspective, while nothing rules out the possibility that individual learners might have reasons of their own for choosing the Queen's English as their target. However, this way of finessing the problem becomes increasingly impossible as we move from individuals to larger collective levels: classes, schools, and national competency levels. Decisions have to be made that are dependent on understanding English as a globally shared entity rather than individual preferences.

This raises the issue of intelligibility, which casts Standard English in a more positive role, cf. Preisler (1995, p. 355): "The evolution of a multiplicity of culturally autonomous Englishes, far from proving the irrelevance of Standard English, means that Standard English will have to be maintained as an instrument of cross-cultural communication". But how does this tally with the ample evidence that native speaker varieties are not necessarily the easiest to understand (Smith and Nelson, 2006; Nelson, 2011; Smith, 2011; Page, this volume)?

At this point it is crucial to observe the distinction between Standard English and 'Native English'. As pointed out earlier, Standard English is not a specific variety of English – it is defined in relation to a set of norms that is shared across different varieties. The social reality of Standard English is most obvious in relation to written rather than spoken English (but the principle is the same), and the practical utility of Standard English, as opposed to relying on separate varieties only, can be illustrated by what would happen to inter-communicability in writing if all varieties of English introduced spellings that reflected variations in pronunciation. This would not be likely to improve the usefulness of English as a shared resource across speech communities. The findings of Smith and Nelson (2006, p. 439) illustrate the difference between the roles of Standard English and Native English in relation to the issue of learning targets: it was found that non-native speakers could equally well be assessed as speaking Standard English; an unmistakably non-native accent was no hindrance.

Part of what makes ELF the burgeoning phenomenon that it is, ironically enough, is in fact a massive teaching effort whose model is overwhelmingly imbued with Standard English. The conclusion must be that while the development away from native varieties and towards a world where English is everybody's property has radically changed the ontology of English as a feature of social reality, it has not provided a new learning target for general-purpose English classes.

6 Summary and Conclusions

The centrepiece of the ontology on which I have based the argument is the understanding of languages as parts of social structures and their causal role as the source of selection pressures. We may compare this causal role with the causality of cellphone coverage. When you move through unknown terrain, you never know whether your cellphone will work or not – that depends on community infrastructure. Similarly, when you move beyond your own home ground, you never know how well your language will work. That, too, depends on community infrastructure. Such features of community infrastructure thereby exert selection pressures on language competencies (and cellphone equipment). I have argued that this constitutes the anchoring of languages in social reality and tried to show what light this can throw on the ontology of English – arguably the most complicated case.

Such operational languages are particulars: you can put colours on a global map of social processes, showing what languages will work in them. As such, operational languages are ontologically primary in relation to 'languages-as-codes' (as universals), but they also provide ontological foundations for languages-as-codes, showing that they, too, exist – as properties of canonical speech communities (something that has occasionally been called into question). Unless the cultural evolution produced abstractable linguistic mappings between expressions and meanings, an operational language could not come into being as a property of the community. Conceptual mappings are necessary, precisely because they are detachable from particulars and hence can be downloaded (through adaptation to community life) into individual brains (as competencies), and form the socially shared targets of status assignments. Through this process they acquire the status of constitutive norms in the speech communities where they occur.

For English, I have argued that the sense in which English can at the same time be one language and a range of different languages can be captured by the notion of a 'language cluster' analogous to 'Scandinavian'. This, however, does not solve the problem of selecting a form of English that can take the place of the Queen's English as the undisputed target of general-purpose English. This does not entail that future students should keep on trying to sound like the Queen. More generally, because adaptive fitness depends on satisficing rather than optimizing, obsession with acquiring complete 'nativelike' competency would be a waste of time for the vast majority of students (it would in fact be a version of 'English for (very) Special Purposes'). As pointed out by Jenkins, 2009 as quoted earlier, adaptation to global coping would instead put a premium on better accommodation skills.

What is hard to get around is the selection pressures emanating from norms for Standard English. Because these norms do not cover a whole language competency, we have seen that they give leeway for some variability, but on those points that they do cover, it would be unprofessional for language experts to underestimate their force (whatever their undesirable side effects may be; cf. Cunningham, this volume). Selection pressures include prestige factors – not only those associated with the sociolinguistic 'high' status of the standard, but also the prestige that goes with perceived closeness to full competency. As an example, we may consider a feature that has been mentioned as a point where ELF differs from English as taught in classrooms now, the third person –s verbal agreement. We may imagine a world where *my client say he have paid* sounds just as convincing as *my client says he has paid*, but it would unwise to wager your – or your students' – money on such a world being at hand any time soon.

Learning targets for general-purpose teaching, in other words, have to evolve at a pace no faster than that of the norms that give rise to selection pressures. We may hope that such norms become less rigid over time, but that is different from hoping that they go away entirely (which is in principle impossible).

References

Baumgardner, R. J. (2006). Teaching World Englishes. In B. B. Kachru, Y. Kachru, and C. L. Nelson, eds., *The Handbook of World Englishes*. Oxford: Blackwell.

Bloomfield, L. (1933). *Language*. New York: Holt, Rinehart and Winston.

Bourdieu, P. (1984). *Distinction: A Social Critique of the Judgement of Taste*. Translation by Richard Nice of La distinction, Critique sociale du jugement. Paris: Les editions du minuit [1979]. New York and London: Routledge.

Croft, W. A. (2000). *Explaining Language Change: An Evolutionary Approach*. London: Longman.

Deacon, T. (1997). *The Symbolic Species: The Co-evolution of Language and the Human Brain*. Harmondsworth: Penguin.

Durkheim, É. (1996/1893). *De la division du travail social*. Paris: Quadrige/Presses Universitaires de France.

Gould, S. J. (1977). Bushes and ladders in human evolution. In S. J. Gould (1991). *Ever Since Darwin: Reflections in Natural History* (pp. 56–62). Harmondsworth: Penguin Books.

Hall, C. J. (2018). Cognitive perspectives on English as lingua franca. In J. Jenkins, W. Baker, and M. Dewey, eds., *Routledge Handbook of English as a Lingua Franca*. London: Routledge.

Harder, P. (2010). *Meaning in Mind and Society: A Functional Contribution to the Social Turn in Cognitive Linguistics*. Berlin/New York: Mouton de Gruyter.

Harder, P. (2014). Variation, structure and norms. In M. Pütz, J. A. Robinson, and M. Reif, eds., *Cognitive Sociolinguistics: Social and Cultural Variation in Cognition and Language Use* (pp. 53–73). Amsterdam: John Benjamins.

Hull, D. L. (1988). *Science as a Process: An Evolutionary Account of the Social and Conceptual Development of Science*. Chicago, IL: University of Chicago Press.

Jenkins, J. (2009). English as a Lingua Franca: Interpretations and attitudes. *World Englishes*, 28(2), 200–207. doi: 10.1111/j.1467-971X.2009.01582.x

Johnstone, B. (2002). *Discourse Analysis*. Oxford: Blackwell.

Kachru, B. B. (1982). *The Other Tongue: English across Cultures*. Urbana, IL: University of Illinois Press.

Kachru, B. B. (1983). *The Indianization of English: The English Language in India*. Delhi: Oxford University Press.

Keller, R. (1990). *Sprachwandel. Von der unsichtbaren Hand in der Sprache*. Tübingen: Francke.

Kristiansen, T. (2009). The macro-social meaning of late-modern Danish accents. *Acta Linguistica Hafniensia*, 41, 167–192.

Labov, W. (1972). *Sociolinguistic Patterns*. Philadelphia, PA: University of Pennsylvania Press.

Labov, W. (2014). What is to be learned: The community as the focus of social cognition. In M. Pütz, J. A. Robinson, and M. Reif, eds., *Cognitive Sociolinguistics: Social and Cultural Variation in Cognition and Language Use* (pp. 23–51). Amsterdam: John Benjamins.

Makoni, S. and Pennycook A. (eds.). 2007. *Disinventing and Reconstituting Languages*. Clevedon: Multilingual Matters.

Medgyes, P. (2017). Elfies at large – Beware! *AngloFiles*, 184, 74–78.

Milroy, J. and Milroy, L. (1991). *Authority in Language,* 2nd ed. London: Routledge.

Mortensen, J. (2013). Notes on English used as a lingua franca as an object of study. *Journal of English as a Lingua Franca*, 2(1), 25–46. Accessed 30 June 2018 from doi: 10.1515/jelf-2013-0002

Nelson, C. N. (2011). *Intelligibility in World Englishes*. New York and London: Routledge.

Pennycook, A. (2007). The myth of English as an international language. In S. Makoni and A. Pennycook, eds., *Disinventing and Reconstituting Languages* (pp. 90–115). Clevedon: Multilingual Matters.

Preisler, B. (1995). Standard English in the world. *Multilingua*, 14(4), 341–362.

Putnam, H. (2001). *Enlightenment and Pragmatism* (The Spinoza Lectures). Amsterdam: Koninklijke van Gorcum.

Richerson P. J. and Boyd, R. (2005). *Not by Genes Alone: How Culture Transformed Human Evolution*. Chicago, IL: University of Chicago Press.

Rorty, R., ed. (1967). *The Linguistic Turn. Recent Essays in Philosophical Method*. Chicago, IL: Chicago University Press.

Searle, J. R. (1995). *The Construction of Social Reality*. Harmondsworth: Penguin.

Seidlhofer, B. (2004). 10. Research perspectives on teaching English as a lingua franca. *Annual Review of Applied Linguistics*, 24, 209–239.

Seidlhofer, B. (2011). *Understanding English as a Lingua Franca*. Oxford: Oxford University Press.

Simon, H. A. (1956). Rational choice and the structure of the environment. *Psychological Review*, 63(2), 129–138. doi: 10.1037/h0042769

Smith, L. (2011). Foreword to C. L. Nelson, *Intelligibility in World Englishes*. New York and London: Routledge.

Smith, L. E. and Nelson, C. L. (2006). World Englishes and issues of intelligibility. In B. B. Kachru, Y. Kachru, and C. L. Nelson, eds., *The Handbook of World Englishes*. Oxford: Blackwell.

Spencer, H. (1864). *The Principles of Biology*. London and Edinburgh: Williams & Norgate.

Tomasello, M. (1999). *The Cultural Origins of Human Cognition*. Cambridge, MA: Harvard University Press.

Tomasello, M. (2008). *Origins of Human Communication*. Cambridge, MA: MIT Press.

Trudgill, P. (1998). Review of John Honey: Language is power. *Journal of Sociolinguistics*, 2(3), 457–461.

VOICE (2011). *Vienna-Oxford International Corpus of English. Frequently Asked Questions*. Online. Accessed 12 October 2012 from www.univie.ac.at/voice/page/faq

VOICE (2013). *Vienna-Oxford International Corpus of English. Frequently Asked Questions*. Online. Accessed 6 July 2018 from www.univie.ac.at/voice/page/faq

Wittgenstein, L. (1953). *Philosophical Investigations*. Oxford: Basil Blackwell.

4 From Constructions to Social Action

The Substance of English and Its Learning from an Interactional Usage-Based Perspective

Søren Wind Eskildsen

1 Introduction

The fundamental question to be explored in this chapter is what people actually learn when they learn 'English', and from this empirical basis distil the categories of the English language and the social-interactional roots of its learning. To this end, I draw on usage-based linguistics (UBL) and ethnomethodological conversation analysis (EMCA). The two-pronged approach combines into an interactional usage-based approach and allows me to capture development over time along two dimensions of L2 learning, namely development of L2 constructional inventories as seen through the lens of UBL and development of interactional competence as evidenced through moment-to-moment microanalyses of interactions (EMCA) over time.

The chapter lays out the foundations of UBL and CA before moving on to the empirical section in which I trace English L2 learning in terms of changes in how L2 speakers of English put language to use over time. This can be done in two ways: by tracing changes in the interactional uses of particular linguistic constructions over time or by tracing change across time in peoples' methods for carrying out particular social actions in talk-in-interaction (Eskildsen, 2018b; Pekarek Doehler, 2018; Eskildsen and Kasper, 2019).

2 Usage-Based Linguistics

UBL is a cover term for a range of linguistic theories that, in brief terms, abolish the syntax-lexis distinction and ascribe massive importance to language use as the driving force for language development and language learning. Derived from the theory of Cognitive Grammar (Langacker, 1987) and predominantly arising from scrutiny of examples from the English language, UBL insists that linguistic structures emerge as a function of human communicative needs and therefore correspond to the human perception and categorization of the world. Although UBL claims that use is the driving force of language emergence, it has been primarily concerned with semantics and the semiotic nature of language, i.e. the form-meaning pairings of which language is seen to consist.

These form-meaning pairings are called symbolic units. All units of a language are symbolic units, described along a continuum of specificity (from fixed, perhaps idiosyncratic, concrete formulas to abstract schematic templates that in turn sanction the single instantiations) and complexity (from morphemes to full utterances). Language knowledge, in this conception, is a structured inventory of these symbolic units. This means that the syntax-lexis division is done away with; there is no principled distinction between something rule governed and something formulaic. These are instead seen to occupy opposite ends of the continuum of symbolic units ranging from the totally specific to the maximally general (Achard, 2007).

Constructions, then, are cognitive schemas that carry meaning. They range from the fairly simple, such as the English schema for 'plural', which consists of two symbolic structures, two form-meaning pairings, namely the noun and the plural morph, to the more complex, such as the 'double-object' construction. This construction can be exemplified by *he gave her flowers, they baked us a cake,* and *she smiled him her love*. What binds these examples together as one construction is the shared syntagmatic structure and the meaning with which it is coupled, namely that of 'object transfer'.

Constructions become imbued with meaning through their foundation in use and language users' meaningful behaviour in the world. This implies that constructions are conventionalized linguistic means for presenting different conceptualizations or construals of an event (Langacker, 2008; Robinson and Ellis, 2008; Ellis and Cadierno, 2009). So a particular situation or event can be construed in different ways through different linguistic resources depending on participants' changing perspectives. Two English examples from Taylor (2002) will serve as illustration. One is the difference between active and passive constructions; they constitute a choice that we, as language users, have between alternatives that describe a situation in slightly different ways. Another is spatial perspective; if we say that "the roof slopes downwards", we are taking a perspective from above, whereas if we say about the same roof that it "slopes upwards", we are taking a perspective from beneath.

2.1 Usage-Based Linguistics and Language Development

Since MacWhinney (1975) argued and empirically showed that child language acquisition is a bottom-up usage-driven process, heavily reliant on recurrence, usage-based L1 research has revealed how a creative linguistic inventory comes into being on the basis of recurring linguistic material in use (e.g., Bates and MacWhinney, 1988; Tomasello and Bates, 2001; Ellis, 2002; Tomasello, 2003; Lieven et al., 2009; Brandt et al., 2011). This research has found L1 learning to be concrete, exemplar based, and rooted in usage, following a trajectory from specific recurring multi-word expressions to partially fixed, partially schematic utterance schemas to increasingly schematic constructions based on systematic commonalities among patterns. The commonalities, derived by the language user through social interaction, come to be represented in the mind, at the most advanced levels of learning, as schemas sanctioning the use, understanding, and learning of novel expressions of the same kind. Although adults learning L2 are operating on years of experience as language users and learn in different contexts than children, similar learning trajectories have been observed in adult English L2 learning (Mellow, 2006; Ellis and Ferreira-Junior, 2009a, 2009b; Eskildsen, 2012, 2017; Tode and Sakai, 2016). UBL has helped us understand how linguistic categories emerge as a result of language use – but we are only beginning to understand precisely the mechanisms of this experiential, usage-driven learning process in which people ascribe function and meaning to linguistic expressions in situ (Eskildsen and Kasper, 2019).

3 EMCA

This brings us closer to the importance of *use*. I have recently argued (Eskildsen, 2018b; Eskildsen and Kasper, 2019) that UBL's roots in Langacker's Cognitive Grammar has brought with it a focus on human cognition, perception, construal, and categorization of the world and that there is something more primordial than that, namely peoples' situated communicative purpose, their reasons for construing scenes and for putting together language to form strings of talk, which is to get some response from some co-participant(s) in some situation, primarily in social interaction. Humans may construe and categorize the world through language, but not in a social vacuum. If we say in English "the roof is sloping downwards" we are likely to do so in a situation where it can be made sense of by co-participants as an action occasioning a response (e.g. an assessment, a token of surprise or something else). Talk-in-interaction is the primordial scene of human social life (Schegloff, 1996) and so social interaction remains key to our understanding of usage-based L2 learning, in particular to our understanding of how people establish links between linguistic expressions and the actions they can be used to accomplish. To understand how social interaction works and how communicative purposes are constructed and made visible for people to learn (from) them, UBL therefore needs to be complemented by a theory of social action.

To redress this balance, I have drawn on ethnomethodological conversation analysis (Eskildsen, 2011, 2012, 2017, 2018c; Eskildsen and Wagner, 2018; Eskildsen and Kasper, 2019) to which I now turn. Rooted in sociology and emerging in the 1950s and 1960s, particularly in the work of Garfinkel (e.g. 1967), ethnomethodology (EM) is concerned with the achievement of social order. It is thus differentiated from predominant ways of thinking in sociology by not starting from the question of how macro-structures of society inform and define human behaviour (for example, how independent variables such as socio-economic status might explain ultimate educational achievement; cf. Markee, 2011). Instead, EM is concerned with the establishment of social order through peoples' methods of achieving everyday actions and practices in situ and in vivo, the key being specifically that social order is primarily to be understood from a participant's perspective (Goffman, 1983; Schegloff et al., 1996; Garfinkel, 2002).

Whereas EM is not particularly interested in how people use language to accomplish these everyday practices, conversation analysis (CA), which derives from EM, seeks to explain the methods whereby the various interactional practices that specify social order are achieved in and through *talk-in-interaction*. It should be observed, however, that CA is not solely concerned with the modality *talk* but with all interactional behaviour, including embodied actions such as gesture, gaze, and body posture, and uses of and orientations to configurations of space, objects, tools in the environment, etc. (a position consistent with that advocated by Canagarajah, this volume). Crucial to an understanding of CA are two notions: (1) intersubjectivity and (2) the next-turn proof procedure. Intersubjectivity concerns the ongoing work people carry out to ensure a common understanding of what is currently happening in interaction, and CA is concerned with explicating peoples' methods for achieving this. CA's focus, then, is on the interactional methods – people's production and displayed understanding of actions in interaction – whereby people achieve the shared understanding at the heart of Tomasello's joint attentional frame as discussed by Harder (this volume). The next-turn proof procedure is the analytic tool analysts use to scrutinize peoples' methods of achieving and maintaining intersubjectivity. It derives from the basic CA finding that conversation consists of turns-at-talk and that these are done in adjacency pairs (Sacks et al., 1974) – that is, when an action is produced, the next relevant action is occasioned, and this next action gives meaning to the prior one. In other words, by providing an answer to a question, or accepting an invitation, or mitigating and producing an objection to a produced comment or assessment (etc.), people show their understanding of what their co-participant just said, thus ensuring the constant building of the architecture of intersubjectivity (Heritage, 1984). If intersubjectivity is challenged, people can initiate repair and work through the challenge to restore intersubjectivity (for further detail on CA, see introductory texts such as that by ten Have, 2007).

The gap between UBL and CA may, at this point, seem to be a matter of interest: the former is interested in semiotic categorization on the basis of humans' cognitive skills, and the latter studies how social order emerges in and through talk and other embodied behaviour. There is, however, a potential for overlap, too. While CA is often held to be non-cognitive, it does in fact make certain assumptions about cognition as a socially shared, publicly visible phenomenon. Cognition, that is, can be studied through peoples' observable behaviour in and through talk and other embodied behaviour in interaction (Garfinkel, 1967; Heritage, 1984; Schegloff, 2006). Cognition, learning, and language thus all emerge as embedded, embodied, and distributed – a point that is also slowly making its way into usage-based second language acquisition (SLA) research (Ellis, 2014, 2015; Eskildsen and Cadierno, 2015; Eskildsen and Markee, 2018).

4 CA-SLA

Concerned with L2 learning as a socially observable phenomenon, i.e. as something that people do and demonstrably orient to in and through talk, conversation analytic SLA, or CA-SLA, has predominantly focused on the here-and-now and demonstrated that L2 speakers in and of themselves are not defective communicators, that people have ways and methods to display learning behaviour, and that repair practices, definition talk, or metalingual talk might lead to situated opportunities for learning. The research is too rich to be discussed at length here, but the interested reader should consult Brouwer (2003), Gardner and Wagner (2004), Markee and Kasper (2004), Pallotti and Wagner (2011), Hall et al. (2011), Kasper and Wagner (2011), and Eskildsen and Markee (2018).

Longitudinal CA-SLA is a more recent addition to the field and has generally taken one of two directions, either focusing on interactional practices or on linguistic/semiotic resources (Kasper and Wagner, 2014). The former has been concerned with exploring L2 speakers' interactional competence, that is methods of accomplishing particular actions, such as repair, turn openings and closings, storytelling, dispreferred responses, and how those methods change over time (e.g. Brouwer and Wagner, 2004; Hellermann, 2008; Hall et al., 2011; Pekarek Doehler and Pochon-Berger, 2015; Pekarek Doehler, 2018). The longitudinal linguistically semiotically oriented CA research traces changes in the interactional use of particular linguistic items over time (Markee, 2008; Ishida, 2009; Kim, 2009; Eskildsen, 2011; Masuda, 2011; Hauser, 2013; Eskildsen and Wagner, 2015, 2018; Eskildsen and Kasper, 2019). These studies have shown how people develop their interactional competencies with respect to the deployment of particular words and other lexically specific items in an increasing variety of interactional contexts. In addition to this, I have combined CA with UBL to carry out investigations of development at the level of utterance schema, which covers a set of interrelated linguistic expressions, rather than particular linguistic items. This research has shown how generic constructions grow out of recurring exemplars in experience (Eskildsen, 2012, 2015, 2017). The remainder of this chapter applies the UBL-CA combination to explore English L2 learning empirically in terms of the following, sometimes overlapping, phenomena: (1) situated social action, (2) change in accomplishment of social actions, (3) establishment of a particular expression, (4) change in the deployment of a particular expression, (5) change in the composition of the expression through pattern expansion (e.g. verb variation), and (6) change in function through increased structural variation (e.g. emergence of interrogative, inversion).

5 Empirical Data and Analysis

The data used here come from The Multimedia Adult English Learner Corpus (MAELC), an audio-visual classroom interaction L2 database at Portland State University. Collected from 2001–2005, the data consist of almost 4,000 hours of classroom interaction. The recordings in the classrooms were made using ceiling-mounted cameras (six) and microphones (four) and personal, wireless microphones. These were worn by the students on a rotational basis (two students per session), and the teacher always wore a wireless microphone. In this chapter, as well as in most of my previous work, I will use data from two Mexican Spanish-speaking students in the corpus, Carlos and Valerio. Both progressed through the levels of the program (known locally as levels A, B, C, and D; cf., Reder, 2005), Carlos from level A, and Valerio from level B (see also Eskildsen, 2015, 2017; Eskildsen et al., 2015).

5.1 Learning as Social Action: Collaborative Word Search

Learning as social action may take on many forms, but the defining principle is that learning is analyzed as something people demonstrably orient to through interactional conduct; it is "a conversational process that observably occurs in the intersubjective space between participants" (Markee and Kasper, 2004, p. 496). More recently, research has been concerned with establishing learning behaviours in more specific terms, such as planning and spelling (Kunitz and Skogmyr Marian, 2017), engaging in language contracts (Eskildsen and Theodórsdóttir, 2017), word searches as self-initiated other-repairs, lexical inquiries to preempt trouble, and re-indexing of previously learned items (Eskildsen, 2019). In the interest of space, I will limit the empirical discussion to word searches. Brouwer (2003) discussed word searches as opportunities for L2 learning, but the practice concerns how speakers initiate and carry out repair in the face of lacking or uncertain vocabulary. The practice concerns, in other words, the interactional organization of orienting to problems in producing and understanding language and maintaining intersubjectivity (Schegloff et al., 1977; Schegloff, 1992). Word searches can be initiated through the use of a lingua franca, explicitly marked through language (e.g. *how do you say x?*) or implicitly marked through turn-design (e.g. pauses and try-marking) (Brouwer, 2003; Kurhila, 2006; Mori, 2010; Eskildsen, 2011, 2018a, 2019; Theodórsdóttir and Eskildsen, 2011). As such, word searches have been shown to be collaborative learning activities. One reason why word searches work as learning opportunities is that the actions of the practice designate learner and expert identities in situ (Brouwer, 2003; Kasper and Wagner, 2011; Theodórsdóttir and Eskildsen, 2011). The L2 speaker is identified as a learner as she displays trouble and initiates repair, thereby inviting a co-participant to help solve the trouble. When the word search has been successful and the troubling item delivered, the learner typically displays having noticed the new item by picking it up and using it. Until recently, the nagging question was whether word searches constitute long-term L2 learning and not only *opportunities for learning* (Brouwer, 2003). However, Eskildsen (2018a) demonstrates that (some) word searches have long-term consequences, and, moreover, there is also an increasing amount of evidence from longitudinal usage-based/CA research indicating that encounters with new L2 vocabulary leave traces in peoples' experience and that learning is a matter of appropriation in multiple encounters over time (Eskildsen, 2015, 2017, 2018a; Eskildsen and Wagner, 2015). Word searches constitute one kind of encounter, a practice for language learning where new L2 items are brought to the fore of the interaction as "learnables" (Majlesi and Broth, 2012; Eskildsen and Majlesi, 2018), and are therefore important stepping stones on the path to increased L2 vocabulary.

Extract 1 is an example of a word search from the MAELC database. Carlos is standing by the white board, having just written yesterday's date as part of a daily routine (Eskildsen, in press). He says something in Spanish (line 1) and begins to correct his own writing, changing the 'y' in *yesterday* to a capital 'Y'. The teacher, noticing his actions, initiates repair (line 2; see p. xx for transcription conventions).

Extract 1 Word search

```
01   CAR:    ((spn))
02   TEA:    say tha:t what what say it again (.) what
03   CAR:    heh?
04   TEA:    huh?
05           (0.8)
05   CAR:    hh. .hh the::h letter
06           (0.5)
07   TEA:    the let[ter
08   CAR:           [is e:h (2.1) is: arh ((looks down)) (1.8)
                   ((looks up)) how d' you say e:h ((shifts gaze to
                   teacher))
09   TEA:    capital let[ter
10   CAR:               [capital letter ((nods))
11   TEA:    uhuh
12   CAR:    (   ) ((puts pen to whiteboard))
13   TEA:    I nee::d
14   CAR:    I need eh put the capi- capital letter
15   TEA:    very good I need to put a capital letter very good
```

Carlos does not immediately show understanding of the teacher's turn; his *heh* with rising intonation usually works as an open-class repair initiator (line 3) but in return the teacher seems to merely mimic him (line 4). Following a pause, Carlos then takes the next turn, as he tentatively produces two words, *the letter* (line 5). Following another pause, the teacher repeats his words, which Carlos treats as an invitation to continue (lines 6–8) but he soon runs into trouble, seen in prolonged sounds, pauses, a speech perturbation and so-called thinking faces (Goodwin and Goodwin, 1986) in the form of gazes away from the co-participant. The phrase *how do you say* may work both as an explicit word search marker and as a display of doing thinking while holding the floor (Brouwer, 2003; Eskildsen, 2011), and it is not until he establishes mutual gaze with the teacher that she steps in with a candidate solution to his trouble, suggesting that he is searching for the word *capital (letter)* (line 10). He confirms by way of a repeat and a head-nod and the teacher acknowledges this (lines 11–12). Carlos says something inaudible and reorients to making the correction (changing 'y' to 'Y') (line 13). The teacher then initiates a new sequence as she embarks on what turns out to be a designedly incomplete utterance (Koshik, 2002) that invites Carlos to step in. He does so, completing her utterance to form *I need put the capital letter* which the teacher commends him for although she implicitly corrects him, adding the infinitival marker *to* and changing the definite article to the indefinite article (lines 14–16).

In a usage-based perspective this encounter is part and parcel of Carlos's experience as a user of English and as such this interaction is as a learning opportunity. The focus word here is *capital (letter)*; this is the first time Carlos utters these words in the class, but it is not the first time he encounters them. I know that because I have followed him in the database but his action in line 10 may actually indicate this, too: he is displaying recognition of the teacher's candidate solution, as seen in his overlap and his head nod. Interestingly, moving ahead, he uses the term *capital letter* spontaneously nine days later and then on several occasions throughout his time in class. The encounters with the term, from the teacher's introduction to the term three weeks prior to this situation, all leave traces in his experience, enabling him to use the term in the end.

Collaborative word searches constitute L2 learning as a social undertaking in which participants orient to the goings-on as learning as they engage in sometimes lengthy sequences of focusing on language. The word search practice is one empirical, in situ unfolding of 'languaging' as discussed by Hall (this volume). The word search sequences, moreover, leave traces, or sediments, in the L2 speakers' experience so that they may draw on these later on (Eskildsen, 2018a, 2019). This is the interactional reality underlying the distilled, empirically harvested insight from usage-based linguistics that English L2 development is the conspiracy of all the utterances in any one L2 English speaker's entire biography as L2 user (Ellis, 2015; Eskildsen and Cadierno, 2015); all language derives from first instances of use (Tomasello, 2003). It is to developmental issues that we turn next.

5.2 Change in Accomplishment of Social Action

Eskildsen and Markee (2018) showed, through fine-grained analyses of particular L2 practices, that L2 talk is a social accomplishment. Language, cognition, and learning are fundamentally embedded in the local circumstances of talk-in-environment and distributed across participants and inherently embodied. We showed how a teacher taught her students the two phrases *it's incorrect* and *let me help you* in a highly contextualized fashion, in environments where she explicitly linked the expressions to particular actions of pointing out mistakes and volunteering to correct the mistakes. She has afforded the L2 students opportunities to use specific semiotic resources for specific actions in specific environments. Carlos learns and uses these expressions in these recurring environments around activities that occasion the uses. He displays the interactional competence in the classroom as community of practice to be able to volunteer, write on the communal board, correct himself and others, and help others. Through an understanding of those practices, he learns the linguistic tools, taught by the teacher, to index and/or express the upcoming action. Whether or not other teachers would have preferred to teach other linguistic tools for accomplishing these particular actions is irrelevant to our point, which is that language is here taught and learned as a semiotic resource for social action (Eskildsen, 2018b, 2018c).

In Extract 2 the teacher is introducing "I don't think so, let me help you" (line 6). This is occasioned by what happened just prior, namely a student's rather blunt display of noticing another student's mistake on the whiteboard (For the full transcription and analysis, please see Eskildsen and Markee, 2018.).

Extract 2 *"Let me help you"*

```
06    TEA:                      [how abou:t £o:h ] no
07    TEA:   I don' t think so let me help you:.£
08    UNI:   what what
09    CAR:   wha- one more[time
10    TEA:                [let me help you
11    MUL:   ((attempts at repeating "let me help you"))
12    TEA:   let me help you
13    CAR:   o:[h
14    TEA:     [come. ((summons another student))
15    CAR:   [let me- ] let me- let me [help you
```

The teacher's action results in heavy repair and repetition work on the part of the students (lines 8–12). Our focal student, Carlos, requests a repetition as one of the repair initiations and, following multiple repetitions of "let me help you", he produces a change-of-state token that works as a claim of understanding (Heritage, 1984). His repetition in line 15 then displays his understanding, if not of the phrase per se, then of the activity that is currently going on.

After this interaction, the teacher writes "let me help you" on the whiteboard. This inscription emphasizes and authorizes the phrase as an important focal point (Streeck and Kalmeyer, 2001; Mondada and Pekarek Doehler, 2004; Eskildsen and Theodórsdóttir, 2017). As we showed (Eskildsen and Markee, 2018), Carlos learned, over the next days, to use "let me help" to indicate his upcoming action of helping a student to correct his or her writing on the board. Essentially, Carlos was learning to accomplish particular actions, namely to indicate errors and to indicate his upcoming action of volunteering to help, in new ways. This happened through repeated correction activities in which, among other things, the teacher repeatedly oriented to her writings on the whiteboard, and in response to these actions the students, in particular Carlos, also oriented to them. These orientations indicate that cognition and learning are deeply embedded in and contingent upon the materiality and configuration of the local space (cf. Canagarajah, this volume). We know this not because we can see the writing on the board, but because of participants' visible orientations; i.e., the participants constantly display their current thinking through verbal and bodily actions. They do not just speak; they enact, point, nod, shift gaze, etc. Cognition is, then, not only embedded, it is also embodied and socially shared.

As Carlos was learning to accomplish actions in new ways, he was also learning (the English) 'language'. Language learning is therefore best viewed as locally contextualized; language emergence is situated, occasioned, socially shared and locally contingent, and understanding and learning an L2 is grounded in understanding of social practices (Wagner, 2015). Calling for an epistemology of SLA research that views language, learning, and cognition as essentially socially distributed, this continues the work of others who have made similar points over the years (e.g., Markee, 1994; Firth and Wagner, 2007; Kasper, 2009; Burch, 2014).

It could be argued that a 'language' is epiphenomenal to social practices, but a less radical standpoint is that social practices simply envelop language and cognition; L2 learners learn to act in situated, locally calibrated ways that adapt to their co-participants. In the case of "let me help", this was discovered by tracing Carlos's conduct in recurring activities. However, L2 learning as the development of acting in situated, locally calibrated ways can also be demonstrated by tracing particular linguistic expressions empirically.

5.3 The Social History of a Particular Expression: Establishment and Change

In the first study in which I combined UBL and CA (Eskildsen, 2011), I showed how Valerio used and learned "what do you say?" and related constructions. I traced the utterance schema *do you verb* and showed that it emerged from the formulaic multi-word expression (MWE) *what do you say* and expanded towards an increasingly schematized and diversified inventory of language knowledge, as new closely related patterns emerge. It may also be noted that the initially occurring patterns, e.g. *what do you say* and *do you like*, are retained and put to use on and off throughout development, alongside the use of the more differentiated structures.

The recurring MWE *what do you say* was found to constitute Valerio's first three occurrences and 50 per cent of all *do*-uses in his first term in class. The inventory then expands on this exemplar-based basis towards an increasingly diversified, perhaps schematized, inventory:

What do you say? Do you like? When do you use? What did he say? (WH) DO X VERB

What do you say is put to use throughout development alongside the differentiated structures, but is continuously recalibrated to accomplish new actions. Valerio used the phrase for four interrelated purposes, as outlined in Table 4.1, which also shows the periods in which Valerio was using the expression for the actions and in what extracts below they are represented.

In Extract 3, Valerio is using the expression to elicit help in a word search. He is involved in pair work but has run into lexical trouble. He then asks a peer, Laura, for help. Laura is not the one Valerio is doing pair work with; instead she is sitting across the room. Hence the summons and the mutual gaze before he proceeds to ask for help (line 1). Laura provides the help, Valerio asks to have it confirmed

Table 4.1 *"What do you say" by action and chronology*

Action	Period of use	Extract
Request for help	July–August 2003	3
Display of doing thinking	July–March 2004	4
Re-indexing previous action	August 2003–June 2005	5
Eliciting a co-participant's opinion	March–July 2004	6

which Laura does, and he finally thanks her (note that *estuvo* does not correspond to *I went*, but that is besides the analytic point here).

Extract 3 Request for help

```
01    VAL:    Laura ((mutual gaze)) what do you say estuvo
02    LAU:    estuvo? (.) I went
03    VAL:    I went?
04    LAU:    uhuh
05    VAL:    alright thank you
```

In the collection of instances, this is how the practice runs off in general: Valerio uses the phrase to ask for help with an item and gets the help following which there is some acknowledgement on his part.

Extract 4 is an example of doing thinking. The students are doing a task intended to elicit the short answer forms "no I don't" and "yes I do". In line 1, Valerio asks Danny (Chinese) if he likes Mexican food. After a pause, Danny offers a tentative answer and Valerio nods in response following which Danny repeats the word *maybe* (lines 2–5). Then Valerio begins a turn that he abandons as he nods in response to Danny's second *maybe* (line 6). He continues with displays of trouble, the use of the expression *what do you say* accompanied by downward gaze, and eventually a restart as he asks Danny, "you eating food Mexican?" In Danny's response, *no never*, we see his understanding of the question as meaning "have you ever eaten Mexican food?" (lines 7–10).

Extract 4 Display of doing thinking

```
01    VAL:    do you like meh eh food Mexican?
02            (2.2)
03    DAN:    maybe but I didn't uh ((starts making a waving gesture
04            with right hand)) but I do not taste
05    VAL:    ((nods))
06    DAN:    maybe
07    VAL:    you ((nods briefly)) you:: ts (1.3) what do you say
08            ((looks down)) (1.0) you eating mex you eating food
09            Mexican?
10    DAN:    no ((shakes head)) never
```

Note how the two examples show the use of *what do you say* in different sequential positions and in different turn-positions. When used to elicit help, the action is always pre-indexed by interactional work, for example a summons, whereas in the uses of the phrase to display doing thinking, the phrase is accompanied by embodied conduct showing momentary detachment from the current interactional space, for example, downward gaze, and participants stick to the preference for self-repair (Schegloff et al., 1977).

The use of the phrase in word search environments can be traced back to Valerio's first day in class, as outlined in Table 4.1. Seven weeks into his time in class, he begins using it to perform another function, namely to re-index a previous action made by a co-participant (Extract 5). Importantly, as Table 4.1 indicates, the new use overlaps chronologically with the previous uses, which suggests that the phrase is one unit that is carried across contextual boundaries. On the day when the interaction in Extract 5 was recorded, one of the students had brought her young daughter to the class. Prior to the extract, the teacher commented that the girl was cute, which spawned questions about the word *cute* and what adjective to use about boys. The teacher explained that cute also works for boys but that when boys get older, handsome may be more apt. This is line 1. Valerio repeats *pretty* in overlap with the teacher and after a few seconds (omitted lines) Valerio uses the phrase to ask again for the word for boys (line 8). Olivia, a fellow student, marks it as a joint inquiry (line 10), following which the teacher repeats the word, *handsome*. Valerio picks it up and has it confirmed (lines 11–13).

Extract 5 Re-indexing previous action

```
01   TEA:   pretty for a girl [ and handsome for a boy
02   VAL:                     [ pretty. ((nodding))
((omitted lines))
08   VAL:   what do you say for bo boy
09          (1.2)
10   OLI:   [ for boy?
11   TEA:   [ handsome
12   VAL:   handsome?
13   TEA:   handsome mhm
```

The final function for which the phrase was used, elicitation of a co-participant's opinion, is displayed in Extract 6. Valerio and the teacher are discussing Valerio's level placement in the following term. At lines 1–2, the teacher is asking Valerio if he prefers level C or D. He gives a tentative answer and then asks for the teacher's opinion, using the target phrase (lines 3–4). After asking him how many times he has done level C she advises him to take level C once more, which he accepts (lines 5–8).

Extract 6 Eliciting a co-participant's opinion

```
01   TEA:   okay (1.2) would you like to stay in level cee or try
02          level dee.
03   VAL:   ehm (2.0) I like level dee but I don' t know (1.1) what
04          do you say (1.2)[ mmm
05   TEA:                  [ how many times have you been in
                level cee
06   VAL:   two
07   TEA:   just two times? (1.0) three times is okay.
08   VAL:   ((nods))
```

Eskildsen (2011) thus documented learning along four of the dimensions mentioned earlier. The data showed the establishment through recurring use of a particular expression, *how do you say?* Investigating the usage event in more detail revealed that Valerio was also learning in terms of change in his deployment of the expression: *elicit help, display doing thinking* → *re-index previous action* → *elicit opinion*. Moreover, the study documented learning beyond the usage events discussed as Valerio's linguistic inventory grew in terms of change in the composition of the expression through expansion: *what do you say?* → *what do you VERB? / WH-Q do you VERB?* Finally, the data also revealed that constructional learning was happening as change in function through increased structural variation; Valerio learned to use *do you VERB?* for other purposes than *what do you VERB?*

6 Conclusion and Implications

This chapter has discussed English L2 learning in terms of the following, sometimes overlapping, phenomena: (1) situated social action, (2) change in accomplishment of social actions, (3) establishment of a particular expression, (4) change in the deployment of a particular expression, (5) change in the composition of the expression through pattern expansion (e.g., verb variation), and (6) change in function through increased structural variation (e.g., emergence of interrogative, inversion). The research is informed by a particular conceptualization of the English language, namely one that is based on an inventory of constructions, as found in UBL. However, recent analyses have confirmed what was already evident in Eskildsen (2011): peoples' linguistic repertoires need to be considered in light of how they accomplish particular social actions (cf. Canagarajah, this volume). It was shown that Valerio was developing his repertoire in response to environmental requirements. His constructional development from establishment of a pattern to increased structural variation happened in and through social interaction in situations that called for the deployment of the linguistic constructions in question. This insight informed the research in Eskildsen and Markee (2018) where we showed Carlos's learning and uses of the phrases "it's incorrect" and "let me help you/her" as situated in recurring environments in which he, while he was learning the phrases, was learning to carry out particular social actions, and similarly, Eskildsen (2018c) showed how Carlos's learning of subordinate and coordinate constructions was inextricably linked with the ongoing discourse in the sense that the constructions were found to be building as much on previous turns by co-participants as on his own previous talk. Moreover, the establishment of the constructions was found to be bound to his developing interactional competence, again suggesting that the constructions grow in response to situated change.

The implication is that there is more to constructions than form-meaning correspondences. In fact, taking the social embeddedness of linguistic behavior and the notion that social interaction is the primordial scene of human sociality as the point of departure, I propose that UBL moves away from the purely semiotic to include actional aspects of linguistic meaning. By this I mean that we have come a long way in describing form-meaning relations in terms of constructions, or symbolic units, but it really is the link between these constructions and the actions they can be used to perform that drives their emergence (Eskildsen and Kasper, 2019). Social interaction is the bedrock of the human experience that is thought to be the root of schemas and constructions in UBL. Therefore, UBL needs to attend more closely to the specifics of social interaction and the array of functions that linguistic expressions can be used to perform in order to investigate the "construction – action" correspondences rather than "form – meaning pairings". We do not usually say things like "the roof is sloping downwards" in a social vacuum; rather, we say these things to perform particular actions that call on reactions form co-participants. The inventory of constructions constituting English, therefore, is best thought of as a semiotic repertoire for social action.

References

Achard, M. (2007). Usage-based Semantics: Meaning and Distribution of Three French 'Breaking' Verbs. In M. Nenonen and S. Niemi, eds., *Collocations and Idioms 1: Papers from the First Nordic Conference on Syntactic Freezes,*

Joensuu, May 19–2 0, 2007. *Studies in Languages, University of Joensuu,* Vol. 41. Joensuu: Joensuu University Press.

Bates, E. and MacWhinney, B. (1988). What is functionalism? *Papers and Reports on Child Language Development, 27,* 137–152.

Brandt, S., Verhagen, A., Lieven, E., and Tomasello, M. (2011). German children's productivity with simple transitive and complement-clause constructions: Testing the effects of frequency and variability. *Cognitive Linguistics,* 22(2), 325–357.

Brouwer, C. E. (2003). Word searches in NNS-NS interaction: Opportunities for language learning? *Modern Language Journal,* 87(4), 534–545.

Burch, R. A. (2014). Pursuing information: A conversation analytic perspective on communication strategies. *Language Learning,* 64(3), 651–684.

Ellis, N. C. (2002). Frequency effects in language processing – A review with implications for theories of implicit and explicit language acquisition. *Studies in Second Language Acquisition, 24*(2), 143–188.

Ellis, N. C. (2014). Cognitive *and* social language use. In *Studies in Second Language Acquisition,* 36, 397–402. [Special Issue *Bridging the Gap. Cognitive and Social Approaches to Research in Second Language Learning and Teaching,* J. Hulstijn, R. F. Young, and L. Ortega, eds.]

Ellis, N. C. (2015). Cognitive and social aspects of learning from usage. In T. Cadierno and S. W. Eskildsen, eds., *Usage-Based Perspectives on Second Language Learning* (pp. 49–74). Berlin: Mouton de Gruyter.

Ellis, N. C. and Cadierno, T. (2009). Constructing a second language: Introduction to the special section. *Annual Review of Cognitive Linguistics,* 7, 111–139.

Ellis, N. C. and Ferreira-Junior, F. (2009). Construction learning as a function of frequency, frequency distribution, and function. *Modern Language Journal,* 93 (3), 370–385.

Eskildsen, S. W. (2011). The L2 inventory in action: Conversation analysis and usage-based linguistics in SLA. In G. Pallotti and J. Wagner, eds., *L2 Learning as Social Practice: Conversation-Analytic Perspectives* (pp. 337–373). Honolulu: University of Hawai'i, National Foreign Language Resource Center.

Eskildsen, S. W. (2012). Negation constructions at work. *Language Learning,* 62 (2), 335–372.

Eskildsen, S. W. (2015). What counts as a developmental sequence? Exemplar-based L2 learning. *Language Learning,* 65(1), 33–62.

Eskildsen, S. W. (2017). The emergence of creativity in L2 English – A usage-based case-study. In N. Bell, ed., *Multiple Perspectives on Language Play* (pp. 281–316). Berlin: Mouton de Gruyter.

Eskildsen, S. W. (2018a). "We're learning a lot of new words": Encountering new L2 vocabulary outside of class. *Modern Language Journal,* 102(Supplement), 46–63.

Eskildsen, S. W. (2018b). Building a semiotic repertoire for social action: Interactional competence as biographical discovery. *Classroom Discourse* 9(1), 68–76.

Eskildsen, S. W. (2018c). L2 constructions and interactional competence: Subordination and coordination in English L2 learning. In A. Tyler, L. Huang, and

H. Jan, eds., *What Is Applied Cognitive Linguistics? Answers from Current SLA Research* (pp. 61–96). Berlin: Mouton de Gruyter.

Eskildsen, S. W. (2019). Learning behaviors in the wild: How people achieve L2 learning outside of class. In J. Hellermann, S. W. Eskildsen, S. Pekarek Doehler, and A. Piirainen-Marsh, eds., *Conversation Analytic Research on Learning-in-Action: The Complex Ecology of L2 Interaction in the Wild*. Dordrecht: Springer.

Eskildsen, S. W. (in press). "Let me help you": Learning to do and correct public writing in the L2 classroom. In S. Kunitz, O. Sert, and N. Markee, eds., *Emerging Issues in Classroom Discourse and Interaction: Theoretical and Applied CA Perspectives on Pedagogy*. Dordrecht: Springer.

Eskildsen, S. W. and Cadierno, T. (2015). Advancing usage-based approaches to L2 studies. In T. Cadierno and S. W. Eskildsen, eds., *Usage-Based Perspectives on Second Language Learning* (pp. 1–18). Berlin: Mouton de Gruyter.

Eskildsen, S. W. and Kasper, G. (2019). Interactional usage-based L2 pragmatics. From form-meaning pairings to construction-action relations. In N. Taguchi, ed., *The Routledge Handbook of Second Language Acquisition and Pragmatics* (pp. 176–191). New York: Routledge.

Eskildsen, S. W. and Majlesi, A. R. (2018). Learnables and teachables in second language talk: Advancing a social reconceptualization of central SLA tenets. Introduction to the special issue. *Modern Language Journal*, 102(supplement), 3–10.

Eskildsen, S. W. and Markee, N. (2018). L2 talk as social accomplishment. In R. A. Alonso, ed., *Learning to Speak in an L2*. Amsterdam: John Benjamins.

Eskildsen, S. W. and Theodórsdóttir, G. (2017). Constructing L2 learning spaces: Ways to achieve learning inside and outside the classroom. *Applied Linguistics*, 38, 148–164.

Eskildsen, S. W. and Wagner, J. (2015). Emodied L2 construction learning. *Language Learning*, 65(2), 419–448.

Eskildsen, S. W. and Wagner, J. (2018). From trouble in the talk to new resources – The interplay of bodily and linguistic resources in the talk of a novice speaker of English as a second language. In S. Pekarek Doehler, J. Wagner, and E. González-Martínez, eds., *Longitudinal Studies on the Organization of Social Interaction*. Basingstoke: Palgrave Macmillan.

Eskildsen, S. W., Cadierno, T. and Li, P. (2015). On the development of motion constructions in four learners of L2 English. In T. Cadierno and S. W. Eskildsen, eds., *Usage-Based Perspectives on Second Language Learning* (pp. 207–232). Mouton de Gruyter.

Firth, A. and Wagner, J. (2007). S/FL Learning as a social accomplishment: Elaborations on a 'reconceptualized' SLA. *Modern Language Journal*, 91 (focus issue), 800–819.

Gardner, R. and Wagner, J. (2004). *Second Language Conversations*. London: Continuum.

Garfinkel, H. (1967). *Studies in Ethnomethodology*. Englewood Cliffs: Prentice Hall.

Garfinkel, H. (2002). *Ethnomethodology's Program*. Lanham: Rowman & Littlefield.
Goffman, E. (1983). The interaction order. *American Sociological Review, 48*, 1–17.
Goodwin, M. H. and Goodwin, C. (1986). Gesture and co-participation in the activity of searching for a word. *Semiotica, 62*, 51–75.
Hall, J. K., Pekarek Doehler, S., and Hellermann, J., eds. (2011). *L2 Interactional Competence and Development*. Clevedon: Multilngual Matters.
Hauser, E. (2013). Stability and change in one adult's second language English negation. *Language Learning, 6*(3), 463–498.
Hellermann, J. (2008). *Social Actions for Classroom Language Learning*. Clevedon: Multilingual Matters.
Heritage, J. (1984). A change-of-state token and aspects of its sequential placement. In J. M. Atkinson and J. Heritage, eds., *Structures of Social Action: Studies in Conversation Analysis* (pp. 299–345). Cambridge: Cambridge University Press.
Ishida, M. (2009). Development of interactional competence: Changes in the use of *ne* in L2 Japanese during study abroad. In H. T. Nguyen and G. Kasper, eds., *Talk-Interaction: Multilingual Perspectives* (pp. 351–386). Honolulu: University of Hawai'i.
Kasper, G. (2009). Locating cognition in second language interaction and learning: Inside the skull or in public view? *International Review of Applied Linguistics, 47*, 13–36.
Kasper, G. and Wagner, J. (2011). A conversation-analytic approach to second language acquisition. In D. Atkinson, ed., *Alternative Approaches to Second Language Acquisition* (pp. 117–142). New York: Taylor & Francis.
Kasper, G. and Wagner, J. (2014). Conversation analysis in applied linguistics. *Annual Review of Applied Linguistics, 34*, 171–212.
Kim, Y. (2009). Korean discourse markers in L2 Korean speakers' conversation: An acquisitional perspective. In H. T. Nguyen and G. Kasper, eds., *Talk-in-Interaction: Multilingual Perspectives* (pp. 317–350). Honolulu: National Foreign Language Resource Center.
Koshik, I. (2002). Designedly incomplete utterances: A pedagogical practice for eliciting knowledge displays in error correction sequences. *Research on Language and Social Interaction, 35*(3), 277–309.
Kunitz, S. and Skogmyr Marian, K. (2017). Tracking immanent language learning behavior over time in task-based classroom work. *Tesol Quarterly, 51*(3), 507–535.
Kurhila, S. (2006). *Second Language Interaction*. Amsterdam: John Benjamins.
Langacker, R. W. (1987). *Foundations of Cognitive Grammar*. Vol. 1 of *Theoretical Prerequisites*. Stanford, CA: Stanford University Press.
Langacker, R. W. (2008). Cognitive grammar as basis for language instruction. In P. Robinson and N. C. Ellis, eds., *Handbook of Cognitive Grammar and Second Language Acquisition*. New York: Routledge.
Lieven, E., Salomo, D., and Tomasello, M. (2009). Two-year-old children's production of multiword utterances: A usage-based analysis. *Cognitive Linguistics, 20*(3), 481–508.

MacWhinney, B. (1975). Pragmatic patterns in child syntax. *Stanford Papers and Reports on Child Language Development, 10,* 153–165.
Majlesi, A. R. and Broth, M. (2012). Emergent learnables in second language classroom interaction. *Learning, Culture and Social Interaction, 1,* 193–207.
Markee, N. (1994). Toward an ethnomethodological respecification of second-language acquisition studies. In E. E. Tarone, S. M. Gass, and A. D. Cohen, eds., *Research Methodology in Second-Language Acquisition* (pp. 89–116). Hillsdale: Lawrence Erlbaum.
Markee, N. (2008). Toward a learning behavior tracking methodology for CA-for-SLA. *Applied Linguistics, 29*(3), 404–427.
Markee, N. (2011). Doing, and justifying doing, avoidance. *Journal of Pragmatics, 43,* 602–615.
Markee, N. and Kasper, G. (2004). Classroom talks: An introduction. *Modern Language Journal, 88*(4), 491–500.
Masuda, K. (2011). Acquiring interactional competence in a study abroad context: Japanese language learners' use of the interactional particle *ne*. *Modern Language Journal, 95*(4), 519–540.
Mellow, J. D. (2006). The emergence of second language syntax: A case study of the acquisition of relative clauses. *Applied Linguistics, 27*(4), 645–670.
Mondada, L. and Pekarek Doehler, S. (2004). Second language acquisition as situated practice: Task accomplishment in the French second language classroom. *Modern Language Journal, 88*(4), 501–518.
Mori, J. (2010). Learning language in real time: A case study of the Japanese demonstrative pronoun "are" in word-search sequences. In G. Kasper, H. T. Nguyen, D. Yoshimi, and J. K. Yoshioka, eds., *Pragmatics in Language Learning,* Vol. 12 (pp. 15–42). Honolulu: University of Hawai'i, National Foreign Language Resource Center.
Pallotti, G. and Wagner, J., eds. (2011). *L2 Learning as Social Practice: Conversation-Analytic Perspectives.* Honolulu: University of Hawai'i, National Foreign Language Resource Center.
Pekarek Doehler, S. (2018). Elaborations on L2 Interactional Competence: The Development of L2 grammar-for-interaction. *Classroom Discourse, 9* (1).
Pekarek Doehler, S. and Pochon-Berger, E. (2015). The development of L2 interactional competence: Evidence from turn-taking organization, sequence organization, repair organization and preference organization. In T. Cadierno and S. W. Eskildsen, eds., *Usage-Based Perspectives on Second Language Learning* (pp. 233–268). Mouton de Gruyter.
Reder, S. (2005). The "Lab School". *Focus on Basics, 8*(A). Available online: www.ncsall.net/fileadmin/resources/fob/2005/fob_8a.pdf.
Robinson, P. and Ellis, N. C., eds. (2008). *Handbook of Cognitive Linguistics and Second Language Acquisition.* New York: Routledge.
Sacks, H., Schegloff, E. A., and Jefferson, G. (1974). A simplest systematics for the organization of turntaking for conversation. *Language, 50,* 696–735.
Schegloff, E. A. (1992). Repair after next turn: The last structurally provided defense of intersubjectivity in conversation. *American Journal of Sociology, 97* (5), 1295–1345.

Schegloff, E. A. (1996). Issues of relevance for discourse analysis: Contingency in action, interaction, and co-participant context. In E. H. Hovy and D. R. Scott, eds., Conversational and Computational Discourse: Burning Issues – An Interdisciplinary Account (pp. 3–35). New York: Springer.

Schegloff, E. A. (2006). Interaction: The infrastructure for social institutions, the natural ecological niche for language, and the arena in which culture is enacted. In N. J. Enfield and S. C. Levinson, eds., *Roots of Human Sociality* (pp. 70–96). London: Berg.

Schegloff, E. A., Jefferson, G., and Sacks, H. (1977). The preference for self-correction in the organization of repair in conversation. *Language, 53*, 361–382.

Schegloff, E. A., Ochs, E., and Thompson, S. A. (1996). Introduction. In E. Ochs, E. A. Schegloff, and S. A. Thompson, eds., *Interaction and Grammar* (pp. 1–51). Cambridge: Cambridge University Press.

Streeck, J. and Kalmeyer, W. (2001). Interaction by inscription. *Journal of Pragmatics 33*, 465–490.

Taylor, J. R. (2002). *Cognitive Grammar*. Oxford: Oxford University Press.

ten Have, P. (2007). *Doing Conversation Analysis: A Practical Guide*, 2nd ed. London: Sage.

Theodórsdóttir, G. and Eskildsen, S. W. (2011). Achieving intersubjectivity and doing learning: The use of English as a Lingua Franca in Icelandic L2. *Nordand, 6*(2), 59–85.

Tode, T. and Sakai, H. (2016). Exemplar-based instructed second language development and classroom experience. *International Journal of Applied Linguistics*, 167(2), 210–234.

Tomasello, M. (2003). *Constructing a Language*. Cambridge: Cambridge University Press.

Tomasello, M. and Bates, E., eds. (2001). *Language Development: The Essential Readings*. Malden: Blackwell.

Wagner, J. (2015). Designing for language learning in the wild. Creating social infrastructures for second language learning. In T. Cadierno and S. W. Eskildsen, eds., *Usage-Based Perspectives on Second Language Learning* (pp. 75–104). Berlin: de Gruyter Mouton.

5 Native and Non-native Speakers of English in TESOL

Rachel Wicaksono

1 Introduction

This chapter explores ideas about '(non-)native' speakers of English, with particular reference to the professional context of teaching English to speakers of other languages (TESOL). The use of '(non-)native' speaker to describe a person's use of English remains common in a variety of domains, despite much scholarly and professional argument against the term. Given that learners and teachers comprise the educational context of this chapter, I have chosen to focus on the native and non-native speakers themselves, rather than on their (so-called) native and non-native uses of English. In doing so, I hope not to fall into the trap of thinking of people as permanent members of closed categories, but, on the contrary, show how we might raise awareness of the (potentially negative) effects of such thinking on speakers of English, in the TESOL profession.

In the first section of the chapter, I consider how 'native' has been used to describe speakers of English: in popular discourse, by TESOL scholars, and in teacher recruitment. Next, I explore contestations of the native speaker idea and add to these, using work on ontologies of English (see Hall, this volume), language cognition, English as a Lingua Franca, and identities. Finally, I suggest what might be done to re-frame, alleviate, or resist some of the negative effects of the native speaker idea on (individuals associated with) the TESOL profession.

2 The Use of the Native Speaker Idea …

2.1 … in Popular Discourse

The idea of a 'native speaker' continues to circulate widely in popular discourse. Aside from multiple dictionary definitions and online encyclopaedia entries, an internet search shows many examples of the phrase: on news websites, for example, "The message, written in English, was sent by a native speaker" (Morrison, 2016); in a UK government report, "This research relates to the presence of native speakers in A level modern foreign languages" (Taylor and Zanini, 2017); and on recruitment websites, for example, "searching for native speakers of British English" (Rosetta Stone, n.d.). At the time of writing this chapter, it is probably fair to say that the phrase 'native speaker' is regarded as entirely unproblematic by most users of English.

These uses of 'native speaker' in popular discourse are attached to other ideas about English. The first two examples in the previous paragraph seem to imply an (inevitably high) level of competence in the use of English – 'competence' is a concept I return to in Section 3.2. The third example implies competence and the importance of place: the combined, and common, assumption that people born in certain parts of the world (in this example, the United Kingdom) (all) speak the best English. This brings us to the next section, in which I give more examples of such place-based definitions.

2.2 . . . in Scholarly Work on TESOL

Often, a place-based definition of 'native speaker' uses countries and nationalities to delimit the members of the category, and there are examples of this use in scholarly work on TESOL. Medgyes (1992, p. 340), for example, in answer to the question 'who is a native speaker?' says, "A Briton is. A Hungarian is not. An Australian is. A French national is not". Such definitions may acknowledge the use of English in places where there is a history of the use of English, such as India, and of intervening variables such as education, age, migration, and home language. Place-based definitions may also allow for less competent 'native' users of English, such as this early example in a fifteenth century poem, published by William Caxton: "And I conuersaunte and borne in the partes, where my natyf langage is moost corrupt [trans: And I am familiar with, and was born in, the region where my native language is very unsound/spoiled]" (Harvey, 1984). Despite these types of allowances, using the 'all other things being equal' argument, proponents of place-based definitions argue that a non-native speaker can never achieve the level of competence of a native speaker, because he or she was, or is, in the wrong place.

Place-based definitions of 'native speaker' conflate a nation-based identity with language use. Political borders are assumed to map directly onto borders between languages and language is considered to be a defining characteristic of national identity. This is part of what

Hall (this volume) calls "Englishry": the use of 'English' to mean a practice or product of 'the English'. More specifically, this use of 'English' implies that being a native speaker of English is an essential component of English identity. As Hall points out in Chapter 2, this conflation incorrectly assumes that the 'national language' has clear dividing lines between English and not-English, and that these lines are the same as the borders between countries.

Scholarly work that aims to correct discrimination against non-native speaker teachers in the TESOL profession (for more on this discrimination, see Section 2.4) may have had the effect of unintentionally reinforcing place-based definitions of 'native speaker'. Medgyes, for example, proposes that native and non-native teachers of English have the same potential to become successful teachers of English, despite what he describes as the non-native speaker's "deficient command of English" (Medgyes, 1992, p. 340). Potentially compensating for their 'deficient' English, non-native teachers, according to Medgyes (1992, pp. 346–347) have the following advantages over native English-speaking teachers: in monolingual classes of students whose language they share, 'non-native' teachers may be able to use this (other) shared language to support learning; the non-native speaker teachers' own 'struggle' to learn English may make them more empathetic towards their students' struggle to learn; non-native speaker teachers may be able to anticipate their learners' difficulties with English; non-native speaker teachers may have acquired (meta-)knowledge about how English works from their own study and be able to pass this on to their students; non-native speaker English teachers may have acquired a range of language learning strategies and be able to pass these on to their students; and the non-native speaker teacher's use of English may provide a more achievable model for their learners. In his defence of the equal value of non-native teachers, Medgyes (1992) maintains the two categories, and the implicit judgement of the English of the speakers born in the 'wrong' place as deficient.

Early work on World Englishes, which recognises the Englishes used in countries other than those traditionally seen as the source of native speakers (the United States, United Kingdom, Australia, Canada, Ireland, South Africa, and New Zealand), also uses place-based definitions of speaker-hood. The seminal work of Braj Kachru, for example, which aims to correct an overemphasis on what he describes (1992, p. 3) as 'native speaker' varieties of English, uses countries in his 'concentric circles' model; the 'Inner Circle' comprising "UK, USA, Australia ...", i.e. those countries in the previous list, the 'Outer Circle' of some ex-colonies of the United Kingdom (such as India, Sri

Lanka, Singapore, and Malaysia) and the 'Expanding Circle' comprising "Holland, Italy, Japan, Brazil ..." The place-based nature of Kachru's model has been critiqued for (amongst other things) its basis in "geography and genetics" by Jenkins (2003, p. 17), who proposes instead a model with a greater focus on *who* is using English, rather than *where* the person is from (I come back to models of English as a Lingua Franca in Section 3.3). An important consequence of Jenkins' emphasis on *who* not *where* is her suggestion that 'native' will come to be seen as a pejorative term in multilingual, international contexts (2013, pp. 39–40). However, having said that "(non-)native speaker" is starting to be seen as an obsolete term, Jenkins does say that it remains relevant in 'English as a Foreign Language' learning situations, where, "it is self evident that those learning English as a second or subsequent language are not native speakers of the language they are learning" (Jenkins, 2013, p. 38). Even in work that aims to undermine assumptions about birth/place/language, Jenkins is prepared to allow 'native speakers' in educational settings; despite the potential for circular reasoning (they are learning English because they are non-native speakers = they are non-native speakers because they are learning English).

There is, of course, potential for paradox in scholarly work that uses the term 'native speaker' to argue against the disadvantage associated with being categorised as a 'non-native speaker': paradox that is compounded by the allowance of 'non-native speaker' to describe learners of English in educational settings (see also Moussu and Llurda, 2008). I argue, however, that what can seem like paradox is in fact a result of the unexamined use of different ontological perspectives on 'English' (for a detailed framework that categorises these various ways of thinking about English, see Hall, this volume). Jenkins' comments about non-native speakers of English being better international communicators than native speakers, for example, assume an idea of English as a notional resource, in some way connected to place (England) and nationality (English). At the same time, she uses 'English' to mean a social resource, something that accounts for communication between individual users in specific contexts. The claim that non-native speakers can be successful teachers (Medgyes, 1992) is also underpinned by the place/nationality understanding, as well as by an idea of English as a cognitive resource, able to be learnt. As Hall (this volume) argues, different conceptualisations of English are useful for different purposes, in different contexts. Here, I want to emphasise the importance of careful thinking, for TESOL scholars/professionals, about how 'English' is being used and the assumptions that underpin these uses.

2.3 ... in Teacher Recruitment

The use of 'native speaker' in teacher recruitment remains current, despite the ongoing efforts of professional organisations to campaign against it. In the United Kingdom, for example, the British Association of Applied Linguistics (BAAL) has said that their online contact service should avoid distributing "[t]eaching post announcements for 'native' language speakers, as this goes against BAAL's policy on not discriminating between native and non-native speakers" (British Association of Applied Linguistics, 2017). Similarly, the US-based professional association, Teachers of English to Speakers of Other Languages (TESOL), has issued a position statement that opposes discrimination against English language teachers on the basis of their 'native language' (TESOL, 2006). Despite these and other efforts, schools operating in, or recruiting from, Inner Circle contexts, as Section 2.1 shows, continue to ask for native speakers and, in many cases, give them preferential treatment (Selvi, 2011; Mahboob and Golden, 2013; Selvi, 2014).

These recruitment practices are underpinned by the assumption that the desired outcome of additional language learning is, in all cases, 'native' competence in 'standard English' (see Cunningham, this volume, for more on standard English as a target in language learning contexts), and that native speakers have, therefore, an inbuilt advantage as language teachers (for a contrasting view, see Medgyes, 1992). Conflating English with 'standard English', combined with a belief that learners learn what teachers teach, might seem surprising in the language teaching business (for a convincing account of the usefulness of other languages in the English language learning classroom, for example, see Cook, 1999). It is, however, entirely possible that the kind of recruitment practices our professional organisations campaign against are nothing at all to do with either language or learning. Instead, they may simply be about (literally) selling an identity that is perpetually out of reach, and therefore requires a lifetime of financial commitment. The 'native speaker' identity (as understood in popular discourse) is an identity that cannot, in fact, be achieved, even with unlimited access to resources. Successfully selling the 'means' to an unobtainable goal sounds like an excellent business proposition and, indeed, a fairly recent report shows that the approximately 650,000 students who came to the United Kingdom in 2014 to study English (this number does not include 'international' students enrolled at UK universities) added about £1.2 billion to the UK economy (in fees, accommodation, and other living costs) and £194 million in tax revenue to the UK government (Chaloner et al. n.d.). While many of those 650,000 students may have enjoyed their experience in the United Kingdom, and learned new ways of communicating, none of them will have become 'native speakers' in the sense of the term as it is popularly understood. With this in mind, in Section 4 I suggest ways in which we can continue to actively challenge the use of the phrase in teacher recruitment.

2.4 Summary

The use of the idea 'native speaker', in popular discourse, in scholarly work on TESOL, and in teacher recruitment, draws on assumptions about *place* (this includes place of birth and age of acquisition), competent language use, and the nature of 'English' (as a static, homogeneous, and bounded object). In the next section of this chapter, I look at these assumptions in turn.

3 Contestations of the Native Speaker Idea

This section begins with a consideration of what could be thought of as 'input' variables, including place (already mentioned); the age at which a person starts, and finishes, learning a language; and some variables related to task and identity. I also look at the complex and interesting issue of what might be thought of as 'outputs' – competence and proficiency in language use. Finally, I turn to conceptualisations of 'English' and implications of what we think 'English' is for what we think a native speaker of English is.

3.1 'Input' Variables

'Nativeness', as we saw earlier, is often conflated with nationality and/or place. But since national borders are not consistent with linguistic ones, this geography-based native/second/foreign typology is so problematic as to be utterly useless. Age, as an 'input variable' also poses significant problems. Research on age-related factors (such as the age at which acquisition began; the period of time over which a person has been acquiring; and the person's level of attainment) can find these factors difficult to separate from each other. This means that the specific effects of age on language processing and ultimate achievement (particularly in the case of additional languages) cannot be independently measured. In addition to the difficulty of separating out *within*-age variables, there is also the problem of separating age-related effects from the effects of the other variables. This means that, despite neurolinguistic evidence that suggests that the brains of monolingual and multilingual people *are* different in several ways, we are presently unable to say anything more specific about age-related effects other than that age *seems to influence* language acquisition and use.

The problem of interacting variables is acknowledged in a review of literature on multilingualism and the brain (Higby et al., 2013), which nevertheless concludes that recent language acquisition research continues to support the critical period hypothesis (CPH). The CPH, first proposed by Lenneberg (1967), claims that there is a limited window during which input must be received and processed before innate mechanisms in the brain change, making subsequent acquisition more difficult. There is some evidence to suggest (Higby et al., 2013) that, although later-learned languages use the 'usual' left-hemisphere language areas of the brain, they also require the use of additional areas to handle the extra work associated with later learning and/or lower levels of attainment. A person who is exposed to English after the end of the critical period, therefore, might process, and use, English in ways that are different from someone who is exposed to English from birth.

From a cognitive perspective, it seems that the age at which a person begins to acquire a language could provide some justification for the two distinct categories of native speaker (exposed to English from birth) and non-native speaker (exposed to English after the critical period), although the evidence for this is by no means clear (see Hall, 2018). Certainly, there are other factors that influence language processing and use. For example, the type of task a language user is engaged in, and his or her level of competence, also interacts with age in a way that makes it very difficult for researchers to isolate these factors from each other. The level of a speaker's general education may also play a role in language production, as experimental research on the use of complex grammar, in which non-native speakers outperformed native speakers, has shown (Street, 2017).

Equally importantly, while the effects of age on language processing and on attainment can be studied in the laboratory, the interpretation of the results needs to be underpinned by an awareness of what 'competence' or 'proficiency' and 'the language' might be taken to mean in different contexts. For example, in this summary of the effects of age on language acquisition, "most bilinguals never attain native-like linguistic competence in the L2 ... a feat that is especially hard for individuals who begin acquiring the new language after puberty" (Higby et al., 2013, p. 75), the authors assume that a language exists as a stable, definable entity, which is consistently used by the group of people who identify, or who are identified, with these uses. From this perspective, there is only one 'English' for speakers of other languages to learn: a complex series of external facts that can be modelled by textbooks, native speaker teachers, and tests. The learner's job, according to this assumption, is to internalise these facts, and any differences between their use of English and their native speaker teacher's use of English is interpreted as a cognitive deficit on the part of the learner, or, in other words, a failure to learn. According to this view of learning, learners of English as an additional language can only very rarely achieve a successful learning outcome.

Cognitive perspectives on language acquisition and processing provide us with important insights into age- and place-related differences, although the contribution of age to these differences is mediated by other variables such as task type. This alone makes it very problematic for anyone who would claim that age of exposure to English is the basis for categorising a speaker as either 'native' or 'non-native'. In addition to the difficulties caused by these interacting variables, we are faced with the problem of what counts as *competent* use of a language, as well as what counts as 'the language'. All learners of English, wherever and whenever they are learning, will construct a version of English that is different from that of their teacher's/parent's/peer's version (an 'I-LANGUAGE' in Hall's framework, this volume). The judgement about whether their version is 'native-like' relies on an assumption about what is, and isn't (good) English. These judgements are social and, unless the assumptions about language (use) that underpin them are carefully examined, they run the risk of being wrong.

In an effort to contest over-simplification and more accurately reflect speaker- and situation-dependent variation, Leung, Harris, and Rampton (1997) have suggested the description of speakers' linguistic repertoires in terms of *expertise* (the ability to achieve specific tasks in specific situations); *inheritance* (the age at which a language in the repertoire began to be used, under what circumstances it was learned); and *affiliation* (level of comfort in using the language, feelings of belonging to a community of language speakers). This is a welcome recognition of the complex interaction between input variables and variable outputs.

Clearly, the term (non-)native speaker generalises about what are extremely heterogeneous groups of language users (Canagarajah, 1999). For example, we know that there is:

- lexico-grammatical and phonological variation within all languages (depending on variables such as age, place, job, hobbies, religion, ethnicity, subculture, and gender);

- no accent-free version of any language;
- variation within the speech and writing of individuals (depending on variables such as their role in a conversation and their relationship with their interlocutor, their languaging purpose, their emotional state, and the social conventions for the context);
- mixing of languages and varieties for maximum communicative effect by multilingual speakers (Dewaele, 2018, proposes *L1 user* for monolingual 'native speakers' and *LX user* for all multilingual users of English).

It is to these output variables that we turn in the next section.

3.2 Outputs: Competence and Proficiency

From the perspective of 'English' as communication ('Englishing', see Hall, this volume), to be a competent user of English requires intelligibility. The same applies for many other judgements of users, such as proficient, good, effective, successful, clear, and so on. There is little agreement, however, about what constitutes intelligibility or about how to measure it (Jenkins, 2000; Derwing and Munro, 2005; Munro et al., 2006). The traditional TESOL position relies on an assumption that intelligibility is the responsibility of *L2 learners/users* of English. Where intelligibility is judged to be a problem (perhaps because of so-called interference from their first language), TESOL practitioners have assumed the solution to be their students' acquisition of *more* ('native-like') English.

The World Englishes and English as a Lingua Franca (ELF) paradigms have challenged the idea of Inner Circle speakers as norm providers for all learners and users of English, and this has led to a new interest in intelligibility issues for speakers of English as an international language. In this section, I review current research on intelligibility, beginning with work in the ELF paradigm, and contrast this with the world Englishes approach.

Early work on ELF proposed the need for a description and possible codification of the English used by speakers in Kachru's Expanding Circle (for example, China, Greece, Poland, Thailand). In contrast to a world Englishes approach, ELF scholars were, and are, less interested in national varieties of English and more concerned with describing the English that is used between speakers of different L1s, who are using English as a Lingua Franca (cf. Part V, this volume). For example, using corpus data collected from mainly Expanding, but also Inner and Outer Circle users, Seidlhofer (2004) proposed a list of typical features of the lexicogrammar of ELF users, while Jenkins

(2002) documented a similar list for phonology. According to Jenkins (2006, p. 170), Seidlhofer's intention in creating and researching the Vienna-Oxford International Corpus of English (VOICE) of ELF data was to "find out which items are used systematically and frequently, but differently from native speaker use and without causing communication problems, by expert speakers of English from a wide range of [first languages]".

In contrast to this early work in ELF, World Englishes scholars (for example, Smith and Nelson, 1985; Kachru, 2008; Nelson, 2008) have tended to focus on the relative nature of intelligibility rather than on its 'core' features. Smith and Nelson (1985, p. 333), for example, state that "intelligibility is not speaker or listener-centred but is interactional between speaker and hearer", and Nelson notes that "being intelligible means being understood by an interlocutor at a given time in a given situation" (1982, p. 59). This conceptualisation of intelligibility as interactionally accomplished links intelligibility to specific contexts of use, involving factors related to the speaker, the listener, the linguistic and social context, and the environment.

The co-constructed nature of intelligibility identified by Smith and Nelson has, in fact, long been a feature of the sociolinguistic literature outside the world Englishes paradigm, which has firmly established the context-sensitive, adaptive, idiosyncratic, unpredictable nature of language use (for example, Giles and Powesland, 1975; Gumperz, 1982; Giles et al., 1991). While 'lingua franca' is one possible context, we are not able to predict in advance what purchase this context (as opposed to all the other contexts in simultaneous operation) will have over the actual language use of speakers. Corpus analyses such as those carried out by ELF researchers can obtain traces of consistent use of phonological and lexico-grammatical features by a selected group of speakers who are assumed to have their communicative context in common. But the basis of the selection cannot be shown to account entirely, or even at all, for the traces of regularity, nor can the regularities be assumed to be 'as a result' of the context.

Intelligibility is a contested construction, even within the relatively small subfield of (applied) linguistics represented by the World Englishes and ELF paradigms. What scholars in this subfield are most likely to agree upon, however, is that there is no causal relationship between speaking an Inner Circle (native speaker) variety of English and being intelligible in an international context. Instead, they stress that it is vitally important for all speakers of English (including those in the Inner Circle) to practise adjusting their speech in order to be intelligible to interlocutors from a wide range of language backgrounds. The potential consequences of this position for TESOL are profound, undermining all previous assumptions about users of Inner Circle English as the ideal users and teachers of English. Successful/clear/competent/proficient users of English are, in the words of Canagarajah over a decade ago (see also this volume), "able to monitor each other's language proficiency to determine mutually the appropriate grammar, lexical range and pragmatic conventions that would ensure intelligibility" (2007, pp. 923–924).

These monitoring and accommodating strategies may play out in very complex ways. The extent and frequency of use of the strategies can vary within a conversation, shaped by changing awareness of a partner's needs (Hwang et al., 2015); speakers may both converge on and diverge from each other's use of English at different points and in different, perhaps contradictory, ways. Beliefs about group identity (for example 'people like us' versus 'foreigners') have been shown to influence understanding/task achievement (Neuliep and Speten-Hansen, 2013) and prejudicial beliefs about 'other people' can result in a perception of difficulty in understanding them (Hansen and Dovidio, 2016), as well as in perceptions of lower intelligence and competence generally (Au et al., 2017). In other words, in addition to ontologies of the language itself, actual 'successful' uses of English depend partly on a nesting of perceptions about the current task, beliefs about your own and another person's identity, your own and other's relational goals, and the outcome of your interaction (Wang et al., 2013).

There is, thankfully, some evidence to suggest that TESOL practitioners are less biased in their judgements than those with no experience of teaching English (Huang, 2013; Sheppard et al., 2017), when judging the overall proficiency of a speaker or the content of their language use. And it is also important (including for teachers) to remember that what might be seen as 'unsuccessful' uses of English could provide effective ways of demonstrating loyalty to an individual or group associated with such (so-called) 'unsuccessful' uses (Trofimovich and Turuševa, 2015).

Suffice to say that, when it comes to definitions and judgements of a speaker's competence, the picture is very complex and there is no escape from peoples' (including our own) subjective assessments; indeed, we *need* such judgements in order to formulate a way of speaking to others. But we can, and should, pay attention to how these judgements advantage or disadvantage the people we are speaking to, and attempt to make subsequent adjustments in order to avoid careless, or even deliberate, discrimination. This is a point I return to in Section 4.

3.3 Conceptualisations of 'English'

In this section, I argue that the question of who is a native speaker is an ontological one (What is 'English'?) but not, as it is often presented, a matter of age or place of acquisition (discussed previously). The practice of dividing up speakers into the two mutually exclusive categories of 'native' and 'non-native' requires a belief in 'English' as a monolithic object, with clear borders between users of 'native speaker English' and users of 'non-native speaker English'. There are similar issues with the division of speakers into the two groups of 'learners' and 'users', given that all users are also (to some extent) learners, and all learners are users (Firth and Wagner, 1997; Canagarajah, 2007).

An important element of monolithic approaches to language is a focus on a core, or 'standard', against which other varieties are judged. The belief in a standard form of English is a very popular one, even though so-called 'standard' varieties of English are inevitably social rather than cognitive entities (Hopper, 1998; Hall, 2005, 2018; Cunningham, this volume). In fact, all individual speakers have their own ultimately unique linguistic repertoires ('I-LANGUAGES'). Groups of speakers *do* share different degrees of awareness of a set of conventions about acceptable, prestigious, and desirable sounds, words, and syntax in specific situations ('N-LANGUAGE'), but again, these are beliefs rather than actually/exactly the same set of linguistic resources, deployed in consistent, entirely predictable ways.

We have argued elsewhere that monolithic conceptualisations of English are not true, fair, helpful, or sustainable (Hall and Wicaksono, 2019). Despite this, such ways of thinking about language continue to underpin the use of 'native' or 'non-native' to categorise speakers of English, with both benefits and drawbacks for individuals and groups of English language users.

3.4 Summary

In this section, I began by thinking about the concept of 'place' and the interaction with another input variable, 'age'. I showed how the framing of these concepts as having a predictable impact on 'competent' language use is challenged by the complex and difficult problem of defining 'competence'. I ended the section with the question of what counts as 'English', a question that has profound implications for the TESOL profession and for debates about 'nativeness'. In the final section of this chapter, I consider what might be done to take account of these contestations of the idea of a native speaker, the potential danger of the concept for members of the TESOL profession, as well at its use, in certain cases, to justify the operations of some of its educational institutions.

4 What Action Can We Take against the Use of 'Native Speaker' in English Language Teaching?

Given our previous conclusions, it is clearly essential for TESOL professionals/scholars to think very carefully about how the categories of native and non-native speaker emerge through a discursive process, a process that Aneja (2016a, b) refers to as "(non)native speakering". Accepting that these categories are discursively constructed, and not 'natural', forces us to notice the complexity of, variation within, and fluidity between, the categories. It is the first step towards taking action against the unexamined use of the categories. Thinking carefully about our naming practices and of the rights of members of groups to identify themselves (and to change their mind, and to disagree with each other about the name of their group) is not just so-called 'political correctness'. It is an important (and easy!) way to avoid thoughtless and damaging generalisations and is, therefore, an essential first step in avoiding discrimination (for more about labelling/naming practices, see Hall et al., 2017, pp. 52–57).

In addition, we need to raise awareness about what 'English' is, and consider the implications of definitions of 'competence' for teaching and testing (see Part IV, this volume). There are implications too for teacher training and recruitment, some of which are considered later.

4.1 Raising Awareness about What Language Is

Organisations that represent the TESOL profession have already recognised (over a decade ago) the importance of challenging monolithic conceptualisations of language that privilege the idea of a 'standard' above other uses. The TESOL International Association, for example,

> encourages the recognition and appreciation of all varieties of English, including dialects, creoles, and world Englishes. In terms of language teaching, TESOL does not advocate one standard or variety of English over another. Rather, TESOL urges English language teachers to make informed decisions at local, regional, and/or national levels, taking into account the purposes and contexts of use that are most relevant to their learners.
>
> (TESOL, 2008)

For this goal to be achieved, however, there continues to be a need for awareness-raising tasks that are accessible to teachers. The online, free-of-charge course *Changing Englishes* (Hall and Wicaksono,

2019) is an example of this kind of resource, but more, and more locally relevant, resources are still needed. The design, publication, and use of such resources would be a valuable contribution towards efforts to challenge the untrue, unfair, unjust, and unsustainable monolithic conceptualisations of English and related ideas about (non-)native speakers.

4.2 Raising Awareness about the Implications of Definitions of 'Competence'

It has been suggested that what gets taught and tested in language classrooms has little effect on how English is actually used outside of the educational environment, despite (all?) our governments' attempts to regulate what kind of English is taught in schools (Anderson, 2018; Goodwyn, this volume; Goddard, this volume). It is possible, however, that tasks that encourage students to consider the context in which they are using English, the beliefs about appropriacy that are embedded in that context, and how successful communicative outcomes might be defined and measured, would be useful. Training students to notice the effects of their language use on others, and on task achievement, could be part of a series of such tasks (see Wicaksono, 2013, for an example). More research is needed into this interesting and important issue, as is more sharing of relevant classroom resources.

The challenges to monolithic thinking about what 'English' is also have serious implications for testing. Hall (2014, p. 383) argues for a 'plurilithic' (i.e. not a monolithic) perspective, claiming:

> Recognition of the plurilithic reality of English necessitates a radical rethinking of the nature and purpose of English testing. Consistent with a plurilithic perspective would be the assessment of a learner's Englishing: what they do with the language in specific situations ... [W]hat should be assessed (where possible and appropriate) is learners' performance on communicative tasks in English that are appropriate to their own goals and contexts, rather than their knowledge and use of 'English itself'.

Such a perspective could mean using a range of varieties of English to test for understanding and reward for the use of the kind of accommodation/task achievement strategies mentioned earlier.

4.3 Raising Awareness about Implications for Teacher Training and Recruitment

In a study of trainees from around the world on the Cambridge ESOL Certificate in English Language Teaching to Adults and the Trinity

College London CertESOL, Anderson (2016, p. 271) concludes, "current initial teacher training courses are not well suited to the needs of NNS participants, who may require a very different type of course to NS participants". I would argue even more strongly that such courses urgently require an updated approach to language for all trainees, equipping them to challenge the untrue and unjust beliefs about language that underpin discriminatory hiring practices in their profession.

Once again, professional organisations provide advocacy on this issue: "The use of the labels 'native speaker' and 'nonnative speaker' in hiring criteria is misleading, as this labelling minimizes the formal education, linguistic expertise, teaching experience, and professional preparation of teachers. All educators should be evaluated within the same criteria. Nonnative English-speaking educators should not be singled out because of their native language" (TESOL, 2006). At my own institution, conversations with our Careers Service have led to a policy that requires members of the team to contact schools who send through advertisements that use the term 'native speaker' and ask them about their rationale for the term. This is a new effort (based on an idea proposed by Kamhi-Stein, 2016) and we are yet to see what the impact of our decision might be.

5 Conclusion

This chapter has explored the idea of a '(non-)native' speaker of English, in the context of teaching English to speakers of other languages (TESOL). Despite much scholarly and professional argument against the term, the use of '(non-) native' speaker to describe a person's use of English remains common in a variety of domains. This is due to a lack of understanding of how and where English is used, a general confusion about what we mean by 'English', and, perhaps, a deliberate undermining of the rights of large groups of users to think of themselves as competent (and therefore deserving of higher pay – in the case of teachers – or not requiring further classroom instruction – in the case of learners).

Contestations from the point of view of ontologies of English, language cognition, English as a Lingua Franca, and identities add up to a strong case for abandoning the (non-)native speaker of English idea. Not just because there is no evidence for any kind of definable 'nativeness', but also because there is still a lot more work for scholars and language teachers to do on what 'English' means. In the meantime, we are all language users of varying degrees of (localised) success, depending on the definition and measurement of 'success'. The relevance of whether or not our language is considered 'English' to the achievement of a communicative task is limited and the unthinking (or cynical) use of the native speaker idea is potentially damaging. I propose that language teachers should focus on 'Englishing', rather than on teaching their students 'English'. This would require working in collaboration with students to identify specific tasks, work out how they (and others) might judge their successful achievement of these tasks, and then locating and acquiring the resources they need for successful task achievement.

As we learn more about language and 'languages', the (arbitrary) naming of languages and problematic assumptions about who is (dis)-counted as a 'speaker', should become less interesting and relevant. We can contribute towards the contestation of arbitrary names and problematic assumptions by asking 'What is English', as well as 'What is needed to communicate here/now?' The answer to both questions might be that nobody agrees, but at least in the ensuing discussion our competing assumptions will be made visible.

References

Anderson, J. (2016). Initial teacher training courses and non-native speaker teachers. *ELT Journal*, *70*(3), 261–274.

Anderson, J. (2018). Reimagining English language learners from a translingual perspective. *ELT Journal,* *72*(1), 247–249.

Aneja, G. A. (2016a). Rethinking nativeness: Toward a dynamic paradigm of (non)native speakering. *Critical Inquiry in Language Studies*, *13*(4), 351–379.

Aneja, G. A. (2016b). (Non)native speakered: Rethinking (non)nativeness and teacher identity in TESOL teacher education. *TESOL Quarterly*, *50*(3), 572–597.

Au, T., Kwok, A., Tong, L. et al. (2017). The social costs in communication hiccups between native and nonnative speakers. *Journal of Cross-Cultural Psychology*, *48*(3), 369–383.

British Association of Applied Linguistics (BAAL). (2017). BAALmail. https://baalweb.wordpress.com/baalmail/

Canagarajah, A. S. (1999). On EFL teachers, awareness, and agency. *ELT Journal* 53(3), 207–214.

Canagarajah, S. (2007). Lingua Franca English, multilingual communities, and language acquisition. *Modern Language Journal*, *91*, 923–939.

Chaloner, J., Evans, A., and Pragnell, M. (n.d.). *Supporting the British Economy through Teaching English as a Foreign Language: An Assessment of the Contribution of English Language Teaching to the United Kingdom Economy*. English UK. www.englishuk.com/uploads/assets/members/newsflash/2015/11_nov/Economic_impact_report_44pp__WEB.pdf

Cook, V. (1999). Going beyond the native speaker in language teaching. *TESOL Quarterly*, *33*(2), 185–209.

Derwing, T. and Munro, M. (2005). Second language accent and pronunciation teaching: A research-based approach. *TESOL Quarterly, 39*(3), 379–397.

Dewaele, J. (2018). Why the dichotomy 'L1 Versus LX User' is better than 'native versus non-native speaker'. *Applied Linguistics, 39*(2), 236–240.

Firth, A. and Wagner, J. (1997). On discourse, communication, and (some) fundamental concepts in SLA research. *Modern Language Journal,* 81(3), 285–300.

Giles, H. and Powesland, P. F. (1975). Accommodation theory. In N. Coupland and A. Jaworski, eds., *Sociolinguistics: A Reader and Coursebook*. London: Macmillan.

Giles, H., Coupland, J., and Coupland, N. (1991). Accommodation theory: Communication, context, and consequence. In H. Giles, J. Coupland and N. Coupland, eds., *Contexts* of Accommodation: Developments in Applied Sociolinguistics. Cambridge: Cambridge University Press.

Gumperz, J. J. (1982). *Discourse Strategies*. Cambridge: Cambridge University Press.

Hansen, K. and Dovidio, J. (2016). Social dominance orientation, nonnative accents, and hiring recommendations. *Cultural Diversity and Ethnic Minority Psychology, 22*(4), 544–551.

Hall, C. J. (2005). *An Introduction to Language and Linguistics: Breaking the Language Spell*. London: Continuum.

Hall, C. J. (2014). Moving beyond accuracy: From tests of English to tests of 'Englishing'. *ELT Journal, 68*(4), 376–385.

Hall, C. J. (2018). Cognitive perspectives on English as a Lingua Franca. In J. Jenkins, W. Baker, and M. Dewey, eds., *Routledge Handbook of English as a Lingua Franca* (pp. 74–84). London: Routledge.

Hall, C. J. and Wicaksono, R. (2019). *Changing Englishes: An online course for teachers (v.02)*. Online. www.changingenglishes.online

Hall, C. J., Wicaksono, R., Liu, S., Qian, Y. and Xu, X. (2017). Exploring teachers' ontologies of English: Monolithic conceptions of grammar in a group of Chinese teachers. *International Journal of Applied Linguistics, 27*(1), 87–109.

Harvey, E., ed. (1480/1984). *The Court of Sapience*. Toronto: University of Toronto Press.

Higby, E., Kim, J., and Obler, L. K. (2013). Multilingualism and the brain. *Annual Review of Applied Linguistics, 33*, 68–101.

Hopper, P. J. (1998). Emergent grammar. In M. Tomasello, ed., *The New Psychology of Language* (pp. 155–175). Mahwah: Lawrence Erlbaum.

Huang, B. H. (2013). The effects of accent familiarity and language teaching experience on raters' judgments of non-native speech. *System, 41*, 770–785.

Hwang, J., Brennan, S., and Huffman, M. (2015). Phonetic adaptation in non-native spoken dialogue: Effects of priming and audience design. *Journal of Memory and Language, 81*, 72–90.

Jenkins, J. (2000). *The phonology of English as an International Language*. Oxford: Oxford University Press.

Jenkins, J. (2002). A sociolinguistically based, empirically researched pronunciation syllabus for English as an international language. *Applied Linguistics*, 23(1), 83–103.

Jenkins, J. (2003). *World Englishes: A Resource Book for Students*. London and New York: Routledge.

Jenkins, J. (2006). Current perspectives on teaching world Englishes and English as a lingua franca. *TESOL Quarterly*, 40(1), 157–182.

Jenkins, J. (2013). *English as a Lingua Franca in the International University: The Politics of Academic English Language Policy*. Abingdon, Oxon, and New York: Routledge.

Kachru, B., ed. (1992). *The Other Tongue – English across Cultures*, 2nd ed. Urbana, IL: University of Illinois Press.

Kachru, B. B. (2008). The first step: The Smith paradigm for intelligibility in world Englishes. *World Englishes*, 27(3–4), 293–296.

Kamhi-Stein, L. D. (2016). The non-native English speaker teachers in TESOL movement. *ELT Journal*, 70(2), 180–189.

Lenneberg, E. H. (1967). *Biological Foundations of Language*. New York: Wiley.

Leung, C., Harris, R., and Rampton, B. (1997). The idealised native speaker, reified, and classroom realities. *TESOL Quarterly*, 31(3), 543–560.

Mahboob, A. and Golden, R. (2013). Looking for native speakers of English: Discrimination in English language teaching job advertisements. *Voices in Asia Journal*, 1(1), 72–81.

Medgyes, P. (1992). Native or non-native: Who's worth more? *ELT Journal*, 46(4), 340–349.

Morrison, L. (2016). Native English speakers are the world's worst communicators. www.bbc.com/capital/story/20161028-native-english-speakers-are-the-worlds-worst-communicators

Moussu, L. and Llurda, E. (2008). Non-native English speaking English language teachers: History and research. *Language Teaching*, 41(3), 315–348.

Munro, M. J., Derwing, T. M. and Morton, S. L. (2006). The mutual intelligibility of L2 speech. *Studies in Second Language Acquisition*, 28(1), 111–131.

Nelson, C. L. (1982). Intelligibility and non-native varieties of English. In B. B. Kachru, ed., *The Other Tongue: English across Cultures*. Urbana, IL: University of Illinois Press.

Nelson, C. L. (2008). Intelligibility since 1966. *World Englishes*, 27(3–4), 297–308.

Neuliep, J. and Speten-Hansen, K. (2013). The influence of ethnocentrism on social perceptions of nonnative accents. *Language and Communication*, 33, 167–176.

Pae, T. (2017). Effects of the differences between native and non-native English-speaking teachers on students' attitudes and motivation toward learning English. *Asia Pacific Journal of Education*, 37(2), 163–178.

Rampton, M. B. H. (1990). Displacing the 'native speaker': Expertise, affiliation, and inheritance. *ELT Journal*, 44(2), 97–101.

Russo, M., Islam, G., and Koyuncu, B. (2017). Non-native accents and stigma: How self-fulfilling prophesies can affect career outcomes. *Human Resource Management Review*, 27, 507–520.

Seidlhofer, B. (2004). Research perspectives on teaching English as a lingua franca. *Annual Review of Applied Linguistics*, 24, 209–239.

Selvi, A. F. (2011). The non-native speaker teacher. *ELT Journal*, 65(2), 187–189.

Selvi, A. F. (2014). Myths and misconceptions about nonnative English speakers in the TESOL (NNEST) movement. *TESOL Journal*, 5(3), 573–611.

Sheppard, B., Elliott, N., and Baese-Berk, M. (2017). Comprehensibility and intelligibility of international student speech: Comparing perceptions of university EAP instructors and content faculty. *Journal of English for Academic Purposes*, 26, 42–51.

Smith, L. E. and Nelson, C. L. (1985). International intelligibility of English: Directions and resources. *World Englishes*, 4(3), 333–342.

Street, J. A. (2017). This is the native speaker that the non-native speaker outperformed: Individual, education-related differences in the processing and interpretation of object relative clauses by native and non-native speakers of English. *Language Sciences*, 59, 192–203.

Taylor, R. and Zanini, N (2017). Native speakers in A level modern foreign languages. OFQUAL. www.gov.uk/government/publications/native-speakers-in-a-level-modern-foreign-languages

TESOL. (2006). Position Statement against Discrimination of Nonnative Speakers of English in the Field of TESOL. www.tesol.org/docs/default-source/advocacy/position-statement-against-nnest-discrimination-march-2006.pdf?sfvrsn=2

TESOL. (2008). Position Statement on English as a Global Language. www.tesol.org/docs/pdf/10884.pdf?sfvrsn=2

Trofimovich, P. and Turuševa, L. (2015). Ethnic identity and second language learning. *Annual Review of Applied Linguistics*, 35, 234–252.

Wang, Z., Arndt, A. D., Singh, S. N. et al. (2013). "You Lost Me at Hello": How and when accent-based biases are expressed and suppressed. *International Journal of Research in Marketing*, 30(4), 185–196.

Wicaksono, R. (2013). Raising students' awareness of the construction of communicative (in)competence in international classrooms. In J. Ryan ed., *Cross Cultural Teaching and Learning for Home and International Students: Internationalisation of Pedagogy and Curriculum in Higher Education*. London and New York: Routledge.

Part III
English in Schools

6 The Origins and Adaptations of English as a School Subject

Andy Goodwyn

1 Introduction

This chapter will consider the particular manifestation of English as a 'school subject', principally in the country called England and using some small space for significant international comparisons, and it will mainly focus on the secondary school version. We will call this phenomenon School Subject English (SSE). The chapter will argue that historically SSE has gone through phases of development and adaptation, some aspects of these changes inspired by new theories and concepts and by societal change, some others, especially more recently, entirely reactive to external impositions (for an analysis of the current position of SSE, see Roberts, this volume). This chapter considers SSE to have been ontologically 'expanded' between 1870 and (about) 1990, increasing the ambition and scope of the 'subject' and the emancipatory ideology of its teachers. This ontological expansion was principally a result of adding 'models' of SSE, models that each emphasise different epistemologies of what counts as significant knowledge, and can only exist in a dynamic tension. In relation to this volume, SSE has always incorporated close attention to language but only very briefly (1988–1992) has something akin to Applied Linguistics had any real influence in the secondary classroom. However, with varying emphasis historically, there has been attention (the Adult Needs/Skills model, see later) to the conventions of language, especially 'secretarial' issues of spelling and punctuation, some understanding of grammar, and a focus on notions of Standard English, in writing and in speech; but these have never been the driving ideology of SSE. Of the two conceptual giants 'Language' and 'Literature', it is the latter that has mattered most over those 120 years.

As with all education systems, a particular element, such as a school subject, has become truly important once it becomes formally assessed. Literature has been recognised in this way for many decades at school and university levels. England has long held a tradition of examining almost all sixteen year olds (currently called General Certificate of Secondary Education, GCSE), and SSE is a compulsory subject and has always included considerable attention to grammar and spelling. For eighteen year olds, the tradition has become to specialise to three or four subjects at 'Advanced Level' ('A' level), these qualifications having always been seen as decisive in indicating if a student is capable of moving on to degree level. The relatively recent growth of English Language at 'A' level is a significant but minor evolution, probably less significant than the very rapid growth of Media Studies, at GCSE, 'A' level, and degree level in many universities.

SSE does exist, to an extent, in primary schools (in statutory terms from 1989) and this will be touched on, but there will be more consideration of English also as the 'discipline' of Higher Education English (HEE) that is fundamentally where SSE began, principally influenced by the ontologies of the university subject. There is only modest space to consider SSE from a more global perspective, but there are many fascinations in the ontological status of SSE in, for example, the obvious major English-speaking countries that include the United States, Canada, Australia, New Zealand, and Ireland, with a profound historical relationship to England and 'English'. These countries have enough in common for there to be shared theoretical constructs of SSE and practical similarities, meaning that there is a sharable history, specifically of SSE, with some key figures having powerful influences at the conceptual and the classroom levels in different countries. Those countries were 'colonies', but SSE has a much more fraught existence in, say, the Caribbean or Gibraltar and an extraordinarily powerful place in nation states such as India and Singapore. The unquestionable global dominance of English as the language of communication in so many countries means that a 'hybrid' SSE also exists there as a second language for many millions of students. In order, therefore, to have any depth of analysis in examining SSE, there must be a necessarily microscopic focus upon it in England and an acceptance that such an attempt is rather like a clinical post mortem, hygienic and sterilised, while the dynamic organism itself continues its energetic and messy evolution in the 'real world'.

In considering that ongoing evolution, I attempt to trace the principal origins and the 'coming into being' of the 'quicksilver' (Dixon, 1975) school subject of English and its development in the twentieth century. Dixon's metaphor is based on the fact that 'quicksilver' is the popular name for mercury, a liquid metal at room temperature that can be poured into a container of any shape. It is also a beautiful silver, and the 'quick' comes from the Latin for 'living'. As this chapter shows, the debate about 'what is English and what are its elements' still continues.

Any discussion of SSE must be framed socially and politically as it has been consistently the focus of political debate much reported in the media (cf. Cunningham, this volume), and increasingly regulated by the nation state; hence there are numerous official reports and documents, and, in the last third of the century and early twenty-first, constant and direct 'interference' into how SSE should be defined. This is also a global phenomenon (Goodwyn, 2011a, 2011b, 2017). Equally, SSE was part of the lived experience of almost every English citizen (and therefore politician) and so becomes part of a living memory, generating endless views and opinions about what SSE is *now* but refracted through vaguely recalled school experiences.

Some of SSE's relentless public attention is partly explained by its pre-eminence as the basis for literacy (a term that only really enters the debate in the late twentieth century and remains in itself a debatable term; Goodwyn and Fuller, 2011). SSE also has a dominating concern with literature as a cultural force, in part a form of heritage project infused with the nationalism of being 'British' (actually mostly English); therefore, what texts are chosen from the literary canon captures public and political attention at every iteration.

SSE is also a key 'credential' with one of the highest 'values' as a 'qualification'. In fact, not to have an English qualification (at whatever is the agreed contemporary benchmark, for example, from about 1989 to 2016, a 'C' at GCSE) was a major detriment to life chances; for example, a 'D' grade meant being barred from becoming a teacher at primary level or of *any* subject in secondary schools. It has always been a key subject, but from 1989 (see below), the National Curriculum made it, explicitly, a compulsory subject for all students from ages five to sixteen. Therefore, even students who were not entered for a GCSE at sixteen had to study SSE throughout their compulsory schooling. Schools even then retained control over the timetable, so how many lessons per week were involved is not officially recorded. I would suggest, based on working with a very large number of secondary schools over the last thirty years, that about three to four hours per school week were devoted to SSE and perhaps one to two of homework, so using the typical school year of thirty-nine weeks, a 'typical student' in her or his five years experienced about 1,000 hours of SSE, which works out as perhaps 15 per cent of school time.

The exact figure is of no real importance; the point is that SSE therefore has a huge place in the mind of the nation, regardless of their class, gender, or ethnicity, and is a powerful collective memory of schooling; this is not just a feature of England but certainly of all the major English speaking countries. It is worth commenting on the additional ontological tension existing in, say, the United States, where English is the main language of the nation (although there is much discussion that it might have been German, when Congress in 1795 considered printing laws in English and German), but the official language is a variant on British English, i.e. 'American English', where high school students take British literature courses separately from American literature. In the United States (and Canada), SSE tends actually to be called 'English and the Language Arts'. In Australia, teachers of SSE are often called teachers of English and Literacy and they approve of this conjunction. In contrast, one finding from my research (Goodwyn, 2003, 2004), was that teachers in England passionately rejected being labelled as teachers of literacy. It might be argued by some that maths has equal status, but I would argue (see below) that it does not in England – it may well in other cultures, hence, Shanghai's premier global league status (e.g. in PISA, the Programme for International Students Assessment; cf. OECD, 2015), which summarises student performance in PISA 2015 and examines inclusiveness and fairness in participating education systems. Put simply, SSE has 'double weight', there being two SSE credentialisers: one is 'English' (usually a combination of language and literature); the other is a separate 'English Literature'.

Finally, this chapter summarises 120 years of history and change and is necessarily selective and, in some ways, unavoidably reductive of important complexities.

2 SSE in the Past and Present Tense

When viewed historically, the discipline of English is considered to somehow materialise in HEE form in the mid- to late nineteenth century (see later). However, in an ontological sense, the version that still prevails today had most of its origins in the 1920s, crucially coming after the devastation of the First World War with The Cambridge School (Richards, 1924, 1929; Leavis and Thompson, 1933) declaiming the sanctity of literature for an elite reader. There was a paradigm shift after the Second World War because of the reaction to the elitist version by The London School in the 1960s and 1970s (Barnes et al., 1971) arguing for the primacy of language, including speaking and listening, a repudiation of elitism and foregrounding of the everyday language of the urban working class. However, the 'turn to language' did not, in terms of SSE's existence, replace it; instead, it added on new facets.

It is important here to turn to a distinction that is both ontological and epistemological, i.e. how it exists but also what is its knowledge. SSE can be considered to exist principally in two forms of knowledge. The most accessible form is historical and textual; we might call it 'the textual domain', whether it is books about English (e.g. by F. R. Leavis), reports about English (e.g. Departmental Committee of the Board of Education, 1921), or a myriad of syllabi now called 'specifications' and, in a different way, a thousand dusty text books; this now also includes a myriad of websites whose rapid changes mean that texts are constantly replaced and 'disappeared' as policy changes. All these texts have some significance; a few have great significance, e.g. Dixon's *Growth through English* discussed later. In all these texts we find explicit or implicit ideologies of SSE that we can analyse and deconstruct. But in the community of practice that exists always in the present tense, we have the practical knowledge of the English teachers and of their students. This knowledge for the teachers is both 'subject knowledge' but also what Shulman (1986, 1987) has defined as 'Subject Pedagogical Knowledge', knowing how to make SSE learnable for students. In that sense, SSE 'happens' in real time in a myriad of classrooms enacted and embodied by teachers and students in what is, almost all of the time, a private drama, between the one teacher and the many-headed class; this is the 'existential domain'. The students, as mentioned previously, keep that version of SSE in their unreliable memories where it will resonate as they become, for example, a parent or a politician.

Over a career in teaching, the wise teacher accumulates a deep and profound knowledge of SSE, becoming an expert in its enactment. Perhaps the one place where the 'living' SSE and the textual SSE are almost indistinguishable is, for the teacher, in the more ephemeral texts of the lesson plan, the scheme of work, the work sheet, and multiple visualisations that adorn all classrooms: for the students it is the 'work' of SSE, their stories, their essays, at some point literally 'marked' by their teacher. So, to make an obvious but crucially important epistemological distinction, for all the enduring importance of the 'significant' texts and their very real influence in, and on, the classroom, SSE exists in the private dramas of lessons and memories of the participants.

Given all these complexities, it makes sense to start 'in media res' with the climacteric year of 1989, in some ways a simple and specific moment as the year when the state of England took strong control of the state of SSE and, in a sense, sought to become the owner of its ontological status.

3 Models of English?

This highly significant moment in the history of SSE occurred in 1989 when the very first National Curriculum for English was published, carrying with it the legal apparatus of being 'statutory'. It is worth noting that the construction of a National Curriculum is a global phenomenon but by no means a universal one and subject to many and different controversies. Federal countries, e.g. the United States and Australia, do their prescribing about SSE at state levels; e.g. 'Victorian English' in Melbourne is the version of the state of Victoria, not some old and long dead queen. They are still arguing in Australia whether there really is an Australian literature, never mind what you teach in high school.

The story of how this version of SSE in England (and technically Wales) came into being is a story in itself, one version of which has been written by Brian Cox, the committee chair and lead author of The Cox Report (see Cox, 1991, 1992). One very striking claim of Cox and his committee was that, in 1988, when the document was being written, there were 'Five Models of English'. They claimed that these 'models' were understood and used by all English teachers.

The term 'model', as any linguist will tell you, can be defined in many ways. Perhaps the simplest explanation is that a model is usually a concrete representation of something else or a version, as in 'this is the new model'. However, it also implies 'modelling', showing what is best or to be emulated. One reason why the Dixon book (1975) was so important was that he chose to discuss (without definition of the term) three 'models of English' – I have argued he means *versions* (Goodwyn, 2016, 2017). Dixon argued emphatically that the Personal Growth model was *the* best version of English.

So the Cox committee simply adopted the term 'model', drawing on Dixon (without acknowledgement or revised definition). They made a bold claim based, as it was, on no real research but simply on much conversation and consultation with the profession.

Their models were as follows (Cox, 1991; numbers mine).

1. A Personal Growth view focuses on the child: it emphasises the relationship between language and learning in the individual child, and the role of literature in developing children's imaginative and aesthetic lives.

2. A Cross-curricular view focuses on the school: it emphasises that all teachers (of English and of other subjects) have a responsibility to help children with the language demands of different subjects on the school curriculum; otherwise, areas of the curriculum may be closed to them. In England, English is different from other school subjects, in that it is both a subject and a medium of instruction for other subjects.
3. An Adult Needs view focuses on communication outside the school: it emphasises the responsibility of English teachers to prepare children for the language demands of adult life, including the workplace, in a fast-changing world. Children need to learn to deal with the day-to-day demands of spoken language and of print; they also need to be able to write clearly, appropriately, and effectively.
4. A Cultural Heritage view emphasises the responsibility of schools to lead children to an appreciation of those works of literature that have been widely regarded as amongst the finest in the language.
5. A Cultural Analysis view emphasises the role of English in helping children towards a critical understanding of the world and cultural environment in which they live. Children should know about the processes by which meanings are conveyed, and about the ways in which print and other media carry values.

The section outlining the models was just a few paragraphs in a very lengthy document (Department for Education, 1989), but it was a rare attempt to 'capture' the subject paradigm succinctly. It seemed to me, at the time and still now, that these 'Cox models' deserved real acknowledgement and also some challenge.

The work of the two previous decades had generated some other versions; indeed, one of the most well known was *Versions of English* (Barnes and Barnes, 1984). It was especially important because it was based on a three-year study based in six schools and four Further Education colleges, focusing essentially on fifteen to seventeen year olds. It, in turn, owed much to Dixon's *Growth through English*, first published in 1967 (Dixon, 1975). That text is a perfect illustration of how debate and discussion lead to new knowledge (Goodwyn et al., 2019), as it followed on from the 'Dartmouth' seminar held in the United States. At this seminar, leading figures from around the English-speaking world met to debate the nature and purpose of the subject. Dixon's seminal book was the outcome as it attempted to capture how the subject English was conceptualised in England.

4 Looking Back to the Grand Narrative

I now attempt a summary and selective ontological history of English as a subject, principally SSE. There are plentiful histories of the origins of English as a 'discipline' and plenty of disagreements about how it came into being (see, for example Eagleton, 1975). For our purposes in understanding how Cox could posit five models of English, we will briefly examine three phases of emergence and note their key 'theorists' ('ideologues' may be a better descriptor). My terms for the early phases are (1) *Ennobling the vernacular*; (2) *Conventions and conditions*; (3) *Culturing the citizenry*; later we move on to (4) *Growth through language*; (5) *English in harmonious practice*; and to the present day (6) *Building the panopticon, the coming of control, conformity, and self-regulation*. I speculate, finally, on the hope for a new and emancipatory phase.

Compulsory state education in England began in 1870. Before that, schooling was the privilege of the elite and essentially private, in schools confusingly (still) called *public schools*. Their curriculum was dominated by studying classical texts from Greek and Roman literature in ancient Greek and Latin. Such knowledge was the mark of a gentleman; attention to language in use was focused on rhetoric. The vernacular language and literature were considered vulgar; English did not exist as a subject at any level of education.

4.1 Ennobling the Vernacular

Phase 1, *ennobling the vernacular*, is marked by the displacement of the classics and emergence of the vernacular in both linguistic and literary terms, approximately from the 1850s to 1914. This period is marked by English becoming first an HEE and then, increasingly an SSE, not least because from 1870 onwards, going to school became a normative part of English culture. The extraordinarily influential figure of Matthew Arnold, poet, critic, and essayist but also school inspector, lights up this period with his passionate espousal of English Literature as the birthright of all citizens. By 1914 English had emerged as a substantive HEE with a professoriate and some academic credibility, and SSE had become a normal subject in ordinary schools, although England's (private) 'public schools' retained a largely classical culture. Cox's Model 4, Cultural Heritage, is emerging with some attention to 3, Adult Needs, but the school system does not yet look beyond the elementary stages.

4.2 Conventions and Conditions

Phase 2, *Conventions and conditions*, approximates 1918–1954. One reaction to the Great War was the Newbolt Report (Departmental Committee of the Board of Education, 1921), named after the minor poet who chaired the committee. In terms of SSE, this report marks a point by which English has come into being with its *schoolish* characteristics. Those characteristics are explicated into what became known later as the four language modes of reading, writing, speaking, and listening. A simple but profound point is that all four were considered both 'teachable' and 'necessary': the state was simultaneously adopting universal literacy as an entitlement and demanding that its citizens conform to using 'good' English in writing and in speech. One member of the committee was George Sampson, who produced 'English for the English' that is a very powerful argument for the centrality of SSE and for the relocation of the classics of Latin and Greek to the category of 'exotics'. His *English for the English: A Chapter on National Education* provides a passionate argument for an Adult Needs model of English, for a literate nation who understand and can use 'Standard English' (Sampson, 1921).

4.3 Culturing the Citizenry

Culturing the citizenry, phase 3, runs from 1929 to 1954. In 1929, I. A. Richards published *Practical Criticism* (1929), a follow up to his *Principles of Literary Criticism* (1924), and F. R. Leavis married Queenie Leavis, having recently secured a position at Downing College, creating a formidable union and part of what later became the Cambridge School of English (Gibbons, 2017). This school of thought was united by a fierce advocacy, especially from Leavis, of the supreme value of studying English literature imbued with a strong evangelical spirit of its moral integrity.

Richards grappled theoretically with the nature of literary response and with what later morphed into both New Criticism in one direction, and its opposite direction, Reader Response theory (see Rosenblatt, 1938/1970). But *Practical Criticism* was a genuinely empirical study of 'real' readers – as much as Cambridge undergraduates in the 1920s can be considered real readers; what matters was that they could not read 'properly' if left to their own devices. What Richards did was simply to give the students unseen passages and poems to evaluate and write about with no author or contextual information. As a result, Richards formulated his ten difficulties in the making of meaning and quite brilliantly problematised how we make our meaning from literary texts and therefore inviting the English teacher to develop a kind of literary pedagogy. He makes specific reference to Sampson's book and to the importance of English teachers (Richards, 1929). Richards also accidentally invented the extraordinarily enduring practice suffered/enjoyed since by millions of students of literature all around the world, of doing 'practical criticism', that is, reading a passage from a text, or a complete poem, with no indication of author or date and 'making a meaning'.

The Leavis's marriage was the beginning of a new critical force, imbued with a version of Richards's practical criticism that became 'close reading' of 'the words on the page'. For F. R. Leavis in particular, coming from his stern nonconformist background, this also became a moral and evangelical campaign to elevate HEE to be the most important of all university subjects and no less than the saviour of a declining civilisation constantly corroded by the emerging powers of the mass media. This was captured most neatly in his textbook for SSE teachers and students, *Culture and Environment* (Leavis and Thompson, 1933), which launched his battle cry, "Discriminate and resist!" Leavis, in texts such as *The Great Tradition* (1962), argued for the supremacy of English literature over all other literatures, therefore making it the most important subject to study at university. In that sense he was imbuing Cultural Heritage with a profound Englishness that persists to this day and is currently enshrined in both official documentation (Department for Education, 2018) and all the specifications of the examination boards, credentialising the English Cultural Heritage model.

However, one unintended consequence of Leavis's taking the effects of the popular media so seriously was, unwittingly, to invent 'Media Studies', a discipline that emerged powerfully in the 1960s, sometimes called 'Cultural Studies'. It can therefore be argued that Leavis's cocktail version of Richards's theories of reading and invention of practical criticism engendered Cox's model 5, Cultural Analysis. The stance, 'discriminate and resist', was later reconceptualised as 'Inoculation theory' (see Goodwyn, 1992b) and certainly English teachers, who have long held very mixed views of the popular media, generally share an ideological stance in which Cultural Heritage and Cultural Analysis exist in considerable and irresolvable creative tension. The Cambridge School in this period defined the ontology of SSE at both secondary and university levels. In this period primary practice was fundamentally focused on basic literacy; most students left school by the age of fourteen and never experienced SSE.

4.4 Growth through Language

In 1954, James Britton, a graduate of English Literature and secondary English teacher in outer London joined the University of London's Institute of Education, spending the rest of his long career there and becoming the most influential theorist of the field to this day. With other very notable figures such as Harold Rosen, Douglas Barnes, and John Dixon, he became part of what is often called the London School (that is, school of thought) and may be considered the key figure in the 'turn to language'. This was not a reinforcement of Phase 2 *Conventions and conditions*; it was a partial rejection of the conventions of language seen as part of the establishment's dismissal of working class language and culture. It was also a move to elevate the importance of expression and creative uses of language seen as the capacity of all human beings, including children. Britton in particular championed the vital place of speaking and listening in the process of developing knowledge in all subjects, developing the idea of language across the curriculum (Cox, model 2).

Turning to language did not displace literature but it did dislodge it from pre-eminence. Inevitably, SSE must be understood as part of the history of schooling and the move over the twentieth century from establishing universal primary education to creating a secondary provision with increasing inclusiveness of all types of student but also for a longer period of adolescence. For the majority of the population, this happened between 1945 and about 1980. The secondary sector for older school students, i.e. aged fourteen to eighteen, was the privileged spaces of the public schools (about 5 per cent of the school population) and the grammar schools (20 per cent), and this was where the English Cultural Heritage and the production of elite readers of Leavis's aspiration were enshrined. But the rise of other kinds of school, particularly the secondary modern after the Second World War (for the 'other' 75 per cent), raised some profound questions about what SSE should become. There were many factors at play throughout the 1950s and 1960s; for our purposes, the most important were the emergence of new forms of mass media such as television; burgeoning popular youth culture, especially music; significant increases in immigrant populations, and the concept of nationalisation as egalitarianism, which led to the establishment of the comprehensive school and therefore the abolition (with a few exceptions) of the grammar/secondary modern binary.

All the theorists from the London School mentioned earlier produced important bodies of work. Britton, unquestionably having the greatest international reputation and influence, wrote mostly about language and its development in children and young people. For our purposes, *Growth through English*, which is really a report on the seminal Dartmouth conference (see Goodwyn, 2017), provides an extraordinarily vivid snapshot of SSE in its emergent ontology of the 1960s, with a resonance that continues to this moment.

As outlined earlier, Dixon identified three dominant 'models' (his word) of English (SSE) in the 1960s. First, there was 'skills'. This approach was about 'drills' and exercises undertaken to improve basic literacy and was marked by decontextualised use of language. Second came 'Cultural Heritage', the notion that there was a well-defined high culture and that by passing on knowledge of this culture, students would become more civilised and unified nationally through an appreciation of their great heritage. However, Dixon's own proposal, based on the work of James Britton in particular, was for a 'Personal Growth' model. Dixon's emphasis was much more on processes than content, hence, his 'quicksilver' metaphor.

Central to Dixon's model was the placing of the individual learner at the heart of English and through various processes involving language use, developing that individual. His approach was essentially a constructivist theory of learning, arguing that individuals create new knowledge and then order and consolidate this knowledge. His manifesto also included considerable attention to using drama as a learning medium, especially elements like role play, again emphasising speaking and listening. The Personal Growth approach is profoundly infused with the work of the US pragmatists, with John Dewey a powerful (although unacknowledged) presence throughout *Growth through English*, and this association places SSE in the progressive 'camp' and with a mission for emancipation that continues to this day, however contested.

Dixon did not reject literature or high culture but he saw them, in their current formation, as having a negative impact, as the students became too passive and the teaching too transmissive. He thus took a stand against the Leavisite tradition (usually categorised as the Cambridge School) that fundamentally viewed high culture as a form of literary salvation. He very much rejected the skills model because it was decontextualised and he placed a very strong emphasis on students using their own writing and local language. He was much concerned with the nature of the city schools and drew much of his examples from London where he taught, giving rise to the tag of the 'London', as opposed to the Cambridge, School of English (Gibbons, 2017). It is important to note that the revised 1975 edition of Dixon's book adds a counterbalancing chapter where additional weight is given to communication and discursive writing, and slightly amends Personal Growth to have a more explicit social dimension.

The Personal Growth model, I would certainly argue, has remained the most quietly influential force in the community of practice itself, despite much criticism of it by some theorists, for example Hunter (1987, 1988). There has been much critique of Dixon's text and of the Personal Growth model, but it has not been displaced and was identified by Cox and his committee as central to English teaching in the late 1980s, twenty years after *Growth through English* first appeared. Dixon's achievement was to bring together much of the best thinking of the 1960s and to challenge the grammar school orthodoxy. His text was essentially a manifesto for change and provided a real catalyst that energised English teaching and still does. I would argue that the revised ontology of SSE, formulated in the 1960s, continues today in the existential domain of the classroom, despite all the colonising of the textual domain by officialdom of all kinds.

Between Dixon and Cox there was much debate, and Barnes's (1984) *Versions of English* was especially important because it was much more research-based. Whereas Dixon's evidence was almost exclusively of students' work, Barnes and his team focused on the teaching through observation. There were also more sociological studies of English, for example, Mathieson's (1975) influential *The Preachers of Culture* that argued that Leavis's dogma was still central, and that also remains partially true even now. Terry Eagleton, the famous Marxist literary critic, commented that all English teachers are Leavisites whether they know it or not (Eagleton, 1975).

The Cox models capture a shift in the subject paradigm that is still reflected in practice today. The full report contains a short, but very important, chapter on Information Technology and on Media Education. The authors are eminently uncertain quite 'what to do' with these new areas, but are emphatic about their growing importance to society and to its young people. The Cox curriculum itself includes Media Education in English and this was its first real recognition (in England) as a part of formal schooling (Goodwyn, 1992b), encapsulated as Cultural Analysis; more evidence of the 'quicksilver' subject.

Cox started with Personal Growth because he had come to realise that this was at the heart of English teachers' beliefs. However, Cox and his committee also recognised that Cultural Heritage remained a real force in English and that most teachers related to it, often critically, but nevertheless it had a certain dominance and also a loyal following. The Adult Needs model is partly the Dixon skills model and partly what came to be the great Literacy paradigm of the late 1990s and beyond. The most important 'new' model was Cultural Analysis as it signalled the paradigm shift towards accepting the study of media, popular culture and to developing a critical approach to all texts. This was an expansive ontological shift; having knowledge about media texts was now important.

Clearly, these 'models' are both complementary and contradictory, but this is their collective strength, and Cox was quite right to set them out in this way. Cox was, however, wrong about Cross curricular. Although he was essentially right in recognising the powerful influence of the 1975 Bullock Report, *A Language for Life* (Department for Education, 1975), he was mistaken in thinking this was part of the English paradigm. My surveys of teachers and student teachers over twenty-five years (Goodwyn, 2011) are quite consistent in their findings: English teachers state that 'Language Across the Curriculum' is a whole school approach and is chiefly important to teachers of other subjects who need to recognise their responsibility (as Bullock actually proposed) to monitor their own use of language in their teaching and to pay attention to helping their students develop as language users (Goodwyn, 1992a; Goodwyn and Findlay, 1999; Goodwyn, 2004).

4.5 English in Harmonious Practice

For a brief period of time, probably 1980–1992, the ontology of SSE was in a kind of alignment with all the various forces in a form of consensus. It existed, in other words, in a collective vision. The following elements were 'lined up'.

The fundamentally egalitarian comprehensive system was fully in place. In 1984, the new assessment system to fit with a comprehensive school, the GCSE, replacing 'O' levels and CSEs, was operational and drew heavily on the innovative practices of the CSE (the certificate developed for less academic students from the Secondary Modern Schools, that is, the 80 per cent of students who did not attend grammar schools). This model incorporated all the thinking of the London School, foregrounding speaking and listening, writing as expression, and reading as personal response and growth; and it put assessment completely in the hands of teachers. Politically, English teachers were seen as autonomous professionals and responsible for all aspects of student learning and 'outcomes' (not a word in use at the time). This autonomy included textual choice, with the Cox Report strongly advocating multicultural literature and a very wide range of texts, including plenty of contemporary writers and non-fiction, supporting the use of media artefacts in the classroom. The only compulsory author was Shakespeare, something English teachers were very content with. This was also the last decade before the coming of the

Office for Standards in Education (Ofsted, responsible for inspecting every school in the country every three years and pronouncing whether the school should continue or 'fail' and be closed), the Teacher Training Agency (which regulated all teacher education), and School League Tables (where all schools appeared in their local newspapers ranked by test results). The alignment was such that my research in 1990 (Goodwyn, 1992a) found that, while English teachers were deeply apprehensive about centralised control (and how right they were), they actually agreed with the spirit and the letter of the first National Curriculum for English. Certainly, secondary teachers believed in this version of SSE.

For primary teachers, the introduction in 1989 of the National Curriculum meant that suddenly there was something called English for ages five to eleven. Their practice had always named what they did as 'language work', with the four modes incorporated in a very child-centred pedagogy. This imposition was not welcomed, and there is not much evidence of sudden change in primary schools (see Goodwyn and Fuller, 2011). The monolithic National Literacy Strategy, which would drive a juggernaut through primary education, was a few years away.

In this period, reading and writing, speaking and listening, were seen as equal dynamics in enabling the development of young people as future citizens in a participatory democracy; English was emancipatory. Most departments organised their classes into fully mixed ability groupings, while maths departments stuck rigidly to ability setting. SSE was in a highly active period of development and the existential and textual domains were harmoniously aligned, with teachers allowed full creative engagement with curriculum, assessment, and pedagogy. It was a Personal Growth National Curriculum and a Personal Growth classroom existence.

4.6 Building the Panopticon: The Coming of Control, Conformity, and Self-Regulation

Between about 1992 and 2007, SSE became profoundly schismatised and all alignment disappeared. In an ontological sense, SSE fragmented into three existences with differing epistemological stances. Beginning with the first revisions of the National Curriculum for English (NCE) as early as 1992, the state's version of SSE was increasingly of a nationalistic English, a highly formalised SSE, dominated by performance indicators for students and teachers, fiercely inspected by Ofsted; this is the version seen from the panopticon. The panopticon concept originated with nineteenth century English philosopher

Jeremy Bentham, who designed a prison where every individual cell is separated and one guard in the centre of the structure can watch every single prisoner. The idea was developed by Foucault who saw it as the way state (or any) surveillance power structure induces self-regulation in every individual within the sphere of the power.

Teachers have held on to their own, the second version, an ideological SSE. In their minds, SSE continued to be an emancipatory project imbued with Personal Growth. The third SSE existed uneasily in practice, in constant tension between the demands of the state and the beliefs of the teachers. This can be easily pictured in the different practices being displayed in 'panopticon lessons' 'put on' for inspectors and observations by senior management when compared to a 'real' and ordinary lesson (cf. Goodwyn, 2010). However, the effect of the panopticon is to produce performative anxiety that creates a mode of self-regulation. The fragmentation of the school system, for example, generating hundreds of academies 'free' from the NCE and no longer in a relationship with a local authority, means the schools are independent, whilst still subject to Ofsted. But practice, version 3, seems to persist in a self-regulating mode.

In explaining this final period of the panopticon, there are some key indicators. Two significant texts appeared in the 1980s, written by the 'old school', Her Majesty's Inspectors of Schools (HMI), who were viewed by the profession as critical friends, not the 'enemy' (Ofsted inspectors were certainly viewed as the enemy; see Goodwyn, 2011a). The first text foreshadowed in its name *English for Ages 5–16* (Department for Education, 1984) and in tone, the various versions of the NCE from 1992 onwards, with its emphasis on formal language teaching and suggesting that some of the rigour of language study had been lost. However the pivotal document is in *English for Ages 5–16, a Response* (Department for Education, 1986). Historically, it was most unusual for HMI to write in response to criticisms and signalled the establishment's need to reinforce its arguments through the proxy of an 'independent' and respected institution – it might be argued that that experience began the process of developing Ofsted in its aggressive and punitive form in the nineties and noughties.

The response also recommended the project that became Language in the National Curriculum that itself came from the 'investigation' led by John Kingman (a mathematician) that reported in 1988 as *Knowledge about Language* (Department for Education, 1988) and was then overtaken by the sudden establishment of the Cox committee. For a fuller account, see Goodwyn, 2011a. For (Applied) Linguists, this was a very striking moment in the ontology of English and, perhaps, the promise of some recognition of what linguistics might finally offer in SSE. What has actually happened is the growth of 'A' level English language, and in that sense, SSE has changed its ontological status but, I would argue, only marginally for 'mainstream' SSE 11–16 (cf. Goddard, this volume).

Kingman argued for Knowledge about Language (KAL), *not* a return to formal grammar teaching. This theme was supported by Cox, and so the first NCE had a section on KAL as desirable, but did not demand much knowledge of linguistics from students. However, it remains to this day a well-known phenomenon that SSE teachers tend to have strong literary knowledge and relatively weak linguistic knowledge (see Myhill et al., 2011), and what is often deemed an anxiety about grammar. Kingman's recommendations were largely adopted in 1988 and, despite the overtaking of that report by the Cox Report in 1989, the Language in the National Curriculum (LINC) project, led by Professor Ron Carter, was set up to improve the KAL of all SSE teachers in service and in training, and to develop supporting materials. This was broadly welcomed by the profession (Goodwyn, 2011b) and was part of the confluent alignment of the time. The training was somewhat problematic, being a 'cascade model' where one teacher from each English department received training from regional advisors and then was supplied with all the emergent materials. There was also a strand for Initial Teacher Training, enthusiastically adopted by University Post Graduate Certificate in Education tutors, this author being one.

The work of LINC was completed by 1992, but its model of a fundamentally sociolinguistic approach to texts and a focus on criticality rather than formal grammar knowledge led to a most extraordinary political reaction from the contemporary right-wing government. The materials were literally banned from schools, with much media furore, with about £25 million being wasted, and leading to a BBC *Panorama* documentary investigating what happened. This act remains an outrageous intervention by the state and a barbaric piece of censorship; however, it is now largely forgotten and hurriedly photocopied versions of the LINC materials gather dust, if they exist at all. What might have led to an ontological revision of SSE with a new model of English, the KAL model, that teachers would have welcomed, was instead an aborted project, signalling, yet again, the state's intention to control SSE and its teachers.

The final leg on this journey began in 1997, with the bringing in of New Labour's flagship policy, the National Literacy Strategy, and ended in 2011, when it, and its secondary companion, the Framework for English (FWE), were discontinued. It was a remarkable sign of the (ironically) higher status of English, compared to maths (in England), that the parallel National Numeracy Strategy was a modest and uncontentious affair. For our purposes the FWE was another element in the schismatisation of SSE, and it was the period when SSE teachers – with no irony – became opposed to 'Literacy'. There is extensive research (Goodwyn and Fuller, 2011) about the way SSE teachers reviled and resisted the dogmatic approaches of the FWE, quite liked the materials produced, but found nothing new in them, and began to live in the three ontologies that still persist.

5 PG and SSE Teachers

The other major finding of my surveys over twenty-five years is that Personal Growth (PG) remains the most important model to English teachers regardless of age and experience. They generally put Cultural Heritage last and Cultural Analysis and Adult Needs close together, but they do 'recognise' that these models capture what goes on in the community of their practice. When asked to identify what the official curriculum demands, they often put Cultural Heritage first, illustrating perfectly the difference between the prescribed form of English and its lived reality in practice. Surveys are, of course, self-reports, and might well reflect espoused models rather than realities; nevertheless, their consistency is remarkable and there has been no major empirical study to challenge these findings. An interesting critique is contained in Marshall's (2000) *English Teachers – The Unofficial Guide: Researching the Philosophies of English Teachers*. One observation-based study, *English in Urban Classrooms* (Kress et al., 2005), brought a valuable multimodal perspective to understanding how SSE teachers carry out their practice with some attention to SSE in its embodied present tense rendition.

6 Closing Remarks

I will not summarise what is already a summary. However, School Subject English (SSE) in England has clearly passed through several formative phases and, fundamentally, has expanded its 'territory' consistently, as the number of models has increased to four, Personal Growth, Cultural Analysis, Adult Needs, and Cultural Heritage. I argue that SSE's existence in the early part of the twenty-first century has, for its teachers, been fragmented into three: (1) the state's, mostly textual version, (2) the inner, ideological beliefs of its teachers, and then (3) the messy reality of practice where these two ontologies interact under a panopticon gaze, enforced externally but also acting as a self-regulating force. Compared to the situation in the 1980s, SSE is a much less emancipatory project and has actually shrunk in scope and ambition. For example, in 2000, the revised National Curriculum included several references to the importance of the moving image, all of which have been removed from the current and statutory NCE. Simultaneously, the NCE has no longer any force in academies and free schools, but this neoliberal policy has not produced a flourishing of bold and innovative teaching. However, this current phase will be just that, a phase. If educational policy can recapture an egalitarian and emancipatory vision, not social mobility but social justice, then English teachers will once more aim for the personal growth of each student and the collective benefits of social empowerment for the nation, perhaps a phase 8, of *Emancipation, Agency, and Social Justice* (Goodwyn, 2017, 2018).

References

Barnes, D. and Barnes, D. (1984) *Versions of English*. London: Heinemann.
Barnes, D., Britton, J., and Rosen, H. (1971). *Language, the Learner and the School*. Harmondsworth: Penguin.
Cox, B. (1991). *Cox on Cox: An English Curriculum for the 1990s*. London: Hodder and Stoughton.
Cox, B. (1992). *The Great Betrayal: Memoirs of a Life in Education*. London: Chapmans.
Departmental Committee of the Board of Education. (1921). The Teaching of English in England (known as The Newbolt Report). London: His Majesty's Stationery Office.
Department for Education. (1975). *A Language for Life* (known as The Bullock Report). London: Her Majesty's Stationery Office.
Department for Education. (1984). *English for Ages 5–16*. London: Her Majesty's Stationery Office.
Department for Education. (1986). *Responses to English for Ages 5–16*. London: Her Majesty's Stationery Office.
Department for Education. (1988). *Knowledge about Language*. London: Her Majesty's Stationery Office.
Department for Education. (1989). *English for ages 5–16*. London: Her Majesty's Stationery Office.
Department for Education. (2018). www.gov.uk/government/publications/national-curriculum-in-england-english-programmes-of-study.
Departmental Committee of the Board of Education. (1921). *The Teaching of English in England (The Newbolt Report)*. London: His Majesty's Stationery Office.
Dixon, J. (1975). *Growth through English: Set in the Perspective of the Seventies*. Oxford: Oxford University Press.
Eagleton, T. (1975). *Literary Theory: An Introduction*. Oxford: Blackwells.
Gibbons, S. (2017). *English and Its Teachers: A History of Policy, Pedagogy and Practice*. Abingdon: Routledge.

Goodwyn, A. (1992a). Theoretical models of English teaching. *English in Education*, 26(3), 4–10.

Goodwyn, A. (1992b). *English Teaching and Media Education*. Buckingham: Open University Press.

Goodwyn, A. (2003). Literacy or English: The struggle for the professional identity of English teachers in England. In D. Homer, B. Doecke, and H. Nixon, eds., *English Teachers at Work: Narratives, Counter-Narratives and Arguments* (pp. 123–135). Kent Town, South Australia: Wakefield Press.

Goodwyn, A. (2004). Literacy versus English: A professional identity crisis. In A. Goodwyn and A. Stables, eds., *Learning to Read Critically in Language and Literacy Education* (pp. 192–205). London: Sage.

Goodwyn, A. (2010). *The Expert Teacher of English*. London: Routledge.

Goodwyn, A. (2011a). The impact of the Framework for English: Teachers' struggle against 'informed prescription'. In A. Goodwyn and C. Fuller, eds., *The Great Literacy Debate* (pp. 117–135). London: Routledge Falmer.

Goodwyn, A. (2011b). Becoming an English teacher: Identity, self knowledge and expertise. In J. Davison and J. Moss, eds., *Debates in English* (pp. 18–36). London: Routledge.

Goodwyn, A. (2016). Still growing after all these years? The resilience of the 'Personal Growth model of English' in England and also internationally. *English Teaching, Practice and Critique*, 15(2), 7–21.

Goodwyn, A. (2017). From Personal Growth (1966) to Personal Growth and Social Agency – Proposing an invigorated model for the twenty-first century. *English in Australia*, 52(1), 66–73.

Goodwyn, A. (2018). From personal growth [1966] to personal growth and social agency [2016] – Proposing an invigorated model for the twenty-first century. In A. Goodwyn, C. Durrant, W. Sawyer, and L. Scherff, eds., *The Future of English Teaching Worldwide and Its Histories: Celebrating 50 Years from the Dartmouth Conference*. London: Routledge.

Goodwyn, A. and Findlay, K. (1999). The Cox Models revisited: English teacher's views of their subject and the National Curriculum. *English in Education*, 33(2), 19–31.

Goodwyn, A. and Fuller, C., eds. (2011). *The Great Literacy Debate*. London: Routledge.

Goodwyn, A., Durrant, C., Sawyer, W., Zancanella, D., and Scherff, E., eds. (2018). *The Future of English Teaching Worldwide and Its Histories: Celebrating 50 Years from the Dartmouth Conference*. London: Routledge.

Hilliard, C. (2012). *English as a Vocation: The Scrutiny Movement*. Oxford: Oxford University Press.

Hunter, I. (1987). Culture, education, English: Building "the principal scene of the real life of children". *Economy and Society*, 16, 568–588.

Hunter, I. (1988). *Culture and Government: The Emergence of Literary Education*. London: Macmillan.

Kress, G., Jewitt, C., Bourne, J. et al. (2003). *English in Urban Classrooms: A Multimodal Perspective on Teaching and Learning*. Oxford: Routledge.

Leavis, F. R. (1962). *The Great Tradition*. Harmondsworth: Penguin.

Leavis, F. R. and Thompson, D. (1933). *Culture and Environment*. London: Chatto and Windus.

Marshall, B. (2000). *English Teachers – The Unofficial Guide: Researching the Philosophies of English Teachers*. London: Routledge.

Mathieson, M. (1975). *The Preachers of Culture: A Study of English and Its Teachers*. Oxford: George Allen and Unwin.

Myhill, D., Lines, H., Watson, A., and Jones, S. (2011). Rethinking grammar: The impact of embedded grammar teaching on students' writing and students' metalinguistic understanding. *Research Papers in Education*, 27(2), 139–166.

OECD. (2015). *Excellence and Equity in Education*. Vol. 1. http://dx.doi.org/10.1787/9789264266490-en.

Richards, I. A. (1924). *The Principles of Literary Criticism*. London: Routledge and Kegan Paul.

Richards, I. A. (1929). *Practical Criticism*. London: Routledge and Kegan Paul.

Rosenblatt, L. (1938/1970). *Literature as Exploration*. New York: MLA.

Sampson, G. (1921). *English for the English*. Cambridge: Cambridge University Press.

Shulman, L. S. (1986). Those who understand: Knowledge growth in teaching. *Educational Researcher*, 15(2), 4–14.

Shulman, L. S. (1987). Knowledge and teaching: Foundations of the new reform. *Harvard Educational Review*, 57(1), 1–22.

7 A 'Godlike Science'
English Teaching in Secondary Schools

Rachel Roberts

1 Introduction

In Mary Shelley's gothic creation *Frankenstein*, the Creature's learning of language is described as something sublime: "[he]... perceived that the words they spoke sometimes produced pleasure or pain, smiles or sadness, in the minds and countenances of the hearers. This was indeed a godlike science" (Shelley, 1818/2000, p. 103). In terms of linguistic development, the Creature's learning that occurs from simply watching and listening to the day-to-day lives of a family of French exiles through a hole in the wall is quite naïve; there is no interaction between the Creature and the family, Shelley presumably conceiving him as a blank slate. Over time, the Creature realises an association between the signs in the books read by the exiles and speech, a tacit acknowledgement of the arbitrary link between word symbols and the nature of the sounds when spoken. The Creature does not explain exactly *how* he was able to learn what he calls the 'science of letters'; his focus is on describing how learning to read "opened before me a wide field of wonder and delight" (p. 108). The affective impact of understanding language underlines the tragedy of the Creature: now that his mind has been 'opened' by language, he begins to wonder about the world and himself. In a Cartesian sense, the Creature *thinks* himself into existence as he grapples with his own identity through language: "the words induced me to turn towards myself... And what was I?" (p. 108). Language has provided thought, identity, and therefore existence.

The centrality of language, of its relationship with thought, and its role in learning, is fundamental to education. This chapter will explore the nature of School Subject English (SSE) teaching in secondary education in contemporary England. Where Goodwyn's chapter (this volume) examines the historical narrative of SSE's ontology, this chapter will focus on its current position as a secondary school subject.

A 'Godlike Science': English Teaching in Secondary Schools 123

In this exploration, I will consider the ontology of English (what it is); its relationship with epistemology (how knowledge is positioned); pedagogy (how it is taught); and ideology as implied through current government policy. The oxymoron of Shelley's "godlike science" contains within it what I will argue in this chapter is not only the heart of English but the heart of *learning*.

My own ontological understanding of SSE is that it is fundamentally constructivist; the world is socially constructed, and SSE provides ways of understanding and negotiating the world via texts and language. This world view would suggest an interpretivist understanding of epistemology; however, it is the question of what *knowledge* is and how we can acquire it that seems to generate the most controversy in current educational discourse.

The metaphors used to describe learning can indicate an epistemological perspective. Shelley's conception of the Creature as a blank slate directly draws on Locke's *tabula rasa* (Locke, 1690/2004). In current discourse around education in England, this kind of thinking about learning is cast as a traditional or a progressive approach (Boulter, 2017). Learning as acquisition ("Pupils gained knowledge about Shakespeare from their learned teacher") would be traditional; learning as construction ("Discussion about Macbeth's character flaws generated a range of interpretations") is the predominant metaphor for a progressive understanding of learning. (A shorthand for distinguishing between the two would be to define traditional teaching methods as 'teacher centred' and progressive teaching methods as 'child centred'.) There is therefore a conflict, or at least a mismatch, between the ontology and epistemology in SSE, from some quarters. The influence of the so-called 'knowledge-rich curriculum' as advocated by Hirsch (1999) is evident in both wider educational discourse and in the thinking of current ministers of education (Gibb, 2015).

As an epistemological battlefield, the educational debate around traditional/progressive approaches to teaching is hardly new; the opening of John Dewey's *Experience and Education*, first published in 1938, comments on the divide (Dewey, 1938/1997). It is, I believe, founded on spurious arguments and leads to a false dichotomy (Husbands, 2015; Boulter, 2017). The metaphors used to describe learning are important *because* they imply an epistemological perspective; although construction metaphors for learning provide agency on the part of the learner, learning is still regularly conceptualised as an entity to be obtained or transferred (Sfard, 1998). Learning *is* ownership of knowledge in these terms, as indicated by the lexicon of words used in relation to learning (*knowledge, idea, fact,* and so on). The participation metaphor moves away from static ownership to a dynamic *doing* of learning – becoming part of a community. In matters of discourse, and perhaps SSE particularly, this latter metaphor is particularly attractive. It chimes with a dialogic understanding of English teaching (Mercer, 2008). It is thus especially important to address epistemology in English teaching; indeed, Medway (1980) argues that this is a fundamental part of what English *is*: "nothing less than a different model of education: knowledge to be made, not given; knowledge comprising more than can be discursively stated; learning as a diverse range of processes, including affective ones; educational processes to be embarked on with outcomes unpredictable; students' perceptions, experiences, imaginings and unsystematically acquired knowledge admitted as legitimate curricular content" (cited in Rosen, 2017, p. 86).

The difficulty lies in the linguistics of discourse for education: 'knowledge', even in its infinitive verb form 'to know', conforms to the acquisition metaphor, whereas 'to learn' implies a process of communication; 'knowing' and 'learning' belong to different semantic classifications of verb: of *having* and *action*. The distinction between 'knowing how and knowing that' (Ryle, 1949, p. 20) does not bridge this gap and *learning* should not be considered as a sub-set of 'knowing how' (see further discussion regarding procedural and declarative knowledge in Ryle, 1949, chapter 5; Hall, this volume, Section 2.1). However, it is worthwhile heeding Sfard's (1998) observation that 'too great a devotion to one particular metaphor can lead to theoretical distortions and to undesirable practices' (p. 4). Epistemology is therefore subject to ideology.

How does the 'godlike science' of SSE fit in this debate? In a world of 'two cultures' (Snow, 2008), in which the STEM subjects of science, technology, engineering, and maths are considered more valuable because of a more obviously measurable output (Alsup, 2015), we might read Shelley's 'godlike science' of language as a contrast between the metaphysical, spiritual, unknowable ('godlike') and the technical, rational, declarative facts ('science'). In this comparison, the act of reading combines these two into one, a fitting metaphor for a subject that struggles to have a unified definition of *what it is*. What follows is a contemporary conceptualisation of SSE teaching in secondary schools, arguing that it is a subject in a state of ontological and epistemological crisis due its positioning in educational policy. I consider the reasons for this and suggest a way of resolving some of the challenges.

2 What's in a Name?

SSE suffers from its 'awkward status as medium as well as object of study' (Green and McIntyre, 2011, p. 6): part of the 'polysemy' described by Hall (this volume). As an academic subject, English was born of a mishmash of cannibalised parts of other subjects such as classics and philology (Eaglestone, 2002). As a university discipline, English is repositioned through different schools of theory: close reading, reader response, deconstructionism, and new historicism have all been bolted on over the course of English's hundred-year lifetime. Rather like the difference between catwalk couture fashion and high street shopping, the influence of university-level critical theory on SSE teaching in secondary schools tends to be a watered-down version and filtered through governmental policy and exam board specifications. While university degrees offer courses entitled 'English', these tend not to feature the same content as school-level English in England. Usually a degree in 'English' will be shorthand for a course in English *literature*, with the possibility of optional modules on creative writing, film, or language – see, for example, Royal Holloway's BA programme (Royal Holloway, University of London, 2018). There is a division of subject content in Higher Education; English literature and language (or linguistics) are usually taught as separate disciplines – the content of the latter will include approaches to grammar, stylistics, etc., and universities that offer a true integration between literature and linguistics, such as the innovative BA at Middlesex University (2018), are rare in the United Kingdom. This separation is reflected in the Quality Assurance Agency for Higher Education's benchmark statement for English: "encompassing study of the structure, history and usage of the English language, critical analysis of literature written in English, and the practice of creative writing" (QAA, 2015, p. 5). The 'content' of English in terms of subject bifurcates more clearly at the upper secondary level (ages sixteen to eighteen), where qualifications are offered for English Literature, English Language, or the combination of literature and language (cf. Goddard, this volume).

Why is the subject called 'English'? While the first university to offer an English degree was Oxford in 1893 (Eaglestone, 2002), it was in 1904 that the Board of Education required subjects of English literature and language to be taught in English schools (Davison and Daly, 2014). This coincided with the further establishment of English as a university subject, partly as a reaction to World War I and partly as a 'civilising' means of social control (Eaglestone, 2002). The Newbolt Report of 1921 identified a need for a *functional* English in employees, specifying a general lack of skill in spelling and 'correct' English usage (Knights, 2015), a social anxiety that continues to this day.

The post-World War II conception of English as a subject split into two camps: Cambridge English and London English (Gibbons, 2014), discussed by Goodwyn, this volume. This split can be broadly cast as a traditional and progressive understanding of SSE. The current National Curriculum is avowedly 'traditional'; its architects declare the influence of American educationalist E. D. Hirsch (Gibb, 2015), who promotes a 'knowledge' curriculum, which I will explore more fully in Sections 5 and 6. From its outset as a school subject, English has thus been fraught with anxieties about its nature and purpose. Its very name implies an imperialistic attempt to bring together disparate factions under a nationalistic banner – an indication of efforts to define the subject's ontology.

From the inception of the 1989 National Curriculum, SSE has been neatly atomised for planning and assessment purposes into three distinct areas: reading, writing, and speaking and listening, more recently termed 'Spoken Language' (Department for Education, 2013). In the early years and primary school phase, emphasis is on learning the basics of reading and writing; decoding of language being the necessary first step. The majority of primary schools name this part of the curriculum 'literacy' rather than 'English' – probably a hangover from the now defunct National Literacy Strategy (Department for Education, 2010). While in secondary schools the curriculum subject is 'English' (as opposed to 'language arts' in the United States), there remains a conflict in educational discourse over nomenclature because of what it suggests about subject content. The term 'literacy' has been criticised because of its functional (and therefore limiting) connotations (Barton, 2013). However, this criticism ignores the associations with *learnedness* that 'literacy' has: to be 'literate' is at once to be able to demonstrate skills of reading and writing *and* competence in a range of different aspects of culture and communication (*Oxford English Dictionary*, 2011). Perhaps this indicates that neither designation of 'English' or 'literacy' fully does justice to the subject.

3 Models of English

The values implied by the stated purposes of a subject discipline will underpin the curriculum itself. It is for this reason that analysis of the National Curriculum, the inception of which in 1989 attempted to formalise the subject for schools in England and Wales, is necessary. A subsequent government document containing recommendations for SSE pedagogy included what are now known as 'Cox's Models' of English (see Goodwyn, this volume). The report was not generated by or drawn from practitioners themselves. Tied to government policy and assessment needs, it presented *a* view of English as it should be taught in secondary schools. That it describes five quite different purposes of English echoes the conflicts and contradictions apparent in the subject's inception. Current teachers of English will have been directly affected by this and the National Curriculum (and its different iterations in 1995, 2000, 2007, and 2013) as both pupils and practitioners. The National Curriculum is statutory for state-maintained schools only; independent schools and academies are not required to follow it (Department for Education, 2014), although many do. The National Curriculum also influences examination specifications for end of secondary school qualifications, taken at age sixteen. It is therefore worth using the ideas set forth in Cox's report.

Goodwyn's (1992) research suggests that, at the time, most English teachers perceived the 'personal growth' and 'Cultural Analysis' models to be the most important in terms of their own personal priorities. Indeed, the 'personal growth' model of English (sometimes described as 'progressive' English) arose as a movement from the Dartmouth Conference (Dixon, 1967; Locke, 2015), which might explain this result. Findlay's (2010) more recent research suggests the importance of literature in English teachers' perceptions of their subject, with emphasis on a cultural heritage model. Gardner's (2017) comparative analysis of the English curricula in England and Australia suggests a shift in the curriculum in England from personal growth towards didactic literacy, although he analysed the National Curriculum for SSE at the primary, rather than secondary, level. This reflects the renewed emphasis on the explicit teaching of grammar and grammatical terms at primary level in England that culminates in highly prescriptive, not to say controversial, tests for eleven year olds in their final year of primary school (see Jones et al., 2013, for an informed discussion on the teaching of grammar; cf. also Goddard, this volume). How much government policy through curriculum reform influences secondary English teachers' perceptions of their subject is difficult to determine, and this suggests a need for further research.

4 An Analysis of the English Programme of Study for Key Stage 3

SSE as it is taught between the ages of eleven to fourteen in secondary schools will incorporate most of the following as topics for teaching:

- literature (both from the English canon and modern prose and poetry)

- non-fiction
- media
- drama
- discrete teaching of grammar
- 'reading' lessons (often held in the library), designed to encourage reading for pleasure

The weighting of each will vary from school to school in terms of time spent in lessons on each topic, usually divided into half-termly blocks of six-week 'Schemes of Work'. These schemes are likely to be blended in terms of the content and teaching approaches (drama or information and communication technologies [ICT]-based activities, for example) and may be thematically or genre-based (a scheme on science fiction might, for example, explore extracts from Shelley, H. G. Wells, and Isaac Asimov as well as *Star Trek* or modern dystopian films and non-fiction 'scientific' writing).

What follows here is a critical analysis of the National Curriculum programme of study for Key Stage 3 English (lower secondary school, ages eleven to fourteen) and a comparison to the 'models' of English as described by the Cox Report (DES and the Welsh Office, 1989). This seeks to critique the government policy in terms of its function as a social document and its relationship within the discourse of SSE education. I have concentrated primarily on the section on reading due to constraints of space.

The English programme of study for Key Stage 3, which forms part of the National Curriculum, is a statutory document produced by the Department for Education for the guidance of school curricula as delivered by schools and teachers. All state-maintained schools must, by law, follow it. While the document is not ascribed to any individual author, such as the secretary of state for education, and therefore to any overt political affiliation, it is nonetheless a political declaration of the government's belief of what should be taught in schools (Dominiczak, 2013). Its initial audience is teachers, particularly those who have direct responsibility for designing programmes of study for whole year groups or Key Stages, such as heads of department. The secondary audience is the public including, of course, voters. Written in the indicative mood and present tense, the National Curriculum gives both a sense of authority and reassurance, beginning with the declaration that "English has a pre-eminent place in education and society" (Department for Education, 2013, p. 2). Although this is grandiose, it serves a purpose for the government to demonstrate its belief in the subject's importance. The phrase "high-quality education in . . ." that follows is used in the 'Purpose of

Study' statement for *every* subject in the National Curriculum (Department for Education, 2014). It is a declaration for the need of high standards, which feeds into a wider political discourse about falling standards in comparison to other countries (Coughlan, 2016), contributing to a narrative of anxiety over the economic implications of having a poorly educated population.

The National Curriculum states that the key aims of English teaching are for children to be able to communicate, to develop to become rounded citizens. These aims, which echo both the 'Personal Growth' and 'Adult Needs' of Cox's models, are framed around a distinctly 'traditional' concept of education, the acquisition metaphor of learning: "reading ... enables pupils ... to acquire knowledge" (Department for Education, 2013, p. 2). It also alludes to the 'Matthew Effect', where, in cultural terms, those who are already rich get richer (Rigney, 2010), which is phrased as a warning: "pupils... who do not learn to speak, read and write fluently and confidently are effectively disenfranchised" (Department for Education, 2013, p. 2). (*Disenfranchised* is an interesting choice of verb, again indicating a political agenda: productive "member[s] of society" are those who can *vote*.)

Other verbs used promise that pupils will be *enabled* and *equipped*, which suggest both personal development and being readied for the future, appealing to Cox's 'Adult Needs' model of English. At the forefront of the Department for Education's vision is the role that literature will play in pupils' progress in SSE. The structure of the stated aims for English does suggest a hierarchy:

- reading
- vocabulary and grammar
- literary heritage
- writing
- discussion
- speaking and listening

As a list of subject content, it could be argued that it expands on the previous National Curriculum's Reading, Writing, and Speaking and Listening. However, statements such as "appreciate our rich and varied literary heritage" (Department for Education, 2013, p. 2) suggest an assumption regarding aestheticism and value in literature: *appreciate* implies an intrinsic worth in specific literature that, as a moral imperative, *should* be taught. What is meant by the pronoun *our* in this sentence? Whose literature? *English* peoples' literature? *British* peoples' literature? There is no reference to children's literature or young adult fiction or fiction from a diverse range of writers; the Great Tradition (Leavis, 2008/1948) and English literary canon is implicitly invoked, as phrases such as "challenging material" and "high-quality works" (Department for Education, 2013, p. 4) suggest.

The subject content section divides literature up into the following (Department for Education, 2013, p. 4):

- English literature, both pre-1914 and contemporary, including prose, poetry and drama
- Shakespeare (two plays)
- seminal world literature

There is no clear reason for the 1914 split, and the only named author is Shakespeare – clearly the model of English promoted here is one of 'Cultural Heritage', and an implicitly sexist one in the use of *seminal*. Literature appears to have one role in the National Curriculum's conception of English: to develop cultural knowledge and appreciation and to demonstrate this through knowledge of vocabulary and skills of reading "critically" (Department for Education, 2013, p. 4). While the opening statement of purpose indicated a desire for English to enable pupils to develop personally, there is little reference to this in the main body of the document, other than through knowledge of 'high-quality' literature. Alsup (2015) writes that pupils need to find some point of connection with a text. An emotional connection that is part of empathetic development has the potential to transform as part of social action. If this is the case, choice of literature taught and children being active in their engagement with texts is key.

Grammar and vocabulary certainly feature much more prominently, including explicit "knowledge of grammar" (Department of Education, 2013, p. 5), as well as demonstrating the ability to use it effectively in writing. It is intended to develop knowledge of grammar developed in Key Stages 1 and 2 (primary age), and this is linked to the use of Standard English.

Perhaps more indicative of the state's view of SSE is in what is absent, rather than what is explicitly mentioned in the National Curriculum. There is no reference to creativity in the current version; a sharp difference to the previous National Curriculum, which had creativity as one of its central tenets (QCA, 2007) and only one reference to 'interpretations' (p. 4) (and this only in relation to staging of plays). Media or multi-modal texts are notable omissions; a retrogressive decision as much consumption of texts, particularly by young people, is likely to be in digital format. It seems, therefore, that the 'Cultural Analysis' model of English with a wider definition of 'texts', has less purchase with the current National Curriculum. Spoken language is similarly neglected; despite the admission that spoken language "continues to underpin the development of pupils' reading and writing" (Department for Education, 2013, p. 2), it is relegated to the end of the document. That it is no longer counted as part of the GCSE qualification (taken by most pupils at age sixteen) indicates the *lack* of importance placed on speaking and listening, belying the earlier statement.

One of the justifications for this revised National Curriculum was that it would give schools and teachers greater freedom in terms of *what* is taught (Department for Education, 2013), and this is true, at least theoretically, for Key Stage 3 (Key Stage 4 is rather hamstrung by the set texts and examination system of General Certification of Secondary Education, or GCSE, syllabuses), although it still perpetuates a model of English that does not necessarily reflect English teachers' views. The model of SSE set out conforms more to Cambridge English, focusing on the 'Great Tradition' (Leavis, 2008/1948), close reading and formal writing. The document doesn't quite position children as blank slates, as it acknowledges that "reading ... enables pupils ... to build on what they already know" (Department for Education, 2013, p. 2), although there seems to be little agency or exploration in terms of what pupils are expected to do. At its best, the National Curriculum for English is contradictory; at its worst, it is reductive. There is an acknowledgement of the relationship between reading, writing, speaking, and listening but the weighting in terms of time spent on literature and what studying language *means* in SSE is neglected. The 'progressive' London English influence, which repositioned English in secondary schools as emancipatory, pluralistic, and enjoyable, seems very distant. When asking "what is English in secondary schools?" perhaps we should ask "from whose point of view?"

5 The Question of Subject 'Knowledge'

Given the disparate nature of SSE in the secondary school, what constitutes 'subject' knowledge? Does this consist of knowledge of texts? Only literary ones? Knowledge of criticism? Knowledge of language and demonstration of these skills? What 'skills' are developed or required by English? The Quality Assurance Agency for Higher Education (QAA) benchmark statements for English degrees list a wide range of items for subject knowledge, including a range of literatures, language and its functions, culture and production of texts, criticality, and relationships between different genres and different media (QAA, 2015, p. 7). This is a much more pluralistic conception of English than the National Curriculum's SSE.

The current National Curriculum seems to imply that English subject knowledge revolves around the literary canon and grammatical terms. If SSE is reduced via a movement towards a 'knowledge' curriculum, this is "knowledge of the powerful" rather than "powerful knowledge" (Young, 2009). If we question, as Lyotard (1984) does, the hierarchy of particular kinds of knowledge, I would suggest that what English *does* is consider what and who we are and how we engage with the world around us. English could be described as a postmodern patchwork; a Frankenstein's monster of a subject. The *différance* exists, in this analogy, in the gaps between the parts: inherent interest in language and story; self-expression and exploration through talk and writing; analysis of 'texts' in the widest sense and of lesser value. The 'gap' is interpretation and creation.

6 The Teaching of Reading in SSE

As a secondary school subject, English's engagement with criticism or theory is 'small c' conservative; it would be a rare class below that of A Level (post-compulsory education, aged sixteen to eighteen) that might consider a range of different readings that overtly uses a theoretical lens with which to examine literary texts. It is not necessary, one might argue, for fourteen year olds to have an hour's lecture on post-colonial theory, although they can easily consider Caliban's motivations in *The Tempest* as a direct result of his usurpation by Prospero and subsequent enslavement and link this to a modern understanding of the nature of Empire. If it is the case that effective teachers of SSE will make opportunities to develop multiple readings of text through the implicit use of literary theory, it is likely that there is a dominant ideology or preferred reading. Consider, for example, the character of Curley's wife in Steinbeck's *Of Mice and Men* (Steinbeck, 1937/2000). An initial 'reader response' analysis of her character might (and does, in my own experience) lead to students' intense dislike of her, seeing her as the prime reason for Lennie's death, as a flirt, a troublemaker. These responses echo the ranch workers' impressions of Curley's wife as a "tart" (p. 50). Using a combination of New Historicism and Feminist theory, supported by close textual reading, it is not difficult to re-cast Curley's wife as an innocent ("Coulda been in the movies", p. 125), rather pathetic figure, trapped by lack of education and life choices that was typical for women in the context of the Midwest during the Depression. The same case can be made for the characters of Crooks (racial discrimination), Lennie (learning disability), and Candy (ageism/physical disability). This can lead to 'manufactured responses' and negates the complex and subjective reading experience if particular interpretations are imposed on pupils (Giovanelli and Mason, 2015). An over-emphasis on reading that focuses on detailed textual analysis, "practical criticism" (Richards, 1929) can obfuscate if "it is literature, not literary criticism, which is the subject" (Dixon, 2009, p. 248). Dixon's comment firmly puts the pupil's personal growth at the centre of what 'happens' when reading in SSE teaching.

However, there is an overarching *moral* component to our modern reading of a text such as *Of Mice and Men*: in twenty-first century Britain, we believe in equality and freedom for all. This is enshrined in the Teachers' Standards as we are bound, as part of our professional and personal conduct, to show "tolerance of and respect for the rights of others ... not undermining fundamental British values, including democracy, the rule of law, individual liberty and mutual respect, and tolerance of those with different faiths and beliefs" (Department for Education, 2011, p. 14). Literary criticism has moved towards stances that focus on the reader to "allow for the possibility of disruption, of re-reading, and of a plurality of readings" (Yandell, 2014, p. 6). A curriculum document that only mentions "different interpretations" (Department for Education, 2013, p. 4) in relation to drama texts, positions the text, rather than the pupils' relationship towards texts, at the centre of the subject.

If we assume that GCSE English Language focuses on the analysis and production of non-fiction texts, we would be mistaken; the qualification contains a good chunk of literature, including 'literary non-fiction' texts. The current AQA GCSE syllabus for English Language states that for Assessment Objective 3 'Studying written language', students need to: "Explain and evaluate how writers use linguistic, grammatical, structural and presentational features to achieve effects and engage and influence the reader" (AQA, 2016, p. 18). Specifically, it is the identification of language techniques (such as use of imagery), grammatical choices (such as declarative sentences), structural features (such as discourse markers), and the explanation of their effects on the reader that form the bones of analysis. As part of reforms to national examinations, the only way in which sixteen year olds are assessed for their reading ability is via written analysis and, for literature essays, this involves a very specific and artificial genre of writing:

the development of the essay is decisively skewed by that of the examination system ... When the essay is co-opted for the exam system ... the essay becomes the most functional kind of writing ... the 'naturalness' of the essay as a discourse is illusory. The candidate is being asked to play a role, to write as if from a subject position quite different from the one she is put in by being asked. (Womack, 1993, 44–45)

The artificial mode of essay writing has been exacerbated by the underpinning necessity of providing lots of textual evidence, which has led to the rise of a very proscriptive essay-writing formula: that of the 'P.E.E. paragraph'. *P.E.E.* stands for *Point, Evidence, Explanation* and this was originally designed to help lower ability children achieve a particular level in now-abandoned end of Key Stage 3 (age fourteen) examinations by including direct reference to language in their literature essays (Warner, 2004). The notion of an analytical paragraph that is structured in such a way (and variations on the P.E.E. paragraph proliferate countrywide) as *the only* way to write a response to a text, is indicative of a closing-down of possibilities. This limited structure of essay writing has been recognised by the school inspectorate Ofsted, who commented that the over-emphasis on P.E.E.-style responses "reduced the breadth of students' experience in English" (Ofsted, 2012, p. 22). With fewer opportunities to respond to texts creatively (particularly in Key Stage 4), it is possible to steer a reading of a text to the extent that "the good student is the one who digests the gobbets [of interpretation] and can regurgitate them appropriately – and we are left with something that looks uncomfortably like an English Literature curriculum for bright parrots" (Yandell, 2014, p. 187).

Greater freedom in responses to texts could produce a more dynamic, 'truer' engagement with literature as studied in secondary school, because a range of different responses to texts might allow students to engage with texts on a more emotional level, which is likely to have greater impact on the learner (Alsup, 2015). There has been a recent backlash against the use of P.E.E.-style responses (Enstone, 2017), although the curriculum reforms at GCSE that are now 100% terminal examinations has limited real diversity in responses to literature. I do not mean to criticise English teachers in this observation; rather they are limited by the assessment system (see Goddard, this volume) and high-stakes accountability culture that can lead to a culture of fear and demoralising conflicts of professional autonomy (Perryman et al., 2011). An approach that taps into an *affective* response (Bleiman, 2016), in which pupils are encouraged to think about and discuss texts so that they *have something to say* about them, is likely to yield a much greater response. An affective response is one that is likely to enable 'personal growth' and therefore repositions the reader's relationship to the text.

Part of the difficulty of using P.E.E.-style responses to literature essay questions is *where* the 'point' comes from: the teacher? the text? (In which case, the first part of the response would be the textual 'evidence'.) Frequently, pupils' responses using this rubric would consist of a single declarative sentence (the 'point'); a short quotation and then a re-statement of the point by way of 'explanation'. For example:

POINT: *At the beginning of Hamlet, Shakespeare uses questions to draw in the audience and help set the scene.*

EVIDENCE: *For example, Bernardo says 'Who's there?'*

EXPLANATION: *The question makes us wonder who is there and why Bernardo is asking it.*

Clearly this is a very limited answer, although it does hint at a greater understanding of the text than the formulaic P.E.E. response has allowed. It is the deep thinking about the texts, their effects and possible meanings that is the creative interpretation. A curriculum that is over-focused on essay-style responses, with a focus on the Great Tradition (Leavis, 2008/1948) of literary hierarchy, will mean that personal responses (and therefore ranges of possible interpretations) are likely to be marginalised.

An affective response to texts arises from an emotional connection on the part of the reader (Alsup, 2015). Most English teachers of my acquaintance have strong personal feelings for texts that they like or dislike, and this is often reflected in their choices of texts that they teach in the classroom (within limitations determined by the exam board syllabus and departmental stock cupboards). The English literary canon is promoted in the current National Curriculum for English and could, without careful choices and planning on the part of English teachers, result in the downgrading of contemporary literature. Douthwaite (2015) argues, in a response to a blog post that positions Robert Swindell's *Stone Cold* (1993) (a story about teenaged homelessness) as a novel not worthy of study, that contemporary texts that deal with relevant issues for teenagers are a vital part of what English should *do*. Cox's 'personal growth' model is evident here. What is interesting about this debate is not the status of the text itself, but that it can produce such extreme reactions in English teachers. It is this combination of subjective response, which may change over several readings and be influenced by a critical eclecticism (Locke, 2015), that gives SSE its dynamism as a subject.

7 Conclusion: SSE Is More than 'Machinery'

SSE has always been a politicised subject, which presents its challenges for teachers caught between examination demands and personal views of the subject that may be in conflict. The problem of teacher professionalism, undermined by excessive government interventions and, to an extent, popular discourse (Goodwyn, 2011), suggests the need for English teachers to have greater control over how their subject is defined by government policy and examination systems. My own response to the question of the purpose of English at secondary school, is that we are teaching ways in which texts can 'mean' and different ways in which students can 'mean' when they express themselves, as part of a dialogue. The connection between language, thought, and identity that is developed as part of a social dialogue, is explained by Bakhtin in the following way: "The word in language is half someone else's. It becomes 'one's own' only when the speaker populates it with his own intention, his own accent, when he appropriates the word, adapting it to his own semantic and expressive intention" (Bakhtin, 1975/1981, p. 293).

Thus, it is possible to conceive of English teachers as 'discourse guides'. Reading Neil Mercer's book *The Guided Construction of Knowledge* (2008), from which this term is taken, was a moment of professional epiphany for me; the muddle of teaching nineteenth century novels, modern poetry, writing letters that persuade, spelling strategies, and Shakespeare suddenly became clear: each element of the curriculum was a different *discourse*, each with its own lexicon, grammar, and stylistics. It is the job of the English teacher, therefore, to clarify *how* written texts might be understood in terms of basic comprehension, inference, and interpretation; *how* speech and writing are tools for self-expression.

Figure 7.1 illustrates my understanding of how the complex relationship between pupils and texts interact; it is certainly not a one-way transmission model. Pupils engage with texts on many levels and the meaning-making process is influenced by a range of factors, including that of affective response.

This is the crux, the *heart*, of English. It is the *love* of the subject: of reading, of a genre, of thinking, of debating, of writing, that understands interpretation as a creative act (McCallum, 2012). Finding a voice and forging an identity is part of what SSE ought to do; what sits at the heart of Frankenstein's Creature is the very centre of us. SSE is at the heart of the curriculum *because* it is at the heart of learning.

Barton (2013) states that "the secret of Literacy is making the implicit explicit" (p. 1); while this might suggest that interpretation is limited to *one* reading, there is the anticipation of finding a 'truth' in the exploration of English. The longer I remain involved in the teaching of English, the more I am convinced that we are attempting to demonstrate the nuances of ambiguity, rather than any certainties.

SSE teachers must, with each successive change of government policy, invent anew their conception of subject (Kress, 2006), yet hold true to a personal ideal. But English teachers are located in a specific

A 'Godlike Science': English Teaching in Secondary Schools

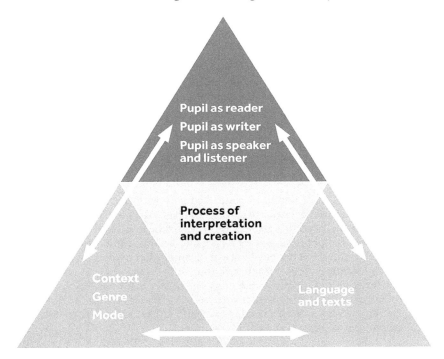

Figure 7.1 A conceptualisation of SSE

time and place, connected to a sense of professional identity by their own experience at school; route through Higher Education; national priorities, strategies, and initiatives; and how this is implemented contextually in their own school, department, and classroom. An English teacher's perceptions of the subject are not straightforward *because* it is shot through with government policy, cultural bias, and political agenda.

This chapter began with a quotation from *Frankenstein* for two reasons. It could be argued that SSE is a Frankenstein's monster of a subject: made up of many parts, sewn together in a postmodern patchwork of (sometimes conflicting) ideology, texts, and purposes. It also reflects my own training in literary analysis and love of over-wrought gothic novels. However, I prefer to think of English as Frankenstein's *Creature*, not monster; a subject of creation, not destruction.

There are sixty-nine references to *creature* in Shelley's novel, the majority of which are in reference to other characters or humanity in general (such as 'my fellow creatures'). Frankenstein refers to his creation as "creature" rather than "monster" more towards the dénouement, having perhaps learnt his lesson of responsibility. Eight uses of *creature* are in reference to Frankenstein himself. That the Creature can be interpreted as a doppelgänger or aspect of Frankenstein is not an original observation, and this is reflected in the number of times that Frankenstein is described as or refers to himself as "creature". At the moment of its birth, Frankenstein refers to "the creature" (p. 60), which then, through his own guilt and horror, turns into "monster" (p. 61). Creation and monstrosity are inseparable in *Frankenstein* and the relationship between language and meaning is, for me, captured in this metaphor:

Literature appears to be a kind of controlled play with the daemonic. It may belong to the logic of literature that Mary Shelley's daemon should
understand that his place lies within the symbolic order of language, that the daemon should fail of arriving at meaning, and become rather the very image of a desire that can never fix or pin down meaning. Yet here we find the logic of desire in literature, desire of the text and for the text. The text solicits us through the promise of a transcendent signified, and leaves us, on the
threshold of pleasure, to be content with the play of its signifiers. At the same time, it contaminates us with a residue of meaning that cannot be explained or rationalised, but is passed on as affect, as taint.

(Brooks, 1979, p. 220)

As a metaphor for English, the Creature is fitting because there is something miraculous about its ability to learn; its desire to understand and interact with the world; to affect and be affected; to create. It is, too, a victim of poor treatment at the hands of those in power. It is this passion, and perhaps the diaphanous nature of the definitions of subject, that motivates teachers to teach SSE in secondary schools. And there is the 'magical' nature of English as a subject – to make meaning through words that stimulate imagination, fuel an opinion, express an inner feeling. One might say English truly *is* a "godlike science".

References

Alsup, J. (2015). *A Case for Teaching Literature in the Secondary School*. New York: Routledge.
AQA. (2016). GCSE English Language Specification. Online. Available from http://filestore.aqa.org.uk/resources/english/specifications/AQA-8700-SP-2015.PDF
Bakhtin, M. (1975/1981). *The Dialogic Imagination*. Austin, TX: University of Texas.
Barton, G. (2013). *Don't Call It Literacy!*. Abingdon: Routledge.

Bleiman, B. (2016). Online. Group Work – Had We But Time Enough. Available from www.englishandmedia.co.uk/blog/group-work-had-we-but-time-enough

Boulter, S. (2017). Education from a biological point of view. *Studies in Philosophy and Education*, 36(2), 167–182.

Brooks, P. (1979). "Godlike Science/Unhallowed Arts": Language, nature, and monstrosity. *The Endurance of Frankenstein: Essays on Mary Shelley's Novel*. Berkley, CA: University of California Press, 205–220.

Coughlan, S. (2016). Online. Accessed 27 June 2018 from www.bbc.co.uk/news/education-38157811

Davison, J. and Daly, C. (2014). *Learning to Teach English in the Secondary School*. Abingdon: Routledge.

Department for Education. (2010). Online. Available from http://webarchive.nationalarchives.gov.uk/20110202094241/http://nationalstrategies.standards.dcsf.gov.uk/primary

Department for Education. (2011). Online. Available from www.gov.uk/government/publications/teachers-standards

Department for Education. (2013). Online. Available from www.gov.uk/government/uploads/system/uploads/attachment_data/file/244215/SECONDARY_national_curriculum_-_English2.pdf

Department for Education. (2014). The National Curriculum in England Framework Document. Online. Available from https://assets.publishing.service.gov.uk/government/uploads/system/uploads/attachment_data/file/381344/Master_final_national_curriculum_28_Nov.pdf

DES and the Welsh Office. (1989). *English for Ages 5–16, (The Cox Report)*. London: HMSO.

Dewey, J. (1938/1997). *Experience and Education*. New York: Touchstone.

Dixon, J. (1967). *Growth through English*. Huddersfield: NATE Publications.

Dixon, J. (2009). English renewed: Visions of English among teachers of 1966. *English in Education*, 43 (3), 241–250.

Dominiczak, P. (2013). Online. Accessed 27 June 2018 from www.telegraph.co.uk/education/educationnews/10166020/Michael-Gove-new-curriculum-will-allow-my-children-to-compete-with-the-very-best.html

Douthwaite, A. (2015). Stone cold: Worthy of study? *Changing English*, 22(1), 14–25.

Eaglestone, R. (2002). *Doing English*. 2nd ed. London: Routledge.

Enstone, L. (2017). Time to Stop PEE-ing? *Teaching English* (13), 33–36.

Findlay, K. (2010). *The Professional Identity of English Teachers in the Secondary School*. Coventry, BERA.

Gardner, P. (2017). Worlds apart: A comparative analysis of discourses of English in the curricula of England and Australia. *Education in English*, 51(2), 170–187.

Gibb, N. (2015). *How E. D. Hirsch Came to Shape UK Government Policy*. London: Policy Exchange. Also online. Accessed 26 June 2018 from policyexchange.org.uk/wp-content/uploads/2016/09/knowledge-and-the-curriculum.pdf

Gibbons, S. (2014). *The London Association for the Teaching of English 1947–67: A History*. London: Institute of Education Press.

Giovanelli, M. and Mason, J. (2015). 'Well I don't feel that': Schemas, worlds and authentic reading in the classroom. *English in Education, 49*(1), 41–55.

Goodwyn, A. (1992). English teachers and the Cox models. *English in Education*, 4–10.

Goodwyn, A. (2011). *The Expert Teacher of English*. Abingdon: Routledge.

Green, A. and McIntyre, J. (2011). 'What is English?'. *Becoming a Reflective English Teacher*. Maidenhead: Open University Press/McGraw-Hill, 6–25.

Hirsch, E. (1999). *The Schools We Need: And Why We Don't Have Them*. New York: Anchor Books.

Husbands, C. (2015). *Which Knowledge Matters Most?* London: Policy Exchange.

Jones, S., Myhill, D., and Bailey, T. (2013). Grammar for writing? An investigation into the effect of contextualised grammar teaching on student writing. *Reading and Writing, 28*(8), 1241–1263.

Knights, B. (2015). English studies: A very brief history. In S. Brindley and B. Marshal, eds., Masterclass in English Education (pp. 5–15). London: Bloomsbury.

Leavis, F. R. (2008/1948). *The Great Tradition*. London: Faber and Faber.

Locke, J. (1690/2004). *An Essay Concerning Human Understanding*. Harmondsworth: Penguin.

Locke, T. (2015). Paradigms of English. In S. Brindley and B. Marshal, eds., *Masterclass in English Education* (pp. 5–15). London: Bloomsbury.

Lyotard, J. (1984). *The Postmodern Condition: A Report on Knowledge*. Manchester, UK: Manchester University Press.

McCallum, A. (2012). *Creativity and Learning in Secondary in English*. Abingdon: Routledge.

Medway, P. (1980). *Finding a Language*. London: Chameleon.

Mercer, N. (2008). *The Guided Construction of Knowledge*. Clevedon, UK: Multilingual Matters Ltd.

Middlesex University. (2018). Online. Accessed 26 June 2018 from www.mdx.ac.uk/courses/undergraduate/english

Ofsted (2012). Moving English Forward. Online. Available from www.gov.uk/government/uploads/system/uploads/attachment_data/file/181204/110118.pdf

Oxford English Dictionary. (2011). Oxford, UK: Oxford University Press. Online. Accessed 31 July 2018 from www.oed.com

Perryman, J., Ball, S., Maguire, M., and Braun, A. (2011). Life in the pressure cooker – School League Tables and English and mathematics teachers' responses to accountability in a results-driven era. *British Journal of Educational Studies, 59*(2), 179–195.

QAA. (2015). Subject Benchmark Statement: English. Online. Available from www.qaa.ac.uk/docs/qaa/subject-benchmark-statements/sbs-english-15.pdf?sfvrsn=4f9df781_12

QCA. (2007). English Programme of Study for Key Stage 3 and Attainment Targets. Online. Available from http://archive.teachfind.com/qcda/curriculum.qcda.gov.uk/uploads/QCA-07-3332-pEnglish3_tcm8–399.pdf

Richards, I. A. (1929). *Practical Criticism*. London: Routledge and Kegan Paul.

Rigney, D. (2010). *The Matthew Effect*. New York, NY: Columbia University Press.
Rosen, H. (2017). Neither Bleak House nor Liberty Hall: English in the curriculum. In J. Richmond, ed., *Harold Rosen: Writings on Life, Language and Learning, 1958–2008* (pp. 73–89). London: UCL, Institute of Education Press.
Royal Holloway, University of London. (2018). Online. Accessed 31 July 2018 from www.royalholloway.ac.uk/studying-here/undergraduate/english/english/
Ryle, G. (1949). *The Concept of Mind*. Chicago, IL: University of Chicago Press.
Sfard, A. (1998). On two metaphors for learning and the dangers of choosing just one. *Educational Researcher,* 27(2), 4–13.
Shelley, M. (1818/2000). *Frankenstein*. Boston: Bedford/St Martin's.
Snow, C. (2008). *The Two Cultures*. Cambridge: Cambridge University Press.
Steinbeck, J. (1937/2000). *Of Mice and Men*. London: Longman.
Swindells, R. (1993). *Stone Cold*. London: Penguin.
Warner, L. (2004). To PEE or Not to PEE? When there's a question. *The Secondary English Magazine,* 20–21.
Womack, P. (1993). What are essays for? *English in Education,* 27(2), 42–48.
Yandell, J. (2014). *The Social Construction of Meaning: Reading Literature in Urban English Classrooms*. Abingdon: Routledge.
Young, M. (2009). *Bringing Knowledge Back in: From Social Constructivism to Social Realism in the Sociology of Education*. London: Routledge.

8 Beliefs about 'Good English' in Schools

Clare Cunningham

1 Introduction

This chapter seeks to evaluate how student users of English are viewed beyond the English-as-school-subject curriculum, both in and out of classrooms. In particular, it exposes some of the tangible effects of ontologies of English in the education context, with important implications for education policy. Despite extensive scholarly work in Applied Linguistics offering positive reconceptualisations of language use in a variety of approaches, such as World Englishes, English as a Lingua Franca, and translanguaging (e.g. Creese and Blackledge, 2010; Hornberger and Link, 2012; García and Wei, 2014; García and Kleyn, 2016), the notion of a 'target' for the learning and teaching of 'good English' for most monolingual mainstream teachers in the United Kingdom remains based on the norms of Standard English, or N-ENGLISH (to adopt the categorisation terminology proposed by Hall, this volume). For more discussion on the nature of linguistic norms, see Harder (this volume). In this chapter, I show how the presentation of Standard English as the ideal, on the assumption that it is "the language we have in common" (DES, 1988, p. 14), alienates not just multilingual learners of English but also many school children who would regard themselves as first-language English speakers.

While the norms of N-ENGLISH are construed from within the 'native-speaker' domain (Wicaksono, this volume) and reflections on the impact of this on multilingual children are important in this chapter, evidence will be assembled showing that some 'monolingual' speakers of similar idiolects of English (I-ENGLISHES in the framework of Hall, this volume) are often constructed and treated even more negatively in the mainstream education system than the 'learner' of English. Drawing on a range of existing research evidence, this chapter will consider teachers' ontologies and beliefs around notions of the target of 'good English' for *all* children in their classrooms, generating new insights into the potentially lifelong legacy of the hidden perils of a using a non-standard variety. This group of children includes those labelled as English as an Additional Language (EAL), whether they are new arrivals to the United Kingdom or whether they are British born and simply classified as EAL due to the presence of a language beyond English in the home environment. Arnot et al. (2014) offer a useful account of the problematic definition of EAL in the United Kingdom. In the United States, much discussion has also been had about the 'deficit model' thinking inherent in terminology for describing 'learners' of English, for example, the use of limited English proficiency (LEP) (Webster and Lu, 2012). However, the group of children concerned here also include those who speak diverse I-ENGLISHES at home, some of which will be further from matching the norms of N-ENGLISH than others. These children are typically *not* those from more socially advantaged backgrounds (Grainger, 2013).

This chapter begins with an exploration of the very notion of the target of Standard English and what that means in practice for those classed as EAL and for those who are considered to be 'native' speakers of English. Next, three fundamental determiners of inequality in education are identified and critically discussed; namely, a lack of explicit linguistic knowledge on the part of educators, a deficit model approach, and the effect of negative ideological discourses within British society. Finally, concrete proposals will be made for how the field of Applied Linguistics can help develop educators' ontologies of English to best serve the needs of a diverse population of children.

2 The Target of 'Good English' for Children in Schools

Bijvoet and Fraurud observe that "taking TL [target language] for granted implies that people agree on what constitutes 'good' language, or the standard norm" (2015, p. 17) and they go on to note that this understanding tends to be more heterogeneous and diverse than traditionally thought to be the case.

Targets for 'good English' also come from a multitude of sources but in essence they involve supressing variation at all levels of language (pronunciation, spelling, grammar, and lexicon), as Milroy and Milroy (1985) suggest in their discussion of the characteristics of standardisation. We will focus here on those targets for 'good English' from within education, but we do also need to pay heed to those that are more political in provenance and those disseminated through mass media coverage of linguistic matters.

2.1 The Target of Standard English: The Language of Education

While the complaint tradition (Milroy and Milroy, 1985) has ensured that 'Standard English' has been held as the ideal model for education since at least the seventeenth century (as discussed by Hall, this volume), this viewpoint was increasingly entrenched in the United Kingdom following the move away from the briefly more pluralistic stances of the 1970s (see Goodwyn, this volume, for more on this). Standard English's supposed status as 'the language *we* have in common' (DES, 1988, p. 14, my emphasis) may also have led to the alienating of some speakers of English as a home language as well as English language learners. The primacy of Standard English influenced the setting of standards in England's National Curriculum and continues to influence educational policy to this day. A teacher in the UK is now tasked with "tak[ing] responsibility for promoting ... the correct use of standard English, whatever the teacher's specialist subject" (Department for Education, 2011, p. 11). However, the difficulties in defining Standard English, due to its abstract nature, have been well documented (Trudgill, 1975), and the reasons behind those problems are further elucidated by Hall (this volume).

Data from a small-scale survey of thirty teachers (Herring, 2017) also revealed the lack of clarity around this issue. While 97 per cent of participants responded that they had a strong or very strong understanding of what Standard English is, the definitions they attempted were as varied as Trudgill (1975) probably would have expected. However, it is also perhaps unsurprising that in almost 60 per cent of the 'definitions' provided, the term 'correct' appeared, demonstrating circularity in thinking. As we have already seen, this foregrounding of correctness and accuracy in place of a more social view on conformity to a norm, such as recognising and explicitly allowing space for local varieties, means that "teachers automatically delegitimize (as incorrect) their pupils' own I-LANGUAGE resources and LANGUAGING practices" (Hall, p. 27, this volume) in the classroom.

It has been suggested elsewhere that teachers' knowledge and awareness of linguistic variety is actually quite nuanced, but that it is rarely explicitly harnessed by individuals or researchers, as it remains largely subconscious (Garrett et al., 1995). In terms of research, it has been noted that different data collection methods in language attitudes research (for example, scales versus labels, matched guise versus questionnaires) elicit different attitudes. These variations in approach dictate whether prestige judgements are foregrounded or not in individual studies. Garrett et al. (1995, p. 106) therefore speculate that there is a potential for concern that "while our teachers' judgements regarding prestige are quietly and without intention permeating their classroom behaviour, a professional norm proscribing acknowledgement of such status prevents them from embarking on talk about language with their learners in such terms, and even acts as a barrier to their own awareness". These potentially silently made and underdiscussed judgements regarding prestige are embedded in the ontological beliefs and societal ideologies that surround educators.

Alongside the requirements for teachers of EAL children to focus on Standard English as stipulated in the National Curriculum documents, a wide variety of scales and continuums to assess children for varying linguistically mediated abilities have been developed over many years (NALDIC, 2005). There is a lack of consistency nationally about which of the assessment scales schools should adopt and no centralised guidance on this additional judging of children's linguistic capacity.

2.2 Societal Notions of What Makes for 'Good English'

Media discourse tends to see stories about linguistic deficit as newsworthy (Grainger, 2013), with journalists often subscribing wholeheartedly to the 'complaint tradition' (Milroy and Milroy, 1985). Alongside tabloid reports of schools 'overrun' with languages beyond English, there are myriad stories about the social and linguistic problems perceived to be caused by the use of regional dialect terms, as well as concerns about the impact of new language inspired by technology and social media. See Section 5.1 for further discussion.

While the focus of this chapter is on the target of 'good English' for education, considering how the concept is discussed outside of education is important since the ideologies around language perpetuated through mass media, for example, cannot fail to have an impact on teachers and form part of their *habitus* (Bourdieu, 1977).

3 Attitudes, Beliefs, and Knowledge Impacting on Both EAL and Low SES Children

Teachers generally feel they are doing a good job under challenging circumstances (Reeves, 2006), being open and encouraging regarding children's languages and identities, but they often disregard the implicit perpetuation of embedded ideologies (Gkaintartzi and Tsokalidou, 2011; Cunningham, 2017) about what constitutes English, and the ontological status of 'good' English in particular. Considerations that, consciously or subconsciously, change perceptions include judgements about linguistic hierarchies and what are seen as elite languages (Romaine, 1998), as well as the issues related to standard language ideology as discussed previously.

Educators' attitudes towards variety, and approaches taken in the classroom to encourage or suppress variety, reflect ideological stances, many of which have been part of the well-established complaint tradition referred to earlier (Milroy and Milroy, 1985). They have been 'a source of social commentary' for centuries (Snell and Andrews, 2017, p. 299), and while it has been observed that most non-linguists do not regularly make a distinction between the spoken and written language (Milroy and Milroy, 1985) or between notions of dialect and accent (Garrett et al., 1995), they certainly have very clear attitudes towards accents and dialects and beliefs about 'incorrect' usage. These attitudes can impact on children in the classroom in differing ways, depending on the linguistic and social backgrounds of the individuals concerned, but I contend that there are aspects of teachers' attitudes, beliefs, and knowledge that impact on both EAL children and those who are monolingual English speakers. In this section, I will discuss the commonalities between EAL and socially disadvantaged children, in terms of the attitudes held and approaches taken educationally with regards to English.

3.1 Deficit Model Thinking Stemming from Lack of Knowledge

It was noted earlier that the abstract concept of Standard English is difficult to grasp. Numerous researchers have also observed that teacher training and subsequent education opportunities do not focus enough on the trainee teacher reaching a high level of understanding of linguistics or second language acquisition processes (Huss-Keeler, 1997; Murakami, 2008; Safford and Kelly, 2010; Wardman, 2012; Safford, 2016). This has an impact on attitudes, policy and practice for EAL children, and also on those children who speak unstandardized varieties of English.

Teachers' lack of linguistic awareness leads to the development of only shallow ontologies about what constitutes English, independently of conscious contemplation (Hall's L-ENGLISH), and the social construction of 'good English' (N-ENGLISH). This means that only a limited number of features are focused on. These features are those that stand out and are easy to hear, or notice in writing, such as particular accent and grammatical features, as well as dialect lexis. Garrett et al. (1995), Munro et al. (2006), and McKenzie (2015) have all concluded that language attitudes and judgements are made both above and below the level of individual consciousness. Even untrained listeners are very attuned to spotting 'foreign accents', and they can have a deleterious effect on evaluation. In a previous study (Bijvoet and Fraurud, 2011, cited in Bijvoet and Fraurud, 2015, p. 22), it was noted that "a single prosodic feature associated with a low-status variety was enough to make listeners also hear what was in reality not there" – intonation patterns were of a particular variety associated with immigrants, and listeners reported hearing grammatical 'errors' that were not, in fact, made. This negative evaluation can be exacerbated by media and film discourse, for example, by the use of characters with certain accents and dialects (or the salient features of certain accents and dialects) to "draw character quickly", often for negative effect (Lippi-Green, 1997, p. 81) since people, including teachers, tend not to have "critically examined their own susceptibility to media influences" (Munro et al., 2006, p. 68).

This lack of conscious knowledge but vague awareness of features that do not adhere to the norms of N-ENGLISH (insofar as the individual has worked out what they might be) can lead to an unconscious bias in the approach taken towards individuals and groups of children. A lack of nuance in the perception of (and understanding of their own perception of) accents, for example, can lead to low expectations of a child or a cohort. In turn, low expectations may lead to low achievement, in terms of success in high-stakes testing. Much has been written about the impact of this for some, particularly 'Pakistani' and 'Bangladeshi' heritage students (Kotler et al., 2001), African American boys in the United States (Martin et al., 2007), and white working-class boys in the United Kingdom (Gillborn and Kirton, 2000) because standardised assessments have been seen to disadvantage these (amongst other) groups.

3.2 Demonisation

Mass media-based moral panics (Cohen, 1972) around immigration and 'chavs', a term used to denigrate young, white, British working-class people (le Grand, 2013), spread societal fear of the 'other', and encourage the pathologisation and medicalisation of children, without any serious consideration of underlying social issues (Edwards et al., 2015). These fears, and their complex roots, need to be better understood and tackled within the education system (and far beyond it). The particular ways in which migrant and working-class pupils are constructed as problematic will be discussed further in the following two sections.

4 Attitudes and Actions of Educators towards the EAL Child

4.1 The Impact of Negative or Shallow Ontologies of 'Good English'

In accent perception studies, it has been observed that classification as 'non-native' is generally backed up with a description of what are described as 'incorrect' features (McKenzie, 2015). McKenzie (2015, p. 164) says that "analysis of participant comments points, rather disappointingly, to the existence of a deficit model in relation to identifications of non-native English speech more generally, with a tendency for the UK-born students to attribute their classifications of Indian, Japanese, Chinese, and Thai English speech to perceived errors the speakers made". It seems that 'non-native' can be more salient than a more fine-grained classification. Knowledge of variations is not overt; for example, the Chinese speaker of English was often classified as 'European' (47 per cent of the respondents). See the limited research on the topic to date (Flynn, 2013; Bailey and Marsden, 2017; Cunningham, 2017).

Other studies back up these findings by offering data that corroborate the conclusion that linguistically untrained listeners consider a 'native-sounding' phonology to be 'correct' and a 'non-native sounding' phonology to be 'incorrect', including cases when the respondents are non-native speakers, for example, the Japanese group that McKenzie (2008, cited in McKenzie, 2015) studied. He also notes that "the results from [other] language attitudes [studies] point towards US-born students' evaluations of L2 English as largely based upon ethnic dimensions, whereby the more 'Caucasian' a speaker is judged to be, the more prestigious his/her speech is likely to be rated" (McKenzie, 2015, p. 165).

With regards to the goal of 'good English', dealing with accent has been a mainstay of the Teaching English as a Foreign Language (TEFL) industry, with Griffen (1991, p. 182) saying that the aim is that "the student ... should learn to speak the language as naturally as possible, free of any indication that the speaker is not a clinically normal native". This pathologisation remains in place for some teachers and speech therapists despite our knowledge that a native-speaker pronunciation norm is considered to be impossible for most adults (Long, 1990). This 'accent discrimination' (Munro et al., 2006, p. 70) is what leads to the idealising of the native-speaker teacher, as discussed by Wicaksono (this volume). A consciousness-raising exercise (Godley et al., 2006) highlighted for participants – prospective English as a second language (ESL) teachers – their biases and prejudices against stereotyped groups. Unconscious bias research also highlights the prevalence in education of stereotyping that is entrenched and, to an extent, beyond most people's control (Van den Bergh et al., 2010).

While accent and the notions of comprehensibility that go along with supra-segmental aspects of pronunciation are important factors, another effect of the lack of linguistic training and awareness provided for educators may be that teachers are often not able to be specific about what may be seen as 'problem areas' for multilingual children. Across the research interviews in a recent study I conducted, there was no attempt on the part of teachers to discuss the specific target or the eventual linguistic goals for the multilingual children in their schools, beyond vague references to success at examination (Cunningham, 2017). In the words of one participant, the rather broad and unspecific "vocabulary" and "tenses", or "markers of EAL," are discussed as principal linguistic problems. For some of the educators interviewed, their focus is on cheerleading the little 'successes' for EAL students, noting how "terrifically" they "picked up our language" (Cunningham, 2017, p. 145).

However, the 'kindness' shown towards L2 learners of English masks a pervasive deficit model: the implied sense that the children will never attain 'good' English, so 'good enough' will probably do. Classifications such as 'EAL' do not help here, as the child is classified as such just by having a language in the home other than English. The term EAL covers a huge range of children and abilities and means that reference to increased success in assessment needs to be nuanced as some groups are outperforming but others not. This classification, however, can culminate in low expectations of teachers (Gkaintartzi and Tsokalidou, 2011; Cunningham, 2017) and the invisibility of other languages. We can see this reflected in teachers' discussions of children who "don't speak" (Greek, in this case, in Gkaintartzi and Tsokalidou, 2011) and of children who come into UK primary schools with "no language", some of whom have mothers who "don't speak" (Cunningham, 2017) and similar statements heard in research studies undertaken in France (Helot and Young, 2002).

4.2 A More Positive Spin for EAL Children

Despite some of the challenges discussed earlier, I contend that children classified as EAL are, in fact, often constructed more positively than those who are first-language speakers of unstandardised varieties and particularly those who are considered to be socially deprived. The expectations of these students actually achieving 'nativelike' norms are often low, leading to virtually no discussion of a linguistic target for EAL students by participants in my study (Cunningham, 2017), but an implied sense that communicative competence is the priority.

Attitudes towards L2 Englishes *can* sometimes mirror attitudes to L1 dialectal Englishes, but the speakers of languages beyond Englishes (and the cultures that are assumed to be attached to them and their languages) are perhaps now more officially 'celebrated' in a school context, as part of a push towards 'multiculturalism' being visible (see Garza and Crawford, 2005, for more on how ideology and practices around notions of multiculturalism may not mesh well). This can be construed as an attempt to manage the demonisation of 'the immigrant' within schools, although the potential for only tokenistic use of languages beyond English in schools as a result of this politically driven agenda is noted elsewhere (Bourne, 2001; DES, 2006; Ludhra and Jones, 2008; Dillon, 2010; Cunningham, 2017) and is beyond the scope of this chapter.

The lack of training in second language acquisition and the lack of multilingualism in most UK teachers' backgrounds (McEachron and Bhatti, 2005) have a number of effects on (and partly determine) teachers' attitudes to working with multilingual students. For example, Saito and Shintani (2016) focused on raters' linguistic backgrounds to ascertain to what extent this is relevant to the judgments of comprehensibility they made when listening to accented speech. They suggest that the disparity they found between monolingual and multilingual hearers has educational implications, especially for testing. Monolingual testers should, for example, be informed about how raters who are more experienced with other varieties of English perceive comprehensibility. This focus on the rater is positive in that it shifts the attention to the perception of the monolingual hearer rather than the multilingual speaker, with the requirement for more effort to be made in understanding than judging.

While there is still a strong model of and focus on transition to English and increasing comprehensibility for EAL children in UK schools, the pace of this transition seems still to be dictated by student need, even if teachers talk negatively about the need to 'still' support particular students (Cunningham, 2017). The increase in research literature on the value of home languages (Conteh, 2007; Kenner, 2010; Wardman et al., 2012; Garrity et al., 2015; Bailey and Marsden, 2017), particularly in the Early Years (four to six years old), has had an impact in certain schools, and the role of the National Association for Language Development in the Curriculum (NALDIC) and their increasing reach through Regional Interest Groups should continue this push.

5 Attitudes and Actions of Educators towards the Socially Disadvantaged Child

As stated in the introduction, I contend that children who are socially disadvantaged are often constructed more negatively than those who are classified as EAL. The negative construction of children and families from low socio-economic backgrounds has been discussed in the sociology and sociolinguistics literature for some time (Reay, 2006; Grainger and Jones, 2013; Jones, 2013; Spencer et al., 2013; Edwards et al., 2015) and the contrast between the treatment of white working-class families and those families from ethnic minorities by schools has already been noted (Reay et al., 2007), although not from a linguistic perspective.

Linguistically, I would argue that children from poorer backgrounds who are monolingual English speakers are judged against the abstract norms of N-ENGLISH because these norms are considered by their teachers to constitute their 'native' language. These children are assumed to be *users,* not *learners,* of English by their educators. Therefore, there is seen to be no excuse for not understanding or using the norms of Standard English in the appropriate contexts. The lack of explicit knowledge of these norms returns as a serious issue here as teachers' ontologies are built on this lack of knowledge.

5.1 Control

The vagueness with which teachers discuss the linguistic markers of an EAL child is a far cry from the highly focused ways that educators have outlawed less prestigious varieties from schools. Indeed, there have been a number of well-documented instances of specific unstandardised features being banned in UK schools. Dixon (2013) reported in *The Daily Telegraph* on one such case in the small town of Halesowen in the West Midlands, where the banned list of terms (transcriptions as in the original document) included:

1. "They was" instead of "they were."
2. "I cor do that" instead of "I can't do that."
3. "Ya" instead of "you."
4. "Gonna" instead of "going to.
5. "Woz" instead of "was."
6. "I day" instead of "I didn't."
7. "I ain't" instead of "I haven't."
8. "Somefink" instead of "something."

9. "It wor me" instead of "it wasn't me."
10. "Ay?" instead of "pardon?"

The head teacher of the school in question said "[w]e value the dialect but we want to encourage children to learn when to use and when not, like for a job interview. It is, of course, fine to use in other situations and we would celebrate that". A lack of linguistic knowledge typical of many in the complaint tradition (Milroy and Milroy, 1985) can be seen here in the lack of distinctions drawn between pronunciation, grammatical, spelling, and lexical concerns.

At another school (in Sheffield in northern England), colloquial language was banned under a policy of 'street stops at the gate', and Bowater (2012) reported in *The Daily Telegraph* that "[t]he trust that runs the academy said it wanted children to cut out slang words and phrases such as 'hiya' and 'cheers' in favour of the more correct 'good morning', 'goodbye' or 'thank you'". And in yet another example, a primary school in Middlesbrough, in northeast England, also issued a list of banned words, including 'gizit ere' and 'nowt'. The head teacher was reported as saying (Furness, 2013):

> You don't want the children to lose their identity, but you do want them to be able to communicate properly with people and be understood. We are going to teach them the rules. If they decide not to use these rules with friends that is fine, but I want them to know that when they are filling in application forms and speaking in a formal situation they should use standard English.

This rare acknowledgement of the role of children in deciding for themselves their own needs for communication, and for maintaining or obtaining social privilege through linguistic choice, is discussed extensively elsewhere (Brice Heath, 1983; Rampton, 1995; Bijvoet and Fraurud, 2015; Willoughby et al., 2015) but is beyond the scope of this chapter where the focus remains on teachers' attitudes, knowledge, and ontologies.

5.2 *The Provenance of the Perceived Deficit*

The demonisation of lower socio-economic groups has rarely been contested in educational contexts by policy makers and educators, and a middle-class vested interest in not contesting the consequential inequalities has been said to exist (Grainger, 2013). The fact that Dianne Reay (e.g. Reay, 2006) has been writing about the same issues for three decades demonstrates the slow pace of change in this regard. Perhaps things are even going backwards in the context of current neoliberal rhetoric of personal responsibility for social mobility and the claims for a connection between linguistic competence and social success (Grainger, 2013). Well-known arguments about a 'word gap' (the difference between the number of words children from a socially advantaged background have in their vocabulary versus those of a child from a less privileged background) prevail (Johnson et al., 2017) and perpetuate a sense of a deficit model for socially disadvantaged children. This embedded deficit thinking does not take into account the 'funds of knowledge' (Moll et al., 1992) and linguistic capacity that are present in all communities (Brice Heath, 1983), because the nature of the language and literacy practices of non-middle-class communities are rarely accorded value in schools (Johnson et al., 2017).

Working-class children and their linguistic practices may be, for the most part, peripheral and excluded in educational contexts, but this exclusion is not explicitly understood or verbalised by teachers. Looking at the terms used to discuss socially disadvantaged children is revealing. Avoidance of the words *working class* and *poor* are seen at policy level and in teachers' talk (Grainger, 2013; Cunningham, 2017). Rather, proxies of deprivation are used in discussing children and parents, with references made to impoverished language, poor role models, and discussions that often suggest that the problem is situated with the parents (Blackledge, 2001; Hanafin and Lynch, 2002; Cunningham, 2017).

Very heavy reliance is placed on a very limited range of peer-reviewed sources in the think tank reports that most directly influence educational policy for socially disadvantaged children (Grainger, 2013). While there are concerns over the stalling in policy and guidance publications within the EAL domain, those that are still in use and read in schools are often highly reliant on good-quality research and academics' work (Bourne, 2002; Conteh, 2003; Gravelle, 1996) even if some of this work was conducted in very different educational contexts (Thomas and Collier, 1997; Cummins, 2000). This perhaps demonstrates a certain "vested interest", as Grainger (2013, p. 99) puts it, in claiming that the failure of the poorest members of the school community to prosper is related to something psychologically or biologically problematic with those groups.

However, vested interests and the accompanying ideologies and ontologies should be something that critically engaged teachers are willing to challenge. Bourne's claim that the teachers have a critical role as agents of social change (2015) makes reflection on these issues the responsibility of educators, as well as policy makers, and implications and recommendations for action for social change following these previous discussions are now considered. These reflections must consider not only pedagogical and policy implications, but also include take into account the necessary shift in ontologies of language learning and language use, of language itself, and of what comprises 'English'.

6 Implications

Following our exploration of teachers' ontologies of 'good English' and the impact of these on EAL children and socially disadvantaged but monolingual children in the United Kingdom, there are recommendations that can be made. Typically, applied linguists call for further education and training and I will make no exception here. Teacher education grounded in understanding linguistic differences and language attitudes may help to address the inequalities of provision for both of these groups of children.

A barrier to teacher preparation for dialectally and linguistically diverse classrooms is the underlying Standard Language Ideology and the fact that teachers actually see their role being to 'correct' pupils' English. Attitudes on these topics are resistant to change, but in the knowledge that "the dominant pedagogical responses to stigmatized dialects are damaging and counterproductive" (Godley et al., 2006, p. 31), we can perhaps take some comfort from the claims of Ball and Muhammad (2003). They reported positive changes in teachers' expressed beliefs about language after undertaking critical discussions around language and power. Contradictory attitudes towards varieties could be exposed through training and education that adopt a critical discourse analysis approach that could be exploited as a way of breaking down some of the entrenched beliefs (Cunningham, 2017). Furthermore, asking teachers to look at their own repertoires could also be a useful starting point. Godley et al. (2006) used recording teachers as a means to allow teachers to realise their oral English was not as 'standard' as they thought.

Knowledge of students' dialects and languages can increase teachers' self-efficacy in giving their students the capacity to notice the differences between their home language and the language required in the education setting. Fogel and Ehri (2006) report on an intervention to sensitise teachers to African American Vernacular English (AAVE), but this could have much worth beyond this variety. These authors discovered that if teachers are taught particular dialectal forms, it can improve their positivity towards unstandardised varieties. This particular study was undertaken under the pretext of improving teachers' ability to teach AAVE speakers to adopt Standard English forms, a transition focus that we may not want to advocate here. Additionally, the results showed that gaining knowledge of

AAVE caused only a slight shift in positive attitudes from slightly negative to neutral, suggesting that more would need to be done to change attitudes significantly than simply exposing teachers to varieties, especially given the social desirability factor that does not seem to have been fully addressed here.

Another option is to decentre Standard English, re-situating it as just one of a range of Englishes available, dependent on context (Murray, 2016). Many teachers are probably already doing this in numerous contexts (Herring, 2017) but it is under-discussed and not officially condoned (Garrett et al., 1995). This has the potential to be transformative for both teachers and children, as they become critically aware of the linguistic repertoires that they already control and can expand, potentially giving them a sense of power over their own language use and choices. Practically, Wheeler and Swords (2004) discussed using contrastive analysis as one of the most beneficial techniques for both teachers and students in terms of raising awareness of the grammaticality of other varieties, and changing attitudes, with teachers challenged to change their terminology from a deficit, prescriptive approach to a descriptive one that emphasised building on students' linguistic repertoires, rather than replacing the stigmatised variety with the 'standard'.

Further implications of some of the issues around teacher's ontologies of 'good' English are discussed elsewhere in this volume. The validity of the focus on N-ENGLISH insofar as assessment is concerned is discussed further in Goddard (this volume). The implications for EAL children and teachers are discussed in more depth by Sharples (this volume). The discussions in Wicaksono (this volume) are also valuable here, despite, or perhaps because of, the fact that the native/non-native distinction appears to remain salient in matched guise language attitudes research (MacKenzie, 2009).

7 Conclusion

Standard English is used to legitimise and perpetuate discrimination in societally structural and systemic ways that most people seem to feel quite comfortable with, including those being discriminated against. It is for this reason that I echo Bijvoet and Fraurud (2015) in calling for further research on perceptions and constructions of the notion of a target.

The advances in the treatment of EAL children up to 2009 (the year that governmental publications on the topic in the United Kingdom ceased) must not be shelved just because this group are no longer in the limelight as far as central government and Ofsted (the government regulator for education in England) are concerned. The work here in the United Kingdom is far from finished, particularly when it comes to issues pertaining to the impact of teacher attitudes and ideologies on working with multilingual children. The limited research on the topic to date (Flynn, 2013; Bailey and Marsden, 2017; Cunningham, 2017) indicates the urgent need for additional work to be undertaken to explore these areas further.

The current pathologisation and medicalisation of socially disadvantaged children have echoes of the way that learners of English and users of creoles, pidgins, and hybrids have been treated over time (cf. Tamura, 1996). The lack of focus on the root causes of the disadvantage (which is, of course, *not* linguistic) must, of course, be rectified for any significant improvement to be seen at an educational level by "shout(ing) louder" about it as Grainger (2013, p. 107) puts it. It is imperative that further research and positive activism is undertaken to work more productively and collaboratively for the benefit of socially disadvantaged children in the battle against the stigmatising impact of the current approach to the linguistic and social challenges faced by this non-homogenous group.

References

Arnot, M., Schneider, C., Evans, M. et al. (2014). *School Approaches to the Education of EAL Students*. Cambridge: The Bell Educational Trust Limited.

Bailey, E. G. and Marsden, E. (2017). Teachers' views on recognising and using home languages in predominantly monolingual primary schools. *Language and Education*, 31(4), 283–206. http://doi.org/10.1080/09500782.2017.1295981

Ball, A. F. and Muhammad, R. J. (2003). Language diversity in teacher education and in the classroom. In G. Smitherman and V. Villanueva, eds., *Language Diversity in the Classroom: From Intention to Practice* (pp. 76–88). Carbondale, IL: Southern Illinois University Press.

Bijvoet, E. and Fraurud, K. (2015). What's the target? A folk linguistic study of young Stockholmers' constructions of linguistic norm and variation. *Language Awareness*, 25(1–2), 17–39. http://doi.org/10.1080/09658416.2015.1122021

Blackledge, A. (2001). The wrong sort of capital? Bangladeshi women and their children's schooling in Birmingham, U.K. *International Journal of Bilingualism*, 5(3), 345–369. http://doi.org/10.1177/13670069010050030501

Bourdieu, P. (1977). *Outline of a Theory of Practice*. Cambridge: Cambridge University Press. http://books.google.co.uk/books?id=WvhSEMrNWHACand printsec=frontcoverandsource=gbs_atb#v=onepageandqandf=false

Bourne, D. (2015). Teachers as agents of social change. *International Journal of Development Education and Global Learning*, 7(3), 63–77. http://discovery.ucl.ac.uk/1475774/1/5. Bourn_Teachers as agents%5B1%5D.pdf

Bourne, J. (2001). Doing 'what comes naturally': How the discourses and routines of teachers' practice constrain opportunities for bilingual support in UK primary schools. *Language and Education*, 15(4), 250–268.

Bourne, J. (2002). *Home Languages in the Literacy Hour*. Southampton: University of Southampton

Bowater, D. (2012, February). Pupils banned from using slang in school. *The Daily Telegraph*. www.telegraph.co.uk/education/educationnews/9081943/Pupils-banned-from-using-slang-in-school.html

Brice Heath, S. (1983). *Ways with Words*. Cambridge: Cambridge University Press.

Cohen, S. (1972). *Folk Devils and Moral Panics: The Creation of the Mods and Rockers*. Abingdon: Routledge.

Conteh, J. (2003). *Succeeding in Diversity: Culture, Language and Learning in Primary Classrooms*. Stoke on Trent: Trentham.

Conteh, J. (2007). Opening doors to success in multilingual classrooms: Bilingualism, codeswitching and the professional identities of ethnic minority primary teachers. *Language and Education*, 21(6), 457–472. http://doi.org/10.2167/le711.0

Creese, A. and Blackledge, A. (2010). Translanguaging in the bilingual classroom: A pedagogy for learning and teaching? *Modern Language Journal*, 94(i), 103–113.

Cummins, J. (2000). *Language, Power and Pedagogy: Bilingual Children in the Crossfire*. Clevedon, UK: Multilingual Matters.

Cunningham, C. (2017). Saying more than you realise about "EAL": Discourses of educators about children who speak languages beyond English. Unpublished Ph.D. thesis. University of York (2017).

Department for Education. (2011). Teachers' standards. Guidance for school leaders, school staff and governing bodies. www.gov.uk/government/publications/teachers-standards

DES. (2006). *Excellence and Enjoyment: Learning and Teaching for Bilingual Children in the Primary Years*. London: Her Majesty's Stationery Office.

Dillon, A. M. (2010). Supporting home language maintenance among children with English as an additional language in Irish primary schools. *WPEL*, 27(2), 76–94.

Dixon, H. (2013, November). Black Country phrases banned from Midlands primary school. *The Daily Telegraph*. www.telegraph.co.uk/education/primaryeducation/10449119/Black-Country-phrases-banned-from-Midlands-primary-school.html

Edwards, R., Gillies, V., and Horsley, N. (2015). Brain science and early years policy: Hopeful ethos or 'cruel optimism'? *Critical Social Policy*, 35(2), 167–187. http://doi.org/10.1177/0261018315574020

Flynn, N. (2013). Linguistic capital and the linguistic field for teachers unaccustomed to linguistic difference. *British Journal of Sociology of Education*, 34(2), 225–242. http://doi.org/10.2307/23356980

Fogel, H. and Ehri, L. C. (2006). Teaching African American English forms to Standard American English-speaking teachers: Effects on acquisition, attitudes, and responses to student use. *Journal of Teacher Education*, 57(5), 464–480. http://doi.org/10.1177/0022487106294088

Furness, H. (2013, February). Middlesbrough primary school issues list of "incorrect" words. *The Daily Telegraph*. www.telegraph.co.uk/education/primary education/9851236/Middlesbrough-primary-school-issues-list-of-incorrect-words.html

García, O. and Kleyn, T., eds. (2016). *Translanguaging with Multilingual Students: Learning from Classroom Moments*. Abingdon: Routledge.

García, O. and Wei, L. (2014). *Translanguaging: Language, Bilingualism and Education*. Basingstoke: Palgrave Macmillan.

Garrett, P., Coupland, N., and Williams, A. (1995). "City Harsh" and "The Welsh Version of RP": Some ways in which teachers view dialects of Welsh English. *Language Awareness1*, 4(2), 99–108.

Garrity, S., Aquino-Sterling, C. R., and Day, A. (2015). Translanguaging in an infant classroom: Using multiple languages to make meaning. *International Multilingual Research Journal*, 9(3), 177–196. http://doi.org/10.1080/19313152.2015.1048542

Garza, A. V., and Crawford, L. (2005). Hegemonic multiculturalism: English immersion, ideology, and subtractive schooling. *Bilingual Research Journal: The Journal of the National Association for Bilingual Education*, 29(3), 599–619. http://doi.org/10.1080/15235882.2005.10162854

Gillborn, D. and Kirton, A. (2000). White heat: Racism, under-achievement and white working class boys. *International Journal of Inclusive Education*, 4(4), 271–288.

Gkaintartzi, A. and Tsokalidou, R. (2011). "She is a very good child but she doesn't speak": The invisibility of children's bilingualism and teacher ideology. *Journal of Pragmatics*, 43(2), 588–601. http://doi.org/10.1016/j.pragma.2010.09.014

Godley, A. J., Sweetland, J., Wheeler, R. S., Minnici, A., and Carpenter, B. D. (2006). Preparing teachers for dialectally diverse classrooms. *Educational Researcher*, 35(8), 30–37. http://doi.org/10.3102/0013189X035008030

Grainger, K. (2013). 'The daily grunt': Middle-class bias and vested interests in the 'Getting in Early' and 'Why Can't They Read?' reports. *Language and Education*, 27(2), 99–109. http://doi.org/10.1080/09500782.2012.760583

Grainger, K. and Jones, P. E. (2013). The 'Language Deficit' argument and beyond. *Language and Education*, 27(2), 95–98. http://doi.org/10.1080/09500782.2012.760582

Gravelle, M. (1996). *Supporting Bilingual Learners in Schools*. Stoke on Trent: Trentham Book, 1–14.

Griffen, T. D. (1991). A nonsegmental approach to the teaching of pronunciation. In A. Brown, ed., *Teaching English Pronunciation: A Book of Readings* (pp. 178–190). London: Routledge.

Hanafin, J. and Lynch, A. (2002). Peripheral voices: Parental involvement, social class, and educational disadvantage Peripheral Voices: Parental involvement, social class, and educational disadvantage. *British Journal of Sociology*, 23(1), 35–49. http://doi.org/10.1080/0142569012010284

Helot, C. and Young, A. (2002). Bilingualism and language education in French primary schools: Why and how should migrant languages be valued? *International Journal of Bilingual Education and Bilingualism*, 5(2), 96–112.

Herring, T. *Standard English in the Primary Classroom: Teacher's Attitudes to Standardised Language*. Unpublished undergraduate dissertation. York: York St John University. (2017).

Hornberger, N. H. and Link, H. (2012). Translanguaging and transnational literacies in multilingual classrooms: A biliteracy lens. *International Journal of Bilingual Education and Bilingualism*, 15(3), 261–278.

Huss-Keeler, R. L. (1997). Teacher perception of ethnic and linguistic minority parental involvement and its relationship to children's language and literacy learning: A case study. *Teaching and Teacher Education*, 13(2), 171–182.

Johnson, E. J., Avineri, N., and Johnson, D. C. (2017). Exposing gaps in/between discourses of linguistic deficits. *International Multilingual Research Journal*, 11(1), 5–22. http://doi.org/10.1080/19313152.2016.1258185

Jones, P. E. (2013). Bernstein's 'codes' and the linguistics of 'deficit.' *Language and Education*, 27(2), 161–179. http://doi.org/10.1080/09500782.2012.760587

Kenner, C. (2010). Multilingual learning: Stories from schools and communities in Britain. *International Journal of Bilingual Education and Bilingualism*, 13(1), 125–128. http://doi.org/10.1080/13670050802670783

Kotler, A., Wegerif, R., and Levoi, M. (2001). Oracy and the educational achievement of pupils with English as an Additional Language: The impact of bringing 'Talking Partners' into Bradford Schools. *International Journal of Bilingual Education and Bilingualism*, 4(6), 403–419.

le Grand, E. (2013). The "chav" as folk devil. In C. Critcher, J. Hughes, J. Petley and A. Rohloff, eds., *Moral Panics in the Contemporary World* (pp. 215–236). London: Bloomsbury.

Lippi-Green, R. (1997). *English with an Accent: Language, Ideology, and Discrimination in the United States*. London: Routledge.

Long, M. H. (1990). Maturational constraints on language development. *Studies in Second Language Acquisition*, 12, 251–285.

Ludhra, G. and Jones, D. (2008). Conveying the "right" kind of message: Planning for the first language and culture within the primary classroom. *English Teaching: Practice and Critique*, 7(2), 56–70.

MacKenzie, P. (2009). Mother tongue first multilingual education among the tribal communities in India. *International Journal of Bilingual Education and Bilingualism*, 12(4), 369–385. http://doi.org/10.1080/13670050902935797

Martin, D., Martin, M., Gibson, S., and Wilkins, J. (2007). Increasing prosocial behavior and academic achievement among adolescent African American males. *Adolescence*, 42(168), 689–698. https://69.32.208.13/library/journal/1G1-172832253/increasing-prosocial-behavior-and-academic-achievement

McEachron, G. and Bhatti, G. (2005). Language support for immigrant children: A study of state schools in the UK and US. *Language, Culture and Curriculum*, 18(2), 164–180. http://doi.org/10.1080/07908310508668739

McKenzie, R. M. (2015). The sociolinguistics of variety identification and categorisation: Free classification of varieties of spoken English amongst non-linguist listeners. *Language Awareness*, 24(2), 150–168. http://doi.org/10.1080/09658416.2014.998232

Milroy, J. and Milroy, L. (1985). *Authority in Language: Investigating Language Prescription and Standardization*. London: Routledge.

Moll, L. C., Amanti, C., Neff, D., and Gonzalez, N. (1992). Funds of knowledge for teaching: Using a qualitative approach to connect homes and classrooms. *Theory into Practice*, 31(2), 132–141.

Munro, M. J., Derwing, T. M., and Sato, K. (2006). Salient accents, covert attitudes: Consciousness-raising for pre-service second language teachers. *Prospect*, 21(1), 67–79. www.nnest-evo2009.pbworks.com/f/21_1_4_Munro.pdf

Murakami, C. (2008). 'Everybody Is Just Fumbling Along': An investigation of views regarding EAL training and support provisions in a rural area. *Language and Education*, 22(4), 265. http://doi.org/10.2167/le767.0

Murray, N. (2016). An academic literacies argument for decentralizing EAP provision. *ELT Journal*, 70(4), 435–443. http://doi.org/10.1093/elt/ccw030

NALDIC. (2005). *NALDIC Briefing Paper Guidance on the Assessment of Pupils Learning English as an Additional Language*. London: NALDIC. www.naldic.org.uk/Resources/NALDIC/Home/Documents/Briefingon Assessment.pdf

Rampton, B. (1995). *Crossing: Language and Ethnicity among Adolescents*. Harlow: Longman Group.

Reay, D. (2006). The zombie stalking English schools: Social class and educational inequality. *British Journal of Educational Studies*, 54(3), 288–307.

Reay, D., Williams, K., Crozier, G., and Jamieson, F. (2007). 'A darker shade of pale?' Whiteness, the middle classes and multi-ethnic inner city schooling. *Sociology*, 41(6), 1041–1060. http://doi.org/10.1177/0038038507082314

Reeves, J. (2006). Secondary Teacher Attitudes toward Including English-Language Learners in Mainstream Classrooms. Faculty Publications: Department of Teaching, Learning and Teacher Education, Paper 116.

Romaine, S. (1998). Early bilingual development: From elite to folk. In G. Extra, ed., *Bilingualism and Migration* (pp. 61–74). Berlin: Walter de Gruyter.

Safford, K. (2016). Teaching grammar and testing grammar in the English primary school: The impact on teachers and their teaching of the grammar element of the statutory test in spelling, punctuation and grammar (SPaG). *Changing English*, 23(1), 3–21. http://doi.org/10.1080/1358684X.2015.1133766

Safford, K. and Kelly, A. (2010). Linguistic capital of trainee teachers: Knowledge worth having? *Language and Education*, 24(5), 401–414. http://doi.org/10.1080/09500781003695567

Saito, K. and Shintani, N. (2016). Foreign accentedness revisited: Canadian and Singaporean raters' perception of Japanese-accented English. *Language Awareness*, 25(4), 305–317. http://doi.org/10.1080/09658416.2016.1229784

Snell, J. and Andrews, R. (2017). To what extent does a regional dialect and accent impact on the development of reading and writing skills? *Cambridge*

Journal of Education, 47(3), 297–313. http://doi.org/10.1080/0305764X.2016.1159660

Spencer, S., Clegg, J., and Stackhouse, J. (2013). Language, social class and education: Listening to adolescents' perceptions. *Language and Education*, 27(2), 129–143. http://doi.org/10.1080/09500782.2012.760585

Tamura, E. H. (1996). Power, status and Hawai'i creole English: An example of linguistic intolerance in American history. *Pacific Historical Review*, 65(3), 431–454. http://doi.org/10.2307/3640023

Thomas, W. and Collier, V. (1997). *School effectiveness for language minority students*. Washington, DC: US House of Representatives, Committee on Education and Labor.

Trudgill, P. (1975). *Accent, dialect and the school*. London: Edward Arnold.

Van den Bergh, L., Denessen, E., Hornstra, L., Voeten, M., and Holland, R. W. (2010). The implicit prejudiced attitudes of teachers: Relations to teacher expectations and the ethnic achievement gap. *American Educational Research Journal*, 47(2), 497–527. http://doi.org/10.3102/0002831209353594

Wardman, C. (2012). Pulling the Threads Together: Current Theories and Current Practice Affecting UK Primary School Children Who Have English as an Additional Language. British Council ELTRP Research Papers (04-12).

Wardman, C., Bell, J., and Sharp, E. (2012). Valuing home languages. In D. Mallows, ed., *Innovations in English Language Teaching for Migrants and Refugees* (pp. 37–48). London: British Council.

Webster, N. L. E. E. and Lu, C. (2012). "English Language Learners": An analysis of perplexing ESL-related terminology. *Language and Literacy*, 14(3), 83–94.

Wheeler, R. S. and Swords, R. (2004). Codeswitching: Tools of language and culture transform the dialectally diverse classroom. *Language Arts*, 81(6), 470–480.

Willoughby, L., Starks, D., and Taylor-Leech, K. (2015). What their friends say about the way they talk: The metalanguage of pre-adolescent and adolescent Australians. *Language Awareness*, 24(1), 84–100. http://doi.org/10.1080/09658416.2014.977387

Part IV
Assessing English

9 *English Varieties and Targets for L2 Assessment*

Claudia Harsch

1 Introduction

Given the widespread use of English, this chapter explores two critical issues: (1) what varieties and standards of English are taught and tested in English as second/foreign language (L2) learning contexts and (2) what role is assigned to communication strategies and plurilingual competences in learning, teaching, and assessing English, particularly in lingua franca contexts.

While the question of what Englishes to teach and assess is a complex one that can only be answered in relation to specific educational and assessment contexts and purposes, it is worth examining the status that standard varieties of English have in teaching and assessment. Mostly, the target language norm in L2 English language classes and tests is to be found in standard varieties of English, whereas the majority of international communication takes place in non-standard varieties of English with at least one communication partner who uses English as second or foreign language. Here, communication and translanguaging strategies (e.g. Pennycook, 2017) play a pivotal role that is insufficiently acknowledged in teaching and assessment.

When reconsidering the targets and varieties of Englishes in teaching and assessment, this chapter will explore the role that the Common European Framework of Reference (CEFR) (Council of Europe, 2001) and its companion volume (CEFR-CV) (Council of Europe, 2018) could play in such reconsiderations, as well as the contributions coming from corpus and discourse analytic approaches. Specific attention will be paid to assessment-related questions, illustrating the (re)-considerations with references to existing language tests and recent assessment research projects. It is, however, impossible to examine targets and varieties of Englishes used in tests without giving due consideration to the targets and varieties that inform teaching and learning, since these form the basis of valid assessment.

The chapter is organized as follows. In Section 2, the contexts of English as second, foreign, and international language are explored with regard to considering what Englishes are appropriate to teach and learn in these three contexts. These considerations inform targeted language usages, norms, and rules against which to assess learner expressions. Section 3 focuses on the most common language use, i.e. English as an international language, with particular focus on communication and translanguaging strategies. Again, these considerations inform assessment targets and norms. These are discussed in Section 4, along with current issues on assessing English varieties and relevant target language usages, illustrated by new perspectives and recent projects that reconceptualize assessment constructs and approaches. Finally, an outlook on innovative ways and future research is provided.

2 Contexts of Language Education and Target Language Use: What Englishes to Teach, Learn, and Assess?

The notion of 'good English' has been explored in the three previous chapters of this volume, with a specific focus on the target Englishes in L1 schooling and education. Predominantly, the construct underlying L1 English education is to be found in what Hall (this volume; also 2014) calls P-LANGUAGE, i.e., an abstracted system of the language used by a specific speech community, most often oriented towards N-LANGUAGE, i.e., the norms and practices derived from the standard variety of English in the national context where the L1 education takes place. Here, ideologies come into play that the previous three chapters have duly analysed and critiqued. Notwithstanding their ideological implications, the norms and standards used in L1 education are widely found as targets in L2 education and assessment. This focus on L1 targets and norms, however, does not necessarily take into consideration the diverse learning contexts and target language uses of the learners. This focus may lead to a narrow construct of the target language when assessing L2 learners, which may not appropriately reflect actual or future target language usages.

2.1 Different Contexts, Different Targets

Admittedly, successful communication in a language requires shared common ground between speakers, be they L1 or L2 users. Hence, L2 education needs appropriate targets and norms that allow successful communication. This may explain why standard Englishes are often adopted as targets in L2 education. However, I argue that in an educational context where English is taught, learned, and assessed as L2, the (future) target language usages should determine what kinds of English varieties, norms, and social rules of interaction are taught and assessed.

SECOND LANGUAGE CONTEXTS

If L2 learners are living, working, and acquiring English in a context where one or another variety is used, the variety(ies) and social rules of interaction used in this context can act as target and input. Learners being exposed to one or several varieties, speaker communities, and their social rules and norms most likely aim to develop their language abilities to a degree that enables successful and effective communication within this community.

Effective communication in this context can be conceptualized in at least two ways, following Hall's framework (this volume). Most obviously, it can be conceptualized by taking into account the 'languaging' of the community in which the L2 learner communicates, with the I-LANGUAGES (idiolects) of all speakers of this community idealized to form the basis of the notional domain of the target language. Exposure to languaging and interaction with a given speaker community in a local context – ENGLISHING, as described by Hall (2014) – ideally enhances language acquisition that is valid for that context and for that speaker community.

On the other hand, there may be reasons for learners to model the target they aspire to on an abstract system (the P-LANGUAGE), which takes an N-LANGUAGE view of one standard variety as its basis, even in contexts where the learner is situated in a specific speaker community. Such reasons could lie in target language use for formal, academic, or legal purposes, where a standard variety is a prerequisite for successful languaging. Moreover, learners most likely will encounter speakers of different English varieties, where a common core of language knowledge is useful for ensuring communication. This common core is most likely to be found in standard varieties. Hence, the fact that a learner interacts with a specific speaker community and is exposed to non-standard varieties does not exclude an orientation towards one or more standard variety(ies).

FOREIGN LANGUAGE CONTEXTS

A large number of learners, however, are situated in educational contexts where English is learned as a foreign language, with limited or no direct exposure to and interaction with a speaker community of the target language. Hence, learners will most likely not be able to experience ENGLISHING in a specific speaker community first hand. In these contexts, the decision about what target variety(ies), norms, and rules to teach and assess requires careful consideration.

In schooling contexts, traditionally one or several standard varieties of English are taught. In the German school system, for example, the main varieties are British and American English, with Australian English being gradually included in the curriculum. Standard varieties are often regarded as the bearers of culture and literature, and at least in the German school system, there seems to be little discussion about including other than standard varieties. They are perceived as the 'least marked' variety, with the clearest pronunciation, closest to the written language, and with the 'widest reach' in order to understand other speakers and to be understood. While these arguments seem logical, they contain a certain circularity: because the standard variety is what learners are most frequently exposed to in schoolbooks and other materials, learners may find this variety the most unmarked and the easiest to understand.

The ideological consequences of adopting N-LANGUAGE as the target in schooling have been explored in previous chapters. Here, I would like to take a pragmatic stance. Foreign language teachers and learners need clear targets, norms, and rules that inform teaching and learning. Without this, feedback on the expressive domain and on where to go in order to develop a learner's I-LANGUAGE resources is not possible, and learners' expressions and their development cannot be assessed.

As I argued earlier for second language contexts, I also argue for foreign language classroom contexts that the (future) target language uses should be informing, if not determining, the target variety(ies), norms, and rules of communication adopted in the classroom. If, for example, the aim is to prepare learners for academic studies in the United States, the United Kingdom, or Australia, the respective standard variety and the rules of general academic communication will be most informative for the students. If, on the other hand, a course aims at preparing German holiday makers for a visit to the Scottish Highlands, the regional variety and the local rules of communication may serve best for this specific learner group. The broader the teaching aims, the wider the target varieties and language use contexts will have to be.

INTERNATIONAL LANGUAGE CONTEXTS

Given the global status of English as an international language, this target language use context should at least be acknowledged in English language education. To date, however, school education has not sufficiently addressed the requirements of using English as an international language. This may be partly due to the fact that international English cannot be described as a variety of its own, as some scholars argue (e.g. Canagarajah, 2007), due to its fluid forms and its interactive, dynamic nature (see Part V, this volume, for an in-depth discussion). Nevertheless, language education would benefit from a principled approach towards selecting and covering a common core of linguistic notions and languaging rules in diverse speaker communities, including exposure to other L2 speakers and relevant aspects of intercultural communication, in order to provide enough overlap between the different user groups to facilitate communication in lingua franca contexts.

2.2 Varieties and Languaging in the CEFR

In language education, the CEFR (Council of Europe, 2001) has had considerable influence on curricula, educational standards, and assessment within Europe and beyond. The CEFR is language and context independent, and conceptualizes language learning as language use (Little and Erickson, 2015). While traditional approaches conceptualized learner language as a deficient system characterised by errors and missing features, the CEFR accepts learner varieties as valid language varieties worth describing positively with a view to what learners already can do with their language and how well they can do it. In 2018, the Council of Europe released the CEFR Companion Volume (CEFR-CV, Council of Europe, 2018) that contains new scales targeting the realms of mediation and plurilingual/pluricultural competence, as well as updated and revised scales for nearly all existing scales. All references in this chapter are made to the scales in the CEFR-CV.

To what extent, then, can the CEFR-CV contribute towards reconceptualizing the target language norms, forms and rules of communication in English as second, foreign, or international language? In this updated version, aspects such as references to *native speakers* as an idealized implicit norm were addressed; all such references have been replaced by terms such as *speakers of the target language, proficient speakers*, or *other speakers*. This is well-illustrated by the new Phonology scales (p. 134), where a shift took place away from any reference to native speakers towards a "focus on intelligibility" (p. 47), as demonstrated by levels C1 and B2 in the scale Overall Phonological Control (p. 136), reproduced here as Figure 9.1.

170 Claudia Harsch

Table 9.1 L2-reference in the CEFR-CV listening and interaction scales

Occurrence of standard	Occurrence of non-standard	Occurrence of variety(ies)	Occurrence of target language
~ form of language: 3 ~ language: 1 ~ speech: 12 ~ spoken language: 4	~ usage: 1	Ø	speakers of the ~: 6

C1	Can employ the full range of phonological features in the target language with sufficient control to ensure intelligibility throughout. Can articulate virtually all the sounds of the target language; some features of accent retained from other language(s) may be noticeable, but they do not affect intelligibility.
B2	Can generally use appropriate intonation, place stress correctly and articulate individual sounds clearly; accent tends to be influenced by other language(s) he/she speaks, but has little or no effect on intelligibility.

Figure 9.1 CEFR-CV *scale* Overall Phonological Control
(© Council of Europe, 2018)

With regard to the reference in the CEFR-CV's scales to target varieties of L2, an analysis of the Listening and Interaction scales in the CEFR-CV reveals that these scales refer to *standard* and *non-standard* usage, as well as to *the target language*, but not once to *varieties*, as Table 9.1 shows. Interestingly, the term *target language* is only used in connection with 'speakers of the target language'.

It appears that the CEFR-CV models its targets of language learning, teaching, and assessment mainly on standard varieties of the target language, while the native speaker is no longer an implicit norm. In the linguistic and communicative scales, the reference to standard language is still noticeable, but the focus is clearly different in the new Mediation scales, where different varieties and registers are acknowledged (see Section 3.2 below). With regard to the CEFR-CV's concept of accuracy, particularly on the higher levels, the scales refer to *appropriate* rather than *correct* language use (e.g. 21 references in the Interaction scales, p. 81), "without imposing strain on either party" (p. 83), thus leaving interpretative room for the varieties and norms that may be appropriate in a given context. The scale Sociolinguistic Appropriateness (p. 138, which has undergone extensive revision; all

English Varieties and Targets for L2 Assessment

C2	Can mediate effectively and naturally between speakers of the target language and of his/her own community, taking account of sociocultural and sociolinguistic differences. Has a good command of idiomatic expressions and colloquialisms with awareness of connotative levels of meaning. Appreciates virtually all the sociolinguistic and sociocultural implications of language used by proficient speakers of the target language and can react accordingly. Can effectively employ, both orally and in writing, a wide variety of sophisticated language to command, argue, persuade, dissuade, negotiate and counsel.
C1	Can recognise a wide range of idiomatic expressions and colloquialisms, appreciating register shifts; may, however, need to confirm occasional details, especially if the accent is unfamiliar. Can understand humour, irony and implicit cultural references and pick up nuances of meaning. Can follow films employing a considerable degree of slang and idiomatic usage. Can use language flexibly and effectively for social purposes, including emotional, allusive and joking usage. Can adjust his/her level of formality (register and style) to suit the social context: formal, informal or colloquial as appropriate and maintain a consistent spoken register. Can frame critical remarks or express strong disagreement diplomatically.
B2	Can with some effort keep up with and contribute to group discussions even when speech is fast and colloquial. Can recognise and interpret sociocultural/sociolinguistic cues and consciously modify his/her linguistic forms of expression in order to express him/herself appropriately in the situation. Can express him/herself confidently, clearly and politely in a formal or informal register, appropriate to the situation and person(s) concerned.

Figure 9.2 CEFR-CV *scale* Sociolinguistic Appropriateness
(© Council of Europe, 2018)

new descriptors are in grey font in Figure 9.2) is a good example of the CEFR-CV's understanding of appropriateness with reference to "proficient speakers of the target language" (C2), the "social context" (C1) and "the situations and person(s) concerned" (B2+).

Here, it becomes apparent that the CEFR-CV has moved away from a formerly implicit assumption of a homogeneous group of (native) speakers towards speaker communities of different target languages. Nevertheless, in order to describe targets in learning, teaching, and assessment, the CEFR-CV needs to generalize to a certain extent. One has to acknowledge the fact that the CEFR aims to cover all European languages and is not tailored to the specific requirements and conditions of the varieties of Englishes used in second, foreign, and international contexts. Hence, the CEFR takes a pragmatic approach to describing target language use contexts in the society where this language is spoken. While the CEFR has to generalize over an abstract speaker community of any target language, users of the CEFR have to define and describe the precise nature of both the language variety and the speaker community that users are targeting.

2.3 Describing Different Varieties and Language Uses

When it comes to describing different language varieties and language uses, corpora and discourse analysis can contribute valuable insights.

Corpora are compilations of authentic language data in different physical media. There are, for example, corpora of spoken and written English for different genres and user groups. Corpus analyses hence examine Hall's 'expressive domain' (this volume), i.e., the linguistic actualizations and products of different speaker communities (e.g. Biber et al., 1998). Processes and practices in Hall's 'social domain' of languaging, on the other hand, are best examined by discourse analysis, which aims to shed light on how things are done with language in different speaker communities (e.g. Gee and Handford, 2012). Corpus and discourse analyses of language products and processes can inform the description of different varieties of Englishes in actual uses across different media, as well as the different rules, norms, and practices found among and across different speaker communities and user groups.

Corpus-based approaches are also used in order to describe learner language. One example is the English Profile project, where corpora of learner texts are compiled and analysed for salient features. While the project claims to "describe ... what aspects of English are typically learned at each CEFR level" (English Profile, n.d.), there may be a certain circularity in the approach: the learner texts in at least one of the corpora used (the *Cambridge Learner Corpus*) stem from tests that are aligned to the CEFR. The learner texts in the corpus are tagged with that CEFR level at which the test operates. Learner features are then described and labelled as being characteristic for a certain CEFR level. However, the tests were designed to elicit certain features that the test designers assumed to be characteristic for a certain CEFR level. So very likely, the occurrence of features in the corpus is caused by test design. Hence, the analysis of this test-driven corpus reveals what is typically elicited by certain tests targeting a certain CEFR level, and not "what is suitable for learning at each level" (English Profile, n.d.).

Corpus and discourse analyses can inform language learning, teaching, and assessment about what kinds of language, norms, and linguistic expressions are actually used and produced by certain user groups and speaker communities, and how languaging is taking place in and across different groups. This in turn can inform decisions about whether a certain form or usage can be regarded appropriate within a certain context or user group, thus informing target language use and norms for teaching and assessment.

2.4 Implications for Assessment

Language educators not only have to (re)consider what varieties of English and what target language use contexts to include in teaching, learning, and assessment materials; they also have to critically reflect on the concepts informing their target language notions, norms, and practices. These concepts can be based – on the one end of a possible spectrum – on standardized, national varieties, which are then abstracted into a linguistic system (Hall's N- and P-LANGUAGES). On the other end of the continuum, the concepts can be informed by actual language usage as practiced by different speaker communities (Hall's E-LANGUAGE and LANGUAGING).

Whether one uses an abstracted language system or actual language usage as the target of teaching and learning has consequences for what counts as error and what as acceptable. An abstracted system of norms and rules oriented towards one standard variety of English leads to a more narrow understanding of correctness, whereas the orientation towards acceptable language uses for different contexts allows for usage that would count as erroneous in a standard variety.

Corpora and discourse analysis can help inform educators and learners about what is actually used and how it is used by different speaker communities, while the CEFR and the revised scales in the CEFR-CV can aid reflection on what kinds of communicative tasks and goals, as well as linguistic features and notions, are important in a given educational context. Yet the decisions about what underlying concepts of language to adopt, and what different varieties and future target language uses to include in teaching, learning, and assessment, have to be made in this specific educational context.

3 Focus on Using English as an International Language: Communication Strategies and Plurilingualism

In some contexts it may suffice to teach towards how one standard variety is used in one native speaker community, for example, in a target language with a small community of speakers and only little languaging diversity. In the case of English, however, where more L2 users exist than L1 users, language educators need to consider the use of English as an international language used in lingua franca contexts.

3.1 English as an International Language: Reconceptualizing Proficiency

When communication in English is taking place between speakers with different L1s and different sociocultural backgrounds, the conditions, practices, and norms differ from contexts where a learner interacts with L1 users from one group or community only. In international communication, participants do not necessarily share a common core of norms, rules, or practices. They come with a repertoire of languaging practices in multiple languages, and they employ a range of communication and translanguaging strategies to achieve their communicative goals (e.g. Byram, 1997; Canagarajah, 2007).

Participants in lingua franca contexts can encompass users of English who have acquired English in formal or informal contexts, as second or foreign language, and are using English in different communities (see Part V, this volume). Hence, it is impossible to generalize to the shared core of linguistic and languaging knowledge that could characterize English as an international language. Consequently, international English is generally not regarded a variety of English (e.g. Canagarajah, 2007). Rather, participants are "shuttling between English varieties" (Canagarajah, 2006, p. 233).

Therefore, researchers demand a reconceptualization of proficiency (e.g. Canagarajah, 2006; McNamara, 2012), away from the traditional static conceptualization of communicative competence (Canale and Swain, 1981; Bachman and Palmer, 1996) that cannot adequately capture the nature of international Englishing (Canagarajah, 2006). Knowing grammatical rules and vocabulary does not suffice to communicate successfully and appropriately in the social domain, nor does it help shaping and developing the I-LANGUAGE of participants in international communication, be they L1 users or learners of English.

Rather, the construct of proficiency in English for lingua franca contexts is characterized by adaptability, by the fluid nature of interaction and co-construction, and by repair and accommodation strategies, as for example Harding (2012) notes. Not surprisingly, there is a great amount of overlap with conceptualizations of intercultural communicative competences, where negotiation, co-construction, adaptability, and accommodation play a central role (e.g. Byram, 1997). The communication and translanguaging strategies employed in lingua franca contexts by plurilingual speakers encompass strategies of adjusting to one's partner, clarifying, circumscribing, code switching, negotiating meaning, reformulating, rephrasing, simplifying, or repairing of breakdowns, amongst others (see e.g. Jenkins et al., 2011).

These strategies need to be accounted for in a reconceptualization of lingua franca proficiency, along with a rethinking of the concept of errors. For languaging, grammatical or vocabulary errors are less grave than pragmatic errors. This reconceptualization of proficiency has implications for teaching and assessment in contexts where English is used as international language, which will be detailed in Sections 3.3 and 3.4.

3.2 The CEFR and English as Lingua Franca

Plurilingualism and interaction between speakers of different languages are at the heart of the European language policy, the original CEFR document, and the CEFR-CV. While mediation, interaction among plurilingual speakers, and translanguaging strategies were not operationalized in a stringent way in the original document, the CEFR-CV has successfully addressed this gap. Here, we find a clear focus on lingua franca contexts and a broad concept of mediating across languages, in "communication and learning, as well as social and cultural mediation" (Council of Europe, 2018, p. 34). The CEFR-CV contains a wide range of new Mediation scales, including aspects such as Facilitating Communication in Delicate Situations and Disagreements and mediation strategies (pp. 103–129). The notes accompanying the Mediation scales clarify the CEFR-CV's concept of target languages: "In the [...] scales, *Language A* and *Language B* may be two different languages, two varieties of the same language, two registers if the same variety, or any combination of the above. [...] users should specify the languages/varieties concerned" (e.g. p. 107), as illustrated in Figure 9.3, an excerpt from "Acting as Intermediary" (p. 124).

This implies that the target language, at least in the realm of mediation, is not modelled on standard varieties. The CEFR-CV explicitly acknowledges and contains scales on plurilingual and pluricultural competences (pp. 157–162). It links its conceptualization to the Framework of Reference for Pluralistic Approaches (Council of Europe, 2012), which lists a taxonomy of plurilingual and intercultural competences. Given the plurilingual situation of most European countries, the status of local varieties and minority languages, as well as the goals of the European language policy, it is very welcome to see

C1	Can communicate fluently in (Language B) the sense of what is said in (Language A) on a wide range of subjects of personal, academic and professional interest, conveying significant information clearly and concisely as well as explaining cultural references.
	Can mediate (between Language A and Language B), conveying detailed information, drawing the attention of both sides to background information and sociocultural cues, and posing clarification and follow-up questions or statements as necessary.
B2	Can communicate in (Language B) the sense of what is said in a welcome address, anecdote or presentation in his/her field given in (Language A), interpreting cultural cues appropriately and giving additional explanations when necessary, provided that the speaker stops frequently in order to allow time for him/her to do so.
	Can communicate in (Language B) the sense of what is said in (Language A) on subjects within his/her fields of interest, conveying and when necessary explaining the significance of important statements and viewpoints, provided speakers give clarifications if needed.

Figure 9.3 CEFR-CV scale Acting as Intermediary
(© Council of Europe, 2018)

the CEFR-CV acknowledging plurilingual realities and translanguaging strategies and giving mediation between speakers of different languages such prominent status.

3.3 Implications for Assessing English as an International Language

Most importantly, teaching and assessment need to take into account communicative and translanguaging strategies as they occur in actual lingua franca contexts. Moreover, learners' plurilingual and pluricultural competences should be acknowledged. Here, the CEFR, and particularly the CEFR-CV with its focus on plurilingual and pluricultural competences, can aid reflection on what kinds of strategies may be important for a given context and for certain target language uses. Discourse analysis can help shed light on how languaging is taking place in such contexts, while corpus analyses can facilitate examining the expressive domain. Insights from research on intercultural communication can inform the reconceptualization of proficiency in lingua franca contexts.

As indicated earlier, the notion of error needs to shift from the notional to the socio-pragmatic domain, taking on board insights from intercultural studies to help understand the impacts that different kinds of errors may have on participants. Language teaching should be informed by intercultural training, taking account of aspects such as teaching repair strategies in cases of communication breakdowns, conveying awareness of what participants can and cannot assume, or teaching strategies to explore what shared concepts (linguistic as well as socio-pragmatic and cultural) the participants have.

While learners of English most likely will gain some insights into the intercultural nature of international communication during their English education, this cannot be presupposed for L1 users of English. Hence, it may be helpful to differentiate between a situation in which only L2 users of English participate and situations where at least one L1 user participates. In the latter situation, the L1 user may bring implicit socio-cultural assumptions and languaging practices to the conversation that the L2 users may not share. This may lead to communication breakdowns, as illustrated by research on air traffic control communication. Analyses of accidents revealed instances where L1 users repeated the same utterance instead of reformulating, rephrasing, or simplifying when an L2 partner did not understand the utterance (e.g., Kim and Elder, 2009; Said, 2011).

Therefore, L1 users should be included in training and assessment of English as Lingua Franca in contexts such as aviation, diplomacy, or health care. Combined with intercultural training, this could help teaching clarification and repair strategies, or raising awareness among L1 English users to not assume that their languaging practices are known by and shared with L2 English users (e.g. Wicaksono, 2012).

4 Assessing English Varieties and Relevant Target Language Usages

For valid language assessment, both the purpose of the assessment and the construct of what is being assessed play a pivotal role. To put it in somewhat simplistic terms, the assessment purpose determines the target language use contexts that the assessment should cover, and the construct needs to validly reflect these contexts and the related language uses. Every assessment needs to transparently define its conceptualization of proficiency, taking into consideration the assessment purpose, the target language uses, and the test-takers.

Since assessment is concerned with judging either the learners' expressive domain or their I-LANGUAGE development, any assessment needs to decide on a clear set of target norms and rules against which learner language and expressions are judged. Hence, assessment contexts need to transparently document all decisions about the targeted English varieties and acceptable languaging practices as expressed in acceptable linguistic expressions and in the use of languaging strategies. These decisions are driven by the same considerations as those outlined earlier for teaching and learning English as second, foreign, or international language. For valid assessment concerned with learner development, it is of utmost importance that teaching aims, learning outcomes, and assessment objectives are constructively aligned (e.g. Little and Erickson, 2015), mirroring and reflecting each other.

4.1 Norms and Varieties of English in Assessments

Any assessment needs to clarify what variety(ies) it regards as acceptable target(s), whether it be standard or non-standard varieties. The accepted varieties influence the assessment in two ways: first, they determine what input is regarded as acceptable to represent the expressive domain used in the assessment; second, these rules and norms determine the judgements of the learners' expressions elicited in the assessment.

The conceptualization of learner language is a further important aspect that needs to be transparently documented, as it has implications, e.g., for the treatment of errors. If learner language is conceptualized as a deficient transition stage towards an idealized target language, errors will likely lead to lower assessment outcomes. If learner language, on the other hand, is regarded as a valid variety of the target language, errors will likely be treated as integral parts of learner language, with a focus on appropriate language use, where only errors that impede successful communication will have an impact on the assessment outcome.

This point is nicely illustrated by a project from the German school context, where tests were to be developed for a large-scale educational monitoring project evaluating whether students reach the educational standards for English as first foreign language at the end of secondary schooling (Rupp et al., 2008). The standards are aligned to the CEFR, as are the tests used for evaluation (Harsch et al., 2010). The tests were developed by trained teachers from all regions and school types in Germany. Initially, the teachers insisted on using only 'formally correct' texts, input and stimuli, whereby they referred to the native-speaker standard varieties of British and American English. When we asked the teachers to define the (future) target language uses of their students, it became transparent that lingua franca contexts played a predominant role.

The target language use contexts were outlined in the test specifications by the teachers, and they accepted all varieties and contexts that were listed in the specification, including the use of English in lingua franca contexts by German and other non-native speakers of English. With regard to the input chosen for the assessment, teachers selected spoken input not only from speakers of the main standard varieties of English, but also from non-native speakers.

When it came to assessing students' output, the teachers, who also developed the initial draft of the rating scale, focused on communicative effectiveness on the lower levels (up to CEFR-level B1), and accepted 'L1 interference' at these levels as a valid and realistic expression of translanguaging. On the higher levels (from B2 onwards), the teachers made a pragmatic decision for the aforementioned standard varieties of English as target norm (in Hall's terminology, P-LANGUAGE based on N-LANGUAGE), not least because these varieties are reflected in the German curricula for secondary schooling. The initial rating scale was refined and validated with a group of raters who confirmed the teachers' approach (Harsch and Martin, 2012).

During the project, a growing awareness amongst teachers and raters emerged about the need to confirm the acceptability of learners' language usage with actual speaker communities in the real world, i.e. by taking the E-LANGUAGE (i.e. actual linguistic expressions used by actual speaker communities) as point of orientation. Here, a 'real-time' corpus would be helpful that could allow insights into what expressions are actually being used by different speaker communities. While Internet search engines permit a quick and very superficial glance, raters and teachers ideally would need more sophisticated tools with options, e.g. to select the speaker communities, different genres, or communicative contexts and purposes.

4.2 International Tests, Varieties of English, and Different Contexts of English Usage

When looking at the varieties of English employed in internationally recognised tests of English, it appears from the information provided online (e.g. Cambridge, IELTS, Pearson PTE, TOEFL, Trinity ISE, as checked in 2017) that the major international test providers use and accept only standard varieties of English as input, in order to ensure that no test-taker is disadvantaged. The Cambridge English Main Suite listening tests, for instance, avoid "accents markedly different from those with which a candidate in a global context can be reasonably expected to be familiar" (Geranpayeh and Taylor, 2013, p. 60). With regard to judging test-takers' output, the learners' expressive domain is usually assessed against standard norms of English. IELTS, for example, states that "all standard varieties of English are accepted" (IELTS, 2015, p. 4).

Test providers generally refer to two main reasons for their orientation towards standard varieties of English (e.g. Geranpayeh and Taylor, 2013). One is the generic purpose of these international tests; i.e., they aim to certify general English proficiency without one specific target language use domain. The second reason lies with the test-takers, who stem from a wide variety of backgrounds and who may have been exposed to very different non-native speaker accents and varieties. Hence, it is understandable that standard varieties are used as the common denominator to ensure test fairness.

The language use contexts captured in internationally recognised tests of English usually encompass everyday, social, or work-related situations. In tests targeting specific English (e.g. academic) usage, the situations are indeed modelled on relevant communication tasks from these contexts. TOEFL iBT, for example, "simulates actual tasks from classrooms – from understanding a lecture to participating in discussions and extracurricular activities" (ETS, n.d.).

As far as communicative strategies in interaction are concerned, most of the internationally recognised tests include a speaking section where test-takers interact directly with an interlocutor or with other test-takers. Some tests are delivered on a computer, such as Pearson

PTE Academic or TOEFL iBT, where the speaking section is also delivered by the computer. Here, the speaking situations do not simulate real interaction, which may have an impact on test-takers' performance. Some students report that they feel uneasy about speaking to a computer (e.g. Harsch et al., 2017). It seems that the potential of interactive online media has not yet been fully exploited in the existing computer-delivered test formats.

With regard to assessment schemes and their conceptualisation of learner language and interactive strategies, test providers take different approaches. Pearson PTE General, for example, takes relevant CEFR descriptors as assessment objectives (Pearson, 2017, p. 37 ff); IELTS uses its own set of descriptors (IELTS, 2017); TOEFL iBT and Pearson PTE Academic employ automated scoring engines. Due to the variety of approaches, it is beyond the scope of this chapter to analyse the rating approaches and underlying conceptualizations of learner language of these tests.

The status of interaction skills and strategies and the ways they are operationalized also differ greatly among internationally recognised tests. One test that explicitly focuses on interaction skills is the Trinity College London GESE exam. Here, interaction strategies are part of the construct. For the intermediate level, for instance, the test-takers are "expected to share responsibility for maintaining and developing the conversation" (Trinity College London, n.d.). Moreover, the Exam Information Booklet of the GESE exam, published by Trinity College London (2016), contains specifications about the interactive nature of the construct for each exam level, including statements on candidate abilities such as "in case of a breakdown in communication, show awareness and take basics steps to remedy it"(Trinity College London, 2016, p. 34).

While some exams do target interactional strategies such as repairing breakdowns in communication, it seems that when it comes to translanguaging and communication strategies relevant for lingua franca contexts, internationally recognised tests do not specifically operationalize and target these skills and contexts.

4.3 Assessing English for Lingua Franca Purposes

Since the usage of English as an international language takes such a prominent role, it is worth considering approaches to assess English specifically for lingua franca contexts. Here, questions such as the following need to be answered, as outlined earlier:

- What target language use contexts need to be covered?
- Should only L2 users be assessed or also L1 users?

- Can the fluid constructs be captured in existing tests, or are new formats and approaches needed to account for a reconceptualized concept of proficiency?
- How can plurilingual and translanguaging competences be accommodated?
- What would appropriate assessment criteria look like?

Aspects such as the impact of learners' L1 also need to be addressed (see Nakatsuhara, Taylor, and Jaiyote, this volume, for the role of L1 in paired speaking tests). Given the intercultural nature of lingua franca communication, a further question arises: What role could and should intercultural competences play in language tests? While scholars such as Byram (1997) and Deardorff (2011) have brought forward approaches to assess intercultural communicative competences, I am not aware of an internationally recognised test of English that coherently operationalizes an integrated approach to encompass languaging, translanguaging, and intercultural communication for lingua franca purposes. In order to fully acknowledge the nature of these contexts, new constructs, formats, approaches, and assessment criteria are needed.

One example for an innovative approach is reported by Harding (2015), using the HCRC (Human Communication Research Centre) map negotiation tasks (Anderson et al., 1991) for research purposes. Harding's construct targets abilities such as tolerating and comprehending different varieties of English, negotiating and co-constructing meaning, using phonological features that are crucial for intelligibility across speakers of different L1 backgrounds, and noticing and repairing breakdowns in communication, as well as the awareness of appropriate expressions of politeness in cross-cultural situations.

Harding (2015) uses paired speaking tests, employing the previously mentioned map negotiation tasks in which non-native participants with different L1s have to negotiate directions according to maps that contain different features. One participant has to direct the other, yet the differences in their maps cause ambiguity and likely lead to a communication breakdown. The goal-oriented task requires the participants to negotiate and co-construct form and meaning.

In order to judge the participants' interaction skills and their languaging, a new set of rating categories is needed that acknowledges the use of strategies required for successful use of English in this lingua franca situation. Harding (2015) suggests including aspects of accommodation (intelligibility, adjustment), negotiation (clarification, self-repair, paraphrasing), and maintaining interaction (turn-taking, politeness strategies). A range of different tasks following these design principles for different communicative situations could be developed to reflect specific lingua franca contexts, as Harding states. This very promising approach can easily be expanded to include L1 users of English in lingua franca contexts, for the reasons outlined previously.

5 Conclusions and Ways Forward

There are a number of promising approaches when it comes to assessing interactive or translanguaging strategies, also in the context of using English as Lingua Franca. Meaning-negotiation tasks and approaches that empower test-takers to take over responsibility for maintaining the conversation are but two possibilities. Another fruitful avenue is to conceptualize learner language as valid language variation, as shown, for example, in the CEFR. Consequently, learner expressions can be assessed not against notions of correctness but rather with a view to judging communicative appropriateness and goals, with errors forming an acceptable part of the learners' I-LANGUAGE as long as they do not impede effective communication. What counts as effective can be negotiated by the participants, shifting control and responsibility to the learners.

It remains challenging for test providers to incorporate all relevant varieties and contexts of English usage and to simulate languaging as experienced in the real world. Tests necessarily have to make a selection from all possible 'universes' of contexts and tasks. Moreover, judging learner development and learner expressions requires a clear target, a set of norms against which to judge. The more specific and clearly defined a test's purpose, target language use contexts, and test-takers, the more focused and narrow will the selection of appropriate targets, varieties, and norms be. Test providers catering for global customers, however, face the challenge to ensure test fairness for their widely differing customers. Hence, they need to base their selection on targets and varieties that they can realistically assume their customers will be familiar with.

Despite these necessary constraints on selecting certain targets and varieties, research can help exploring the potential of corpora, discourse analysis, and the Internet as a worldwide storage of the expressive domain of online English communication in order to address some of the remaining questions. I list but a few of the most urgent challenges here.

In order to study real-time language usage amongst different speaker communities and for different text types, communication contexts, and purposes, it would be interesting to develop tagging systems and search engines for examining online communication and documents stored online. This could feed into exploring innovative computer-based assessment formats to capture relevant interactive features of online communication for assessment purposes.

An empirically based description of communication and trans-languaging strategies along with relevant interactive competences employed in lingua franca contexts would facilitate a conceptualization of the fluid, interactive, and co-constructive nature of successful communication in these contexts. Here, research should include L1 speakers, in order to examine the competences and strategies L1 speakers ideally should possess for successful lingua franca communication. What is also needed is a description of the relevant strategies, practices, and competences for different usage contexts and on different competence levels, so that valid assessment categories and band descriptors can be developed.

Due to the intercultural character of lingua franca communication, it would be worth exploring how these two fields - intercultural and lingua franca communication - can be integrated in assessment. Innovative assessment approaches are needed to validly capture and assess different English usage contexts and their related strategies and languaging practices. Here, I would like to point out the potential of Dynamic Assessment (e.g. Lantolf and Poehner, 2004) as an innovative approach to assessing and developing the skills needed in lingua franca communication. Dynamic Assessment is rooted in socio-cultural theory (Vygotsky, 1962) and it is designed to integrate learner development with assessment, whereby the assessor takes on the role of a mediator, providing a Mediated Learning Experience (Feuerstein et al., 2010). Dynamic Assessment aims at developing learners' cognitive abilities and conceptual understanding while simultaneously assessing their potential for future development. Dynamic Assessment and the integrated mediation procedures are well established in clinical and special needs assessments but apart from one explorative study (Harsch and Poehner, 2016), they have not yet systematically been applied to assessing intercultural and lingua franca communication skills – skills that are characterised by the same dynamic, co-constructive and interactive nature underlying the Dynamic Assessment approach.

While this chapter could only touch the surface of the most urgent challenges in assessing different varieties and target language uses of English, I hope that the reader may take away some inspiration for reconsidering what targets, norms, and practices of Englishing can and should be assessed for different learner groups and their varying language use contexts, thereby using innovative approaches or redesigning and adapting existing ones.

References

Anderson, A., Bader, M., Bard, E. G. et al. (1991). The HCRC map task corpus. *Language and Speech, 34*(4), 351–366.

Bachman, L. F. and Palmer, A. S. (1996). *Language Testing in Practice.* Oxford: Oxford University Press.

Biber, D., Conrad, S., and Reppen R. (1998). *Corpus Linguistics, Investigating Language Structure and Use.* Cambridge: Cambridge University Press.

Byram, M. (1997). *Teaching and Assessing Intercultural Communicative Competence.* Clevedon: Multilingual Matters.

Canagarajah, S. (2006). Changing communicative needs, revised assessment objectives: Testing English as an international language. *Language Assessment Quarterly, 3*(3), 229–242.

Canagarajah, S. (2007). Lingua franca English, multilingual communities, and language acquisition. *Modern Language Journal, 91*, 923–939.

Canale, M. and Swain, M. (1981). A theoretical framework for communicative competence. In A. S. Palmer, P. Groot, and G. Trosper, eds., *The Construct Validation of Tests of Communicative Competence* (pp. 31–36). Washington, DC: TESOL.

Council of Europe. (2001). *Common European Framework of Reference for Languages: Learning, Teaching and Assessment.* Cambridge: Cambridge University Press. Online. Accessed 19 August 2017 from www.coe.int/t/dg4/linguistic/Source/Framework_EN.pdf

Council of Europe. (2012). Framework of Reference for Pluralistic Approaches. Online. Accessed 10 August 2018 from http://carap.ecml.at

Council of Europe. (2018). CEFR Companion Volume. Online. Accessed 7 June 2018 from https://rm.coe.int/cefr-companion-volume-with-new-descriptors-2018/1680787989

Deardorff, D. K. (2011). Assessing intercultural competence. *New Directions for Institutional Research, 149*, 65–79.

English Profile. (n.d.). English Profile - What the CEFR Means for English. Online. Accessed 19 August 2017 from www.englishprofile.org

ETS (n.d.). TOEFL iBT® Test Content. Online. Accessed 19 August 2017 from http://www.ets.org/toefl/institutions/about/content

Feuerstein, R., Feuerstein, R. S., and Falik, L. H. (2010). *Beyond Smarter: Mediated Learning and the Brain's Capacity for Change.* New York: Teachers' College Press.

Gee, J. and Handford, M. (2012). *The Routledge Handbook of Discourse Analysis.* London: Routledge.

Geranpayeh, A. and Taylor, L. (2013). *Examining Listening: Research and Practice in Assessing Second Language Listening.* Cambridge: Cambridge University Press.

Hall, C. J. (2014). Moving beyond accuracy: From tests of English to tests of 'Englishing'. *ELT Journal, 68*(4), 376–385.

Harding, L. (2012). Accent, listening assessment and the potential for a shared-L1 advantage: A DIF perspective. *Language Testing, 29*(2), 163–180.

Harding, L. (2015). Adaptability and ELF communication: The next steps for communicative language testing? In S. Dawadi, J. Mader, and Z. Urkun, eds., *Selected Proceedings from the IATEFL TEA SIG 2014 Conference*. Granada: IATEFL.
Harsch, C. and Martin, G. (2012). Adapting CEF-descriptors for rating purposes: Validation by a combined rater training and scale revision approach. *Assessing Writing, 17*, 228–250.
Harsch, C. and Poehner, M. (2016). Enhancing student experience abroad: The potential of dynamic assessment to develop student interculturality. *Language and Intercultural Communication, 16*(3), 470–490.
Harsch, C., Pant, H. A., and Köller, O., eds. (2010). *Calibrating Standards-Based Assessment Tasks for English as a First Foreign Language. Standard-setting Procedures in Germany*. Münster: Waxmann.
Harsch, C., Ushioda, E., and Ladroue, C. (2017). *Investigating the Predictive Validity of TOEFL iBT® Scores and Their Use in Informing Policy in a UK University Setting*. ETS Research Monograph. Princeton: ETS.
IELTS. (2015). Ensuring quality and fairness in international language testing. Online. Accessed 21 August 2017 from www.ielts.org/-/media/publications/quality-and-fairness/quality-and-fairness-2015-uk.ashx?la=en
IELTS. (2017). Speaking band decriptors. Online. Accessed 22 August 2017 from www.takeielts.britishcouncil.org/sites/default/files/IELTS_Speaking_band_descriptors.pdf
Jenkins, J., Cogo, A., and Dewey, M. (2011). Review of developments in research into English as a lingua franca. *Language Teaching, 44*(3), 281–315.
Kim, H. and Elder, C. (2009). Understanding aviation English as a lingua franca. *Australian Review of Applied Linguistics, 32*(3), 23.1–23.17.
Lantolf, J. and Poehner, M. (2004). Dynamic Assessment: Bringing the past into the future. *Journal of Applied Linguistics, 1*, 49–74.
Little, D. and Erickson, G. (2015). Learner identity, leaner agency and the assessment of language proficiency. *Annual Review of Applied Linguistics, 35*, 120–139.
McNamara, T. (2012). Language Assessments as Shibboleths: A Poststructuralist Perspective. *Applied Linguistics, 33*(5), 564–581.
Pearson. (2017). PTE General. Specification. Online. Accessed 22 August 2017 from www.pearsonpte.com/wp-content/uploads/2017/06/PTE-General-Specification-2017.pdf
Pennycook, A. (2017). Translanguaging and semiotic assemblages. *International Journal of Multilingualism, 14*(3), 269–282.
Rupp, A. A., Vock, M., Harsch, C., and Köller, O. (2008). *Developing Standards-based Assessment Tasks for English as a First Foreign Language – Context, Processes and Outcomes in Germany*. Münster: Waxmann.
Said, H. (2011). *Phraseology: Pilots and Air Traffic Controllers Phraseology Study*. Montreal: International Air Transport Association.
Trinity College London. (2016). Exam Information: Graded Examinations in Spoken English (GESE). Online. Accessed 22 August 2017 from www.trinitycollege.com/resource/?id=5755

Trinity College London. (n.d.). Online. Accessed 22 August 2017 from www.trinitycollege.com/site/?id=3108

Vygotsky, L. S. (1962). Thought and Language. In E. Hanfmann and G. Vakar, eds. and trans. Cambridge, MA: MIT Press.

Wicaksono, R. (2012). Raising students' awareness of the construction of communicative (in)competence in international classrooms. In J. Ryan, ed., *Cross Cultural Teaching and Learning for Home and International Students: Internationalisation of Pedagogy and Curriculum in Higher Education*. London and New York: Routledge.

10 The Role of the L1 in Testing L2 English

Fumiyo Nakatsuhara, Lynda Taylor, and Suwimol Jaiyote

1 Introduction

A number of chapters in this volume have highlighted the role of testing and assessment in contributing to maintaining monolith conceptualisations of English, and conversely the hybrid nature of the language and lack of clear boundaries, especially in L2 versions. Accordingly, this chapter discusses the role of the L1 in assessing L2 English proficiency, focusing particularly on tests of L2 English speaking ability. It first considers Weir's (2005) socio-cognitive framework for developing and validating speaking tests (further elaborated in Taylor, 2011), in order to locate the issue of L1 influence comprehensively within an overall test validation framework. It then describes how the different test purposes for which tests are designed can determine the role of the L1, according to the specific construct of the test. To exemplify differing roles that can be played by the L1 in speaking tests, this chapter then presents two studies on L2 spoken English tests that sought to address the issue of test-takers' L1 in contrastive ways.

The first study explored the impact of test-takers' L1 backgrounds in the paired speaking task of a standardised test of general English provided by an international examination board (Nakatsuhara and Jaiyote, 2015). The key question in the research was how we can ensure fairness for test-takers who perform paired tests in shared and non-shared L1 pairs. The second piece of research is a test validation study conducted as a part of the development of a new English for Academic Purposes (EAP) test administered by a national examination board, targeting a monolingual population of learners who share a single L1 (Nakatsuhara, 2014). Of particular interest is the way in which the test's pronunciation rating scale was developed and validated for the single L1 context.

In light of these examples of research into international and locally developed tests, this chapter aims to demonstrate the importance of the construct of a test and its score usage when considering what Englishes (rather than 'standard' English) should be elicited and assessed, and when/how we can reconcile notions of 'standard' English with local language norms and features without undermining the validity of a test or risking unfairness for test-takers. In so doing, this chapter reiterates the point made by Harsch (this volume) concerning the significance of establishing a transparent test construct with due considerations to the specific context of each test, leading to the best possible way to benefit learners by appropriately selecting the variety(-ies) of English against which their 'I-LANGUAGE' development (Hall, this volume) should be assessed.

2 Test Validity Framework

Since Messick's (1989) seminal paper on a unitary conceptualisation of test validity, there has been a general consensus among language test researchers and practitioners that test validity concerns "an integrated evaluative judgement of the degree to which empirical evidence and theoretical rationales support the *adequacy* and *appropriateness* of *inferences* and *actions* based on test scores or other models of assessment" (Messick, 1989, p. 13, italics in original). According to this understanding, validity is not a property of the test itself, but rather a concept pertaining to the meaning, interpretations, and inferences made on the basis of test scores. Messick (1989, p. 20) explains the centrality of construct validity and the significance of taking social dimensions into account within his unified theory of validity.

Building on Messick's validity conceptualisation, Weir (2005) proposed a socio-cognitive framework for test development and validation, which is now widely recognised as a sound and comprehensive framework on the basis of which validity judgements can be made more confidently (e.g. Shaw and Weir, 2007; Khalifa and Weir, 2009; O'Sullivan and Weir, 2011; Taylor, 2011; Geranpayeh and Taylor, 2013). The framework pays special attention to the cognitive processing theory that underpins equivalent operations in real-life language use, and it views the use of language in performance tasks as a social rather than a purely linguistic phenomenon. In the socio-cognitive framework for validating speaking tests illustrated in Figure 10.1, Weir (2005; further elaborated in Taylor, 2011) proposed six distinguishable elements, for which we need to generate evidence to support a meaningful validity argument. These are *test-taker characteristics, context validity, cognitive validity, scoring validity, consequential*

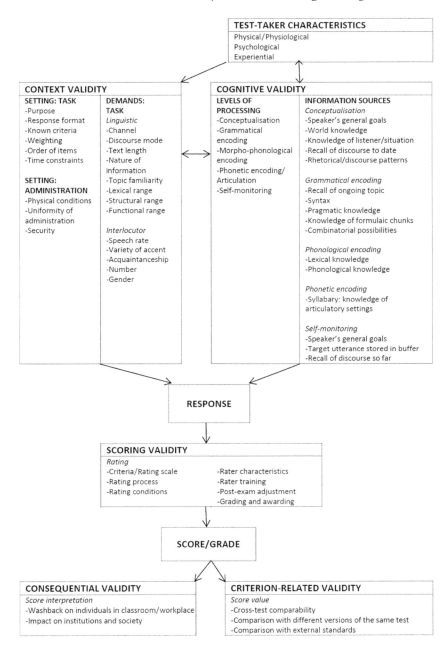

Figure 10.1 Weir's socio-cognitive framework for validating speaking tests (Taylor, 2011, p. 28)

validity and *criterion-related validity*. They are briefly explained as follows (cf. Weir, 2005, pp. 48–49):

- *Test-taker characteristics* concern how the physical/physiological, psychological, and experiential characteristics of candidates are catered for by a test, and whether the test is likely to be appropriate for the target candidates.
- *Context validity* concerns to what degree the test tasks can be judged as being capable of eliciting language under appropriate linguistic and task-based performance conditions that are relevant to and representative of the real-life construct that the test is intended to measure.
- *Cognitive validity* concerns the extent to which the cognitive processes required to complete the tasks are shown to be processes that correspond to the intended underlying theoretical construct of language ability, as well as the extent to which candidates are likely to use the same cognitive processes as they would if performing the same task in a 'real-world' context.
- *Scoring validity* concerns to what extent we can depend on the scores from the test being consistent, reliable, and generalisable in a non-test target language use context, what the scores or grades mean, and whether the relationship between task performance and the rating criteria used to assess the performance is appropriate.
- *Consequential validity* concerns the degree to which test scores are interpreted and acted upon in the intended way, and the extent to which the test has intended or unintended consequences associated with the washback effect on teaching and learning and the impact on society.
- *Criterion-related validity* concerns the extent to which the empirical relationship with external sources (i.e. different versions of the same test, other tests with an identical construct, or the future performance of candidates) supports the way the score is meant to be interpreted.

Echoing Messick (1996, p. 253), Weir (2005) notes that these different components should be seen as complementary forms of validity evidence. The validity of a test relates to all these aspects, and the interpretation of evidence relying on just one aspect in isolation fails to treat validity as a whole.

When evaluating the role of the L1 in an L2 speaking test, we need to take all these validity components into consideration, since the L1 issue could potentially influence all parts of the framework. We will now briefly discuss the relationship between the L1 and each component of the socio-cognitive framework, while making some links to

Hall's (this volume) ontological framework of English whenever possible.

Test-takers' own L1 background belongs to the top box of the framework, *test-taker characteristics*, which will affect the *cognitive* processes that the test-takers will engage while performing test tasks. For example, grammatical, phonological, and phonetic encoding stages could be to some degree influenced by test-takers' L1 transfer. These two aspects of the socio-cognitive framework could relate to what Hall calls 'I-LANGUAGE resources', since both *test-taker characteristics* and *cognitive* parameters are about features pertaining to individual learners and their internal cognitive capacity.

If the test format involves interaction between an examiner and a test-taker or between peer test-takers, then the 'interlocutor' aspect of *context validity* requires careful attention in terms of the L1 background of interlocutors. The selection of such contextual parameters can be considered as specifying the types of 'languaging' we would like to assess in a test.

Test-takers' spoken output, which is in the expressive domain of one's language, is usually assessed by either an examiner who also acts as an interlocutor or a rater who listens to or watches recorded performances of test-takers; as a result, how familiar the examiners and/or raters are with the test-takers' variety of English and how they are trained to assess the performances under *scoring validity* become critical.

Furthermore, consideration for *consequential validity* should also be made, since the resulting scores then have to be interpreted to inform the users of the test score in a way that is appropriate to specific test purposes. Whether and the extent to which the test facilitates positive washback to teachers and learners and provides positive impact on educational systems and society are also key considerations. Finally, since a test is often used to predict learners' future performance in a real-life context, the predictive power of a test and its relation to the role of the L1 needs to be considered under *criterion-related validity*.

The centrality of the construct of a test and the use of test scores (Messick, 1989) means that all parameters relating to the role of the L1 in an L2 speaking test must accord with what the test is designed to measure and what score interpretations are anticipated. Therefore, while advances in research on World Englishes and English as a Lingua Franca are welcomed by language testing researchers and test providers, the actual decision on the treatment of L1-related issues and a variety of Englishes in a language test will need to be made on a case by case basis, depending on the construct of the specific test in question and its intended score interpretations. In doing so, all the validity parameters described above have to be given due consideration.

3 Test Validation Studies Addressing L1-Related Issues

To exemplify how differing L1 roles can be operationalised in actual language tests, we will now present selected parts from two validation studies on two speaking tests that have clearly different test constructs and different purposes to serve for different target test-taker groups, highlighting the differing roles played by the L1 in these two tests.

The first study described in Section 3.1 is taken from Nakatsuhara and Jaiyote (2015) on the *B2 First* examination (formerly known as First Certificate in English or FCE) developed and delivered by Cambridge Assessment English. *B2 First* has a very large international candidature cohort and is one of the most popular general English tests offered by Cambridge English that administers more than 5 million English tests annually in more than 130 countries (Cambridge English, 2018a). For example, *B2 First* was administered in 94 countries in 2016 (Cambridge English, 2018b).

The second study illustrated in Section 3.2 is extracted from Nakatsuhara (2014) on the *Test of English for Academic Purposes (TEAP)*, which is a relatively new admissions test for Japanese colleges and universities. The test was taken by 24,434 test-takers in 2017, and it is expected that *TEAP* will be recognised by all national universities when the current National Centre Test for university admissions (with 550,000 candidates in 2017; National Centre for University Entrance Examinations, 2017) is phased out from 2020 (Tanaka, 2018). Therefore, a significant increase of the test-taker numbers is expected in the next few years.

As such, *B2 First* is a general English test for a multilingual population of international learners, while *TEAP* is an EAP test targeting a monolingual population of learners who share a single L1.

3.1 B2 First: *English Test for International Test-Takers*

The focus of Nakatsuhara and Jaiyote's (2015; see also Jaiyote, 2016 for more details) study was the paired speaking task (Part 3: collaborative task) of *B2 First*. The research investigated the extent to which test-takers having a shared or non-shared L1 partner can affect their performance on the task. More specifically, this research addressed three different aspects of test validation in relation to the role of the L1 in a paired speaking format: fairness in test scores, listening demands imposed by an interlocutor, and communication patterns. Firstly, since *B2 First* is a large-scale, high-stakes test, "issues of quality and fairness must be paramount" (Taylor, 2006, p. 56). The test construct should be comparable in both shared and non-shared L1 pairings, and test-takers should not be advantaged or disadvantaged in terms of awarded scores due to their partners' L1 backgrounds. Secondly, it has been demonstrated that interactive speaking tests tap into both speaking and listening constructs to some degree, because test-takers' listening proficiency is inevitably required in order to respond to their partner appropriately (e.g. Seedhouse and Egbert, 2006; Nakatsuhara, 2012). It is necessary therefore to examine the extent to which the two types of pairing are comparable in terms of the listening demands imposed by the paired partner. Lastly, it is important to investigate how comparable communication patterns are between the two types of pairing. In Jenkins' (1997) study, in which she observed paired discourse in *C1 Advanced (CAE)*, it was found that test-takers with a shared L1 partner deliberately used more L1-influenced pronunciation features to make their utterances mutually intelligible. As her study was relatively small scale, this study also aimed to re-examine whether and to what extent speech accommodation and any other salient communication patterns can be identified in the two types of pairing and what roles the learners' listening proficiency may play in communicating with shared and non-shared L1 partners. In terms of locating the focus of this study within the socio-cognitive validation framework, it relates to *scoring validity* and the 'interlocutor' component of *context validity* in addition to the test-taker's own *test-taker characteristics*.

The research questions for the study were as follows:

RQ 1: Are there any differences in speaking test scores when test-takers are paired with a shared L1 speaker as compared with a non-shared L1 partner?

RQ 2: Are there any differences between shared and non-shared L1 pairs in terms of the impact of their listening proficiency on performance in paired oral tests?

RQ 3: What are the similarities and differences in communication patterns between shared and non-shared L1 pairs?

METHODOLOGY

Forty pre-sessional English programme students at a UK university participated in the study, of which twenty were Thai L1 speakers and twenty were Urdu L1 speakers. To minimise the potential effects of other test-taker characteristics, the participants' test-taker characteristics other than L1 background were controlled as much as possible. Ten males and ten females from each L1 background were recruited, and only single-sex pairs were formed. Most of the participants were in their twenties (Mean = 27.20, SD = 2.84), and their speaking and listening proficiency levels were comparable according to their recent IELTS Band scores (Speaking: Mean = 5.61, SD = 0.35, Listening: Mean = 5.28, SD = 0.39). A demographic questionnaire also confirmed the test-takers' perceived familiarity with the English spoken by shared and non-shared L1 speakers with Likert-scale questions. Unsurprisingly, they were significantly more familiar with the English spoken by the same L1 speakers than the English spoken by the other L1 speakers (i.e. Thai or Urdu).

All forty learners were asked to take four tests: a listening test, two paired speaking tests, and a monologic speaking test. The listening test was to assess the learners' general listening ability, using thirty items taken from *B1 Preliminary (PET)* and *B2 First* practice materials (Cambridge English, 2008, 2009). The reliability of the listening test was acceptable, showing a Cronbach alpha value of 0.91. All participants took two paired speaking tests, one with a shared L1 partner and one with a non-shared L1 partner. Two paired speaking tasks were selected from *B2 First* practice materials (Cambridge English, 2009), and the two tasks were used in a counterbalanced order between the shared and non-shared L1 conditions. The forty learners also took a monologic speaking test. This was to obtain their baseline performance data without any influence of a paired partner. Both the paired and monologic speaking tests were video recorded and double marked by two trained examiners. The paired performance was assessed using the four rating criteria of *B2 First* (i.e. *Grammar and vocabulary, Discourse management, Pronunciation,* and *Interactive communication*), and the monologic performance was assessed using the same rating scales except for *Interactive communication*. Inter-rater reliability between the two raters was relatively high, with Pearson correlations ranging from 0.89 to 0.93. The absolute agreement rate of the two raters was 55.5 per cent (243 of the total 440 score points in total), and the remaining 44.5 per cent (197 scores) fell within one-point difference.

After each paired speaking test, a stimulated recall interview (Gass and Mackey, 2000) was carried out with each of the paired test-takers, to gain insights into the interaction in both shared and non-shared L1 pairings. Using a videorecording of test performance as a stimulus, the test-takers were asked to explain and elaborate on their communicative behaviours to help the researchers to interpret the salient communicative patterns of each pairing.

RESULTS AND ANALYSIS

The listening test scores and paired and monologic speaking test scores were statistically analysed to address RQ1 and RQ2. First, non-parametric Wilcoxon Signed Rank tests were used to examine differences in paired speaking scores between shared and non-shared L1 pairs (RQ1). As presented in Table 10.1, the results show that there was no statistically significant difference for any of the analytic categories in the two types of pairing. This suggests that the type of pairing does not affect the test-takers' paired test scores.

To address RQ2, Spearman correlations were performed to examine the strength of the correlations between the listening test scores and the analytical scores of monologic and paired speaking tests in the whole group, and in shared and non-shared L1 pairs separately. Table 10.2 shows that while none of the correlations between listening and monologic test scores was statistically significant, positive

Table 10.1 Comparison of paired speaking-test scores between the shared and non-shared L1 pairs (N = 40)

Rating category (1–5 points)	Pair type	Median	Mean	SD	Wilcoxon
Grammar and vocabulary	Shared L1	3.50	3.36	1.12	Z = –0.12,
	Non-shared L1	3.50	3.36	1.21	p = .90
Discourse management	Shared L1	3.50	3.13	1.16	Z = –1.90,
	Non-shared L1	3.50	3.45	1.12	p = 0.06
Pronunciation	Shared L1	3.00	3.19	1.16	Z = –0.23,
	Non-shared L1	3.00	3.19	1.10	p = .82
Interactive communication	Shared L1	3.50	3.23	1.20	Z = –0.81,
	Non-shared L1	3.25	3.16	1.28	p = 0.86

Table 10.2 Correlations between listening and speaking scores (N = 40)

	Grammar and vocabulary		Discourse management		Pronunciation		Interactive communication	
Speaking test mode	Mono	Paired	Mono	Paired	Mono	Paired	Mono	Paired
Spearman's rho	0.19	0.32	0.13	0.35	0.19	0.25	–	0.08
Sig.	0.25	0.04	0.44	0.03	0.24	0.13	–	0.63

significant correlations were found between listening and paired speaking scores for *Grammar and vocabulary* (rho = 0.32, p = 0.04) and for *Discourse management* (rho = 0.35, p = 0.03). Although the strength of these correlations was only medium (Cohen, 1998), there seems to be a positive relationship between the learners' listening proficiency and their paired speaking performance displayed for *Grammar and vocabulary* and *Discourse management.*

The same correlational analyses were then carried out for shared and non-shared L1 pairs in the paired test. Interestingly, the identical results were found only for non-shared L1 pairs, but not for shared L1 pairs. As reported in Table 10.3, no significant relationship was found between test-takers' listening and speaking proficiency displayed in paired tests when they were paired in shared L1 pairs. However, their listening proficiency seemed to matter in non-shared L1 pairs for their *Grammar and vocabulary* (rho = 0.37, p = 0.02) and *Discourse management* (rho = 0.38, p = 0.02) scores. That is, although the strength of correlations was only medium, the higher the learners' listening scores were, the higher *Grammar and vocabulary* and *Discourse management* scores they received when they were paired with a different L1 partner.

To address RQ3, all video recordings of paired speaking performance were transcribed following conversation analysis (CA) conventions (Atkinson and Heritage, 1984). CA is a type of discourse analytic approach that Harsch (this volume; cf. also Eskildsen, this volume) also suggests as useful to gain insights into actual 'languaging' instances, and it was carried out to explore communication patterns in the paired tests that were related to test-takers' listening abilities and their L1s. Data from retrospective interviews with test-takers and raters were used to support and elaborate on the researchers' interpretation of the CA analysis. After salient communication patterns were identified in both shared and non-shared L1 patterns, the transcripts were coded by two researchers independently, to count the number of occurrences of each feature and to examine them statistically between the two pair groups. Due to space limitations, only one main difference between shared and non-shared L1 pairs is presented here.

The number of communication breakdowns, the test-takers' attitude towards repairing communication breakdowns, and their success rates seemed different between the two types of pair. Among the entire transcripts of twenty shared and twenty non-shared L1 interactions, twelve communication breakdowns were observed in shared L1 pairs and an attempt to solve the breakdown was made for all twelve cases, all of which were successful. On the other hand, non-shared L1 pairs

Table 10.3 Correlations between listening and paired speaking scores for shared and non-shared L1 pairs (N = 40)

Pair type	Grammar and vocabulary		Discourse management		Pronunciation		Interactive communication	
	shared L1	non-shared L1	shared L1	non-shared L1	shared L1	non-shared L1	shared L1	non-shared L1
Spearman's rho	0.26	0.37	0.26	0.38	0.22	0.22	−0.01	0.14
Sig.	0.10	0.02	0.11	0.02	0.17	0.18	0.97	0.37

encountered as many as twenty-five communication breakdowns, and an attempt to solve the breakdown was observed, however, only for nineteen cases (76 per cent), of which fifteen cases (60 per cent) were successful. That is, non-shared L1 pairs had more than twice as many communication breakdowns as shared L1 pairs, and while 100 per cent of the communication breakdowns were repaired in shared L1 pairs, only 60 per cent were repaired in non-shared L1 pairs. An example of a non-attempt to solve a communication problem in a non-shared L1 pair is exemplified in Excerpt 1 (U08 is an L1 Urdu speaker and T08 is an L1 Thai speaker; see the line with an arrow).

Excerpt 1 *Non-attempt to repair communication breakdown*

```
U08:    er: to become ah:: successful artist it-it basically
        depend upon er:: (.) personality... for person who is
        too shy [ to come and =
T08:           [ mm:: ((frowning))
U08:    = perform in front of many people and especially in
        these days...
→T08:   mm:: ((frowning)) ok my my turn (0.3). hhh in this
        picture
```

Related to the increased level of understanding in shared L1 pairs, it seems that shared L1 pairs understood each other even when a partner's utterance was somewhat confusing – in other words, non-target. For instance, in a Thai L1 pair in Excerpt 2, T19 used the verb *make* instead of the verb *do*. Nonetheless, T20, without even making a clarification request, understood what T19 intended to say, and T20 continued the conversation. In T20's stimulated recall interview, T20 reported, "I knew what she meant. In my language, 'make' and 'do' have the same meaning", indicating that T20's familiarity with the specific variety of English helped her understand T19. Echoing May (2011), the two trained raters in this study also reported that test-takers from the same L1 background seemed to understand each other well, even when they had difficulty in comprehending the talk.

Excerpt 2 *Understanding an utterance with a non-target element*

```
T19:    what do you think about (0.7) er:::: girlfriend and
        (.) boyfriend make something together?
→T20:   i think for girls, they like maybe share feeling or
        talk something
```

It was also noted that misunderstandings occurred in non-shared L1 pairs because of the different cultural backgrounds of the test-takers. Excerpt 3 illustrates miscommunication between U10 (Urdu) and T10

(Thai). T10 suggested that U10 should organise a party to make new friends. U10 then imagined that alcohol would need to be offered at a party, which is not compatible with U10's religious beliefs. In U10's stimulated recall interview, he said, "I am Muslim and our religion doesn't allow us to drink alcohol. I tried to tell my partner about it." However, U10 explained the cause of his unwillingness to organise a party only very implicitly, referring to his lack of skills in arranging parties. T10 did not understand his partner's hidden problem with a party, and proposed that they should move on to a new topic. This example highlights the importance of explicit explanation for successful communication in non-shared L1 pairs.

Excerpt 3 *Misunderstanding due to different cultural backgrounds*

```
U10:   i only have two or three friends
T10:   you- you can do parties if you want to make a lot of
       friends
→U10:  actually problem's that i'm not good at party ha
       ha ha
       .
       .
       (awkward conversation for 16 lines)
       .
T10:   so let's go to the next...
```

Interestingly, there was no instance of speech accommodation as observed in Jenkins's (1997) study. There were two occurrences where two Thai test-takers used L1-influenced back-channelling and an L1 word during the paired test interaction, but both instances were observed in non-shared L1 pairs, and they reported in retrospective interviews that they unconsciously inserted the L1 back-channelling and L1 word.

To summarise the results, there seemed some differences in the construct measured between shared and non-shared L1 pairs. While the construct under the non-shared L1 condition included listening, listening proficiency did not seem to matter under the shared L1 condition. More communication breakdowns and misunderstandings were observed by non-shared L1 pairs, and it seemed harder to repair them. Nevertheless, fairness to test-takers in both pairs was retained, as test scores were not different between the two conditions. These findings will be revisited and interpreted in the Discussion and Conclusions section below in relation to the role of L1 in international tests.

3.2 TEAP: *English Test for Single L1 Test-Takers*

As noted earlier, *TEAP* is a university admissions test in Japan, aiming to assess English skills required by Japanese students to study at the university level in Japan. The *TEAP* Speaking rating scales were therefore developed considering the construct and the use of test scores in this particular context. This section will focus only on its *Pronunciation* scale, and report on how the rating descriptors to be used to assess the single L1 group, Japanese, were developed and validated. Hence, the focus is the *scoring validity* of the *TEAP* Speaking test in relation to the role of L1 in this test.

As was decided from the outset of the project, the CEFR (Council of Europe, 2001) played a central role in designing the *TEAP* test, while making it relevant to the specific Japanese context. To this aim, the test design team built on the CEFR performance descriptors with more descriptors specific to target language use (TLU). In addition to the *Course of Study for High Schools* published by the Japanese government (MEXT, 2008), various rating scales that that were developed for Japanese learners of English such as the Standard Speaking Test rating scales (ALC, 2006) and Kanda English Proficiency Test rating scales (Bonk and Ockey, 2003) informed drafting of the *TEAP* rating scales. Once an early version of the rating scales was drafted, the scales were discussed iteratively between the three test development partners, and based on these discussions, draft rating scales to be used for a pilot study were prepared. The draft scales contained five analytical categories, *Grammatical range and accuracy*, *Lexical range and accuracy*, *Fluency*, *Pronunciation*, and *Interactional Effectiveness*, each of which had four levels (0 = below A2, 1 = A2, 2 = B1, 3 = B2). Of the five scales, this section focuses only on *Pronunciation*. Since the *TEAP* analytic scales are not publicly available, pronunciation descriptors included in the *TEAP* holistic scale are extracted in Table 10.4.

The research questions relevant to the *Pronunciation* scale in this round of a priori validation study are given on the following page.

Table 10.4 Pronunciation descriptors in the TEAP *holistic scale*

B2	Speech easy to understand; accurate stress and intonation; some L1 influence on individual sounds
B1	Speech intelligible; noticeable L1 influence on stress, intonation, and individual sounds
A2	Speech mostly intelligible; heavy L1 influence on stress, intonation, and individual sounds; some mispronunciations impede communication
Below A2	No response OR often unintelligible

Eiken Foundation of Japan (2014).

RQ1: Is there any evidence from test-takers' output language that validates the descriptors used to define the levels on each rating scale?

RQ2: How well is the scoring validity of the *TEAP* Speaking tests supported by the three-facet Multi-faceted Rasch Model (MFRM) analysis (i.e. test-taker, rater, and rating category)?

METHODOLOGY

Twenty-three first-year Japanese university students and three trained raters participated in this study. The three raters were experienced English native speaker teachers at Japanese universities. They all attended a rater training session prior to the pilot test.

All twenty-three students took a trial version of the *TEAP* Speaking test, and all performances were video-recorded, which were then rated by the three trained raters using the draft rating scales. As a method to validate the descriptors used to define the levels on each rating scale, the test-takers' actual speech samples were transcribed and analysed linguistically to address RQ1. Previous studies have employed this approach to validating rating scale descriptors, including Brown (2006) and Iwashita et al. (2008). A variety of linguistic measures were selected to reflect the features of performance relevant to the wording within the draft analytical rating scales, so as to investigate whether these measures differ in relation to the proficiency levels of the test-takers assessed using the rating scales. After that, test scores were analysed using MFRM analysis with the (FACETS) program. The FACETS analysis was carried out with three major facets for the score variance in this study: test-takers, raters, and rating categories. This analysis can identify inconsistencies in test-takers' rating scores, rater severity, and differences in the difficulty levels across the five rating categories.

After the three raters had completed the rating of all recorded performances, they were invited to take part in a focus group session. During the focus group, the raters watched videos of three test-takers once again, and the videos were paused after each task to allow for discussion. The focus group was designed to elicit the raters' reasons for awarding the scores they had given, to provide insights into the rating process(es), and to inform the way in which the results from the linguistic and statistical analyses are interpreted.

RESULTS AND ANALYSIS

Key assessment areas specified in the draft *Pronunciation* scale were intelligibility, prosodic features such as intonation, rhythm, word/

sentence stress, assimilation/elision, and L1 influence. In practice, pronunciation was the hardest category to quantify. Iwashita et al. (2008) employed measures of phonology using specialists' judgements on different phonological features. Brown (2006) dropped phonology analysis because of the difficulty of measurement. Post (2011) used acoustic analysis software to analyse pronunciation features, which is the most accurate way of quantifying pronunciation features. However, it involves extremely labour-intensive work in segmenting and making judgements on each phoneme. Iwashita et al.'s method would have been less labour intensive, but it was not feasible for this project either due to practical constraints. Instead, for the purpose of this study, it was decided to measure only the quantity of L1-influenced (Japanese *katakana*-like) words, by counting the number of obviously L1-influenced words as a percentage of total words produced. Words spoken with noticeable *katakana*-like pronunciation such as inserting extra vowels (e.g. [dogʊ] for [dog]), all syllables evenly stressed without using [ə] or L1 influenced consonants (e.g. [ɹ] for [l], [s] for [θ]) were coded on the transcripts. Examples include

S1–1: and: what's (.) your ah problem [pʊɹobʊɹemʊ] in class.
S2–4: (.) Ah, I: enjoyed (1.5) club [kɹabʊ].

This analysis does not cover all features included in the *Pronunciation* scale, nor does it take it into account that "not all aspects of the English phonological system are equally important for international intelligibility" (Jenkins, 2000; cf. Field, 2005; Tsuzuki and Nakamura, 2009; Sewell, 2013, p. 428). However, it was thought that this measure should tap into the 'intelligibility' and 'L1 influence' aspects of the given rating scale to some extent, which were both important in validating TLU-domain-specific rating descriptors. Approximately 10 per cent of the data were co-coded by another researcher for inter-coder reliability.

Table 10.5 presents the results, showing the extent to which the analysed feature differs between the adjacent levels of the rating scales. Since there was only one student who scored 1 in *Pronunciation*, the analysis combined Levels 1 and 2 students together as one category and compared the group with the Level 3 students. The Level 3 students showed less L1 influence (Mean = 1.14 per cent) than the Level 1 and 2 students (Mean = 1.38 per cent). The results therefore indicated that the L1 influence measure exhibited a change in the expected direction, providing evidence that the rating descriptors on L1 influence are functioning in a way congruent with the test designers' intention.

Table 10.5 Pronunciation features in two proficiency levels (%)

Focus	Measure	Level	N	Min	Max	Mean	SD
L1 influence	Percentage of words pronounced with L1 influence	Level 1 + 2 (A2 and B1)	1 + 15	0.00	8.00	1.38	2.00
		Level 3 (B2)	7	0.00	4.00	1.14	1.35

Table 10.6 Rating category measurement report

Rating category	Fair Average	Measure	Real S.E.	Infit MnSq
Pronunciation	2.07	−0.74	0.31	1.19
Interactional Effectiveness	2.07	−0.74	0.30	1.06
Fluency	1.97	0.08	0.29	0.86
Lexical range and accuracy	1.91	0.57	0.29	1.01
Grammatical range and accuracy	1.87	0.83	0.30	0.75

Regarding the FACETS analysis, we present only the analysis related to five rating categories in Table 10.6. Of relevance to the focus of this section is the second column, Fair Average (which indicates expected average raw score values transformed from the Rasch measure). The analysis showed that the five rating categories exhibited different degrees of difficulty and these differences were statistically significant ($X^2(4) = 23.5, p < 0.005$). In particular, *Pronunciation* and *Interactional Effectiveness* were found to be easier than the other scales.

In the post-rating focus group discussion with the three raters, one of the topics was whether the difficulty level of *Pronunciation* and *Interactional Effectiveness* should be increased to be more aligned to the other scales. However, unlike the *Interactional Effectiveness* descriptors for which ambiguous wording was identified for revising, the raters agreed that changes to wording in the *Pronunciation* scale was not necessary. 'Intelligibility' is central to the construct of pronunciation defined in this rating scale. As Issacs (2008) noted, intelligibility is an 'evasive' concept that is hard to pin down, and a lot of the discussion with raters concerned what 'intelligible' means and how to interpret 'impeding communication' (cf. Wicaksono, this volume). Raters felt that they were able to understand the test-takers because of their familiarity with Japanese speakers' pronunciation of English. They were concerned about whether this would also apply to 'unsympathetic' or 'naïve' listeners. However, the TLU domain for *TEAP* is the EFL context in Japanese universities. Students in the context will be interacting with tutors and peer students who are obviously familiar with pronunciation features that are typical of Japanese EFL learners. Given the target context, it was felt that it was appropriate to judge students' pronunciation on the basis of raters' own ease of understanding that pronunciation. That is, while descriptors on L1 influence seemed to function well, being lenient about the impact of L1 influence on intelligibility and communication effectiveness was perfectly justified. As such, the *TEAP* Speaking test embraces the English variety spoken by Japanese speakers, reflecting the construct of the test and the usage of the test scores.

4 Discussion and Conclusions

Following the description of the socio-cognitive framework for developing and validating speaking tests (Weir, 2005; Taylor, 2011), this chapter has exemplified two studies that highlight the different roles of the L1 in speaking tests. It is believed that the *TEAP* Speaking rating scale offered an example of reconciling notions of 'standard' English with local English norms and features. In contrast, the *B2 First* example showed the complexity in treating L1-related issues in a valid and fair manner in international examinations. Given the increased number of communication breakdowns in non-shared L1 pairings in the paired discussion part of *B2 First*, it would be indeed interesting if non-shared L1 pairs were always formed for such General English tests "to examine [test-takers'] ability to negotiate their own dialectal differences in conversation" (Canagarajah, 2006, p. 239). However, its practicality is highly questionable, since such international tests are administered all over the world, and most of the learners who take a test in their home country are likely to share the same L1. In addition, as Field (2018, p. 60) notes, "the ability to decode strongly accented speech is not a matter of adjusting immediately and flexibly to unfamiliar features, but the result of a period of exposure that is often a matter of chance". Therefore, having only non-shared L1 pairings does not guarantee that the test can measure a more consistent construct. Some learners may happen to be familiar with the particular variety of English spoken by their paired partners, while others may not. And this is essentially impossible to control in large-scale international examination contexts. Taylor (2006, p. 58) pointed out more than a decade ago that testing is "the art of the possible". As discussed previously in conjunction with the socio-cognitive framework for test development and validation, what is important is that every component of 'the possible' is selected in a principled and justifiable way. This is in line with Harsch's argument (this volume) for the necessity of 'pragmatic' decisions that we have to make.

However, this does not mean that international language examination boards have neglected advances in research on World Englishes and English as a Lingua Franca. Most language tests and language benchmark standards no longer make reference to Native Speaker competence (Taylor, 2006: 52; see also Harsch, this volume, about recent changes made in the 2018 CEFR Companion Volume). Furthermore, many interactive speaking tests in interview, paired, and group speaking formats now have a scale to measure *interactional competence* (e.g. Young, 2011), which is "the ability to co-construct interaction in a purposeful and meaningful way, taking into account socio-cultural and pragmatic dimensions of the speech situation and event" (Galaczi and Taylor, 2018, p. 226). Example descriptors that have operationalised the construct of interactional competence include:

- Initiates and responds appropriately, linking contributions to those of other speakers; maintains and develops the interaction and negotiates towards an outcome (Interactive communication scale, *B2 First*).
- Fulfils the task very well; initiates and responds with effective turn-taking; effectively maintains and develops the interaction; solves communication problems naturally, if any (Communicative effectiveness scale, Trinity's *Integrated Skills in English II*).

It is believed that these descriptors are in line with and benefited from a body of research in World Englishes and English as Lingua Franca, valuing what learners can do with their individual communicative resources.

As discussed thus far, the negotiation of the local and global dimension of the English language is a challenging task to address in international examinations (cf. Sewell, 2013). However, a new initiative taken by the British Council's Aptis test seems to suggest a possible way for international examination boards to attempt to reconcile the notions of 'standard' English with local language norms and features and to reconceptualise the role of the L1 in their tests. O'Sullivan (2011) argues for the need for 'localisation' of assessment systems when the conditions of a test are found to be appropriate. He states that localisation is appropriate especially when a test is used to make specific claims about a particular population in a particular domain or context. Namely, when test scores are not meant to be generalised beyond a specific context, such as within a company or a university, then the test that is designed to reflect features of that context (e.g. in the use of visuals, specific language, or cultural references) is far more likely to work, and Aptis was developed to take localisation into account when the conditions are met. O'Sullivan and Dunlea (2015, p. 8) describe different degrees of localisation, and the localisation scheme seems to indicate that Aptis can be localised to reflect local language norms and features. The test also uses the socio-cognitive framework as its validation framework, and special care is taken for test localisation not to undermine the validity of a test or put at risk fairness for test-takers. While we should bear in mind that the test scores generated from localised tests are meaningful only within the specific context for which the tests were localised, this approach taken by the British Council appears to take us a step forward in reconceptualising the role of the L1 in English language testing.

References

ALC. (2006). Standard speaking tests. Available online from www.alc.co.jp/edusys/sst/english.html

Atkinson, J. M. and Heritage, J. (1984). *Structures of Social Action*. Cambridge: Cambridge University Press.

Bonk, W. J. and Ockey, G. J. (2003). A many-facet Rasch analysis of the second language group oral discussion task. *Language Testing*, 20(1), 89–110.

Brown, A. (2006). Candidate discourse in the revised IELTS Speaking Test. *IELTS Research Report*, 6, 71–89.

Cambridge English. (2008). *Cambridge Preliminary English Test: Official Examination Papers from University of Cambridge ESOL Examinations (PET Practice Tests)*. Cambridge: Cambridge University Press.

Cambridge English. (2009). *Cambridge First Certificate in English: Official Examination Papers from University of Cambridge ESOL Examinations (FCE Practice Tests)*. Cambridge: Cambridge University Press.

Cambridge English. (2018a). Cambridge English First (FCE). Available online from www.cambridgeenglish.org/exams-and-tests/first/

Cambridge English. (2018b). Grade statistics. Available online from http://gradestatistics.cambridgeenglish.org/2016/fce.html

Canagarajah, S. (2006). Changing communicative needs, revised assessment objectives: Testing English as an international language. *Language Assessment Quarterly*, 3(3), 229–242.

Cohen, J. (1998). *Statistical Power Analysis for the Behavioural Sciences*. Hillsdale, MI: Erlbaum.

Council of Europe. (2001). *Common European Framework of Reference for Languages: Learning, Teaching, Assessment*. Cambridge: Cambridge University Press.

Eiken Foundation of Japan. (2014) *TEAP* Speaking rating scales. Available online from www.eiken.or.jp/teap/construct/sp_rating_crit.html

Field, J. (2005). Intelligibility and the listener: The role of lexical stress. *TESOL Quarterly, 39*, 399–423.

Field, J. (2018). *Rethinking the Second Language Listening Test: From Theory to Practice*. Sheffield: Equinox.

Galaczi, E. D. and Taylor, L. (2018). Interactional competence: Conceptualisations, operationalisations, and outstanding questions. *Language Assessment Quarterly, 15*(3), 219–236.

Gass, S. M. and Mackey, A (2000). *Stimulated Recall Methodology in Second Language Research*. Mahwah, NJ: Lawrence Erlbaum.

Geranpayeh, A. and Taylor, L., eds. (2013). *Examining Listening: Research and Practice in Assessing Second Language Listening*. Cambridge: UCLES/Cambridge University Press.

Issacs, T. (2008). Towards defining a valid assessment criterion of pronunciation proficiency in non-native English speaking graduate students. *Canadian Modern Language Review, 64*, 555–580.

Iwashita, N., Brown, A., McNamara, T., and O'Hagan, S. (2008). Assessed levels of second language speaking proficiency: How distinct? *Applied Linguistics, 29*(1), 24–29.

Jaiyote, S. (2016). The relationship between test-takers' first language, listening proficiency and their performance on paired speaking tests. Unpublished PhD thesis, University of Bedfordshire.

Jenkins, J. (1997). Testing pronunciation in communicative exams. In M. Vaughan-Rees, ed., *A Special Issue of Speak Out! Bringing Together the Interests of the IATEFL Pronunciation and Testing Sigs*, pp. 7–11.

Jenkins, J. (2000). *The Phonology of English as an International Language*. Oxford: Oxford University Press.

Khalifa, H. and Weir, C. J. (2009). *Examining Reading: Research and Practice in Assessing Second Language Reading*. Cambridge: UCLES/Cambridge University Press.

May, L. (2011). *Interaction in a Paired Speaking Test*. Frankfurt am Main: Peter Lang.

Messick, S. (1989). Validity. In R. L. Linn, ed., *Educational Measurement*, 3rd ed. London and New York: McMillan.

Messick, S. (1996). Validity and washback in language testing. *Language Testing, 13*, 241–256.

MEXT. (2008). The course of study for upper secondary school. Available online from www.mext.go.jp/a_menu/shotou/new-cs/index.htm

Nakatsuhara, F. (2012). The relationship between test-takers' listening proficiency and their performance on the IELTS Speaking Test. In L. Taylor and C. J. Weir, eds., *IELTS Collected Papers 2: Research in Reading and Listening Assessment* (pp. 519–573). Cambridge: UCLES/Cambridge University Press.

Nakatsuhara, F. (2014). A research report on the development of the Test of English for Academic Purposes (TEAP) Speaking Test for Japanese university entrants – Study 1 and Study 2. Available online from www.eiken.or.jp/teap/group/pdf/teap_speaking_report1.pdf

Nakatsuhara, F. and Jaiyote, S. (2015). Exploring the impact of test-takers' L1 backgrounds on paired speaking test performance: How do they perform in shared and non-shared L1 pairs? *Paper presented at the BAAL/CUP Applied Linguistics Seminar*. York St John University, 24–26 June 2015.

National Centre for University Entrance Examinations. (2017). Transition in the number of applicants. Available online from www.dnc.ac.jp/data/suii/suii.html

O'Sullivan, B. (2011). Introduction – Professionalisation, localisation and fragmentation in language testing. In B. O'Sullivan, ed., *Language Testing: Theory and Practice* (pp. 1–12). Oxford: Palgrave.

O'Sullivan, B. and Dunlea, J. (2015). Aptis Genearal Techinical Manual Ver 1.0 TR/2015/005. Available online from www.britishcouncil.org/sites/default/files/aptis_general_technical_manual_v-1.0.pdf

O'Sullivan, B. and Weir, C. J. (2011). Test development and validation. In B. O'Sullivan, ed., *Language Testing: Theories and Practices* (pp. 13–32). Basingstoke: Palgrave Macmillan.

Post, B. (2011). Using acoustic analysis software to analyse L2 pronunciation features. *Paper presented at the 3rd BAALTEASIG Conference*. University of Warwick.

Seedhouse, P. and Egbert, M. (2006). The interactional organisation of the IELTS Speaking Test. *IELTS Research Report, 6*, 161–205.

Sewell, A. (2013). Language testing and international intelligibility: A Hong Kong case study. *Language Assessment Quarterly, 10*(4), 423–443.

Shaw, S. D. and Weir, C. J. (2007). *Examining Writing: Research and Practice in Assessing Second Language Writing*. Cambridge: UCLES/Cambridge University Press.

Tanaka, C. (2018, June 13). Private-sector test results to account for 20% of national university English entrance exam scores. *The Japan Times*. Available online from www.japantimes.co.jp/news/2018/06/13/national/private-sector-test-results-account-20-national-university-english-entrance-exam-scores/#.W5aI8uhKhAk

Taylor, L. (2006). The changing landscape of English: Implications for English language assessment. *ELT Journal, 60*(1), 51–60.

Taylor, L., ed. (2011). *Examining Speaking: Research and Practice in Assessing Second Language Speaking*. Cambridge: UCLES/Cambridge University Press.

Tsuzuki, M. and Nakamura, S. (2009). Intelligibility assessment of Japanese accents. In T. Hoffmann and L. Siebers, eds., *World Englishes: Problems, Properties and Prospects* (pp. 239–261). Amsterdam: John Benjamins.

Weir, C. J. (2005). *Language Testing and Validation: An Evidence-Based Approach*. Basingstoke: Palgrave Macmillan.

Young, R. (2011). Interactional Competence in Language Learning, Teaching, and Testing. In E. Hinkel, ed., *Handbook of Research in Second Language Teaching and Learning Volume II* (pp. 426–443). New York: Routledge.

11 *Mind the Gap*
Dis/Continuities in the UK Assessment of L1 English Language

AngelaGoddard

1 Introduction

This chapter explores how the subject of L1 English Language is currently assessed in England at different stages of learning, drawing on official requirements as set out by the United Kingdom Department for Education (DfE), on test papers and assessment arrangements devised by the Standards and Testing Agency (STA), on the subject criteria as defined by the exams regulator for English qualifications (Ofqual), and on the qualifications that have been developed by the various exam boards, termed 'Awarding Bodies' or 'Awarding Organisations', within the United Kingdom.

1.1 What Can Be Learned from Looking at Assessment?

Assessment vehicles arguably offer just as much insight into how L1 English is taught and learned as studies of curriculum requirements. This is because school league tables have focused schools on their exam results and turned assessment into the unwitting driver of curriculum planning and teaching rather than the endpoint (thus continuing to shape and perpetuate Hall's category of N-ENGLISH, this volume). You don't have to look very far to see evidence of this: a brief trawl of courses for teachers and of school textbooks will show you that 'success' is all about getting more students higher grades in their respective tests. This is a reversal of how things are supposed to work: success in assessment is supposed to be the outcome from rich experiences of learning with teachers who are passionate about education and about their subject (see Roberts, this volume). However, this topsy-turvy situation should not be surprising. The 2010 OECD report *Education at a Glance* found that school accountability based on student test results "can be a powerful tool for changing teacher and school behaviour but it often creates unintended strategic behaviour" (Rosenkvist, 2010, p. 1). The strategy of 'teaching to the test', or, as Manchester University's Chair of Educational Assessment describes it rather more graphically, "the grotesque caricature of teaching as coaching" is exactly this kind of unintended outcome (Boyle, response to Ward, 2017).

There is a further consideration that lends weight to the idea of extrapolating from assessment to how the learning and teaching of L1 English is conceptualised in practice, and therefore how the subject itself is understood. In its inception, the National Curriculum for English (NCE) (cf. Goodwyn, this volume; Roberts, this volume) was supposed to be a statement of entitlement for all. But while the curriculum covered state education within England, Wales, and Northern Ireland, there was never a requirement for private or public schools to follow it. Since then, other types of school outside of local authority control, including free schools and academies, do not have to adhere to the National Curriculum. However, all these different types of school still need to enter their pupils for publicly recognised assessments: to do otherwise would be detrimental both to the school's credibility and to the interests of their students. Assessment, then, could be seen as a rare point of commonality in an increasingly fragmented educational landscape. This commonality has in fact intensified within the secondary school sector since the current government excluded International General Certificate of Secondary Education (iGCSEs) – previously preferred by some independent, fee-paying schools – from being credited in league tables.

1.2 Assessment across the United Kingdom

The commonality of assessments only goes so far, however. Devolved parts of the United Kingdom (Scotland, Wales, and Northern Ireland) have developed their own distinctive approaches to the assessment of L1 English, and these may or may not mirror those of England either in frequency or nature. For example, there are currently no Standard Attainment Tests (SATs) in Scotland or Wales; and in Northern Ireland, teacher assessments at the end of Key Stage 1 (Year 2) and 2 (Year 6) subsume 'English' within a cross-curricular framework of communication skills, information technology (IT), and maths.

Assessment arrangements are also constantly on the move (or not) within the different parts of the United Kingdom, producing even more diversity but also more inflexibility and educational 'silos'. Pupils in the devolved areas are now required to take the qualifications offered by their own national exam boards, which means that learners are constrained by whatever conceptualisation of English exists in their own particular part of the United Kingdom. To give one example of this disparity, in Northern Ireland, L1 English AS/A level is a single subject – English literature; in England, it is three subjects – English literature, English language, and English language and literature.

In the face of all these complexities, it is clear that the United Kingdom cannot be discussed as if it were a single entity in terms of assessing L1 English. In research terms, we need to resist any idea of a UK 'grand narrative' and focus on specific, situated contexts in order to arrive at any meaningful description of language policy and practice.

1.3 Aims and Method

Given the complexity of the picture described earlier, this chapter takes a specific approach in order to offer some insights into the models of L1 English Language that lie behind its assessment at the different stages of schooling. The overall aim is to tell the 'story' of L1 English Language assessment as it unfolds through the lifespan of a notional learner in a school in England, drawing on the evidence outlined in the opening paragraph.

Of course, in reality a learner takes many years to progress through the school system, during which time there are likely to be many changes both to curricula for L1 English and to their assessment. So the notional learner at the centre of this chapter is a convenient fiction for thinking about what L1 English language currently 'means' at all those stages simultaneously. However, what this method intends to show is how the various models of L1 English relate to each other: are there elements of continuity and progression within a single model of L1 English? Or is each stage of assessment based on a different understanding of the subject, resulting in multiple shifts of gear? And most importantly of all, how might the subject be experienced by our notional learner? What story of English is being told?

2 *Once Upon a Time*: Key Stage 1 (Age 5–7) Assessments

Key Stage 1 assessments of English language are in three parts:

1. a 'phonics check'
2. a reading comprehension test
3. an English grammar, punctuation, and spelling test (which is now optional).

2.1 The Phonics Check

English primary schools are required to run an assessment termed a 'phonics check' on their Year 1 pupils towards the end of the first year of their compulsory schooling. Pupils who fail – which currently means scoring less than thirty-two out of forty – have to take another test in Year 2. The test is designed to assess pupils' reading skills.

There isn't space here to offer detailed coverage of the extensive literature on how young children learn to read and on how they are best supported in acquiring literacy skills. Instead, I refer readers to the useful overview in Richmond (2015). What can be stated here as a kind of 'headline' is that there is an overwhelming consensus in research that reading involves a range of skills all operating together, of which awareness of the sounds of spoken language and of grapho-phonemic relationships forms a part. A beginning reader draws on many aspects of knowledge in order to determine the meaning of a text, including not only grapho-phonemic, semantic, lexical, morphological, and syntactic information, but also important contextual factors such as the nature and purpose of the text, its visual design, where the text came from, and so on. And these days, of course, we are talking not just about reading matter in the traditional sense of books, but also digital texts of all kinds. Over thirty years ago, Rumelhart conceptualised the act of reading written texts as "simultaneous, multi-level interactive processing" (cited in Lightfoot and Martin, 1988, p. 75) and, after countless studies of reading behaviour over the years, this definition still holds good.

Unfortunately, the United Kingdom Department for Education (DfE) has eschewed notions of this complexity in its adoption of a model of literacy learning termed 'the simple view of reading' (SVR), which underlies the DfE's Primary National Strategy and associated assessments. The SVR model sees reading as a simple decoding process, and emphasises phonic awareness, hence the early 'phonics check'. The model also sees word recognition and language comprehension as separable and therefore assessable in isolation.

To take phonics first: there is, of course, nothing wrong with a teacher assessing a child's phonic awareness. But unfortunately, a particular model of phonics dominates both the assessment of reading and the learning process itself. This is 'systematic synthetic phonics' that, according to the Department for Education, should be "the prime approach used in the teaching of early reading" (Department for Education, 2006, p. 54).

Synthetic phonics takes as its starting point the phonemes of English (in the sense of Hall's 'P-ENGLISH', this volume) and maps these to one or more written letters in a set order that is highly regulated. Once a number of these have been taught, they are combined to make words, with pre-selected lists of words ensuring that the sound-to-symbol correspondences hold. These words are supplemented by the inclusion of invented words in order to reinforce the idea of the correspondence. This means that a young reader will be presented with words that don't exist, sometimes involving sequences of letters that a reader would be unlikely to see in an English word, such as *arnd*. So enamoured was the UK government of this scheme that from 2010 to 2015, matched funding of up to £3,000 was offered to schools that bought approved phonics teaching materials from a particular catalogue and/or that sent teachers to be trained by approved experts listed in the same catalogue. Extreme versions of this scheme actually prohibit children from reading texts beyond the scheme itself until a certain stage has been reached. This is a prime example of what Goodwyn (this volume) refers to as "regulation by the nation state".

The problems associated with the idea of synthetic phonics and its assessment are legion. First, the assumption that acquiring reading competence is a bottom-up process of building from micro-skills into larger frameworks of understanding is deeply flawed.

Those who defend synthetic phonics often justify it as a way to address the issue of poor reading skills in young children. But as a system operating in isolation for learners to rely on, synthetic phonics becomes unreliable very quickly when applied to real texts, because of the complex interrelationships that exist between the twenty-six alphabetic letters and the forty-four or so phonemes of Standard British English. Therefore, there is a danger that if pupils are given an overwhelmingly phonics-based diet, they will be unable to develop and draw on the many other resources needed to become fluent readers. Moreover, if pupils are not at a stage where the 'rules' they are being taught make sense and can be applied, they are unlikely to make progress: "Yes, there are phonic rules, regularities in written English, but to teach them out of context and in advance is to put the analytical cart before the competence-based horse" (Richmond, 2015, p. 39).

There is another issue that also potentially affects children who are progressing normally or even excelling in their literacy development. The idea of being presented with invented words at exactly the same time as learning new, real, ones is likely to be a very confusing experience for learners, especially if the non-real words have odd sequences of letters that cannot be connected with patterns elsewhere in the English spelling system.

Some examples are needed at this point. In the 2016 test, the non-real words included *rird, woats, jigh,* and *shup,* while in 2017, *jash, zued*, *coid*, and *meve* appeared. Because the test is one where pupils have to sound out the words they are presented with, teachers have to check their pupils' articulations against an 'acceptable' list of pronunciations in the mark scheme. This process has echoes of elocution lessons in the days when Received Pronunciation (RP) was perceived as the desired accent to aspire to. Readers who are familiar with some of the regional varieties of English accent within the United Kingdom will recognise that regionally accented speakers in the south-west pronounce /r/ in postvocalic positions; that speakers with a Newcastle upon Tyne accent will say /ɜ/ for /əʊ/; that many northern accents have no /ʌ/ phoneme; and that certain words with an *a* in the spelling are realised as /ɑ/ in RP but /æ/ in some regional accents. So a pupil with a regional accent from the south-west will pronounce the second /r/ in *rird* while an RP speaker will not; *woats* would be /wəʊts/ in RP but /wɜts/ in Newcastle; *shup* would be /shʌp/ in RP but /shʊp/ for some northern speakers; and, if pupils are operating beyond the scope of synthetic phonics and are aware of the *lack* of correspondence between some sounds and symbols in English words, the vowel in *jash* could resemble that in *wash* and *squash*, or in *dash* and *bash* by speakers anywhere in the United Kingdom. Some regional variations are classified as 'acceptable' in the mark schemes, but there is a sense of special dispensation in the very fact of having to say this. Even more bizarre is the fact that some variations are allowed when pronouncing the pseudo-words but none is allowed at all for the real words. This phonics test is a practical illustration of Hall's N-LANGUAGE category in action (this volume).

Richmond (2015, p. 39) sees the fundamental problem of the check as follows:

It utterly fails to represent everything we know about how a successful five- and six year old reader should be operating. And it utterly fails to detect a failing five- and six year old reader, because to be able to pronounce isolated, phonically regular words, half of them non-existent, is no guarantee of being able to read in the sense of being able to make sense of meaningful print.

Richmond also sees the effects of the check as far reaching in terms of how English is taught, referring to instances where pupils are given nonsense words to take home and 'learn' for their homework:

The Year 1 phonics check is a triumph of ideology over reason. Apart from its shortcomings as a brief experience for a child on a particular day in June, its existence has already had a distorting effect on the teaching of reading in many classrooms in the months leading up to that day. The check will one day be looked back on with a mixture of mirth, embarrassment and regret. It should be abolished.

(2015, p. 40)

2.2 The Reading Comprehension Test

This consists of two papers, each with a mixture of fiction and non-fiction texts, with questions to be answered on each text. The SVR rationale for this material would stress its objective nature as a test of decoding skill: can the written words be recognised by a reader and the appropriate information located? But, as Dombey (2008) points out, there is more to reading than this mechanical process:

> The extent to which batteries of 'objective' questions posed on short passages can assess a child's capacity to make sense of more demanding texts such as a long story or a detailed account of global warming has been called into question (e.g. Paris and Stahl, 2005). These kinds of texts require more than decoding and listening comprehension. They need skilled reading.

The notion of 'skilled reading' includes aspects of genre; for example, how the language of fiction and non-fiction texts differ, how these genres organize their information differently, how they have a different relationship to real world events, and so on. The skill to perceive such differences takes a considerable time to develop, and some of the particular language features characteristic of certain types of writing, for example passive verb structures in non-fiction and in scientific writing more generally, are acquired late in children's literacy development (see Perera, 1984, for a thorough scholarly treatment of this topic). In the Department for Education's 2015 sample materials, showing teachers the kinds of texts their pupils will be expected to deal with, a non-fiction text called *Plastics and the Environment* begins as in Figure 11.1.

Even in this short extract, there are four passive verb structures, an example of grammatical ellipsis, four uses of a modal verb, a rare use of a determiner with a noun that we normally encounter as non-count (*a plastic*), and some complex cohesion ("a plastic", "plastic", "plastics"). These features may be characteristic of non-fiction texts but to expect seven year-olds to cope with material such as this is extremely unfair. In concentrating on the level of word recognition, then, the test creator has effectively ignored some significant aspects of difficulty in other aspects of language use.

Unfortunately, the non-fiction texts are never attributed to specific authors, so we are unable to know whether they have any grounding themselves in assessing levels of reading difficulty – or, in fact, whether they have any pedagogic experience at all. A very different situation obtains for the fiction texts, where extracts are taken from published stories. This situation similarly ignores an aspect of larger context for language use, in this case the fact that pupils may already know the

---

What is a plastic?

Plastic is a material we all use every day. The first plastics were made more than 100 years ago from the parts of plants.

Plastics can be useful for people but bad for the planet. Here are some of the reasons.

Good points	Bad points
Plastics can be shaped into almost anything	Plastics can be difficult to recycle
Plastics can be produced in different colours	Plastics are made from oil, which is running out

---

Figure 11.1 An extract from the Reading Comprehension Test

story from their own personal reading. Again, perhaps a foregrounding of the notion of word recognition blinds the test-setters to the larger question about whether knowing the story in the first place is an advantage. The tests are, after all, not supposed to be tests of how well endowed a child's household is for reading matter – or are they?

What the tests certainly all are at this initial stage is a learning experience for children about how tests work. The tests come with very explicit instructions to teachers about administration, including both the physical aspects of how children should be arranged and the psychological aspects of what teachers are allowed to express and how they should interact with pupils. This includes keeping pupils focused on how to arrive at the 'correct' answer, according to the mark schemes. Guidance is given to pupils via teachers talking them through some sample answers to questions, showing pupils what would be a good answer and what would be seen as incorrect. For example, in the 2015 sample materials, a further non-fiction text, entitled *The World of Ants*, has an introductory picture of ants around a hole in the ground and then the text in Figure 11.2.

Question 2 of the test asks pupils to find and copy two places you might see ants. The teacher is told to accept 'garden', 'park', 'pavement', and 'underground' but to tell pupils that if they write "in a hole" this would be wrong because this information has been taken from the picture and "not the text". In the SVR model, word recognition is all, and inferences from any of the cues we normally use as readers are therefore wrong (see Canagarajah's discussion of

Ants are insects that you can often see in a garden, in a park, or just on the pavement. They usually live underground.

Figure 11.2 Another extract from the Reading Comprehension Test

logocentrism, this volume). The assessment's logocentrism is a strangely reductive and narrow idea about how meanings are made, a world away from the rich semiotic, multimodal environments we all experience in everyday life as soon as we go online, and is severely at odds with long-standing academic scholarship about modern text and discourse analysis (for example, see Kress, 2003; Gillen, 2014; Goddard and Carey, 2017). Canagarajah (this volume) usefully refers to the idea of 'assemblage' as the core of meaning making, a notion that goes back to Bakhtinian ideas of 'bricolage' (Bakhtin, 1981).

2.3 The Grammar, Punctuation, and Spelling Test

The spelling part of this test, which was due to be sat for the first time by pupils in May 2016, was mistakenly uploaded to the website of the DfE's own Standards and Testing Agency in January of that year, and since then the whole test has been optional. Institutional embarrassment and ineptitude are only part of the story, however. This test, along with its Key Stage 2 equivalent (see later), which was also accidentally published before it was due to be sat in May 2016, has attracted widespread criticism from parents and education professionals for a number of reasons, including being too demanding and, to use Richmond's earlier expression, for putting the "analytical cart before the competence-based horse". In other words, in the grammar test particularly, children are being asked to analyse language before they can use it with any confidence. In 2016, a groundswell of resistance came from parents, many of whom took their children out of school at the point when the tests were due to be taken; and there were many reports of distress among pupils taking the tests. Similar concerns being reported in 2017 saw headteachers claiming that the whole culture of testing was causing widespread mental health problems among their pupils. Weale (2017) quotes headteachers' examples of children presenting with sleeplessness, bouts of sobbing, low self-esteem, fear of academic failure, depression, anxiety, and loss of eyelashes through stress.

Meanwhile, in 2017, the parliamentary cross-party Education Select Committee reported its own findings on the SATs assessments in primary schools. Their many criticisms went beyond the nature and administration of the tests themselves to include broader questions about the distorting effects that such 'high stakes' tests have clearly had on the whole sector. Using the test results in school performance tables, the committee says, has unbalanced the curriculum and given English too much emphasis in terms of teaching time at the expense of other subjects and activities; also, that undue pressure has been put on pupils to pass the tests for reasons beyond their own development.

In theory, education professionals within the English academic area ought to have welcomed the increased time being devoted to their subject. But this is far from the case, because there are concerns about how that extra time is being spent. For example, in giving evidence to the Select Committee, Dominic Wyse, Professor of Education at UCL (London University) Institute of Education, saw serious problems for children's literacy development in the separation of grammar, spelling, and punctuation from other aspects of English (Wyse, 2017). He outlines 'two major flaws' in the statutory tests conducted in 2016 'and for some years previously':

1. the undue separation of the composition of writing from the transcription elements of grammar, spelling and punctuation;
2. an undue emphasis on decontextualised grammatical knowledge. Both of these flawed features of assessment are contrary to research evidence.

Michael Rosen sees the emphasis on 'SPaG' (the acronym that has come to stand for the focus on and testing of spelling, punctuation, and grammar) as changing the way the whole area of English language is seen, leading to mistaken ideas among pupils about what is valuable and interesting to know about. He sees it both as a waste of 'mind space' within individuals and as misleading in the expectation it gives pupils about how to be good communicators (Rosen, 2016). In essence, the idea of language as an expressive resource is being replaced by N- and P-LANGUAGE abstractions (see Hall, this volume), with an emphasis on the 'secretarial' aspects of communication (see Goodwyn, this volume).

3 *The Emperor's New Clothes*: Key Stage 2 (Age 7–11) Assessments

These SATs are taken by children at the end of Year 6 (age 10–11), which is in effect the end of their primary schooling. The tests are more elaborate in every way than their Key Stage 1 predecessors, including the following:

1. A reading comprehension test, which in 2017 consisted of thirty-nine questions across three texts of different kinds (two fiction extracts and a non-fiction piece). Pupils have one hour to complete the test.
2. A spelling test, where pupils are given a booklet of written sentences with gaps. The teacher reads out a word that pupils have to insert and spell correctly in the gaps. There are twenty sentences and the test lasts for 15 minutes.
3. A grammar and punctuation test lasting 45 minutes and, in 2017, containing fifteen questions.
4. An assessment of pupils' writing based on teachers' evaluations with reference to set criteria.

Some of the problems associated with these assessments have already been rehearsed, and have simply been amplified in these more challenging tests. We are beyond synthetic phonics at this point, but the SVR is alive and well in the reading test; the fiction extracts are from published stories that more literate households might well have encountered; and assessment of SPaG consists of decontextualised batteries of questions and tasks. Again, the level of preparation for, and management of, the assessments by the government's Standards and Testing Agency has been called into question. For example, two-thirds of moderators (people who guide teachers and set the standards for how to assess pupils' writing) themselves failed to assess three portfolios of children's writing accurately in their 2017 training. Some of the 2,547 moderators described the marking system as "crude", "ridiculous", and a "farce" (Ward, 2017).

Most widespread public concern has focused on the SPaG test, however, particularly the nature and extent of the grammatical terms that Year 6 pupils are expected to know. The Key Stage 1 equivalent test required pupils to punctuate sentences; fill in appropriate conjunctions; understand word classes (noun, verb, adjective, adverb), suffixes, noun phrases, verb tenses, and singular and plural nouns. The Key Stage 2 requirements go much further, including determiners, main and subordinate clauses, relative and possessive pronouns, prepositions, subjects and objects, modal verbs, verb voice, mood and aspect, colons, and semicolons. Tim Oates, a key government adviser on the new national curriculum that was developed in 2014, admitted in 2016 that there had been "a genuine problem about undue complexity in demand" in terms of the metalanguage that children are required to know, stating that "naming grammatical constructions is being studied just as something in its own right that needs to be remembered" (Wiggins, 2016). David Crystal has stated that "the SPaG test, and the view of language lying behind it, turns the clock back half a century" (cited in Mansell, 2017).

Given the focus of this volume on ontologies of English, reference to "the view of language lying behind [the SPaG test]" is key. The view that Crystal refers to conceptualises language, not as a form of social behaviour or anything to do with communication (Hall's LANGUAGING, this volume), but rather as an abstract set of narrowly defined grammatical rules referring to written English but originally derived from the study of Latin (P-LANGUAGE following N-LANGUAGE norms). UK public school and grammar school classrooms in the previous century were awash with decontextualised grammatical exercises with highly prescriptive, right-or-wrong answers. This approach, of course, suits a testing system that wants something easy to measure, even if what is being measured has no real value to the individuals concerned. Unfortunately, some aspects of language study invite that kind of deployment all too easily. This is the territory of 'the emperor's new clothes': belief in the study of something at all costs, no matter how ill conceived the enterprise is. And knowing about grammar has that veneer of social status regardless of its usefulness: the opulence of the clothes that the emperor believes he is wearing.

It is problematic enough that the decontextualised approach to language is being exhumed from former times. But at Key Stages 1 and 2, there are many aspects of knowledge about language that pupils would find exciting and intriguing – that they would actually be able to demonstrate knowledge of, rather than associating language with difficulty and failure. The government-funded Language in the National Curriculum (LINC) project (1989–1992), which trained all primary language co-ordinators and all secondary heads of English in knowledge about language, collected many examples of pupils highly engaged with language topics, from the language of their regional communities to the history of place names, and from the language of puzzles, games, and jokes to the patterns of poetry (see, for example, Carter, 1991). Young children are passionate monitors of justice and fairness, and can become very engaged in how language is used to manipulate and persuade in texts such as advertisements and speeches (and bully, in online communication). However, these topics do not lend themselves to quick and easy measurement of the type required by national tests. See Goodwyn (this volume) for an account of the political context surrounding the LINC project.

There was also a serious miscalculation in the constituency of the group who developed the SPaG area, because none of the group had any real experience of primary teaching. Dick Hudson, a key figure in devising the tests, has criticised the whole development process, which was driven by former Education Secretary Michael Gove, as 'chaotic'. Asked whether there was any evidence at the time that a greater emphasis on traditional grammar was developmentally appropriate for children, Hudson acknowledged that "there was no evidence, and we were guessing" (quoted in Mansell, 2017).

The result is a bizarre situation in which the structural aspects that are in place, even if they are taught meaningfully, are actually in the *wrong* place at Key Stages 1 and 2. Where students do need some metalanguage is at A level, which our notional student may or may not go on to study at the point where choice is possible. However, by that stage, he or she will have forgotten the terms and concepts they were introduced to earlier. Worse still, they might arrive with misunderstandings that have to be unpicked before going further. Debra Myhill, another of the panel members who advised on the SPaG developments, submitted her own assessment of the tests to the Education Select Committee. Her view was that the tests should be discontinued because they serve no valid educational purpose, that the test design was seriously flawed, and that "children are developing grammatical misconceptions ... caused by an overemphasis on naming and identifying [terms] for test purposes" (cited in Mansell, 2017). The committee's conclusion was that the test should be optional, like the Key Stage 1 version. Currently, it is still compulsory.

4 *Groundhog Day?* GCSE, Key Stage 4 (Age 14–16)

SATs for Key Stage 3 (age 11–14) were abolished in 2010, amid concerns that students were being over-assessed through their school career. This means that there are no national assessments from Year 7, when most students begin their secondary education, until Year 11, when they take their GCSEs. In theory, then, English teaching during these years offers opportunities for deep learning that is exciting, creative, and relevant to modern life. A report published in 2013 by the Office for Standards in Education (Ofsted) reassures readers that it is perfectly possible for schools to be innovative and still perform well in national tests, but complains that despite the removal of the Key Stage 3 SATs, there has not been enough refreshment of the curriculum. Instead, the report claims, assessment all too often acts as a dead hand as teachers adopt 'watered down' GCSE approaches: "Too many schools offered no rationale to students for Key Stage 3 work, referring instead constantly to the GCSE examinations to be taken at some point in the distant future" (Ofsted, 2013, p. 23). The report observes that anxious senior leadership teams often adopt a prescriptive position that produces a culture of classroom timidity among the teaching staff, who in turn focus far too early on practising a narrow range of GCSE skills. If our notional student is in a very results-driven school with just such a senior team, their secondary school English, at least from Year 9, might consist of endless repetitions: Groundhog Day for three years.

The Ofsted report cited previously notes that in terms of transition between the Key Stages, there is insufficient communication between staff, resulting in unhelpful overlaps and repetition, even to the extent that the same literary texts are covered at Key Stages 2 and 3. However, the transition from primary 'English' to its incarnation at upper secondary level could also involve some radical differences for our student. In their school in England, a subject that they studied previously becomes two subjects, at least where assessment is concerned: English language and English literature part company, each having a different set of content and assessment objectives (AOs) at GCSE. English language has nine AOs, split between reading, writing, and speaking/listening. And what English language involves, in some of those elements of assessment, has changed in emphasis or simply arrived with no obvious antecedents at primary level. Where, for example, primary assessments of reading are focused largely on retrieving information, tests of reading at GCSE involve the critical evaluation of texts, the analysis of the language used by writers, comparisons of different writers' techniques, and the selection and synthesis of information from different texts. Students are expected to analyse texts they have never seen before and are required to respond to material from the nineteenth century as well as the twentieth and twenty-first centuries. This material has to include literary texts and 'literary non-fiction'; despite the subject content requiring the study of multimodality, assessments are not allowed to include what the DfE term 'transient texts' such as digital newsfeeds.

GCSEs and A levels underwent reforms at the behest of Michael Gove (Secretary of State for Education 2010–2014) who demanded that these qualifications become more rigorous and challenging. New qualifications began in 2015. Partly this idea of increased demand can be seen in the English language requirement to read material from former centuries; an equivalent for GCSE literature is to study more canonical literary texts from the past, including nineteenth century novels. Both these requirements follow a 'cultural heritage' model of the subject: see Goodwyn (this volume) for a discussion of models of English as devised by the Cox Committee. But the idea of rigour and challenge in English language is also associated with having to deal with extracts from literary works. In some ways, this is even harder than having to read the whole work, because at least then there is a known context for the material. But what English language students end up with is an exercise that is redolent of practical criticism courses taken in university English literature departments in the 1920s: responding to an 'unseen', the mainstay of liberal humanist literary criticism of former times. See Goodwyn (this volume) and Roberts (this volume) for discussion of higher education epistemologies and their effects on school English teaching.

English language AOs for writing and for speaking and listening are less remarkable than those for reading in terms of what they assess. However, *how* these aspects are assessed has changed considerably. Students' writing skills could previously be assessed by coursework, where they could submit a folder of work drafted and revised through time. Now those skills are tested in timed exam conditions. Critics of coursework would of course say that this is a fairer system as there are no supports for students to call on in an exam, but this in no way resembles anything that we do in reality when we have to undertake a writing task, where in the real world we redraft, look things up online, try ideas out on other people, and so on. If we want assessments to prepare students for the world of work, this is a backward step, as is expecting them to handwrite answers in a paper booklet rather than at a keyboard.

Assessment of speaking and listening, previously part of a coursework submission and therefore contributing to a student's overall grade, is now a separate assessment that does not contribute to any final mark. It exists as a stand-alone statement at either pass, merit, or distinction levels. This is a clear devaluation of oral skills – ironic when communication skills are such a prized part of modern workplaces.

5 *And Then There Were None*: A Level English, Key Stage 5 (Age 16–18)

Our student has coped with the shift from seeing English as an integrated subject in the primary classroom to seeing it as two subjects at GCSE. In moving from GCSE to AS and/or A level, suddenly it's three (in England): English language, English literature, and English language and literature. These different Englishes can be taken at AS and A levels, but the way they are examined changed in 2015. Previously, they were in a modular structure, so that each paper contributed to the final mark and credits could be built up as a student went along. Now A levels are linear courses, with everything depending on a student's performance in final exams – turning the clock back to the 'all or nothing' situation experienced long ago by previous generations. AS levels have been completely separated from A levels, so if our student wants to take English language AS and then go on to take the A level, no marks are carried forward: he or she has to take all the final A level assessments as if they had not done the AS qualification.

Inevitably, this dislocation has resulted in fewer students taking AS levels. Exam entry prices are also a significant factor for schools and colleges, who have, for the same reason, had to trim the range of subjects they can offer. In 2018, entries for AS subjects fell by 60 per cent. While this clearly affects all subjects, English language A level has more to lose than English literature from any drop in take up at AS. This is because, prior to 2015, AS English language was often a fourth or fifth A level for students who, in line with the Curriculum 2000 reforms, wanted to broaden their subjects before specialising further at A level (Curriculum 2000 was an initiative to encourage students to broaden their subject base). The experience of AS English language sometimes acted as a 'taster' and led students to continue with the subject. Now that opportunity is no longer there, making it more difficult for teachers to give potential students a sense of what A level English language is all about. Students often reflect on their experience of GCSE and think that A level is 'more of the same', which is certainly not the case (see Goddard and Beard, 2007, for teachers' comments about transition from GCSE as well as that from A level English language to higher education). English language is not alone in losing A level numbers, however: Busby (2018) notes a 14 per cent drop between 2016 and 2018 in entries for English A levels overall.

At AS/A level, the demarcations of 'reading, writing, speaking and listening', which have formed the mainstay of National Curriculum requirements at secondary level for many years, and which form the basis of English language GCSE assessments, disappear in favour of a set of analytical and creative skills that cut across those earlier distinctions. For English language AS/A level, there are subject-specific requirements, and five assessment objectives in order to test them. These include knowledge of theoretical topics drawn from the academic English language/linguistics field in higher education, for example: language acquisition, language change, and language variation; the ability to analyse and compare texts of all kinds, with an emphasis on authentic texts drawn from everyday life, including multimodal texts and those deemed 'transient' and unworthy of serious study at GCSE; the ability to write in different ways; and the ability to undertake a language research project as a coursework activity.

Although there is some continuity from GCSE in that AS/A level also includes writing skills, the biggest shift in perspective at this point of transition is that English language becomes the subject of study – the topic – rather than simply a set of skills. There are theories and research histories on many aspects of language, and students need to learn about different perspectives and traditions. Students do need some metalanguage, not just about grammar, but also about phonology, semantics, discourse, and semiotics (particularly aspects of textual design). Multimodality is a required area of study, and, given the elaboration of academic research interest in this field, students are able to link their own communication practices with what academic researchers are proposing.

The idea of English language as a topic for study in the sense described previously is likely to elude our student, unless at some point during her or his primary or secondary years, she or he happened to have a confident teacher who encouraged students to explore language actively, for example, interviewing family members about dialect words or conducting a survey about multilingualism. If this has not been the case, then the idea of English language as an open-ended subject intimately connected with personal identity, social behaviour, public attitudes, and institutional power will never emerge.

Before the 2015 reforms, there were some elements of previous English language GCSE qualifications that involved the active exploration of language use. For example, exam boards were required to include "the study of spoken English" in their 2010 specifications. One of the boards, Edexcel, also included an active, creative module entitled 'The Moving Image', where students devised their own moving image texts. Now that coursework is no longer extant at GCSE, such independent student-led enquiry is not easily accommodated.

Coursework, now renamed 'Non-examined Assessment', has been retained for all the A level Englishes, but at a reduced contribution of 20 per cent to the final A level mark (and there is no coursework at AS). This means that, for our students, the A level years, if they get that far, will be the first time they encounter the idea of an ongoing self-directed piece of work. If they are in a school where AS level and A level students are co-taught, they might not experience coursework until the final year of their studies.

One of the aims of reforming A levels was supposedly to ensure "a smoother transition" into higher education (Department for Education, 2015). Given that self-directed coursework is the mainstay of university study, it is hard to see how reducing the coursework potential at A level could possibly be seen as aiding transition. It takes a long time for learners to develop the skills of independent study, including knowing how best to use their tutors as a resource, by coming to tutorials having prepared some questions and ideas, for example. Our students cannot possibly learn these skills within a single year of A level study, or two years at most.

The idea of a 'smoother transition' into higher education also came to have a much narrower meaning as the A level reforms were emerging. A pamphlet called 'Informed Choices' was first produced in 2011 by the Russell Group of universities (the United Kingdom's self-styled 'elite' group of twenty-four institutions, named after the hotel in London where the original group first met). 'Informed Choices' defined a group of subjects called 'facilitating subjects', which were supposedly those subjects that were most often featured on lists of entry requirements for courses at these universities. 'English' was listed, but its meaning was (and still is) 'English literature', further evidence of Goodwyn's assertion (this volume) that literature is the default reference point for the study of English.

The rendering of English language as invisible or as a lesser form of study in the pamphlet has been seen by some as the result of a subject – that is, English more broadly – at war with itself over student numbers (Eaglestone and Kovesi, 2013), and the most recent figures quoted earlier show that the subject of English overall is certainly in decline.

6 Conclusions

It needs to be remembered that there is a difference between the curriculum itself and its assessment. At least, that should be the case, and hopefully there are many examples of good pedagogy where that difference is understood and acted upon. However, if we take the idea proposed at the outset, that assessment has become such a central concern that it has dominated the curriculum, then what can be said from this review of a potential student's experience of English? What story has emerged?

It's clear that English language has suffered from piecemeal reforms in each educational phase, without any serious attempt to look across the whole diet. Our student has had to change gear several times, and some aspects have left him or her ill-served both for further study and for modern living. The intense concentration on grammar at Key Stage 2 will be a dim and distant memory by the time A level arrives, and there are no opportunities to develop in any incremental way the key skills of independent enquiry that are so important both on undergraduate degrees and in professional careers. The language associated with modern technologies is prohibited in GCSE assessments in an age when the ability to critique social media and spot 'fake news' (as well as fake people) is crucial. The paper and pen exams that supposedly prepare our student for contemporary life and work operate in a vacuum that bears no resemblance to how we write either personally or professionally.

More generally, all the reforms to the 'Englishes' seem to have been a vanity project for certain politicians trying to recreate the schooling of former times as they remembered it at their public schools and grammar schools. These seem like items from an English heritage museum: literature "of proven worth" such as canonical nineteenth century novels, grammatical parsing, 'unseen' practical criticism exercises, sink-or-swim end-of-course exams that boast of their 'hardness'. None of it sounds much fun, and it's difficult to imagine that our notional student would stay the course beyond absolute necessity. The English subject area should stimulate a love of reading and a sense that it's possible to read for pleasure without having to do a comprehension test on it; learning about language should be exciting and empowering, not suffused with a fear of failure; and writing should be a creative activity involving a personal voice that articulates exactly what you want to express. Speaking and listening should be central, not an add-on worth nothing.

Eaglestone and Kovesi (2013) suggest that English has been taken for granted, and, likening the situation of the subject to the big banks before the financial crash of 2008, warn that "it is not too big to fail". If the study of English, and English language in particular, does not offer skills that are relevant to modern life, then it could go the way of Classics, taken by a few enthusiasts to get a window on a forgotten world.

References

Bakhtin, M. M. (1981). In M. Holquist, ed. C. Emerson and M. Holquist, trans. *The Dialogic Imagination*. Austin, TX: University of Texas Press.

Boyle, B. (2017). Response to Ward (2017, 19 May). Exclusive: More Sats 'chaos' as two thirds of moderators fail to assess pupils' work correctly. Times Educational Supplement. Online. Accessed August 2017 from www.tes.com/news/school-news/breaking-news/exclusive-more-sats-chaos-two-thirds-moderators-fail-assess-pupils

Busby, E. (2018, 18 May). 'Worrying decline' in pupils choosing English at A level. *The Independent*. Available from https://edition.independent.co.uk/editions/uk.co.independent.issue.250518/data/8368091/index.html

Carter, R., ed. (1991). *Knowledge about Language and the Curriculum: The LINC Reader*. London: Hodder and Stoughton.

Davies, C. (2017). Sats tests for seven-year-olds in England set to be scrapped. *The Guardian*. Online. Accessed August 2017 from www.theguardian.com/education/2017/mar/30/national-sats-tests-for-seven-year-olds-set-to-be-scrapped

Department for Education and Skills. (2006). *Primary National Strategy: Primary Framework for Literacy and Mathematics.* Norwich: OPSI.

Department for Education. (2015). Policy Paper: 2010 to 2015 government policy: school and college qualifications and curriculum. Online. Accessed 1 August 2017 from www.gov.uk/government/publications/2010-to-2015-government-policy-school-and-college-qualifications-and-curriculum/2010-to-2015-government-policy-school-and-college-qualifications-and-curriculum

Dombey, H. (2008). The simple view of reading – Explained. Online. Accessed August 2017. www.teachingtimes.com/news/the-simple.htm

Eaglestone, R. and Kovesi, S. (2013, 31 October). English: Why the discipline may not be 'too big to fail". *Times Higher Education*.

Gillen, J. (2014). *Digital Literacies*. London: Routledge.

Goddard, A. and Beard, A. (2007). As Simple as ABC? Issues of transition for students of English Language A Level going on to study English language/linguistics in higher education. *Report Series 14*. The Higher Education Academy English Subject Centre.

Goddard, A. and Carey, N. (2017). *Discourse: The Basics*. London: Routledge.

Kress, G. (2003). *Literacy in the New Media Age*. London: Routledge.

Lightfoot, M. and Martin, N. (1988). *The Word for Teaching Is Learning: Essays for James Britton*. NATE. Portsmouth: Heinemann.

Mansell, W. (2017). Battle on the adverbials front: Grammar advisers raise worries about Sats tests and teaching. *The Guardian*. Online. Accessed August 2017 from www.theguardian.com/education/2017/may/09/fronted-adverbials-sats-grammar-test-primary

Ofsted. (2013). Improving literacy: Moving English forward. *Ofsted Schools Survey Reports*. Online. Accessed September 2017 from www.gov.uk/government/publications/moving-english-forward

Parliament Education Select Committee Report on Primary Assessment. Online. Accessed August 2017 from https://publications.parliament.uk/pa/cm201617/cmselect/cmeduc/682/68202.htm

Perera, K. (1984). *Children's Writing and Reading: Analysing Classroom Language*. Oxford: Wiley-Blackwell.

Richmond, J. (2015). Reading 3 to 7. *English Language and Literacy 3 to 19: Principles and Proposals*. Leicester: UKLA and Owen Education.

Rosen, M. (2016). How to engage an audience? Good conjunctions and suffixes. [Irony alert]. Online. Accessed August 2017 from http://michaelrosenblog.blogspot.co.uk/2016/05/how-to-engage-audience-good.html

Rosenkvist, M. (2010). Using student test results for accountability and improvement: A literature review. *OECD Education Working Papers*, No. 54. Paris: OECD Publishing. Online. Accessed August 2017 from http://dx.doi.org/10.1787/5km4htwzbv30-en

Rumelhart, D. (1976). Toward an interactive model of reading. *Technical Report No. 56*. San Diego, CA: Center for Human Information Processing, University of California at San Diego.

Russell Group. (2016). Subject choices at school and college. Online. Accessed August 2017 from http://russellgroup.ac.uk/for-students/school-and-college-in-the-uk/subject-choices-at-school-and-college/

Ward, H. (2017). More Sats 'chaos' as two thirds of moderators fail to assess pupils' work correctly. *Times Educational Supplement* online. Online. Accessed August 2017 from www.tes.com/news/school-news/breaking-news/exclusive-more-sats-chaos-two-thirds-moderators-fail-assess-pupils

Weale, S. (2017). More primary school children suffering stress from Sats, survey finds. *The Guardian.* Online. Accessed August 2017 from www.theguardian.com/education/2017/may/01/sats-primary-school-children-suffering-stress-exam-time

Wiggins, K. (2016). Top adviser calls for a rethink over 'really demanding' grammar test for 11-year-olds. *Times Educational Supplement.* Online. Accessed August 2017 from www.tes.com/news/school-news/breaking-news/exclusive-top-adviser-calls-rethink-over-really-demanding-grammar

Wyse, D. (2017). Evidence given to the Parliamentary Education Select Committee: Primary Assessment, 3: Design and Development, Writing, para 34. Online. Accessed 31 July 2019 from https://publications.parliament.uk/pa/cm201617/cmselect/cmeduc/682/682.pdf

Part V
English in Lingua Franca Contexts

12 What Is English in the Light of Lingua Franca Usage?

Iris Schaller-Schwaner and Andy Kirkpatrick

1 Introduction

The origin of the term 'lingua franca' is unclear. According to Ostler (2010, p. 7), lingua franca "seems to be a retranslation of some Eastern-Mediterranean term for 'language of the Franks'". Ostler also notes (2010, p. 4) the "original 'Lingua Franca' was once a particular language ... the common contact language of the Eastern-Mediterranean in the first half of the second millennium, the pidgin Italian in which Greeks and Turks could talk to Frenchmen and Italians". He defines a lingua franca as a "contact language used for communication among people who do not share a mother tongue" (2010, p. 36). Seidlhofer points out that the term has Latin roots meaning something like 'free language'. "It is thus not fanciful to think of 'Lingua Franca' as 'free language' ... a means of intercultural communication not particular to countries and ethnicities, a linguistic resource that is not contained in, or constrained by traditional (and notoriously tendentious) ideas of what constitutes a 'language'" (2011, p. 81).

That a lingua franca is circumscribed as a linguistic resource not constrained by traditional views of language and as a contact language raises the question of what a contact language is and, indeed, what a language is. The idea of language or a language is considered in depth by Hall (this volume). We suggest that a contact language can be seen as the outcome of social and individual bi- and multilingualism so that the use of one shows traces of the other. At the same time, one must be aware that this thinking is steeped in the monolingual mindset that assumes 'normal' languages to be pure. In the context of English as a Lingua Franca (henceforth ELF), this means that ELF can be linguistically influenced by contact with the other languages of the speakers who use ELF. As there is no limit to speakers who use ELF, this, in turn, means that, theoretically in any event, ELF can be linguistically influenced by any of the languages in any ELF speaker's linguistic repertoire. ELF is thus subject to unbounded variation. It is therefore not a stable easily definable 'thing'. ELF, as a form, is often "inherently, chronically, irremediably variable" and "is also inherently hybrid in nature" (Firth, 2009, p. 163). This also leads us to note that the very definition of what a language is becomes slippery, or "notoriously tendentious" as noted. The variation in ELF and its causes – incorporating both the contact between the linguistic resources in the speaker's own head and mouth and contact with speakers of other 'languages' – give us an insight into language itself.

From a multilingual point of view, we would argue that English isn't just English and ELF isn't just English only. It is a way of being and doing English with other 'languages' in (the back of one's) mind and in a specific setting. ELF is a multilingual practice with a largely monolingual surface and with attributes that derive from factors such as: the multilingual work that is going on when English is chosen as a mode of communication used with intentionality or ostentation; as an overt behaviour enhancing salience/drawing attention to itself and thus contributing to content meaning (Scott-Phillips, 2012, 2017); from the mutual permeability of 'languages' in the language users' repertoires; and from the multilingual nature of the encounter or speech event in the context in which it is embedded. Following Bell's (2001) reworking of audience design and what can motivate language choice, ELF can be a 'responsive' choice that caters to one's own and interlocutor's or audience's perceived fit of linguistic repertoires and their incongruent first languages. Yet, ELF can also be an 'initiative' choice motivated by needs, desires, and purposes beyond the sheer negotiation of transactional meaning, a choice that changes and re/co-constitutes the local context into which it is embedded. Even in cases where its use does not emerge as agentively, ELF is essentially always a choice in that a selection has to be made, a decision has to be executed, linguistic resources have to be activated for output and others inhibited.

English is not just one language but a label encompassing many different varieties of a 'plurilithic' entity (Hall, 2013). English, one may argue historically, is itself a contact language influenced over several centuries by many different languages from Germanic, Norman French, classical Greek, and Latin to languages spoken across the world today. Historically, English has also been a multilingual enterprise in that code mixing was common (see for example, the chapters by Fischer, Schendl, and Wright in Schreier and Hundt, 2013).

This is not to deny that languages can be described, as the thousands of grammar books that are available testify. However, most grammar books describe an idealised form of the language – what, in Hall's taxonomy (this volume) would be classified as an N-/P-LANGUAGE – and would imply that speakers constantly use the forms as presented in the grammar books. Even comprehensive descriptive grammars only capture some of the variation inherent in language. However, by appearing in a grammar book, particularly a certain type of prescriptive grammar, a linguistic form is apparently given approval and legitimised as the 'standard' form, thereby rendering other forms as inferior in some way.

So, we are faced with a conundrum. On the one hand, it seems that language is a system, something that is relatively stable and that can be described and compared. This view sees language as an object. Traditional ontologies of language tend to be essentialist; that is to say that they treat language as a thing (Ortega, 2018). On the other hand, language is seen as a form of social practice (e.g. Saraceni, 2015), where language is a process characterised by perpetual change and regulated by contextual factors. We agree that language is a social practice and constantly changing, but we also recognise that it is regarded by its adult, literate users as something that can indeed be described and taught. As Joseph has noted, "so long as people believe that their way of speaking constitutes language in its own right, there is a real sense in which it is a real language" (2006, p. 27). Following Heller (2007), one will also have to bear in mind that 'language' and 'identity' are not natural phenomena but social constructs and that "the messiness of actual usage" (2007, p. 13) cannot be understood if one does not take this into account.

A language, then, is not easy to categorise. On the one hand it is a system; on the other it is a dynamic shifting phenomenon subject to variation along variables ranging from social settings, genres, registers, and influence from other languages to the idiosyncratic uses of an individual. Indeed, familiarity with the linguistic resources and idiosyncrasies of one's interlocutors is a significant aid to mutual understanding in ELF communication. ELF, then, is not a stable 'thing' but rather a description of how English is used by people who share this resource.

A recent definition of lingua franca by Seidlhofer is "any use of English among speakers of different first languages for whom English is the communicative medium of choice" (2011, p. 7). This, we feel, captures the essence of a lingua franca. Two points can be highlighted here. The first is that, as noted, a lingua franca can be regarded as a contact language, as an outcome of bi- and multilingualism, and it is important to note that a lingua franca is a multilingual endeavour. Bi- and multilinguals develop, expand, and refine the resources in their linguistic repertoire in order to communicate with other multilinguals. Multilinguals also have to call on their linguistic resources in the moment that they need to language, while assessing which of their linguistics resources can be or need to be called upon to affect successful communication with their interlocutor(s). The lingua franca will be open to influence from the first languages of the speakers who have adopted the language as a lingua franca. This first language influence is most obviously noted in the different pronunciations that different speakers will have. But first (and other) language influences can be seen at the levels of grammar and discourse, and in phenomena such as code-switching. It is useful to consider and perhaps qualify the current overgeneralisation that ELF researchers are only now discovering multilingualism. While a pedigree in English (applied) linguistics or English language teaching (ELT) may predispose one to see the shape of English before the ground of multilingualism when looking at ELF rather than the other way round, there has been awareness and consideration of the multilingual features of ELF and of ELF as a multilingual phenomenon, explicitly for example in Klimpfinger (2005, 2007, 2009), Smit (2005), Kirkpatrick (2010a, b), Schaller-Schwaner (2011), Cogo (2012), or Hülmbauer and Seidlhofer (2013).

Starting with Grosjean's (e.g. 2001) functional holistic account of how bi- and multilinguals can travel along a continuum of language modes between monolingual and bilingual ends and synthesizing this approach with compatible multilingualism constructs, Schaller-Schwaner (2017, pp. 15–49) has identified cornerstones of multilingualism that can be drawn together as five contingencies "that together lead on to their conceptual relevance for English as a lingua franca". These are (2017, p. 59):

1. assuming that individual bi- and multilingualism is not an accumulation of monolingualisms and that multilingual repertoires and multi-competence are variable, dynamic, and asymmetrical with interacting linguistic resources that are shaped by use
2. given that additional language users may choose their additional language not only to talk to its L1 speakers but to other additional language users
3. provided that we still want to identify, count, describe, or explain (resources from) the languages that wax and wane in people's different modes of functioning in multilingual situations

4. further, in order to explore how languages and languaging (language as a practice) are functioning outside traditional L1 speech communities or stable bilingual communities as well as
5. in order to interrogate traditional notions of ideal communicators (and language teachers), it is highly desirable if not compelling to conceive of individual languages not only in terms of L1 or native language varieties but also in terms of plurilingual uses. One would thus go beyond multilingualism with English (Hoffmann, 2000) and turn the perspective into English with multilingualism, or English as a Lingua Franca.

These points summarise what we take to be the basic tenets of ELF. Having established ELF as inherently dynamic, multilingual, and subject to inherent variation, we want, in this chapter, to investigate how a language is adopted as a lingua franca in different settings. First we describe how English came to be the lingua franca of the Association of Southeast Asian Nations (ASEAN). Then we refer to research conducted by Schaller-Schwaner (2011, 2015, 2017) where she describes how English was adopted as a lingua franca at the University of Fribourg, Switzerland. The University of Fribourg is Switzerland's only bilingual university (German and French are the two official languages) and, as we shall show, the use of English as an academic language was officially discouraged. This provides an example of ELF use in a relatively bounded setting compared with the wide range of settings in which ELF occurs in ASEAN.

2 English as a Lingua Franca in ASEAN

ASEAN was first established in Bangkok in 1967. There were five founding member states, namely, Thailand, the Philippines, Malaysia, Singapore, and Indonesia. The founding document, the Bangkok Declaration, made no mention of language and which language(s) might be official languages of the group. Instead, delegates involved in setting up ASEAN indicated that they simply assumed English would be the working language. Delegates were quoted as saying: "'the idea of English as the common language came out automatically', 'there has been no regulation for the use of English but it has been used in all the actual situations', and 'we took it for granted'" (Okudaira, 1999, pp. 95–96).

That the delegates simply assumed English would be the common language of ASEAN is extremely surprising given that two of the founding member states, Indonesia and Thailand, had no history of English. In contrast, the Philippines, Malaysia, and Singapore had all been colonies of English-speaking nations and were countries where English played an institutional role and had developed their own varieties of English (Kirkpatrick, 2007, 2010a). The acceptance of English as the working language clearly discriminated against Thailand and Indonesia as they had few proficient speakers of English compared with the other three nations. One might have expected Malay/Indonesian to be named the working language, as it was an official or national language of three of the founding member states, Indonesia, Malaysia, and Singapore, and spoken to some extent in both the Philippines and Thailand. When one of the authors of this chapter asked the director general of ASEAN why language had not been discussed, he replied that it would have been like opening Pandora's Box (Edilberto de Jesus, p.c.).

In time, a further five nations joined ASEAN. Brunei joined in 1984, Vietnam in 1995, Laos and Burma (Myanmar) in 1997, and finally Cambodia in 1999. What had been a de facto agreement became de jure with the signing of the ASEAN Charter in 2009, where English was legislated in Article 34 of the Charter as the sole working language of the group.

It is worth pointing out at this stage how linguistically and culturally diverse ASEAN is. For example, Indonesia is home to 700 or so languages and more than 150 languages are spoken in Myanmar and the Philippines. The birth of ELF in ASEAN was therefore attended and potentially shaped by hundreds of languages. When an Indonesian, Filipino, and Burmese are engaged in ELF, many languages may be at work in each speaker's mind.

The legislation of English as the sole working language of ASEAN has had obvious consequences. As Musthafa et al. (2019) point out the official adoption of English as ASEAN's working language has major ramifications on ASEAN member states' educational systems. These ramifications include the increased presence of English in the curricula (Kirkpatrick, 2010b). For example, Indonesia is the only country of ASEAN that has not made English a compulsory subject in primary school. In the other nine countries, English is introduced, typically from Primary 3. In Brunei, English acts as a medium of instruction from Primary 1. In Singapore, it is *the* medium of instruction (Kirkpatrick, 2010a). English is also increasingly being used as a medium of instruction in higher education in the region's universities (Fenton-Smith et al., 2017; Barnard and Hasim, 2018).

Further motivation to learn English for communication within and across ASEAN comes from ASEAN's recent drive to establish an ASEAN identity. The crucial role of English in this enterprise was emphasised by Secretary General of ASEAN Le Luong Minh:

With the diversity in ASEAN reflected in our diverse histories, races, cultures and belief systems, English is an important and indispensable tool to bring our Community closer together ... Used as the working language of ASEAN, English enables us to interact with other ASEAN colleagues in our formal meetings as well as day-to-day communications ... In order to prepare our students and professionals in response to all these ASEAN integration efforts, among other measures, it is imperative that we provide them with opportunities to improve their mastery of the English language, the language of our competitive global job market, the lingua franca of ASEAN.

(ASEAN, 2013)

English is now firmly entrenched as the lingua franca of ASEAN, an area of great linguistic and cultural diversity. As such, it reflects the cultural diversity of its speakers and a decentring away from Anglophone cultures towards more localised and transcultural practices (Baker, this volume). To give just one example, 'English for Islamic Values' is taught in schools attached to mosques in Indonesia (Kirkpatrick, 2015). Its speakers are attuned to the natural diversity and variation of ELF use (see Page, this volume) and use ELF for communication (see Badwan, this volume). Its position as a lingua franca has been the result of a top-down policy, with the ASEAN Charter officially nominating English as the sole working language of the group and the Secretary General of ASEAN stressing the importance of English as a tool to create an ASEAN identity and more interaction between ASEAN member states. The use of ELF in ASEAN has, thus, to a certain extent been motivated by official policy from the top. It occurs across ASEAN in a myriad of varied contexts, comprising speakers of different languages in different circumstances, from official ASEAN meetings to ad hoc interactions. We now turn to a completely different context and set of circumstances where ELF was adopted bottom-up in opposition to official policy, the University of Fribourg.

3 The Choice of ELF in Academic Settings of One Specific Non-Anglophone University

As noted previously, when English is used as a lingua franca, this can be on an ad hoc basis, for example to address someone (whose language repertoire is) unknown (see Wray and Grace, 2007 on exoteric communication, which is relevant in such ELF contexts) or to perform a task/enact a certain role linked with English spontaneously; but ELF can also be part of an explicit or implicit 'indigenous' (in the sense of Jacoby, 1998; Jacoby and McNamara, 1999) (formal) habit and expectation in which the language choice is anchored in a speech event genre for the participants of what might then over time become a community of practice. The way ELF in academic settings at universities outside Anglophone countries can emerge bottom-up to fulfil local needs is a case in point.

The university in question is located in Switzerland, which has four national languages used in their respective territories with rather stable and societally salient language boundaries connecting/separating cantons or areas where French, Italian, or Romansh is spoken, also from the majority-language diglossic German-speaking parts of the country. Most Swiss grow up using either German, French, or Italian, and only the small Romansh-speaking minority become systematically bi- or multilingual. However, school teaching and language exchange within one's own or with neighbouring countries are considered more or less successful ways of learning other national languages. Despite the label 'Latin Switzerland' for the areas in which the Romance languages are spoken and despite the country's Latin designation Confoederatio Helvetica (CH), Switzerland historically had no lingua franca.

Regardless of social or educational background, Swiss Germanophones characteristically use prestigious Alemannic varieties of German orally as well as in informal writing. Standard German is a school subject, the language of print and of formal speech. On the German-medium TV news, for example, the news is read in Standard German but interviews are often conducted in Swiss German. In Francophone cantons, on the other hand, dialect carries very little prestige, and formal literacy in what is perceived as a uniform standard is valued highly. A reluctance to speak an L2 in public or in class can combine with a very assertive use of French in the bilingual canton and town of Fribourg vis-à-vis German speakers, to the extent that French is used in first encounters even by German speakers until they find out that they both are.

Generally, Swiss universities are monolingual institutions whose language depends on the canton in which they are situated. There is one exception, namely Switzerland's Bilingual University, Fribourg/Freiburg, which has since its foundation in the late nineteenth century been institutionally bilingual in the two cantonal languages, French and German. The complexity of institutional bilingualism and the emergence of English as an additional language will be described briefly. There were periods in the history of the university when the local competition between the two languages was more or less pronounced (or more or less volitional), and co-existence vs. co-operation was a more prominent theme. In fact, the most frequent form of institutional bilingualism, termed "parallel" by Brohy (2005), has been a form of twin monolingualism in which studies can be undertaken in either of the two languages to the exclusion of the other. This form requires communicative bridges. A prominent public relations message of the university to this day is its unique position in Europe of offering a complete programme of studies in both French and German. This is not the only form of institutional bilingualism, however. Of Brohy's (2005) tripartite terms, "complementary bilingualism" describes the optional combination of French and German, for example through elements from parallel study programmes. This is intended as an incentive for becoming individually bilingual during one's studies and there are models that lead to certification of the extra effort required in studying through two languages.

The only form of institutional bilingualism that makes an at least passive command of the partner language compulsory without certification is what Brohy (2005) calls "integrated bilingualism", which in fact, somewhat euphemistically, also included English as used in the science faculty. There was no reduplication of programmes and no segregation of languages, but the natural sciences were offered in French or German, depending on the teacher. Students were allowed to choose in which language to write papers or take exams. 'Scientific English' was a given for research publications, but English was also used orally to accommodate students and staff who did not speak either of the local languages. On the basis of interpersonally compatible language repertoires, Italian has sometimes also played a role, for example, as the language of the lab in research teams headed by an Italian-speaking professor. The use of English was condoned by the 1997 University Law granting faculties the right to specify other languages of instruction but was internally contested as 'unruly/wild trilingualism' and 'proliferation' and seen to undermine bilingualism in French and German. In the course of 2005, there was, however, a flurry of activity in language management, for example a special work group on English led by the representative of the Bilingualism Committee who invited representatives from all faculties to report on the use of English in their faculties. The representative of the science faculty stated that English was in daily use and indispensable to the workings and international success of the science faculty. Towards the end of this year, in the Dies Academicus annual ceremony, it was officially announced by the Rektor/Recteur in his speech that the Science Master programmes were being taught through English. English was construed in his speech as a force that acts on its own accord, but at the same time, the point was made that English fulfilled functions comparable to Latin in theology, which had long been a 'lingua academica' without interference with bilingualism.

The situation in the natural sciences that brought about the official acknowledgement in 2005 of the use of English as a primary teaching language in the new master programmes was, however, preceded by and concomitant with the emergence of English in much less visible niches. The 'Beer and Lunch Seminars' in biochemistry and the 'Lunchtime Seminars' in psychology were the first series of disciplinary events in English to emerge during a period of radical change that temporarily culminated in the announcement made at the Dies Academicus referred to earlier. By means of a new genre (Swales, 1990, 2004), English was embedded between the local languages as a lingua franca for disciplinary oral presentations and discussions. A comparison of the two lunchtime events as communal disciplinary and public speaking events shows how the use of ELF was developed within the university in response to surrounding language segregation, fostering of global contacts, and disciplinary socialisation needs for oral use of ELF.

Crucially, in both settings, the use of English emerged bottom-up out of people's own vital communal impetus. In both, English was available at least receptively as an international disciplinary language and the multilingual agents of change appropriated it for their local purposes and on their own terms. The choice of a local language separates local audiences, producing respective 'others'. A common lingua franca thus offers a functional alternative, not only as the only means of communication, but also as an additional one. Instead of code-switching between territorial languages, 'code-sharing' (Schaller-Schwaner, 2010, 2011) in lingua franca mode allows for disciplinary cohesion. The use of ELF in the Fribourg University academic settings examined was the most useful common denominator for every individual and for education and research. The extension of ELF in one's multilingual repertoire and in one's discipline for local academic speech events therefore served individual and institutional multilingualization.

The longitudinal ethnographic contextual analysis of the emergence of ELF in a multilingual academic context, mainly as used for lunchtime oral speech events in two different faculties of a bilingual institution with rather different types of institutional bilingualism (segregated or integrative) and hence, motivations to use English, yielded a picture that was rich in detail as well as complex, fluctuating, and dynamic, not least in reconstituting the academic context and to some extent the multilingual repertoires of its users. What is essential to bear in mind in all this is these users, however. A language does not emerge of its own accord; it does not itself change an institution or the communicative economy of groups of language users. A language has no agency of its own. Speakers have agency (Ahearn, 2001) and may together or individually adapt their communicative repertoires when they are motivated to do so (Gal, 1979). They actualize and co-create the factors that shape their situated English language practices, the ELF code-sharing mode that they adopt for certain purposes, embedded in a highly aware and deliberate way in the local languages but, in the core phases of the speech events, in preference to (code-switching between) the local languages. This is not to deny the influence of structur(ation) but to argue that language users can together try out alternatives and create new experiences that become the new normal (Schaller-Schwaner, 2015, pp. 330–331).

Epistemologically and perhaps also ontologically, these users of English with their awareness, their concerted multilingual effort, and their agency make the difference between English as a language in one of the conventional senses (as an abstraction and idealization in the way they are presented elsewhere in this volume) and our take on ELF as a multilingual practice and code-sharing mode. Together, these multilingual language users shape and make up "the many faces of English" (Schaller-Schwaner, 2017, p. 3) and while it is not entirely clear at this stage if it is just our knowledge that is still blurred or if ELF is indeed, as argued elsewhere, a fuzzy category (Schaller-Schwaner, 2017), one thing seems clear: ELF does not exist without its additional language speakers because it is 'their' English. ELF is about a multilingual language concept much more than about the presence or absence of L1 users of English, but the presence of an L1 user can trigger foreign language anxiety, unwillingness to communicate, and linguistic insecurity connected to a monolingual language concept and habitus/mindset. In the next section, we describe four factors that combined to motivate the use of ELF in the university.

4 The Four-Factor Model

The four factors singled out here appear to be partly overlapping or growing into each other. They will be taken into consideration in turn, starting with the speech event/disciplinary genre factor, moving on to the community of practice factor and the (self)socialization/multilingualization factor before concluding with a brief reappraisal of the foundational ELF concept of the habitat factor for the habitat under consideration.

4.1 The Speech Event/Disciplinary Genre Factor

The speech event/genre factor is a crucial one methodologically as well as in terms of the material manifestations of English and the shared (or not) purposes of its use. Methodologically, a Swalesian situation first approach (Swales, 2004) was motivated in the Fribourg case by the way in which English first became publicly visible as a local oral practice: in two innovative lunch-time event series for presentations plus discussion, which were unprecedented on university timetables not only because they took place at noon but also because the language of presentations was English.

The speech events in biochemistry, the Beer and Lunch Seminars, were open to everyone but compulsory for all members of all research teams. The doctoral student presenters and peer helpers were in charge and not chaired, unlike occasional invited talks during this weekly time slot by established researchers presenting their own work. All talks and almost all introductions of invited speakers took place in English. As other languages were sometimes being used interpersonally in low voices in the preparatory phases preceding the chair's or the presenter's taking the floor in English, initiating the phases of the speech event that were exclusively English sometimes sounded effortless and at other times as if presenters had to collect themselves and overcome the competition of other languages for immediate output, but it was always a matter of course. The biochemistry unit's decision to use English had also been triggered by a large number of doctoral students from India as well as by the unit's desire to socialize everyone into orally engaging in the disciplinary discourse locally. As illustrated in Schaller-Schwaner (2009, p. 257), the unit decided to safeguard disciplinary standards by imposing a regularly updated English-medium textbook for teaching and learning and to familiarize students with cutting-edge publications in the original, English being the "vernacular language" in science. English was also adopted for the speech event 'as a training for students', arguing that keeping to English for the presentation was pedagogically useful as well as easier as it permitted staying in the same language. English was also heard and seen out in the corridors on notice boards and equipment and reported to be used on social occasions that included everyone because it was the only shared language spoken by everyone. While it was thus a responsive choice (in Bell's 2001 sense) to accommodate the Indian students, as elsewhere in the faculty the many other internationals who spoke neither or only one of the local languages, the speech event genre of the Beer and Lunch Seminar was the format that had to be filled with English in a disciplinary role and with a specific academic purpose, locally anchoring English for each individual who had to participate as a member of the audience or as a presenter. Initially, the use of English was perceived as stressful by students, but it became less so with time and experience in the years in which their disciplinary persona developed, together with their English in this lingua franca context.

The choice of English in the psychology department's Lunchtime Seminar, which was observed in its second and third year of existence, was motivated at that time by the desire to create disciplinary synergies between the only recently united linguistically segregated chairs and their teams who went on to develop a trilingual master's programme in psychology.

The disciplinary speech event anchors the language choice and primes the mind and body for activating English. It is a temporal space and communicative opportunity, a disciplinary and linguistic activity for appropriating and repurposing the journal club (in biochemistry) or brown-bag inspired peer research event (as was the case in psychology) as well as marking the boundary from individual language choice to public speaking language choice, the 'gear shift' to English. This language selection is declarative and effortful but becomes less taxing over time as a genre expectation. While in the years of observation in the psychology event series the language of presentations was announced as English, this is taken as read a decade later: the language of presentations is assumed to be English and therefore not announced.

4.2 The Community of Practice Factor

The community of practice (Wenger, 1998) is important for ELF in more than one way, even if ELF encounters may be so transient as to defy a notion of community. In a multilingual disciplinary context, in which disciplinary colleagues are struggling to visibly negotiate, navigate, or transcend the local language boundary and realize synergies, the term 'community of practice' is needed to complement the idea of a discourse community (Swales, 1998) that shares a language and conventionalized ways of using it for the specific purpose. The community of practice (henceforth CoP) factor is also visible in the degrees of involvement and the legitimate peripheral participation of members. ELF is not only the two disciplinary communities' shared resource, however, but is also part of their communal endeavour beyond static language concepts. In psychology the use of ELF was a way of 'getting the German side on board' and 'due to bilingualism' (in whose 'parallel' realization French and German are assumed to index and be intended for its L1 users only), but also an investment in the future of developing (individual repertoires for) a trilingual master's programme. In biochemistry, the international composition of what was at the time a division of the medical department of the science faculty (with its bilingualism type of immersing students in alternate languages of instruction) meant that its members had to become familiar with the impact of nine different L1s and had to grow accustomed to each other's Englishes. The biochemists generally held that no one should have to deny his or her origin when using English but 'difficulty understanding' occurred, despite familiarity. The difficulty of converging on English while face-to-face with audience members with whom one shared other, interpersonally established linguistic resources, and inhibiting these as best one could, also required learning to handle this competition for imminent output, mild alertness and resolve, as well as mindfulness of one's best linguistic behaviour in the disciplinary CoP.

4.3 The (Self)Socialization/Multilingualization Factor

As is becoming clear from the preceding discussion, ELF constellations of dialect-register-genre (James, 2005) can go beyond the typical trigger of no-other-shared-medium scenarios. In fact, linguistic self-determination and agency permit users to language in ELF for their purposes beyond the immediate deictic centre, that is the speakers' here-and-now and immediate interlocutors, to include psychologically important reference points and 'referees'. Doing English for the communicative autonomy of a future self is a form of taking ownership of English (Widdowson, 1994) in the physical sense of embodiment. Language socialization of self and others into an additional academic language is an 'initiative' language choice in the sense of referee design (Bell, 2001) for important absent others with which one wishes to affiliate and a way of changing the situation, but it is also a way of changing oneself in relation to context and changing one's habitus. Multilinguals are usually aware that they need to use a language in order to grow it as part of their own practices. The physical experience of speaking English aloud to an audience, intentionally nurturing English in one's repertoire, and literally incorporating it through the mouth as pathway (also vicariously in experiencing close peers doing it) can counteract structuration and reality-defining restrictions. Multilingualization is as naturally occurring as other ELF languaging but takes time and tolerance of ambiguity. Small audiences on home turf and informality/sociality signals such as beer or food may ease the process, but the waxing and waning of linguistic resources remains a challenge to participation and self-concept.

4.4 The Habitat Factor

The ELF 'habitat factor' that Pölzl and Seidlhofer (2006) established as a foundational aspect both underlines the context sensitivity of ELF and helps one examine how far shared ground between interlocutors furthers and hinders international convergence. As explained and illustrated for a specific case in Schaller-Schwaner (2015), the additional language socialization into ELF that the multilingual biochemistry CoP provided for doctoral students also provided so much situated familiarity and compatible interlingual resources (as well as shared schemata and terminology) that international intelligibility may have become an issue. ELF as a multilingual practice may have a certain contextual *Gültigkeitsbereich* ('scope'; Auer, 2009, p. 94) and does not automatically transfer as autonomously functional into contexts where other interlingual resources are available. In this sense, the habitat factor is also a limiting factor that needs to be taken into account pedagogically.

5 Conclusion

In this chapter, we have considered various aspects of ELF and its origins and stressed its inherent multilingual nature and hybridity. Far from ELF being an easily definable stable form of code, we have argued that it is characterised by inherent variation and flexibility. But does this mean that, to reiterate Firth's notion, ELF, as a form, is "inherently, chronically, irremediably variable" (2009, p. 163)? ELF, as a form, can look much like any English. While it is, as Seidlhofer noted, "a 'free language', a linguistic resource that is not contained in, or constrained by traditional (and notoriously tendentious) ideas of what constitutes a 'language'" (2011, p. 81), it is situated in realities that make languages and different societal language concepts highly relevant. ELF users position themselves within these discursively available categories while their practices may be in the process of creating new experiences and realities and categories.

Given the spectrum of ontologies of English and the facets of ELF, it may be helpful to consider a continuum of blurred understandings with language as a system at one end and language as social practice at the other. Looking for/at the 'language' English as a reified/artefactualised 'thing' (Blommaert, 2010) towards the system end of the continuum does not deny its inherent variation with ELF towards the social practice end of the continuum, which is still possible to identify as some form of English(ing). It would appear, then, that ELF can be more than one thing. What it is not, in our view, is a monolingual construct. ELF needs to be viewed through a multilingual lens.

The complexity of ELF is further underscored by the potential of it being, as we argued earlier, a 'responsive' language choice or an 'initiative' language choice (Bell, 2001). The example of ELF use at the University of Fribourg was bottom up in that it was voluntarily adopted as a choice by its users. In contrast, the use of ELF in ASEAN is the result of a top-down policy decision. We thus underline the importance of context, setting, and the participants themselves, and thus, the need to investigate each case of ELF and where it came from (Dafouz and Smit, 2014). A four-factor model comprising *the speech event/disciplinary genre factor, the community of practice factor, the (self)socialization/multilingualization factor,* and *the habitat factor* was shown to motivate the choice and use of ELF, but with much variation depending on the particular context.

In summary, ELF needs to be viewed through a multilingual lens, understood as a fuzzy category, and one that is contextually determined and open to inherent variation. And it is also English. Named languages may be a discursive reality, an academic paradigm, an argumentative device, an ideological point of identification, and a communicative tool as well as a symbolic claim, perhaps even more in the case of English than in the case of other named languages. English is an emic as well as an etic category and therefore 'plurilithic' and not monolithic.

Schaller-Schwaner (2017) wondered what the etymological stones in the 'plurilithic' concept might actually be. She argued that a metaphor that lends itself to being a conceptual tool worth exploring in further work on English as a Lingua Franca is the image of the beach.

Beaches are inherently dynamic 'landscapes', contact zones and permeable boundary formations shaped by ongoing instability or individual events, they are continually under reconstruction, they have varied and varying forms and the elements and forces they are exposed to and moulded by reinforce or counteract each other in multiple ways. They are also subject to tidal events, global streams and lunar waxing and waning but clearly locally typified and specific to a place.

(p. 327)

She suggests that regardless of the specific composition of the beach, it is recognizable as one by anyone who knows the distinction between being out at sea and out of one's depth (with no means of communication) and the relative security of the beach. The beholder's methodological lens is also involved, however:

The granularity of the beach also depends on the granularity of the data transcription and analysis and on the time scale of observation: the length of observation and the point in time/tide and the season. The point is that while traditional language conceptualisations are rather 'land-locked', a more dynamic metaphor for languaging which accounts for more dynamic functions and purposes can be useful.

(Schaller-Schwaner, 2017, pp. 327–328)

ELF, we suggest, is like a beach, with stones and pebbles shaping each other through constant contact and subject to external influences, including being buffeted by wind and water. ELF can occur wherever and whenever there are multilingual speakers looking to seek out a common language. It is therefore ontologically subjective.

References

Ahearn, L. M. (2001). Language and agency. *Annual Review of Anthropology*, 30, 109–137.

ASEAN. (2013, 24 June). Keynote address by H. E. Le Luong Minh, secretary-general of ASEAN. Presented at the British Council Conference on Educating the Next Generation of Workforce: ASEAN Perspectives on Innovation, Integration and English. Bangkok.

Asian Corpus of English (ACE). Online. Accessed 25 June 2018 from http://corpus.ied.edu.hk/ace/

Auer, P. (2009). Context and contextualisation. In J. Verschueren and J Östman, eds. *Key Notions for Pragmatics*, Vol. 1. Amsterdam and Philadelphia: John Benjamins, 86–101.

Barnard, R. and Hasim, Z., eds. (2018). *English Medium of Instruction Programmes: Perspectives from Southeast Asian Universities*. London: Routledge.

Bell, A. (2001). Back in style: Reworking audience design. In P. Eckert and J. R. Rickford, eds. *Style and Sociolinguistic Variation*. Cambridge: Cambridge University Press, 139–169.

Blommaert, J. (2010). *The Sociolinguistics of Globalization*. Cambridge: Cambridge University Press.

Brohy, C. (2005, 1–3 September). *Overt bilingualism, covert multilingualism? Official languages and 'other languages' in a bilingual French-German university. Paper presented at the conference on Bi- and Multilingual Universities: Challenges and Future Prospects, University of Helsinki.* Online. Accessed 19 June 2017 from www.palmenia.helsinki.fi/congress/bilingual2005/abstracts/brohy.pdf

Cogo, A. (2012). ELF and super-diversity: A case study of ELF multilingual practices from a business context. *Journal of English as a Lingua Franca*, 1(2), 283–313.

Dafouz, E. and Smit, U. (2014, 11 July). Towards a dynamic conceptual framework for English-Medium education in multilingual university settings. *Applied Linguistics*, 37(3), 397–415. Online. Accessed from https://doi.org/10.1093/applin/amu034

Fenton-Smith, B., Humphreys, P., and Walkinshaw, I., eds. (2017). *English Medium Instruction in Higher Education in Asia-Pacific: From Policy to Pedagogy*. Dordrecht: Springer.

Firth, A. (2009). The lingua franca factor. *Intercultural Pragmatics*, 6(2), 147–170.
Gal, S. (1979). *Language Shift. Social Determinants of Linguistic Change in Bilingual Austria*. New York: Academic Press.
Grosjean, F. (2001). The bilingual's language modes. In J. L. Nicol, ed., *One Mind, Two Languages: Bilingual Language Processing* (pp. 1–22). Oxford: Blackwell.
Hall, C. J. (2013). Cognitive contributions to plurilithic views of English and other languages. *Applied Linguistics*, 34(2), 211–231.
Heller, M. (2007). *Bilingualism: A Social Approach*. Basingstoke: Palgrave Macmillan.
Hoffman, C. (2000). The spread of English and the growth of multilingualism with English in Europe. In J. Cenoz and U. Jessner, eds. *English in Europe: The Acquisition of a Third Language* (pp. 1–21). Clevedon: Multilingual Matters.
Hülmbauer, C. (2013). From within and without: The virtual and the plurilingual in ELF. *Journal of English as a Lingua Franca*, 2(1), 47–73.
Hülmbauer, C. and Seidlhofer, B. (2013). English as a lingua franca in European multilingualism. In A-C. Berthoud, F. Grin, and G. Lüdi, eds. *Exploring the Dynamics of Multilingualism. The DYLAN Project* (pp. 387–406). Amsterdam: John Benjamins.
Jacoby, S. W. (1998). Science as performance: Socializing scientific discourse through the conference talk rehearsal. Unpublished doctoral dissertation, University of California, Los Angeles.
Jacoby, S. W. and McNamara, T. (1999). Locating competence. *English for Specific Purposes*, 18(3), 213–241.
James, A. (2005). The challenges of the lingua franca: English in the world and types of variety. In C. Gnutzmann and F. Intemann, eds., *The Globalisation of English and the English Language Classroom* (pp. 133–144). Tübingen: Gunter Narr.
Joseph, J. E. (2006). *Language and Politics*. Edinburgh: Edinburgh University Press.
Kirkpatrick, A. (2007). *World Englishes: Implications for English Language Teaching and Intercultural Communication*. Cambridge: Cambridge University Press.
Kirkpatrick, A. (2010a). *English as a Lingua Franca in ASEAN: A Multilingual Model*. Hong Kong: Hong Kong University Press.
Kirkpatrick, A. (2010b). English as an Asian lingua franca and the multilingual model of ELT. *Language Teaching*, 43(3), 1–13.
Kirkpatrick, A. (2015). The future of English in Asia. In M. O'Sullivan, D. Huddart, and C. Lee, eds., *The Future of English in Asia* (pp. 3–19). Cambridge: Cambridge University Press.
Klimpfinger, T. (2005). The role of speakers' first and other languages in English as a lingua franca talk. Unpublished master's thesis, University of Vienna/ Diplomarbeit Universität Wien.
Klimpfinger, T. (2007). Mind you sometimes you have to mix – The role of code-switching in English as a lingua franca. *Vienna English Working Papers*, 16(2),

36–61. Online. Full text at http://anglistik.univie.ac.at/fileadmin/user_upload/dep_anglist/weitere_Uploads/Views/Views_0702.pdf).

Klimpfinger, T. (2009). 'She's mixing the two languages together' – Forms and functions of code-switching in English as a lingua franca. In A. Mauranen and E. Ranta, eds., *English as a Lingua Franca – Studies and Findings* (pp. 348–370). Newcastle-upon-Tyne: Cambridge Scholars Publishing.

Musthafa, B, Hamied, F.A. and Zein, S. (2019). Enhancing the quality of Indonesian teachers in the ELF era: policy recommendations. In Zein, S. ed., *Teacher Education for English as a Lingua Franca. Perspectives from Indonesia*. London and New York: Routledge.

Okudaira, A. (1999). A study on international communication in regional organizations: The use of English as the 'official' language of the Association of South East Asian Nations (ASEAN). *Asian Englishes*, 2(1), 91–107.

Ortega, L. (2018). Ontologies of language, second language acquisition and world Englishes. *World Englishes*, 37, 64–79.

Ostler, N. (2010). *The Last Lingua Franca*. London: Penguin.

Pölzl, U. and Seidlhofer, B. (2006). In and on their own terms: The 'habitat factor' in English as a lingua franca interactions. *International Journal of the Sociology of Language*, 177, 151–176.

Saraceni, M. (2015). *World Englishes: A Critical Analysis*. London: Bloomsbury.

Schaller-Schwaner, I. (2009). Under the microscope: English for plurilingual academic purposes. In D. Veronesi and C. Nickenig, eds., *Bi-and Multilingual Universities: European Perspectives and Beyond*. Bolzano-Bozen: Bozen/Bolzano University Press, 245–264.

Schaller-Schwaner, I. (2010). ELF(A) in the eye of the beholder: Multilingual or monolingual practice. *Paper presented at the 11th International CercleS Conference: University Language Centres–Language Policy and Innovation*, University of Helsinki, 2–4 September.

Schaller-Schwaner, I. (2011). The eye of the beholder: Is English as a Lingua Franca in academic settings a monolingual or multilingual practice? *Language Learning in Higher Education*, 1(2), 423–446.

Schaller-Schwaner, I. (2015). The habitat factor in ELF(A) – English as a Lingua Franca (in academic settings) – and English for plurilingual academic purposes. *Language Learning in Higher Education*, 5(2), 1–23.

Schaller-Schwaner, I. (2017). *The many faces of English at Switzerland's Bilingual University: English as an academic lingua franca at the institutionally bilingual University of Freiburg/Fribourg – A contextual analysis of its agentive use*. Unpublished doctoral thesis, University of Vienna.

Schreier, D. and Hundt, M., eds. (2013). *English as a Contact Language*. Cambridge: Cambridge University Press.

Scott-Phillips, T. C. (2012). The origins of human communication. Signalling signalhood. *The Psychologist*, 25, 2–3.

Scott-Phillips, T. C. (2017, 8–10 February). Miscommunication, relevance, and the evolution of human communication. *Plenary presentation at the COM-COG 2017 Conference Communication and Cognition – Miscommunication: Getting Lost in Language(s)*. Fribourg: University of Fribourg.

Seidlhofer, B. (2011). *Understanding English as a Lingua Franca*. Oxford: Oxford University Press.
Smit, U. (2005). Multilingualism and English: The lingua franca concept in language description and language learning pedagogy. In R. Feistaur, I. Cullin, C. Cali, and K. Chester, eds., *Favorita Papers 04 Mehrsprachigkeit und Kommunikation in der Diplomatie* (pp. 66–75). Diplomatische Akademie Wien/ Vienna School of International Studies.
Swales, J. (1990). *Genre Analysis: English in Academic and Research Settings*. Cambridge: Cambridge University Press.
Swales, J. (1998). *Other Floors, Other Voices. A Textography of a Small University Building*. Mahwah and London: Lawrence Erlbaum.
Swales, J. (2004). *Research Genres: Explorations and Applications*. Cambridge: Cambridge University Press.
Wenger, E. (1998). *Communities of Practice. Learning, Meaning and Identity*. Cambridge: Cambridge University Press.
Widdowson, H. (1994). The ownership of English. *TESOL Quarterly, 28*(2), 377–388.
Wray, A. and Grace, G. (2007). The consequences of talking to strangers: Evolutionary corollaries of socio-cultural influences on linguistic form, *Lingua, 117*, 543–578.

13 English as a Lingua Franca and Transcultural Communication

Rethinking Competences and Pedagogy for ELT

Will Baker

1 Introduction

Research into global uses of English, and particularly ELF (English as a Lingua Franca), has highlighted the diversity and fluidity of communicative practices in intercultural and transcultural communication through English. Successful intercultural/transcultural communication involves the ability to make use of and negotiate multilingual/plurilingual linguistic resources, a variety of communicative practices and strategies, and movement between global, national, local, and emergent frames of reference. This is a very different conception of competence to that typically utilised in English language teaching (ELT) with its pre-determined 'code' consisting of a restricted range of grammatical, lexical, and phonological forms and minimal concern with the sociocultural dimension of communication. The need for a reconceptualisation of language in applied linguistics and more recently ELT has begun to receive serious scholarly attention. However, this needs to be accompanied by a focus on the wider intercultural and transcultural communicative practices in which language is embedded and enmeshed. This entails recognition of the central place of intercultural competence and the awareness that is necessary to manage such complexity, variation, and fluidity in communication. As such, this chapter addresses Hall and Wicaksono's (this volume) call to interrogate and be "explicit about what we, as applied linguists, think English is – our *ontologies of English* – and how these ontologies underpin our educational ideologies and professional practices", with a particular focus on the intercultural and transcultural dimensions to both English use and education policy and practice.

This chapter will begin by examining how research on ELF, which emphasises the multilingualism and multiculturalism of such communicative scenarios, forces us to reconsider what we mean by intercultural communication. When it is no longer possible to clearly discern and delineate the languages and cultures that are being mixed and hybridised, then the term *inter-* may be misleading and limiting. Instead, transcultural communication in which linguistic and cultural boundaries are seen as both transcended and transgressed may be more appropriate. This perspective links transcultural communication research in ELF with other translanguaging and translingual approaches in applied linguistics (e.g. García and Li, 2014). This is followed by an exploration of the significance of reconceptions of language and intercultural communication for understanding successful communication, and particularly the concept of communicative competence. I will argue that, in order to account for the fluidity and complexity of both intercultural and transcultural communication, a wider view of competence is needed. A number of different concepts including intercultural communicative competence (Byram, 1997) and intercultural awareness (Baker, 2015a) will be explicated.

The chapter will then turn to an exploration of the implications for ELT. I suggest that the current simplistic view of communication in ELT results in essentialised perspectives that fundamentally misrepresent the processes of intercultural and transcultural communication, and thus serve as a poor model for English language learners and users. A range of alternative approaches to ELT will be discussed that focus on post-methods (Kumaravadivelu, 2012) and post-normative (Dewey, 2012, 2015) conceptions of teaching, where languages and communication are viewed as variable processes rather than products. This will also include a discussion of the cultural dimensions to ELT, arguing strongly for a decentring of ELT away from Anglophone cultures towards more localised, intercultural, and transcultural perspectives (e.g. Baker, 2012, 2015a). While there are many pressures that may limit the extent to which teachers can, or would wish to, implement an ELF and transculturally 'informed' pedagogy, there are also nascent signs of a recognition of ELF and intercultural communication in students' and teachers' beliefs and attitudes (see Page, this volume), as well as in education policy and even testing in ELT. Through the discussion of implications for ELT and recommendations for alternative approaches, this chapter will also address one of the other core aims of this volume to "take a more activist stance to challenge dominant monolithic conceptualisations of English, chiefly by promoting awareness of users' actual knowledge and practices and the alternative ontologies that these imply" (Hall, 2017, p. 137 cited in Hall and Wicaksono this volume).

2 English as a Lingua Franca: From Intercultural Communication to Transcultural Communication

The aim of this chapter is not to provide a comprehensive overview of ELF, as this is given in the previous chapter (Schaller-Schwaner and Kirkpatrick, this volume). Nonetheless, given the variety of definitions of ELF, as well as the potential for misunderstanding, it is important to state how ELF as a term is used here. First, following Seidlhofer (2011), it is viewed from a functional perspective as "any use of English among speakers of different first languages for whom English is the communicative medium of choice, and often only option" (p. 7). English native speakers are included in this definition since they too use English in intercultural communication as a lingua franca; however, they do not form the linguistic or communicative reference point. Second, in line with Jenkins (2015), the multilingual aspects of ELF are emphasised in which it is viewed as "multilingual communication in which English is available as a contact language of choice, but is not necessarily chosen" (p. 73). As Schaller-Schwaner and Kirkpatrick (this volume) make clear, ELF use cannot be properly understood without situating it in the multilingual context in which it inevitably occurs and also, I will argue here, equally important is situating it in the corresponding multicultural settings. Third, taking up the research dimension, Baird et al. (2014) define ELF "as a field that enquires into various aspects of the use of English among speakers who do not share a first language" (p. 191). Taken together, these three perspectives underscore how ELF as both a use of English and a research field is fundamentally concerned with multilingualism (different first languages) and variability and fluidity in communicative practices (a contact language). Furthermore, the use of different first languages in ELF communication almost inevitably introduces an intercultural dimension, since interlocutors will typically have a variety of linguacultural (linguistic and cultural) backgrounds and it is this intercultural dimension that this section will focus on.

It is also beyond the scope of this chapter to provide an overview of intercultural theory, but, as with the previous discussion of ELF, it is helpful to clarify how the term is understood here. This is particularly important given that I will argue that ELF research forces us to reconsider some of the fundamental concepts in intercultural communication and to even question the use of the term itself. A key distinction needs to be drawn between cross-cultural communication and intercultural communication. Although there is some debate concerning how the two terms are used, here cross-cultural communication will be viewed as exploring cultural differences between groups of people by comparing intracultural communicative practices at the national scale (e.g. Hofstede et al., 2010). Such approaches have been criticised as essentialist and stereotyped in their assumption of a one-to-one correlation between language, culture, and nation and failing to take into account the complexity and variety of cultural identifications an individual may have (Holliday, 2011). Equally significantly in comparing cultures and communicative practices at a national scale, cross-cultural perspectives fail to account for the fluidity, adaptability, and negotiation of communicative practices in individual instances of intercultural communication (Scollon et al., 2012). Lastly, in uncritically foregrounding national conceptions of culture, cross-cultural approaches frequently ignore the underlying ideologies behind particular cultural characterisations and the power imbalances that this may lead to in intercultural communication (Piller, 2011).

In contrast, intercultural communication research typically focuses on actual instances of communication between interlocutors from different cultural groups in which the relationships between language and culture are approached as an empirical question rather than a pre-given. Here, cultures are seen as variable, contested and negotiable, and with boundaries between them blurred. Culture is not simply equated with nation but may also be related to many other groupings such as ethnicity, gender, generation, profession, and sexuality (Scollon et al., 2012). A critical perspective is introduced where the concept of culture itself is questioned, exemplified by Scollon and Scollon's call to ask "[w]ho has introduced culture as a relevant category, for what purposes, and with what consequences?" (2001, pp. 544–545). Thus, while all instances of communication between interlocutors with different linguacultural backgrounds could be seen as intercultural communication, in order for investigations to be meaningful, intercultural communication research focuses on communication where cultural and linguistic differences are perceived as relevant to the interaction by participants and/or researchers (Zhu Hua, 2014; Baker, 2015a). It is this intercultural perspective that much ELF research has adopted in understanding issues of culture, identity, language, and communicative practices (e.g. Pölzl and Seidlhofer, 2006; Baker, 2009; Kalocsai, 2014). However, empirical data suggest that while intercultural communication approaches have been productive in ELF research, we need to take another step beyond them to fully understand how cultures and cultural practices are negotiated and constructed in ELF communication.

ELF studies have underscored, through the (super-)diversity and complexity of languages and cultures present in many communicative scenarios, the difficulty and inappropriateness of attempting to establish set language–culture connections. This is especially relevant for English at the national scale (e.g. associating English language with the culture of Anglophone countries) but also for any other language and culture correlation. ELF research (e.g. Pitzl, 2018; Baker and Sangiamchit, 2019) demonstrates participants orientating to multiple cultural groupings within the space of a single interaction and also negotiating such orientations in situ. In such cases, the *inter-* of *intercultural* communication becomes problematic since it is not clear what cultures participants are in between. Instead the prefix *trans-*, which implies moving through and across, rather than in between, seems more appropriate. In these instances, ELF communication would be better approached as transcultural communication in which interactants are seen moving through and across cultural and linguistic boundaries in which those very borders become blurred. Furthermore, this boundary-crossing and blurring, whether as an unconscious part of everyday communicative practices or as a deliberate act, highlights the transgressive nature of such interactions, whereby 'named' languages and cultures can no longer be taken for granted. This approach thus directly links the theoretical orientation of transcultural communication to the growing field of translingual approaches in applied linguistics such as global Englishes (Pennycook, 2007), superdiversity (Blommaert, 2013), translanguaging (Canagarajah, 2013; Li and Zhu Hua, 2013; García and Li, 2014) and metrolingualism (Pennycook and Otsuji, 2015).

It is important to clarify that this does not constitute a rejection of intercultural communication research or the role of national conceptions of language and culture. Empirical studies (e.g. Holliday, 2011; Baker, 2015a) show that nationalist ideologies are frequently drawn on in research participants' perspectives on languages and cultures and thus need to be accounted for in research. Nonetheless, as researchers, we need to approach such ideologies critically as one of many possible linguistic and cultural scales that can be drawn on, crossed and transgressed in communication. Furthermore, while intercultural communication research emphasises the mixing and hybridity of groupings, transcultural communication research focuses on scenarios where participants both transcend cultural and linguistic boundaries and also, critically, where such boundaries cannot easily be discerned. Viewing ELF communication as a form of transcultural communication has important implications for how we approach it as a subject of study and many of its core concepts.

3 Rethinking Communicative Competence for Intercultural and Transcultural Communication through ELF

ELF research, and many other approaches in applied linguistics, as illustrated in other chapters throughout this volume, have identified the variable and fluid way in which English, and language generally, is used in intercultural/transcultural communication. However, in ELF and intercultural communication research, it is not only language or linguistic forms that are crucial to understanding communication. The importance of communicative and pragmatic strategies and linking this to language use has been highlighted as key to understanding communication (e.g. accommodation, cooperation, pre-empting misunderstanding, and clarification requests; e.g. Jenkins et al., 2011). Yet, as with linguistic forms, these strategies need to also be approached as equally variable and fluid in use (Baker, 2011; Canagarajah, 2013). Beyond language and pragmatic strategy use, communication is also accompanied by a wider range of knowledge, skills, and attitudes related to the processes of intercultural/transcultural communication, including a willingness to adapt and negotiate communicative and other cultural practices (see Canagarajah, this volume). At the same time, we need to recognise power issues that may result in unequal willingness to engage in adaptation from all participants. All these factors have implications for how we view 'successful' communication, how we might model it, and how we teach it. These topics have frequently fallen under discussions of communicative and intercultural communicative competence.

In applied linguistics, and ELT in particular, communicative competence has typically been conceived in a narrow manner, with linguistic competence emphasised over other competencies (e.g. Canale and Swain, 1980). This competence has also focused around the linguistic competence of an idealised monolingual native speaker rather than the multilingual competence more appropriate to ELF communication. While Hymes' (1972) original characterisation gave a higher weighting to the sociocultural aspects of competence, it was still conceived in relation to a relatively homogenous speech community, which is clearly not the case in much ELF communication or other forms of intercultural/transcultural communication. Furthermore, when the sociocultural aspects of communication are taken up, especially in ELT, they are most frequently based on the intuition of one particular social group (Anglophone, male, white, middle class; cf. Leung, 2005; Hall, 2013). As such, communicative competence as traditionally conceptualised can be critiqued for its static representation of communication and reification of language that misrepresents the fluid, hybrid, and adaptable nature of linguistic resources in intercultural/transcultural communication. Indeed, reconceptualisations of language in communicative competence have received extensive treatment (e.g. Brumfit, 2001; Widdowson, 2012; Hall, 2013) and are also beginning to be discussed in relation to ELT (e.g. Hall et al., 2013; Dewey, 2015). However, as made clear in the previous discussion of transcultural communication, successful communication involves a lot more than mastery of linguistic forms and, as such, communicative competence in ELT is missing much that is crucial.

Within intercultural communication, and intercultural education research, the intercultural dimensions to communicative competence have, unsurprisingly, received more attention. The most well-known model is Byram's (1997, 2008) intercultural communicative competence (ICC) that builds on the core elements of communicative competence (linguistic, sociolinguistic, and discourse competence) but adds an intercultural competence element. This intercultural element consists of the five *savoirs* (Byram, 1997, p. 73), which centre around critical cultural awareness (*savoir s'engager*). The five *savoirs* emphasise a wider range of knowledge, skills, and attitudes, beyond communicative competence, related to critical evaluation of, engagement with, and negotiation and mediation between "own and other cultures and countries" (Byram, 1997, p. 54). As such, Byram's model of ICC has been very influential in recognising the intercultural orientation of most second language use and learning, and the need to incorporate this in models of communicative competence. Correspondingly, the model of the intercultural speaker has replaced the native speaker as a goal in successful intercultural communication. However, there are a number of limitations to ICC, the most significant of which is the focus on the national scale in relation to both language and culture, and the resulting danger of essentialist language, culture, and nation correlations (see Baker, 2011, 2015a; Holliday, 2011). This clearly limits its relevance to understanding ELF, where such correlations cannot be taken for granted.

More recently, a number of dynamic conceptions of competence that transcend the national scale, and that are better suited to the multilingual and multicultural nature of intercultural/transcultural communication through ELF, have been presented. Two especially relevant perspectives to this discussion are Kramsch's (2009, 2011) symbolic competence and Canagarajah's (2013) performative competence. Symbolic competence underscores the flexibility and contextually dependent nature of any competence, and emphasises the importance of criticality and reflexivity more than understanding of a cultural other and one's own culture (although this is still needed).

Symbolic competence is also about understanding the fluidity of numerous "discourse worlds" (Kramsch, 2011, p. 347) in which change, multiple meanings, and diverse interpretations are the norm. It is thus a notion of competence that is clearly well suited to the multiplicity and diversity of ELF communication, although this is not a direction that Kramsch has pursued herself. Performative competence (Canagarajah, 2013) builds on Byram's (1997) ICC but, as its title suggests, focuses on those aspects of ICC that concern the *how* rather than the *what* of communication. Most crucially though, performative competence explicitly deals with translinguals' "competence for plural language norms and mobile semiotic resources" (Canagarajah, 2013, p. 173) rather than a competence related to distinct cultures and languages. Similar to symbolic competence, the lack of pre-established norms in intercultural communication is recognised, resulting in the need for flexibility, negotiation, and cooperation in conceptualising competence. However, Canagarajah's characterisation of English in ELF research as a value-free and culturally neutral form of English (2013, p. 175) is clearly very different from the research discussed here and in other chapters in this volume, and so limits his ability to engage in current debates on these issues.

A conception of competence that incorporates many of the features of ICC and the more dynamic and critical competencies discussed previously and that applies specifically to intercultural/transcultural communication through ELF, is my own research on intercultural awareness (Baker, 2011, 2015a). Intercultural awareness is defined as "a conscious understanding of the role culturally based forms, practices and frames of reference can have in intercultural communication, and an ability to put these conceptions into practice in a flexible and context specific manner in communication" (Baker, 2011, p. 202). Here, awareness is used in an extended sense to incorporate cognitive, behavioural, and attitudinal aspects of competence and performance, at the same time functioning as a more holistic replacement for the problematic competence/performance distinction. As with symbolic competence and performative competence, there is an emphasis on process and practice in communication, with negotiation and fluidity of communicative and other cultural practices in meaning-making viewed as central. Furthermore, the focus in both theory and empirical support on intercultural/transcultural communication through ELF means that the national scale for language and culture is only one of many, and frequently is not relevant. Instead, cultural resources are often seen as emerging in situ and transcending pre-defined cultural and linguistic boundaries (Baker, 2015a). Therefore, English (and any other 'named' languages present in multilingual

ELF interactions) is used to represent and construct cultural practices and references that can be far removed from 'Anglophone cultures' or any other pre-established cultural grouping (Baker, 2011, 2015a).

In sum, the variable and fluid ways in which English is used as a lingua franca in intercultural/transcultural communication needs to be incorporated in any conception of 'competent' communication. This entails a recognition of the intercultural/transcultural dimension of communication and hence, a move from communicative competence to intercultural communicative competence/awareness. Such a move means going beyond linguistic forms to include communication and pragmatic strategies. At the same time, these strategies need to be included as part of the wider linguistic and intercultural awareness in which such knowledge, skills, and attitudes are embedded. Given the dynamic nature of such intercultural/transcultural communication, any specification of competences/awareness must necessarily be general since specific features will be situationally dependent. Thus, a focus on process and criticality becomes central, and three approaches that do this have been presented here: symbolic competence (Kramsch, 2009), performative competence (Canagarajah, 2013) and intercultural awareness (Baker, 2011, 2015a).

4 Implications for ELT: Alternative Approaches to Methods and Content

The recognition of the multilingual and intercultural/transcultural nature of much communication through English results in a need to re-examine the subject matter of ELT. This will entail reconceptualising teacher knowledge both of language (Dewey, 2012, 2015; Hall et al., 2013) and communication/ intercultural communication (Byram, 1997, 2008; Holliday, 2011; Baker, 2015a). As Hall et al. note, "in a world of multiple Englishes, ELT needs to readdress the subject matter of its pedagogical mission. We suggest that the ways in which English is traditionally conceived, and is currently being reconceived, have fundamental implications for the theory and practice of language learning and teaching" (p. 16). Due to the central place that communicative competence has had in ELT, any reconceptualisation of this, as outlined in the previous section, will have significant consequences.

Yet, despite much discussion at the theoretical level of the diversity of Englishes and the intercultural nature of communication, current ELT teaching practices, materials, and examinations remain focused on a fixed linguistic code based on a narrow interpretation of the already limited notion of communicative competence (Dewey, 2012;

Widdowson, 2012; Hall et al., 2013). This bounded code typically consists of a set of predefined features of syntax, lexis, and phonology associated with an idealised model of an 'English native speaker'. Similarly, if sociocultural or intercultural elements of communication are incorporated into ELT, they are frequently associated with Anglophone cultures and a restricted section of that world (white, middle class, male, and monolingual) presenting an essentialised image of 'other' cultures (Leung, 2005; Hall, 2013; Baker, 2015b). For instance, two studies of representations of culture in ELT textbooks found similar stereotypical images of cultures, despite being separated by more than ten years (Cortazzi and Jin, 1999; Vettorel, 2010). However, such a restricted view of English and communication through English is "unlikely to equip learners of English for the variable demands of intercultural communication through ELF" (Baker, 2015a, p. 243).

There are a growing number of approaches to ELT that aim to address this gap between the diversity of practices in intercultural/transcultural communication through ELF and the limitations on how English and communication are presented in ELT. Indeed, there are more approaches than can be discussed in one short chapter, so I will focus on a small selection as an illustration of the key features of such alternative perspectives that place globalisation and intercultural/transcultural communication as the central concern, as opposed to national languages and cultures. These features include a post-methods (Kumaravadivelu, 2012) and post-normative (Dewey, 2012) approach, in which process is given priority over product, intercultural awareness with its emphasis on reflexivity, criticality, and negotiation and, centrally, recognition of the role of English as a Lingua Franca and the multilingual and multicultural nature of this. Given the interests of this chapter, while the linguistic dimensions will be mentioned, the focus will be predominantly on the intercultural aspect of such approaches and will pay particular attention to ELF informed perspectives.

First, the post-methods approach (Kumaravadivelu, 2012) has been very influential in much thinking about alternative ELT practices. Post-methods approaches underscore the importance of contextualisation (particularity), breaking down gaps between theory and practice (practicality), and criticality (possibility) in teaching and language learning (Kumaravadivelu, 2012). In line with this, much discussion of ELF and ELT practices has been careful to avoid prescriptions about what teachers 'should' or 'should not' do, believing that teachers are best placed to decide what aspects of ELF research are most relevant for their teaching practices (e.g. Jenkins, 2012). Nonetheless, recently there has been increasing engagement with pedagogic issues from ELF researchers and ELT researchers interested in ELF: see the edited collections from Bayyurt and Akcan (2015), Bowles and Cogo (2015), and Vettorel (2015). In particular, Dewey's post-normative approach (2012, 2015) builds on post-methods but emphasises the importance of critically reflecting on the appropriacy and relevance of the norms that may underpin teaching and also the necessity and role of norms in general in ELT. Dewey (2012), like other ELF scholars (Seidlhofer, 2011; Jenkins, 2012), suggests that the best opportunity to explore such questions is in teacher training and education. Additionally, a growing number of empirical studies have demonstrated increasingly positive attitudes to global Englishes and ELF among teachers (Sifakis and Fay, 2011) and students (e.g. Csizer and Kontra, 2012).

Turning to the intercultural/transcultural dimension, Baker (2012), Galloway (2013) and Hino and Oda (2015) all offer empirical evidence in support of pedagogies that emphasise the importance of the intercultural in materials and practice, with the former two studies also incorporating aspects of intercultural awareness. Importantly, all three studies explore cultures in a manner that moves away from essentialist correlations between English language-Anglophone nations and instead bring in a range of cultural sources, products, and practices into the classroom through ELF. Kirkpatrick's multilingual model for ELT (2011, 2017) combines both the linguistic and intercultural dimensions. Although specifically developed in relation to the Association of Southeast Asian Nations (ASEAN), in which English functions as both the official language of the organisation and as the predominant lingua franca in the region, Kirkpatrick's model is likely to have significance beyond this region. Especially relevant are Kirkpatrick's recommendations that the linguistic target should be successful English use in multilingual settings (not necessarily with the native English speaker); that local and regional cultures, rather than native English-speaking cultures, are most relevant and that the associated goal should be (ASEAN-focused) intercultural competence; and that "well-trained local multilinguals provide the most appropriate English language teachers" (2017, p. 13).

In my own research, I have presented guidelines for teachers on how intercultural communication, specifically intercultural awareness (ICA) through ELF, can be incorporated in ELT practice alongside a practical example of this in a Thai ELT setting (Baker, 2012, 2015a). These guidelines detail five possible areas for developing ICA in the classroom, including exploring the complexity of local cultures; exploring cultural representations in language learning materials;

exploring cultural representations in the media and arts, both online and in more 'traditional' mediums; making use of cultural informants (including teachers and other students); and engaging in intercultural communication both face to face and electronically (Baker, 2015a, pp. 195–198). Although these recommendations go further than the general teaching principles discussed so far, they are still necessarily quite broad since the content included and how the recommendations are applied will be dependent on the teaching setting. And, of course, not all of these recommendations will be relevant in all contexts. Nonetheless, they attempt to outline how the resources available in many ELT classrooms can be utilised to critically explore and reflect on the cultural and intercultural/transcultural dimensions to language learning and use through English. Through such an approach, learners should become aware of the diverse range of settings in which English is used and the range of cultural practices and references constructed and represented through English. This will almost inevitably result in a de-centring of the Anglophone settings and cultures that currently dominate ELT materials in favour of more locally relevant cultural settings. However, this does not mean Anglophone settings are necessarily ignored and, given their predominance in ELT materials, they are likely to still be present. Yet, as with any cultural representation, these settings will need to be explored in a similarly critical manner as one of many possible cultural associations with English (see Badwan, this volume, for further discussion of critical approaches to culture and nation in ELT).

How these five areas can be put into practice in both materials and teaching was illustrated through a ten-week online course in global Englishes and intercultural communication/awareness offered to thirty-one undergraduate English language students at a Thai university (Baker, 2012, 2015a). Six English language teachers from the same institution were also asked to evaluate and comment on the course. Quantitative data from questionnaires and qualitative data from interviews and observations showed predominantly very positive responses to the course (Baker, 2012, 2015a). Both students and teachers reported interest in, and the relevance of, both intercultural aspects and Global Englishes elements of the programme. Furthermore, there appeared to be a fairly extensive awareness of the multiplicity of Englishes beyond Anglophone settings. However, it was not always clear from participants' responses to what extent ELF was seen as a variable and fluid use of English or as another variety of English. Furthermore, a number of the participants still felt that Anglophone varieties of English were the most prestigious type of English and what they aspired to. In relation to the development of ICA, while participants frequently demonstrated an awareness of the role of culture in communication, the influence of their own linguaculture and the potential differences when communicating with people with different linguacultures, there was less evidence of the advanced levels of ICA. Thus, there appeared to be little understanding of transcultural communication in which linguistic and cultural boundaries are crossed and blurred and cultural practices emerge in situ through interaction. Nonetheless, overall, the course can be viewed as successful both in terms of the practicality of incorporating intercultural and Global Englishes elements into ELT materials, and the relevance and interest of teachers and students to such approaches (Baker, 2012, p. 23).

Despite these positive findings in relation to rethinking the subject matter of ELT in terms of both English and communication, it must be recognised that there are still significant pressures and limitations on teachers that restrict their ability to implement changes. In relation to ELF, there is now a great deal of empirical research demonstrating teachers' somewhat ambiguous attitudes to the English language. Thus, even if the role of ELF is recognised, there is still a strong pull towards standard orientations and idealised native speaker models of English (e.g. Jenkins, 2007; Hall et al., 2013). Previous studies have also shown that the intercultural dimension is frequently low on teachers' list of priorities and is rarely systematically integrated into teaching (Sercu and Bandura, 2005; Young and Sachdev, 2011). This is most likely the result of the lack of attention these issues are given in current materials, teacher education, and especially testing, making it difficult for teachers to envisage how they should be applied to their classrooms. Furthermore, adding a yet wider range of intercultural skills and knowledge to the already demanding scope required for communicative competence can be viewed as placing an additional burden on already busy language teachers and classrooms.

Linked to the previous point, incorporating a wider range of Englishes and a more complex notion of intercultural competence/awareness into the classroom may seem to be adding more complexity than can be dealt with by teachers or understood by students. However, as Brumfit (2001) rightly points out, teachers have always had to select and simplify from a complex subject matter, so there is arguably nothing new here. Brumfit also notes that we must always approach selection and simplification critically, and be prepared to re-evaluate what we choose to focus on as teachers. It can thus be argued that, due to the now extensive research on English use as a form of intercultural/transcultural communication through ELF, the time is ripe for such a critical re-evaluation. Perhaps the biggest restraint to innovation that teachers face is language examinations. The need for students to pass exams is clearly of major concern to most ELT teachers and while high stakes language exams such as IELTS and TOEFL remain orientated to a narrow view of communication and 'standard native' English, then it will be difficult to implement change (Jenkins and Leung, 2014; McNamara, 2014). However, there are alternatives to these narrowly focused examinations, as detailed by Harsch (this volume), and also by other researchers in testing (Jenkins and Leung, 2014; McNamara, 2014). Nonetheless, there are powerful vested interests, including the large examining bodies as well as publishers and commercial language schools, to name a few, in maintaining the status quo that favours Anglophone orientations in ELT.

Two recent empirical studies (Boonsuk, 2016; Liu, 2016) have clearly demonstrated the difficulties teachers can face when trying to implement changes based on awareness of ELF and the intercultural nature of English communication. Boonsuk (2016) surveyed teachers', students', and programme administrators' beliefs about the construction of nativeness and its relationship to ELT in Thai higher education settings. He found that there was widespread recognition of English as a language belonging to anyone who spoke it and that his survey participants generally felt that anyone who was suitably qualified and proficient in English could make an effective English teacher. Nonetheless, at the same time, both teachers and programme administrators reported discriminatory hiring practices in which native English speakers were favoured for certain positions and typically received higher salaries than local teachers (see Wicaksono, this volume). This was attributed to outside pressures such as parents and university management, and resulted in resistance to making changes to these inequitable hiring practices for teachers. Liu's (2016) ethnographic study of a Chinese high school illustrated a different range of pressures on high school teachers. She found there was generally awareness among teachers of Global Englishes/ELF and that furthermore the national education curriculum incorporated a range of elements related to both intercultural communication and Global Englishes. However, this was not translated into classroom practices, which were heavily orientated towards examinations focusing on a restricted range of grammar and vocabulary exercises. Teachers reported being under significant pressure (both in terms of professional status and financial reward) to ensure students passed these exams, despite being critical of the effectiveness of the exams in terms of learning and using English. This leads Liu (2016, p. 218) to underscore the importance of the test reforms that are currently underway in China.

In sum, there is a growing recognition of the need to rethink both content and approaches in ELT to reflect the manner in which English is typically used as a lingua franca for intercultural/transcultural communication and to better prepare learners of English for such communication. This entails a re-evaluation of the core concept of communicative competence, widening it beyond its currently narrow focus on a limited code towards a wider range of skills and knowledge associated with intercultural/transcultural communication and the ability to make use of linguistic resources in flexible and variable ways. Perspectives such as Dewey's (2012, 2015) post-normative approach explore how such dynamic conceptions of the English language can be implemented in teacher education and classrooms. Furthermore, studies, including my own research, have examined how the cultural and intercultural content of classrooms can be shifted away from their current focus on Anglophone settings to more global perspectives (e.g. Baker, 2012, 2015a). Kirkpatrick (2017) provides an example of teaching recommendations that includes both this flexible multilingual approach to English, underscoring its use as a lingua franca, and also a de-centring of the cultural content away from Anglophone cultures towards more local and intercultural settings. Such changes may be seen as demanding for already busy teachers and indeed, empirical research has demonstrated the difficulties and limitations to implementing such changes at the 'chalk face' (e.g. Boonsuk, 2016; Liu, 2016). Nonetheless, in emphasising the importance of critical evaluation of content, flexibility, and local contextualisation, these ELF-informed perspectives on ELT offer teachers and students increased agency and freedom in the classroom. Such freedom will, of course, be limited by outside pressures such as curricula and especially testing. However, studies such as Liu's (2016) and a number of chapters in this volume show that change can and is being implemented here too and is generally moving in a direction that increasingly recognises the use of English as ELF in intercultural/transcultural communication.

5 Conclusion

To return to Hall and Wicaksono's (this volume) call to examine and be "explicit about what we, as applied linguists, think English is – our *ontologies of English* – and how these ontologies underpin our educational ideologies and professional practices", a number of perspectives have been outlined here. First, ELF research illustrates the potential complexity and fluidity of communication through English with empirical data clearly demonstrating the multilingual and plurilithic nature of ELF. Furthermore, this complexity and fluidity extends beyond linguistic forms. In order to understand ELF communication, we need to look at communication strategies used alongside the cultural practices and settings in which linguistic forms and communication strategies are embedded. However, these cultural practices and settings should be approached in a parallel manner to linguistic forms in ELF as complex, fluid, and emergent. Thus, I have argued that while much communication through ELF can be viewed as intercultural communication, this approach has failed to explain instances where cultural practices and references could not be attributed to, or positioned between, any defined culture and language correlation. To account for this, the notion of transcultural communication was introduced in which linguistic and cultural boundaries and correlations were transgressed and transcended.

Second, the implications for one of the core concepts in ELT, communicative competence, were considered. Communicative competence was critiqued for its narrow view of language and communication, especially as it is used in ELT practices (e.g. testing). Alternative conceptions that expanded competence to account for the intercultural dimensions were explored (Byram, 1997) as well as recent suggestions for critical approaches (Kramsch, 2009; Canagarajah, 2013), especially those that focused on the use of ELF for intercultural and transcultural communication (Baker, 2015a). Alongside an expanded range of skills, knowledge, and attitudes related to language, communication, and culture, the importance of flexibility, process, and contextualisation in understanding intercultural competence and awareness was explored.

Third, the significance of these alternative views of English, communication, and competence/awareness through ELF for intercultural and transcultural communication for ELT policy and practice was considered. In that section, a more 'active stance' was adopted and a range of recommendations offered that suggested teaching practices and policy needed to take better account of the extensive use of ELF for intercultural/transcultural communication. Taking account of ELF involved a de-centring of the current Anglophone focus with the implications of de-centring in relation to cultural content and references explored in depth in this chapter. I also argued that more emphasis needed to be given to processes of learning; variability at all levels from linguistic forms to cultural references; the importance of local contextualisation; and a critical questioning of norms and models. This criticality, of course, includes the approaches to ELT advocated here and it is important that any recommendations made are wide enough in scope to allow teachers and policy makers the freedom to decide what aspects are most relevant for them. While these alternative approaches may appear demanding for teachers and policy makers, questioning and revision of approaches and content in ELT are an everyday part of ELT practices and, as such, these recommendations may not be as radical as they first appear. Although major changes to the subject matter of ELT are advocated here, in practice this may not lead to radical new teaching processes, but rather selection from a different range of content sources. Despite empirical studies showing mixed findings in relation to uptake of ELF and intercultural communication in ELT policy and practice, recent research also shows a nascent awareness of both an ELF and intercultural (although perhaps not transcultural at this time) 'informed' policy and practice. Due to this increasing interest from both ELT practitioners in ELF research, and ELF researchers in pedagogy, the synergy between research and practice is likely to grow in the future with potentially significant implications for the content and approaches to English and communication in ELT.

References

Baird, R., Baker, W., and Kitazawa, M. (2014). The complexity of English as a lingua franca. *Journal of English as a Lingua Franca, 3*(1), 171–196.

Baker, W. (2009). The cultures of English as a lingua franca. *TESOL Quarterly*, 43(4), 567–592. doi: 10.1002/j.1545-7249.2009.tb00187.x

Baker, W. (2011). Intercultural awareness: Modelling an understanding of cultures in intercultural communication through English as a lingua franca. *Language and Intercultural Communication, 11*(3), 197–214.

Baker, W. (2012). Using online learning objects to develop intercultural awareness in ELT: A critical examination in a Thai higher education setting. *British Council Teacher Development Research Papers*. www.teachingenglish.org.uk/publications

Baker, W. (2015a). *Culture and Identity through English as a Lingua Franca: Rethinking Concepts and Goals in Intercultural Communication*. Berlin: De Gruyter Mouton.

Baker, W. (2015b). Research into practice: Cultural and intercultural awareness. *Language Teaching, 48*(1), 130–141.

Baker, W. and Sangiamchit, C. (2019). Transcultural communication: Language, communication and culture through English as a lingua franca in a social network community. *Language and Intercultural Communication*. doi: 10.1080/14708477.2019.1606230

Bayyurt, Y. and Akcan, S., eds. (2015). *Current Perspectives on Pedagogy for ELF*. Berlin: De Gruyter Mouton.

Blommaert, J. (2013). *Ethnography, Superdiversity and Linguistic Landscapes: Chronicles of Complexity*. Bristol: Multilingual Matters.

Boonsuk, Y. (2016). Thai university students, teachers and program administrators, construction of nativeness in English language teaching. Unpublished PhD thesis, University of Southampton.

Bowles, H. and Cogo, A., eds. (2015). *International Perspectives on English as a Lingua Franca: Pedagogical Insights*. London: Palgrave Macmillan.

Brumfit, C. (2001). *Individual Freedom in Language Teaching: Helping Learners to Develop a Dialect of Their Own*. Oxford: Oxford University Press.

Byram, M. (1997). *Teaching and Assessing Intercultural Communicative Competence*. Clevedon: Multilingual Matters.

Byram, M. (2008). *From Foreign Language Education to Education for Intercultural Citizenship: Essays and Reflections*. Clevedon: Multilingual Matters Ltd.

Canagarajah, S. (2013). *Translingual Practice: Global Englishes and Cosmopolitan Relations*. London: Routledge.

Canale, M. and Swain, M. (1980). Theoretical bases of communicative approaches to second language teaching and testing. *Applied Linguistics, 1*(1), 1–47.

Cortazzi, M. and Jin, L. (1999). Cultural mirrors: Materials and methods in the EFL classroom. In E. Hinkel, ed., *Culture in Second Language Teaching and Learning* (pp. 196–219). Cambridge: Cambridge University Press.

Csizer, K. and Kontra, E. (2012). ELF, ESP, ENL and their effect on students' aims and beliefs: A structural equation model. *System, 40*(1), 1–10.

Dewey, M. (2012). Towards a post-normative approach: Learning the pedagogy of ELF. *Journal of English as a Lingua Franca, 1*(1), 141–170.

Dewey, M. (2015). Time to wake up some dogs! Shifting the culture of language in ELT. In Y. Bayyurt and S. Akcan, eds., *Current Perspectives on Pedagogy for ELF* (pp. 121–134). Berlin: De Gruyter Mouton.

Galloway, N. (2013). Global Englishes and English language teaching (ELT) – Bridging the gap between theory and practice in a Japanese context. *System, 41*(3), 786–803.

García, O. and Li, W. (2014). *Translanguaging: Language, Bilingualism and Education*. Basingstoke: Palgrave Macmillan.

Hall, C. J. (2013). Cognitive contributions to plurilithic views of English and other languages. *Applied Linguistics, 34*(2), 211–231.

Hall, C. J., Wicaksono, R., Liu, S. et al. (2013). *English Reconceived: Raising Teachers' Awareness of English as a 'Plurilithic' Resource through an Online Course*. ELT Research Papers. London: British Council.

Hino, N. and Oda, S. (2015). Integrated practice in teaching English as an international language (IPTEIL): A classroom ELF pedagogy in Japan. In Y. Bayyurt and S. Akcan, eds., *Current Perspectives on Pedagogy for ELF* (pp. 35–50). Berlin: De Gruyter Mouton.

Hofstede, G. H., Hofstede, G. J., and Minkov, M. (2010). *Cultures and Organizations: Software of the Mind: Intercultural Cooperation and Its Importance for Survival*, 3rd ed. New York and London: McGraw-Hill.

Holliday, A. (2011). *Intercultural Communication and Ideology*. London: Sage.

Hymes, D. (1972). On communicative competence In J. B. Pride and J. Holmes, eds., *Sociolinguistics* (pp. 269–293). Harmondsworth: Penguin.

Jenkins, J. (2007). *English as a Lingua Franca: Attitude and Identity*. Oxford: Oxford University Press.

Jenkins, J. (2012). English as a Lingua Franca from the classroom to the classroom. *ELT Journal, 66*(4), 486–494.

Jenkins, J. (2015). Repositioning English and multilingualism in English as a Lingua Franca. *Englishes in Practice, 2*(3), 49–85.

Jenkins, J., Cogo, A., and Dewey, M. (2011). Review of developments in research into English as a Lingua Franca. *Language Teaching, 44*(3), 281–315.

Jenkins, J. and Leung, C. (2014). English as a Lingua Franca. In A. Kunnan, ed., *The Companion to Language Assessment* (pp. 1607–1616). Malden, MA: John Wiley.

Kalocsai, K. (2014). *Communities of Practice and English as a Lingua Franca: A Study of Erasmus Students in a Central-European Context*. Berlin: DeGruyter Mouton.

Kirkpatrick, A. (2011). English as an Asian lingua franca and the multilingual model of ELT. *Language Teaching, 44*(2), 212–224.

Kirkpatrick, A. (2017). Language education policy among the Association of Southeast Asian Nations (ASEAN). *European Journal of Language Policy, 9* (1), 7–25.

Kramsch, C. (2009). *The Multilingual Subject*. Oxford: Oxford University Press.

Kramsch, C. (2011). The symbolic dimensions of the intercultural. *Language Teaching, 44*(3), 354–367.

Kumaravadivelu, B. (2012). *Language Teacher Education for a Global Society: A Modular Model for Knowing, Analyzing, Recognizing, Doing, and Seeing*. Abingdon and Oxon: Routledge.

Leung, C. (2005). Convivial communication: Recontextualizing communicative competence. *International Journal of Applied Linguistics, 15*(2), 121–144.

Li, Wei and Zhu Hua. (2013). Translanguaging identities and ideologies: Creating transnational space through flexible multilingual practices amongst Chinese university students in the UK. *Applied Linguistics, 34*(5), 516–535.

Liu, H. (2016). Language policy and practice in a Chinese junior high school from global Englishes perspective. Unpublished PhD thesis, University of Southampton.

McNamara, T. (2014). 30 years on – Evolution or revolution? *Language Assessment Quarterly, 11*(2), 226–232.

Pennycook, A. (2007). *Global Englishes and Transcultural Flows*. London: Routledge.

Pennycook, A. and Otsuji, E. (2015). *Metrolingualism: Language in the City*. Abingdon: Routledge.

Piller, I. (2011). *Intercultural Communication: A Critical Introduction*. Edinburgh: Edinburgh University Press.

Pitzl, M. (2018). Transient international groups (TIGs): Exploring the group and development dimension of ELF. *Journal of English as a Lingua Franca, 7*, 25.

Pölzl, U. and Seidlhofer, B. (2006). In and on their own terms: The "habitat factor" in English as a lingua franca interaction. *Language and Intercultural Communication,* 177, 151–176. doi: 10.1515/IJSL.2006

Scollon, R. and Scollon, S. W. (2001). Discourse and intercultural communication. In D. Schiffrin, D. Tannen, and H. Hamilton, eds., *The Handbook of Discourse Analysis* (pp. 538–547). Oxford: Blackwell.

Scollon, R., Scollon, S. B. K., and Jones, R. H. (2012). *Intercultural Communication: A Discourse Approach*, 3rd ed. Chichester: Wiley-Blackwell.

Seidlhofer, B. (2011). *Understanding English as a Lingua Franca*. Oxford: Oxford University Press.

Sercu, L. and Bandura, E. (2005). *Foreign Language Teachers and Intercultural Competence: An International Investigation*. Clevedon: Multilingual Matters.

Sifakis, N. and Fay, R. (2011). Integrating an ELF pedagogy in a changing world: The case of Greek state schooling. In A. Cogo, A. Archibald, and J. Jenkins, eds., *Latest Trends in ELF Research* (pp. 285–297). Newcastle: Cambridge Scholars.

Vettorel, P. (2010). EIL/ELF and representation of culture in textbooks: Only food, fairs, folklore and facts? In C. Gagliardi and A. Maley, eds., *EIL, ELF, Global English: Teaching and Learning Issues* (pp. 153–187). Bern: Peter Lang.

Vettorel, P., ed. (2015). *New Frontiers in Teaching and Learning English*. Newcastle: Cambridge Scholars Publishing.

Widdowson, H. G. (2012). ELF and the inconvenience of established concepts. *Journal of English as a Lingua Franca,* 1(1), 5–26.

Young, T. J. and Sachdev, I. (2011). Intercultural communicative competence: Exploring English language teachers' beliefs and practices. *Language Awareness,* 20(2), 81–98.

Zhu Hua. (2014). *Exploring Intercultural Communication: Language in Action*. Abingdon: Routledge.

14 *Exploring Standards-Based, Intelligibility-Based, and Complex Conceptions of English in a Lingua Franca Context*

Nathan Page

1 Introduction

This chapter aims to engage with wider discussions in this volume regarding ontologies of English and how language can be productively conceptualized by English teachers, learners/users, and other stakeholders. As indicated by the title, the work is intended to make a specific contribution towards uncovering complexity in ontologies of language that do not map cleanly onto dichotomies such as 'monolithic versus plurilithic' (Hall, 2013), 'difference versus deficit', or 'standards-based versus intelligibility-based'. As also indicated, these ontological discussions are framed by a study carried out in a lingua franca context of pedagogy and usage, where (1) Japanese voluntary workers use English as a Lingua Franca to communicate with local interlocutors in diverse global locations and (2) an English language course is taken by these volunteers prior to their departure from Japan that is specifically designed to facilitate that communication. Further details on this context are provided in the following section before the focus returns to conceptions of English.

1.1 Research Context

The Japan International Co-operation Agency (JICA), Japan's equivalent of the US Peace Corps, is a governmental organisation that co-ordinates global voluntary work opportunities for Japanese volunteers (JICA, 2018). Large numbers of volunteers are regularly dispatched by JICA to live overseas and work on projects related to international development for a period of two years, working in fields such as health care, education, and engineering. Before departure, the volunteers must pass a ten-week training course in Japan. This is focused on language lessons that prepare volunteers for using a specific target language in their destination countries. For example, volunteers going

273

to most parts of East Africa, South Asia, the Pacific nations, and the Caribbean would take English lessons, although many other languages are also learned at the two JICA training centres in Japan.

The English language courses at JICA are intensive, comprising roughly five hours of language lessons per day, six days a week for the ten-week duration. Students are ranked according to proficiency as determined by an admissions test, and grouped into classes, each containing approximately six students. These learners take a morning 'home class' to practice general English and an afternoon 'technical class' focusing on specific language for their particular field of work. The general principle underlying the course is to develop the communicative skills of the volunteers in preparation for working overseas. However, the assessment of grammatical accuracy is also included in JICA's final language test that must be passed before volunteers can be dispatched.

JICA is a dynamic context for applied linguistics research, notable for the target language usage (post-pedagogy) taking place in linguistically diverse locations around the world, and in a globally significant way as it relates to international development. The context represents a unique opportunity for examining how English is conceptualized in relation to the diversity of global English.

1.2 Conceptualizing English in Lingua Franca Contexts

Key research in English as a Lingua Franca (ELF) such as that by Jenkins (2000) and Seidlhofer (2001) has championed a view of language that prioritizes intelligibility over adherence to grammatical standards. Defining ELF situations as whenever speakers of different (non-English) mother tongues are in communication, these seminal works showed that numerous features of pronunciation and lexicogrammar that are commonly emphasised in the practice of ELT may not be wholly relevant to the learners, as they have little or no impact on their mutual intelligibility when communicating with other speakers. ELF research tends to contain the underlying argument that teachers and other professionals working with language should be open to intelligibility-based rather than standards-based perspectives, as this would be fairer and more beneficial to the learners.

Although there were initially many controversies and debates associated with ELF, there was an underlying humanistic and egalitarian motive that has contributed greatly to a shift towards an acceptance of the diversity in how English is used and a contribution to other areas such as the erosion of the privileging of the native speaker over the

Complex Conceptions of English in a Lingua Franca Context   275

non-native speaker (see Wicaksono, this volume). This overall shift can be traced in the work of many other scholars working in ELF and related fields. More traditional prescriptivist, standards-based views of language have of course been prevalent historically (Crowley, 2003), in line with historically more essentialist views of constructs such as culture (Piller, 2011). A great deal has been written about the historical privileging of standard forms of language over regional dialects (see Hall, this volume), and attempts to impose the former while stamping out the latter. This was the case both in the United Kingdome (Crowley, 2003) and in many other countries such as Japan (Seargeant, 2009).

In fields relating specifically to ELT and applied linguistics, a key event facilitating the conceptual acceptance of diversity in English (and the movement from standards- to intelligibility-based views in academic research) was the Quirk–Kachru debate from the mid-1980s. This focused on the relevance of traditionally accepted, standard forms of English in the global enterprise of ELT. Kachru argued that diverse forms of English in localized contexts such as India and Africa should be afforded legitimacy, and went on to spearhead the World Englishes movement that continues to foster the acceptance of global diversity in English with research into localized forms of the language around the world. Kachru's original three circles model (Kachru, 1985) has since been critiqued, with many now viewing it as an oversimplification, albeit still useful and important (e.g. McKay and Bokhorst-Heng, 2008).

Before the key ELF research referred to previously, other relevant publications included Firth (1990), Widdowson (1994), and Firth and Wagner (1997), which all progressed the emerging notion in academic fields that diverse forms of English should be viewed as legitimate and valid, whether conforming to a standard variety or not. These important publications can be associated with the so called 'critical turn' in applied linguistics and ELT in the 1990s. Related to the idea of accepting diversity in English and eroding the power associated with idealized notions of standard English were other powerful and critical concepts such as the importance of identity in language learning, rather than viewing learning as a purely mechanical process without unique individual factors (Pierce, 1995). As Firth and Wagner (1997) pointed out, learners had been typically viewed by the research community in terms of deficit rather than what they could already achieve with the language. Their paper called for the established Second Language Acquisition (SLA) paradigm to afford more legitimacy to second language users of English and for a reconceptualization that would move the field away from negative terminology such as 'interlanguage' and 'fossilization'.

1.3 Further Issues in the Conceptualization of English

Complementing the ideas just reviewed are many contemporary perspectives that align with the conceptual acceptance of diversity in English, not only specifically for ELT and other global dimensions of the language, but more generally. Leung and Street (2014) describe English as a 'protean entity' and state that "its fabric and its uses are being constantly re-shaped and transformed in multiple ways" (p. xxi), a view that is incompatible with standards-based views of the language. Hall et al. (2011, p. 25) point out that many people see languages "as single objects, like rocks, but they are in fact more like sandy beaches, rain clouds or galaxies: collections with no one central point and no sharply defined borders".

The metaphor of a rock is allied to Hall's (2013) discussion of 'monolithic' as opposed to 'plurilithic' views of language. Monolithic views are of the standards-based, prescriptivist type whereas plurilithic views recognise the changeable, fluid nature of language as it is actually used for communication. Monolithic versus plurilithic conceptions of language, along with difference versus deficit and standards-based versus intelligibility-based perspectives, are all binary distinctions with related meanings. They indicate the extent to which a person is tied to decontextualized, idealized notions of language when conceiving of it, or are more likely to be cognizant and accepting of variation in how language is used. The three binaries are represented in Figure 14.1.

These three distinctions are viewed here as interchangeable, although the third has been adopted for the title of this chapter. To unpack the subtle differences and connections between them, the first most clearly relates to overall ontologies and conceptualizations of language (see Hall, 2013, also Hall this volume). The second (e.g. Firth and Wagner, 1997) relates to value judgements applied to specific examples of language and instances of its use. The third relates to the values underpinning those judgements, which form part of a person's overall ontology of language.

When considering the different conceptualizations of language that an individual might hold, it is important to acknowledge that the term

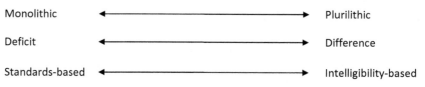

Figure 14.1 Three related binaries for depicting conceptualizations of English

'language' can be used to refer to different entities. Hall (2013) lists eight different senses of the word language, which were subsequently categorized into four domains (cognitive, expressive, social, and notional) in Hall et al. (2017) and in Hall (this volume). A key concept here is that our ideas about English might unintentionally conflate conceptualizations of idealized forms of the language (from the notional domain) with specific acts of expression (expressive) or uses of language to achieve a social aim (social). An individual tied to a notional view of English is likely to see it as an idealized entity that is defined by its official codified structures; however, this would not account for the type of variation that occurs in meaningful, successful, and legitimate communication in the real world.

The notional versus expressive/social distinction can be mapped onto Agar's (1996) discussion of 'the perfect circle' in conceptions of language. He states that we may refer to language inside an imagined circle, representing idealized forms of language that conform to officially recognised standards, or language outside of it, that is the more messy reality of how language is actually used for real-life communication, being open to a great deal of diversity, variation, and change. To map the same concept one more time, it can also be equated with Widdowson's (2003) notion of English as subject and object: the subject is the idealized version that might be taught in school whereas the object is the more diverse entity that exists in real-life communication. These concepts, along with Hall's distinction between notional, expressive, and social domains, indicate the need for reconceptualizing English for any ELT practitioners who have not considered the difference between idealized versions of language and the daily realities of it.

The notion of linguistic repertoire (e.g. Snell, 2013) is also relevant here. This demonstrates how we have access to different styles and types of language that can be deployed based on our current situation. Snell's (2013) research shows that school children in the North East of England have access to features of both the local dialect and standard forms of English and can use them flexibly as they wish to suit their current interlocutors and type of speech activity. The same concept can be applied to global diversity in English where, for example, a speaker in Jamaica has access to standard forms of English and Jamaican Creole, being able to skilfully move between the two along a cline of linguistic structures (Irvine, 2008). The point here is that it could be misleading to assume that either of the 'non-standard' forms from these examples is the only version of the language that the speakers have access to. The notion of a linguistic repertoire allows us to take a holistic view of a person's language usage and capabilities, acknowledging the role of context. This is plurilithic in the sense of variation of language resources within the same individual in addition to across individuals.

1.4 Complexity in Conceptualizations of English

Just as with Kachru's three circles model, binary distinctions such as standards-based versus intelligibility-based conceptions of language may be oversimplifications, even though they are a useful point of departure. The reality is likely to be more complex and as with so many areas of English studies and ELT, it may be that context is an important driver of decision making and particular conceptual positions that we might take up. We can see, for example, that if our students are preparing for an International English Language Testing System (IELTS) exam, the nature of their learning needs might require us to take a more standards-based approach, whereas if their only target is to communicate verbally then an intelligibility-based approach might be more appropriate (see Sifakis, 2017; also Harsch, this volume). This then becomes a rather complex issue when it comes to conceptualizing English: should our conceptions depend on what English is appropriate for what purposes? This seems inevitable given the earlier example of learner needs and only contributes to the idea of complexity in conceptions of English, given the fact that both external (contextual) and internal (ontological) factors go towards orientating our approach to language as standards- or intelligibility-based. This is in addition to the fact that English as used in lingua franca contexts is in itself inherently complex and should not be considered reductively or without accounting for context (see Baird et al., 2014 for a full discussion; also Schaller-Schwaner and Kirkpatrick, this volume).

As a related point, some ELF research has been critiqued for arguing the case for an intelligibility-based perspective too strongly (Sewell, 2012) and overgeneralizing concepts (Friedrich and Matsuda, 2010). Seargeant (2009) has pointed out that the ELF terminology itself, and the central tenet that the adherence to idealized grammatical standards is not important in communication, cannot account for the multiple situations around the world where knowledge of 'standard' grammatical forms is important in reality for the individuals involved (cf. Harder, this volume).

2 The Study

The study reported here investigates JICA volunteers' conceptualizations of English, as informed by their experiences of communicating in lingua franca contexts associated with their overseas voluntary work. The focus will be on how these map onto either standards- or intelligibility-based conceptions and any areas of complexity in between. This will be supplemented by the analysis of a JICA volunteer interacting with a local volunteer in Kenya.

2.1 Research Methods

In what follows, I draw on data extracts from research conducted in 2012–2013 as part of my wider research into the JICA context (Page, 2015). This involves sampling data from:

1. *Focus groups with JICA English learners prior to dispatch*, who responded to prompts on topics such as their expectations of English usage overseas and whether they felt that studying grammar was good preparation for this or not.
2. *Interviews with JICA volunteers after being dispatched*, which were conducted either in person during my fieldwork or remotely via Skype and were primarily about the experience of using English and other languages for voluntary work and everyday life in their specific context.
3. *Interactions between JICA volunteers and local interlocutors after being dispatched*, which were collected through a combination of volunteers self-recording conversations and through my recordings while on location doing fieldwork.

Data from points 1 and 2 look at participants' conceptualizations of English (as related to lingua franca usage and pedagogy) and the third is used as an example of actual language usage in that kind of context. In terms of data analysis methods, my major influences are linguistic ethnography (e.g. Rampton, 2006) and a discourse analysis-based approach to research interviews (e.g. Mann, 2011) and focus groups. Following Rampton (2006), transcribed audio recordings were analysed using methods derived from Conversation Analysis and Interactional Sociolinguistics, involving a close turn-by-turn analysis of spoken interaction and also drawing in elements from interview and observational data in order to build up interpretations. The turn-by-turn interactional analysis was seen as compatible with the strategies suggested for interview analysis by Mann (2011), and was therefore applied to all three types of data previously described. For reasons of space, brief extracts from the interview and focus group data will be used here. Pseudonyms have been used for the participants in order to maintain confidentiality.

2.2 Analysis and Findings

USAGE OF ENGLISH DURING VOLUNTARY WORK

An illustrative example of what communication is like for JICA volunteers in their host countries (post-pedagogy) is provided in Extract 1, where Riko, a Japanese volunteer working in health care in rural Kenya, is visiting what she refers to as a 'feeding centre' for malnourished children. During this visit, Riko is discussing the centre with two Kenyan health care workers, Belinda and Florence, primarily with the purpose of learning about the services that it offers.

Extract 1

```
01   R:   okay (.) so:: right now how many: (.) how many
02        childrens are there here
03   B:   we have one hundred and eighty
04   R:   one hundred and eighty
05   B:   yes
06   R:   children
07   B:   yeah
08   R:   you are feeding
09   B:   mmm
10   R:   okay: (.) uh-huh (.) so::: (.) out of a hundred
11        eighty how many children are malnourished
12        (1.1)
13   B:   you know the s- the chil- the- (.) the:: support here
14
15   R:   uh-huh
16   B:   it was a result of (.) malnourished children in the
17        community
18   R:   okay
19   B:   and so we were just trying ( ) some student
20        who maybe going to school so it's like all of them
21        were malnourished
22   R:   uh-huh
23   B:   but some are rehabilitated by now [so
24   R:                                     [okay
25   B:   that's why we- you can identify them from their
26        hairs
27        and [maybe the loss of
28   R:       [mmm
29   B:   body weight
30   R:   mm
31   B:   so
32   R:   mm-hm
33   B:   it's that way
```

Complex Conceptions of English in a Lingua Franca Context 281

```
34   R:   mm-hm (.) okay
35   B:   yes
36        (.)
37   R:   wh- when will you discharge those children
38   B:   mmm?
39   R:   discharge? like (.) ((laughter))
40   B:   how
41   F:   ( )
42   R:   mm?
43   F:   what do you mean by discharge
44   R:   [er: like er you
45   B:   [if you want to
46   R:   mm you like you register those children
47   B:   [yes
48   R:   [but then (.) wh- mm up to when are you going to
49        take care of them
50   F:   ( )
51   B:   it's like er:
52   F:   ((speaks in a local language))
53   B:   it's like er:: (2.5) it's like er:: if you look at
54        er: the time er of maybe (.) releasing them
55   R:   mm-hm
56   B:   we just give them chance even up to when they are
57        doing their secondary school
58   R:   mm-hm
```

There are numerous points of interest in this extract that can be commented upon. Taking an overview of the unfolding interaction, there is an initial question by Riko (1–2) that gets a non-problematic response from Belinda (3) and then a second (10–11) that requires a longer response from Belinda (13–33). Both of Riko's initial questions were intelligible to Belinda, and there is no evidence to suggest that Riko cannot comprehend her replies. It is Riko's third question (37) that very clearly does cause interactional trouble as, although Belinda knows the key word *discharge* (she finds it intelligible in the sense used by Smith and Nelson, 1985), she cannot comprehend or interpret what Riko means by it in this context, therefore the question is not understood. There are numerous markers to indicate that this process takes place, for example, Belinda's initial *mmm* made with rising intonation (38), Riko's repetition with rising intonation followed by laughter (39), and Florence's intervention of *what do you mean by discharge* (43). Riko then paraphrases her question (46, 48–49), and Belinda ultimately replies to it in a way that demonstrates that she now does comprehend what Riko is asking (51–57). This is clearly an example of speakers negotiating meaning in order to maintain intelligibility, a process that is thought to be common in ELF communication (e.g. Firth, 1990; Cogo and Dewey, 2006). Interestingly, *discharge* was not the only vocabulary item that needed to be negotiated in the full interaction; there were also *groundsman* and *thrice*, both occurring in the opposite direction of Belinda producing and Riko receiving.

Beyond this most distinctive feature – Riko's skilful paraphrase of the problematic word to maintain mutual intelligibility – it is important to point out that grammatically non-standard features of English are used in the interaction (Riko's *childrens* (2), Belinda's *give them chance* (56)) with no effect on mutual intelligibility, following key assertions about lexicogrammar in ELF (Seidlhofer 2001, 2004). There are also numerous back-channels in the interaction: small discourse markers such as Belinda's *yes* (5) and Riko's *uh-huh* (15) to indicate interest on the part of the listener when their interlocutor is speaking. Such back-channels are also said to be common in ELF interaction (Meierkord, 2000) as they work to scaffold smooth interaction and intelligibility. There are also indicators that Riko is accommodating to her Kenyan interlocutors in terms of accent, although this cannot be seen in Extract 1. Riko's *childrens* (2) is pronounced distinctively as /tʃɪldʒrenz/ with features including the final vowel sound being very similar to what we would expect from speakers of English in Kenya (e.g. Skandèra, 1999). Converging on the local accent is a notable phenomenon and is likely to be related to Riko's identity along with the desire to maximize intelligibility. These features are broadly consistent across the other interactions in my data set, including the analysis presented in Page (2014).

What can Extract 1 and its analysis tell us about appropriate conceptualizations of English for the JICA context? It would problematize, at least to some extent, conceptions by teachers, learners, and other stakeholders that are overly focused on standards and grammatical correctness. Although Riko must of course know a certain amount of grammar to be able to construct her utterances and comprehend those of her Kenyan interlocutors, the communication is fluid and does not always adhere to 'standard' grammatical norms. We can see therefore that class time spent with Riko prior to dispatch that overly emphasized the standard usage of plurals, for example, would not have been a good use of resources. A focus on pragmatic moves and vocabulary might be more important: although Riko skilfully paraphrases when needed, other volunteers may not have the confidence or ability to do this; therefore, they may need to 'let pass' (Firth, 1990) or change topic completely when interactional trouble comes up, such as the problematic vocabulary in Extract 1. Therefore, the extract presented here fits with many of the existing assertions about ELF communication and serves as a warning against too much focus on grammatical norms in the pre-service language training at JICA.

LEARNER/USER CONCEPTUALIZATIONS OF ENGLISH

Turning now to learner/user conceptualizations of English in the JICA context, a series of quotations from my interview and focus group data will be presented to illustrate these. When I interviewed Ryuta, a volunteer based in South Africa, and asked him whether his interlocutors there were using English with strict adherence to grammatical rules, he replied:

R: It's not so strict ... they can catch even when I speak not proper grammar ... I think it comes from the characteristic of different cultures, they use eleven official language ... so there's some gap between people who speak English.

The concept being referred to here is lingua franca usage, whereby English is used as a bridging language to connect different mother tongues. Ryuta is making a connection here between a flexibility in his use of English – in that the grammar is not 'proper', in other words, contains errors relative to standard forms – and the fact that the language around him is used flexibly due to historical and cultural reasons. Ryuta is clearly displaying an intelligibility-based conception of English as his primary orientation, and this was fairly consistent among the volunteers. For example, when I asked another volunteer – Kozue, working in Uganda – if she would have any advice for future volunteers for how to study English prior to dispatch from Japan, she responded:

K: Well just to be open-minded ((laughter)) I think just try not to get caught by the rule that we learned in school ... in textbook and just try to not to speak with one rule because English is like ... you know I don't know what rule is correct because everyone use it in different ways ((laughter)) and I think that's what makes English very unique and enjoyable

This extract continues Ryuta's theme of flexibility in usage of English, de-emphasizing the importance of adherence to standard grammar rules in JICA contexts of usage. Kozue introduces a new element in response to the idea of giving advice to future volunteers, in that she cautions specifically against Japanese volunteers trying to adhere too

284   Nathan Page

much to grammatical rules that they learned in school as this is likely to inhibit their ability to communicate. It has been widely reported elsewhere (e.g. Bolton, 2008) that although Japanese students spend an enormous amount of time studying English at school, this is largely based on learning 'standard' grammar rules, resulting in learners typically not being able to communicate with any fluency or confidence (see Hall, this volume, Section 5.2). Kozue is specifically warning against a preoccupation with following grammatical rules when communicating as a JICA volunteer. Elsewhere in her data, she refers to the idea of needing not to worry about making mistakes and the fact that she sees English as a neutral tool of communication.

Beyond the two examples that have been given, there were numerous other examples in the data set of JICA volunteers displaying intelligibility-based conceptions of English. Standards-based conceptions were very rare in the data set overall, except where some volunteers with self-perceived lower proficiency were concerned about not knowing enough grammar to construct meaningful utterances and to understand the talk of others. One volunteer – Shinobu, working in the Marshall Islands – displayed somewhat standards-based conceptions when she responded as follows to my question about whether it is important to follow grammatical rules there:

```
S:   I think not really important ... you know if you want to
     speak with Marshallese people in English ... grammar
     rules of course maybe are important but we can understand
     each other even if it's not perfect English
```

The point to note here is that although Shinobu is here making roughly the same point as the other volunteers who have been quoted, she tended to use terms that hinted at a deficit type conception of language such as perfect/imperfect, good/bad, and with frequent reference to mistakes and errors in the language of local users in the Marshall Islands. Some would argue that this terminology is legitimate, especially or perhaps because Shinobu is a teacher of English herself. However, such language does belong to a more standards-based conception of language in contrast to the other two volunteers quoted earlier.

Now turning to the notion of complexity in conceptualizations, including instances when both standards-based and intelligibility-based conceptualizations are displayed, some relevant data for this will now be demonstrated. Returning to Kozue, who was quoted earlier in the context of enjoying the freedom and flexibility that she found with English, she also reported instances when those around her had cared very much about grammatical standards in English:

K: it's surprising that I have regular like monthly meetings with the officers and there is a man who is in charge of ... recording minutes, and he comes back to me a few weeks after the meeting with the minutes and we correct together, and at the next meeting with the rest of the group members we go through the minutes, but surprisingly the very first thing they do is correcting the mistakes, the grammar, but it's so interesting that they spend so much time correcting this person's mistakes rather than the content

It is interesting to note here the experience that her colleagues in Uganda – the same people who she has said were very flexible when it comes to grammatical standards in spoken language – are preoccupied with grammatical 'correctness' in official documentation. We can only speculate about why this might be, for example, standards-based conceptions coming to the forefront when language is actually written down or pressure from senior management for such documents to be written in a standard form of English. This is therefore an important element to add to our picture of Kozue's experiences of English and how she is required to use it. It also hints at the fact that an 'intelligibility only' conception of English might be inappropriate for JICA learner/users who are required to produce and deal with such official documentation, perhaps both for the volunteers themselves and for the teachers who are responsible for preparing them for this experience. As for Kozue, even though it may not be her own opinion that the documents need to be in standard English, this pressure becomes part of her conceptualizations of English, as she understands that she will move through certain situations where standard grammar will be important and others where it will not. This kind of multiplicity or contextualization of ideas about English was also demonstrated in Kozue's input to the focus groups in Japan, where she and another volunteer – Rika, going to Malawi – said that although they personally have relaxed attitudes towards standards in English and feel that mutual intelligibility is the most important thing, there are certain times when it might be necessary to use standard grammar. The next sequence follows an indication by Kozue that during her time spent in the United States, she was initially nervous about making mistakes, and then *got over it*:

N: does it really matter do you think if you make mistakes
K: as long as you try ... because English is a tool of communication and for example when I'm speaking to a Japanese speaker I don't really care if that person's making mistakes if it makes sense

R: I totally agree with what she said but I'm just worried about the formal English because ... I think we might have a chance to speak with someone in a really high position and we're representing the country

These points raised by Kozue and Rika are expanded by further comments made by them in the focus group:

K: I've spoken with people from different countries before and I've never felt too nervous although I still make many mistakes and sometimes when the other person is you know kinda judgemental I might feel a bit nervous

R: I think I will be speaking English at work and sometimes ... I will have to meet someone in a higher position, in that case you know English helps a lot and if I don't speak higher English there might be a problem

Kozue and Rika both present different reasons for why an 'intelligibility only' perspective on language would be inappropriate for them, even though that is their main inclination. For Kozue this is primarily out of concerns for when others might be 'judgemental' of her mistakes in English, and for Rika this is related to concerns over using formal English when meeting senior figures.

Another example of a complex conceptualization came from the same focus group as Kozue and Rika. The speaker is Yoshi, a volunteer preparing for dispatch to Ghana to work as a primary school teacher. As part of his response to the elicitation statement 'in order to communicate successfully with people in my host country, I think it is important to learn English grammar rules as they are written in textbooks', he said:

Y: I have two reasons, of course I'm a teacher so I have to speak correctly, so the grammar is probably important for me but on the other hand when I was in London my friends were Spanish and Polish and Italian, their English was terrible, er not terrible, they had fluency but their grammar is not correct ... I was a very shy student so I couldn't speak well ... but they spoke each other fluently at pub ... so to communicate and make friendship with Ghanaian people ... too nervous for grammar is not good for me

This portrays a complex and layered conception of English wherein for general communication, intelligibility is the most important factor, whereas in his teaching role, he feels that standard English is important. This fits with an intelligibility-based perspective for his everyday communication but also highlights a limit to how far that can be applied to him as a learner of English. His perspective is that standard English is still needed for his teaching role, although we are left to guess the exact reasons for this, as with the example of official documentation previously. Perhaps the two examples are linked in that standard, grammatically 'correct' English is seen as important for professional domains in contrast to when it is used for interpersonal communication. This distinction can be applied to the 'language in and outside the circle' concept (Agar, 1996) that was referred to in the introduction. It also links with the finding by Hall et al. (2017, p. 97) from their participants of "a generalized perception that a monolithic 'standard' variety must serve as a pedagogical model, but is inappropriate for actual use (languaging)". Overall, we have seen here that although volunteers predominantly took up intelligibility-based conceptualizations of English before and during their voluntary work, there were areas of communication for which grammatical standards in English were seen to be important, including when connected to educational contexts/teaching, official documentation, or where interlocutors were seen to be of a high status and/or potentially judgemental of non-standard forms of English. This certainly adds complexity to the idea of a distinction between standards-based and intelligibility-based conceptualizations of English in learners/users.

3 Discussion

3.1 Summarizing and Interpreting the Findings

To summarize the data analysis presented here, an interaction between a JICA volunteer and two local interlocutors from Kenya was presented that demonstrated interactional trouble caused by a vocabulary item used by the Japanese volunteer, which was resolved primarily by the volunteer paraphrasing its meaning. The extract also included examples of non-standard forms of English used by both speakers that had no effect on mutual intelligibility and numerous examples of backchannels from both speakers that served to indicate active, interested listening and that support the ongoing interaction.

Following this, interview and focus group data from learners/users in the JICA context were drawn upon and comments were categorized as adhering either to standards-based or intelligibility-based orientations, or to complex conceptions where both positions were represented. The learners/users primarily displayed intelligibility-based conceptions linked to the perceived flexibility of language usage in their host countries. In cases where complex conceptualizations were displayed, this was linked to the flexibility of spoken informal language on the one hand, and the perceived need to use standard language in work situations such as teaching or where official documentation was involved. There were also references to where grammatically correct, standard forms of English might need to be used with 'judgemental' interlocutors or people of a high official status.

How then can these results be interpreted? The findings from the interactional analysis connect with many other findings from the field of ELF studies (see earlier citations). Whereas it is important not to generalize or essentialize too strongly, as every situation can be unique, it seems clear that the English usage of JICA volunteers in general situations is similar to that reported elsewhere in ELF literature, meaning that many of the claims made about the need not to overemphasize grammar – especially redundant features that do not affect mutual intelligibility – are relevant here.

The perspectives of learners/users on such issues have not featured heavily in the research literature to date. The findings here can be equated to those of Hall et al.'s (2017) investigation of teachers, as both sets of participants seemed to indicate conceptions that were multiple, inconsistent, and complex. The complexity of viewing language as intelligibility-based in social domains and standards-based in professional roles is a notable finding, and can be teased out using constructs that were discussed in the introduction: notional, idealized language versus social/expressive (Hall et al., 2017), language in and outside the circle (Agar, 1996), and language as subject versus language as object (Widdowson, 2003). Essentially, it seems that the learners/users conceptualize English in multiple ways depending on the context and the interlocutor, often prioritizing intelligibility but occasionally based on adherence to grammatical standards.

3.2 Implications for Teachers and Learners/Users

One implication of these findings is that teachers in the JICA context and beyond should become aware of the issues related to global diversity in English and associated issues in learner/user conceptions of the language (see Page, 2015 for evidence that some JICA teachers demonstrated a lack of understanding and awareness in this area). Awareness raising could take the form of in-house teacher training activities for contexts such as JICA and also other kinds of private language institutions. As this is now such an important dimension of applied linguistics and ELT practice, arguably all teachers should be given some kind of exposure to it; therefore, the topic could also be featured as a core component of Cambridge Assessment English Certificate in Teaching English to Speakers of Other Languages (CELTA), Cambridge Assessment English Diploma in Teaching English to Speakers of Other Languages (DELTA), Master's in Teaching English to Speakers of Other Languages (MA TESOL), and other kinds of professional teaching qualifications. As for the nature of this training, Sifakis (2017) is a strong advocate of reflection on extracts of real-life communication between international users of English as a means to raise teacher awareness of the issues involved. Recordings and transcripts of such interactions are widely available and can be found for the JICA context specifically in Page (2014, 2015), including interactions between Japanese volunteers and local interlocutors in Kenya, India, and Jamaica.

In conjunction with a guided-discovery approach based on exposure to examples of real interactions, structured training sessions would be recommended. These could be based on the kind of published materials referred to in the introduction of this article – essentially presenting facts about global diversity in English and the possible pedagogical responses to it – for discussion and awareness raising. It must be noted that the manner in which such content is framed and pitched at practicing teachers is essential as it is not uncommon for teachers to reject such ideas if they are presented too forcefully or in a way that undermines existing practice. The degree to which teachers modify their practice based on such ideas will vary widely due to a number of legitimate reasons including the immediate purposes and needs of learners. Arguably, however, it would empower all teachers to make good pedagogical decisions if they have a good level of awareness of issues in diversity. Even for teachers who do not modify what they teach *explicitly* at all, they may find that they want to *implicitly* foster a perspective on language that accepts diversity. This is one of the potential benefits of activities such as those proposed at the end of Matsuda (2012), for example, a YouTube listening activity featuring Ban Ki-Moon that contains non-standard features of English but is nonetheless fully intelligible. However, the findings of this research indicate that an intelligibility-only position – in other words, not paying any attention to the promotion of grammatical accuracy beyond what is required to maintain intelligibility – would not be wise as this would not be fulfilling the needs of all the volunteers. This assertion can be seen to act as a counterpoint to some of the stronger arguments associated with the ELF research literature.

As a final recommendation for teacher training, Hall and Wicaksono (2019) is an interactive web resource that can be used for teacher awareness raising in formal training situations as mentioned previously, or for the purposes of individual teacher self-development. The resource features interactive units that guide the user through topics and issues relating to diversity in English and language pedagogy, such as those that have been touched upon here. The material by Hall and Wicaksono (2019) or similar material is also likely to be beneficial to many of the JICA learner/users. This would mean that any learners who hold standards-based views – or are "caught in the rules they learned in school" (to borrow Kozue's terminology) – could be opened up to more intelligibility-based perspectives that might facilitate both their learning and their actual communication in the host countries.

Beyond this, the issues discussed here indicate the need for critical approaches to education, considering when tests can be re-designed to avoid washback effects and so on (see Harsch, this volume). As a basic starting point for this kind of enterprise, it is important for all professionals working with language to become aware of some of the ontological categories and concepts under discussion in this chapter and elsewhere in the volume, such as the distinction between idealized forms of standard language and the more fluid nature of real-world communication. Conceiving only of the idealized form of language when seeking to understand and teach English will have unintended negative effects. To conclude, it is recommended that all professionals involved with applied linguistics and the ELT profession ensure that they are aware to some extent of the issues touched upon here, as this can work to erode negative practices and attitudes, facilitating informed teaching and learning practices.

References

Agar, M. (1996). *Language Shock: Understanding the Culture of Conversation*. New York: HarperCollins.

Baird, R., Baker, W., and Kitazawa, M. (2014). The complexity of English as a Lingua Franca. *Journal of English as a Lingua Franca*, 3(1), 171–196.

Bolton, K. (2008). English in Asia, Asian Englishes, and the issue of proficiency. *English Today*, 24(2), 3–12.

Cogo, A. and Dewey, M. (2006). Efficiency in ELF communication: From pragmatic motives to Lexico-grammatical innovation. *Nordic Journal of English Studies*, 5(2), 59–93.

Crowley, T. (2003). *Standard English and the Politics of Language*, 2nd ed. London: Palgrave Macmillan.

Firth, A. (1990). 'Lingua franca' negotiations: Towards an interactional approach. *World Englishes*, 9(3), 269–280.

Firth, A. and Wagner, J. (1997). On discourse, communication, and (some) fundamental concepts in SLA research. *The Modern Language Journal*, 81(3), 285–300.

Friedrich, A. and Matsuda, P. (2010). When five words are not enough: A conceptual and terminological discussion of English as a lingua franca. *International Multilingual Research Journal*, 4(1), 20–30.

Hall, C. J. (2013). Cognitive contributions to plurilithic views of English and other languages. *Applied Linguistics*, 34(2), 211–231.

Hall, C. J., Smith, P. H., and Wicaksono, R. (2011). *Mapping Applied Linguistics*. London: Routledge.

Hall, C. J. and Wicaksono, R. (2019). *Changing Englishes: An online course for teachers*. Online. Accessed 31 July 2019 from www.changingenglishes.online

Hall, C. J., Wicaksono, R., Liu, S. et al. (2017). 'Exploring teachers' ontologies of English: Monolithic conceptions of grammar in a group of Chinese teachers'. *International Journal of Applied Linguistics*, 27(1), 87–109.

Irvine, A. (2008). Contrast and convergence in Standard Jamaican English: The phonological architecture of the standard in an ideologically bidialectal community. *World Englishes*, 27(1), 9–25.

Jenkins, J. (2000). *The Phonology of English as an International Language*. Oxford: Oxford University Press.

JICA. 2018. Online. Accessed 4 July 2018 from www.jica.go.jp/english/

Kachru, B. (1985). Sociolinguistic realism: The English language in the outer circle. In R. Quirk and H. G. Widdowson, eds., *English in the World: Teaching and Learning the Language and Literatures* (pp. 211–226). Cambridge: Cambridge University Press.

Leung, C. and Street, B. V. (2014). Introduction. In C. Leung and B. Street, eds., *The Routledge Companion to English Studies* (pp. xxi–xxx). Abingdon: Routledge.

Mann, S. (2011). A critical review of qualitative interviews in Applied Linguistics. *Applied Linguistics*, 32(1), 6–24.

Matsuda, A. (2012). *Principles and Practices of Teaching English as an International Language*. Bristol: Multilingual Matters.

McKay, S. L. and Bokhorst-Heng, W. D. (2008). *International English in Its Sociolinguistic Contexts: Towards a Socially Sensitive EIL Pedagogy*. New York: Routledge

Meierkord, C. (2000). Interpreting successful lingua franca interaction: An analysis of non-native-/non-native small talk conversations in English. *Linguistik Online*, 5(1). Online. Accessed 10 May 2015 from https://bop.unibe.ch/linguistik-online/article/view/1013/1673

Page, N. (2014). English in a global voluntary work context: A case study of spoken interaction and its implications for language pedagogy. *Asian Journal of Applied Linguistics*, 1/2, 84–101.

Page, N. (2015). *English in global voluntary work contexts: Conceptions and experiences of language, communication and pedagogy*. Unpublished PhD Thesis, University of Leeds.

Pierce, B. N. (1995). Social identity, investment, and language learning. *TESOL Quarterly*, 29(1), 9–31.

Piller, I. 2011. *Intercultural Communication: A Critical Introduction*. Edinburgh: Edinburgh University Press.

Rampton, B. (2006). *Language in Late Modernity: Interaction in an Urban School*. Cambridge: Cambridge University Press.

Seargeant, P. (2009). *The Idea of English in Japan: Ideology and the Evolution of a Global Language*. Bristol: Multilingual Matters.

Seidlhofer, B. (2001). Closing a conceptual gap: The case for a description of English as a Lingua Franca. *International Journal of Applied Linguistics*, 11(2), 133–158.

Sewell, A. (2012). English as a lingua franca: Ontology and ideology. *ELT Journal*, 67(1), 3–10.

Seidlhofer, B. (2004). 10. Research perspectives on teaching English as a Lingua Franca. *Annual Review of Applied Linguistics*, 24, 209–239.

Sifakis, N. C. (2017). ELF awareness in English language teaching: Principles and processes. *Applied Linguistics*, 1–20. doi https://doi.org/10.1093/applin/amx034

Skandera, P. (1999). What do we really know about Kenyan English? A pilot study in research methodology, *English World-Wide*, 20(22), 217–236.

Smith, L. and Nelson, C. L. (1985). International intelligibility of English: Directions and resources. *World Englishes*, 4(3), 333–342.

Snell, J. (2013). Dialect, interaction and class positioning at school: From deficit to difference to repertoire. *Language and Education*, 27(2), 110–128.

Widdowson, H. G. (1994). The ownership of English. *TESOL Quarterly*, 28(2), 377–389.

Widdowson, H. G. (2003). *Defining Issues in English Language Teaching*. Oxford: Oxford University Press.

Part VI

English and Social Practice

15 *English as a Resource in a Communicative Assemblage*

A Perspective from Flat Ontology

Suresh Canagarajah

1 Introduction

Ontology (i.e. thinking about what's out there) is intimately connected to epistemology (i.e. questions such as, "how can we know what's out there?"). Both are also connected to ideology (i.e. whose interests do those perspectives on ontology and epistemology serve?). The once dominant cognitivist and structuralist orientations on language and communication are increasingly challenged by new thinking about what is out there. This new thinking is in turn changing the way we engage in inquiry about language and communication. Among the many philosophical paradigms challenging cognitivism and structuralism, I present the set of theories espousing a flat ontology as facilitating a more inclusive and dynamic understanding of language in communication. Flat ontology questions binaries such as mind/body, cognition/matter, human/nonhuman, and verbal/nonverbal, with the former in each pair treated as agentive and more significant. It considers all resources as working together in the construction of meaning and activity. Flat ontology is adopted by philosophical schools such as posthumanism (Braidotti, 2013), new materialism (Barad, 2007), actor network theory (Latour, 2005), and spatiality (Massey, 2005). In this chapter, I will articulate how such schools provide a different orientation to the ontology of English, with new implications for meaning and communication, and for changes in the way we conduct language analysis and teaching in the future.

2 Beyond Structuralism and Cognitivism

Linguists consider Saussure's work as foundational for modern linguistics. His version of structuralism has become disciplinary common sense in some parts of our field, lending to "folk structuralist discourses" (Prior, 1998, pp. 273–274) that find representation in teaching, scholarship, and language attitudes. Under this influence, we think of language as a self-defining, autonomous, grammatical structure. From this perspective, we assume that English has a structure that exists out there and is independent of other languages. Its structure is also separate from other semiotic resources such as gestures, images, and artefacts. Saussure's distinction between *langue* and *parole* (or the underlying abstract grammar of a language and its realization in communicative practice, respectively) also suggests that the former is worthy of analysis while the latter is of secondary or incidental relevance. Also, his focus on synchronic analysis presented the static, abstract, and objectified grammatical structure as the proper focus of analysis, treating the diachronic (i.e. the spatial and temporal life of language) as secondary.

Chomsky provided a cognitive and individual locus to Saussure's structure, as Hymes (1971) has observed. Chomsky's *competence/performance* distinction (similar to *langue* and *parole*) located grammatical structure in one's mind. He exacerbated dichotomies such as mind/body and cognition/materiality, drawing from Cartesian philosophy and privileging the mind as more real, generative, or foundational than the body or the material world. The mind enjoys the agency to shape passive matter according to its will. With this, we also get a strong version of *representationalism*. This is the view that the grammatical structure located in our mind encodes the knowledge that shapes meanings and activities in our social and material life. There is thus an equation made between mind, language, thinking, and knowledge in shaping communicative and other human activities. Representationalism has continued to have significance for epistemology, as I will elaborate later. Chomskyan linguistics also reinforced notions such as native speakerism and language ownership, which have attained ideological significance. They have implications for fostering inequalities such as the following: monolingualism is treated as the norm; multilinguals are treated as interlopers, lacking legitimacy in other languages they speak; and native speaker norms are treated as authoritative and definitive in a language, becoming the target for learning for others (see also Wicaksono, this volume).

However, recent developments in theoretical physics motivate us to reconsider these orientations to the mind and matter. In European Enlightenment thinking, especially in the paradigm popularized by Descartes, matter was conceived as an undifferentiated and solid mass that depended on human shaping. Newtonian physics gave more importance to matter, conceiving it as a machine or a clock that can run with predictability once it was wound. However, contemporary physics treats physical nature as unpredictable, even random, with its own complex and self-regulating processes (Coole and Frost, 2010).

Such a reorientation to matter (which constitutes the theory of new materialism) has significant implications for epistemology. In our knowledge-making activities, we used to make a distinction between organic and inorganic sciences, treating biology as having to do with entities that had life, and physics or chemistry as dealing with entities that didn't have life. But, as Coole and Frost (2010) remind us, "new materialists discern emergent, generative powers (or agentive capacities) even within inorganic matter" (p. 9). Moreover, we distinguished between symbolic and natural sciences. The former included the human and social, such as linguistics, literature, cultural studies, which studied meaning-making practices. The latter included physical sciences, which we treated as dealing with mute and passive objects. This distinction between the symbolic and natural also has to be re-examined now. Critiquing social scientists for their disciplinary territoriality, Latour (2005) argues: "For the social scientists, there were some serious motives behind the need to ceaselessly patrol the border separating the 'symbolic' from the 'natural' domain. This is an artificial division imposed by the disciplinary disputes, not by any empirical requirement" (p. 83).

Such shifts call for a different epistemological orientation. Scholars influenced by the new materialist orientation call for analysing activities, processes, or meanings in a more inclusive manner, without adopting predefined boundaries on what any discipline can study. The new mode of transdisciplinary inquiry as described by Coole and Frost (2010) is "to track the complex circuits at work whereby discursive and material forms are inextricable yet irreducible" (p. 27). Latour's (2005) actor network theory and Barad's (2007) performative method adopt a similar process of inquiry and consider texts and activities as an assemblage configured by diverse social, material, and semiotic resources and networks. Latour's work theorizes how social and material resources are networked in generating meanings and knowledge. Barad theorizes how such meanings and knowledge emerge in and through practice (i.e., in the process of getting things done), and not given beforehand.

Geographers see in this new materialist orientation potential for more complex knowledge making and inclusive ideologies. Adopting the metaphor of *space* to index physical nature, Doreen Massey (2005) points out: "The stasis of closed systems robs 'the spatial' of one of its potentially disruptive characteristics: precisely its juxtaposition, its happenstance arrangement-in-relation-to-each-other, of previously unconnected narratives/temporalities; its openness and its condition of always being made" (p. 39). From her perspective, space is everything structuralism tried to evade. Space presents events and activities in all their messy complexity. Its concreteness is always resistant to model building, theorization, or normativity, presenting resources for the generation of diverse possibilities. Matter is always in a process of becoming, when structures present meanings and activities as already constructed. Therefore, Massey theorizes spatiality as opening up more inclusive, responsive, and dynamic analyses on the 'becoming' of meaning and activities. Since the structures that produce generalizations and abstractions serve the partial and partisan interests of those who formulate them, spatiality has the potential of deconstructing dominant ideologies and reconstructing more inclusive understandings of activities and meanings. For example, the purportedly universal grammatical structures are informed by the values and interests of those formulating them, as in the preference of some communities to structure languages as separated, territorialized, and owned. In deconstructing these structures lies the politics of new materialism.

New materialist orientations lead to what is becoming known as a flat ontology (Marston et al., 2005). It means the following for analysing meaning-making activities: going beyond binaries and hierarchies, such as human/thing, mind/body, cognition/matter, language/objects; treating all resources as equal in status and mediating each other; questioning the primacy of structures that define activities and events, or treating them as separately constituted or secondarily generated; and perceiving everything as connected to everything else. From this perspective, we have to reconsider the logocentricism in linguistics that treats language (or verbal resources) as a superior medium for meaning making. We have to be open to diverse resources as capable of making meaning, with body and objects having different meaning-making capacities paralleling language. Though developments in *multimodality* have introduced certain communicative resources beyond language as meaningful (Kress, 2009; Mondada, 2014), flat ontology would question that each is organized into different modes. Moreover, these modes of semiotic resources are not already endowed with meanings (i.e. each gesture coupled with their respective meanings; cf. Kendon, 2004), but generate meanings in relation to the other resources participating in an activity. A term that might capture this understanding of meaning-making resources is *assemblage* (Deleuze and Guattari, 1987). Assemblage also accommodates the idea that the coming together of these resources is performative. That is, resources are configured in activities to make meaning in a situated manner in relation to the social and material networks characterizing that activity. Their coherence is not to be accounted for by an originary or foundational cognition, individual, or structure.

In other words, meanings are not to be attributed to the mind of a person who produced the text, or an underlying genre and language structure that determine it. Meanings emerge in relation to the different ecological resources and social networks participating in the communicative activity in different spaces and times. As such, meanings are always in a process of 'becoming'.

From the perspective of flat ontology, as articulated earlier, we have to note an important implication for English. 'English' is itself made up of diverse resources. Its ideological status as a separately labelled language might hide the verbal resources from many languages constituting it. Furthermore, resources from what is labelled 'English' might form an assemblage with diverse other semiotic resources (gestures, visuals, sound), and diverse material resources (objects, artefacts), to form meaning. Though I will subsequently make a case for still referring to 'English' as a labelled language from ideological considerations, we have to first adopt the understanding that its linguistic resources will participate with equal status with diverse other material, social, and semiotic resources and networks, to make meaning at the level of practice. This is becoming known as the *translingual* orientation in applied linguistics (see Canagarajah, 2013).

3 Conceptual Shifts

A flat ontology will lead to a shift from other familiar constructs adopted in language analysis and teaching. I will further elaborate on eight examples of these shifts before articulating the pedagogical implications later.

3.1 From Representational to Performative

As we discussed earlier, the structuralist orientation gives centrality to words located in the mind as representing knowledge and regulating one's life. From this point of view, grammatical competence shapes one's communicative activities and social practice. The flat ontology perspective treats practice as shaping meanings and thinking. Meanings emerge from activities. This performative orientation doesn't simply mean that words are action, as in J. L. Austin's famous *How to Do Things with Words*. Such an orientation to performativity also informs the theories of those like Judith Butler. For Butler, repeated use of language constructs bodies and identities. For the new materialist orientation, on the other hand, activity comes first. Discourses and identities emerge from activities, as if to "do words with things" (to reverse Austin's book title). Such an orientation would lead to non-representationalist thinking and communication (Thrift, 2007). While representationalism focuses on propositional knowledge for accounting for communicative competence, non-representationalist thinking focuses on procedures, processes, and strategies as generative. That is, representationalism asks what grammatical norms, linguistic knowledge, discourse paradigms, or pragmatic values an individual needs to communicate successfully, as in structuralist orientations. The performative orientation of non-representationalist thinking, in contrast, asks what collaborative, negotiated, responsive, and situated strategies generate meanings.

3.2 From Grammar, Discourse, or Genre Structures to Spatial Repertoires

Representationalism treats constructs such as grammar, discourse, or genre systems as the units of analysis in language studies and pedagogy. However, the unit of analysis or pedagogical consideration in flat ontology is 'spatial repertoires'. This orientation, developing through the recent work of applied linguists (Rymes, 2014; Pennycook, 2017), focuses on semiotic resources that transcend the grammatical structure of labelled languages. In this sense, verbal resources from different labelled languages can form a unit of consideration. Furthermore, non-verbal semiotic resources that configure a situated activity can also be part of spatial repertoires. Verbal grammar is part of these spatial repertoires and works in concert with them. Grammar is a sedimentation of verbal semiotic resources used in repeated situated activities. What gives coherence to the spatial repertoires is space; for example, the resources that characterize a communicative activity (such as buying/selling in an urban market) in a specific spatiotemporal location. We might consider this as the resources characterizing a genre of activity. However, the fact that we label them repertoire rather than 'structure' or 'norm' suggests that the resources that characterize these activities are fluid, emergent, generative, and negotiated. Though there could be a coherence given by the situated activity, the resources can be changing and variable, based on the mix of participants. Some scholars thus see a personal dimension to repertoires. As people become familiar with particular activities with specific social networks in situated spatiotemporal locations, they might develop a proficiency in the set of resources relevant for those genres. Pennycook and Otsuji (2015, p. 83) define spatial repertoires as "link[ing] the repertoires formed through individual life trajectories to the particular places in which these linguistic resources are deployed". As in Blommaert's (2010, p. 23) notion of "truncated multilingualism," these repertoires may cut across labelled languages. While someone may not have advanced competence in the grammatical structure of English, he or she might have the proficiency in the mix of verbal and non-verbal resources required for the successful performance of the communicative activity relating to a scientific discipline, for example.

I find spatial repertoires a useful construct to help explain the successful teaching of international science scholars in American classrooms. In a focused analysis of a Chinese math graduate teacher, I found that the repertoire he needed included the following: deixis to point to visuals and equations on the board; Latinate technical terms belonging to his subject matter; hand gestures to simulate processes; body positioning to shift attention to the board, his mini lecture, or students' time for questions; body movements that convey affect; and the use of the board to present visuals and texts (see Canagarajah, 2018). That he didn't have an elaborate lexical corpus or grammatical competence in English didn't affect his communication in the classroom.

3.3 From Text/Context Binary to Entextualization

Under the influence of structuralist linguistics, applied linguists distinguished text from context in their analysis. The text, whether spoken or written, was our focus of analysis. Context was there to bring the text into relief. Linguists also traditionally treated context as static, monolithic, and of secondary importance. In some studies, there was a deterministic treatment of context as a container, such as the community or nation-state that both governed and explained the norms and terms of the interaction. Flat ontology would suggest the following about context: many nonverbal resources relegated to context would actively mediate and shape communication; such resources would make context agentive and dynamic rather than being static or monolithic; the context can be layered and expansive, constituting many levels of space and time scales. From these perspectives, flat ontology would go beyond the binary of text/context and consider how diverse semiotic resources of different scales of space and time are 'entextualized' to constitute the communicative activity. This notion also adopts a process oriented (non-representationalist) approach to communication in focusing on the emergence of meanings. It treats texts as a social and historical process that involves the collaborative activity of transforming semiotic resources into a spatial repertoire in situated activity. The strategic selection of resources in the environment and in one's repertoire to entextualize meaning, with its uptake by interlocutors, constitutes successful communication.

302 *Suresh Canagarajah*

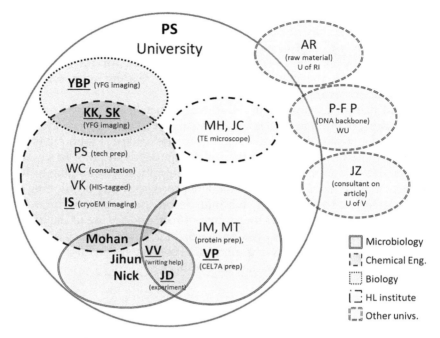

Figure 15.1 *Jihun's social networks*

Consider, for example, the way a published article by a Korean scholar (whom I will call Jihun) was put together. To begin with, a range of participants collaborated in the construction of the text. At a local spatial scale, his collaborator was Nick, the senior professor of his lab and principal investigator in the grant funding this research. Both came from the Department of Microbiology. A junior faculty member from the Department of Chemical Engineering, Mohan, was also an active member of this research group and played an important role in shaping the text. These three scholars worked closely on the manuscript, with many rounds of reading, commenting, and revising. Beyond these three, two other post-doctoral research associates from Jihun's department, JD and VV, collaborated less actively on the experiment and writing. Five others are listed as authors (whose names are bolded and underlined in Figure 15.1). Nine others are listed in the Acknowledgements as having made additional contributions. They come from four other departments in Jihun's own university and from departments in three other universities. The last mentioned fourteen scholars were not involved in face-to-face interactions during the writing, in conversations in the research group meetings, or in conducting the experiment in Jihun's lab. However, they made substantial contributions to both the research and the article at more distant space and time scales. They conducted related parts of the experiment, prepared raw materials, provided chemicals and instruments for the study, analyzed the data, or offered technical assistance. In some cases, they provided consultation on particular aspects of the manuscript or on the experiment. As they come from distant universities and departments, they represent influences from different spatial scales. The metaphor of 'scales' helps us focus on the complex relationship between these locations, considering their overlapping, variously proximous, and networked nature of the interactions, as depicted in Figure 15.1. The term 'locations' is too monolithic to accommodate their layered nature. Also, as some contributions come from much earlier in the experiment or writing, such as the preparation of the raw materials by AR that preceded the experiment or the imaging work of KK, SK, YBP that followed much later, they come from different time scales as well. Jihun's role as the lead author lies in assembling all these resources from different spatiotemporal locations to put together the successive drafts. The article emerges through the activity of reading, writing, and commenting on the resources assembled in the text. The activity of writing is thus one of turning diverse material and semiotic resources into a coherent text, and hence engaging in entextualization.

3.4 From Metaphysics of Presence to Distant Spatial Scales

Flat ontology would also challenge the dominant approach of treating the tangible and immediate as the data for meaning-making activity or mediating meanings. The latter approach is encouraged also by the empirical tradition in many fields, where the datum immediately available to the senses is treated as the only valid proof for claims. These tendencies follow the metaphysics of presence (Derrida, 1973), identified as characteristic of human inquiry in the western Enlightenment tradition. Flat ontology would accommodate invisible and distant influences in analysis of meaning-making practices. Some scholars are adopting scalar metaphors borrowed from geography and political science (see Canagarajah and DeCosta, 2016, for a review) to address influences from expansive spatial and temporal locations. These scales can be layered and relative, as depicted in Figure 15.1. Blommaert's (2005) notion of 'layered simultaneity' accommodates the possibility that such expansive and invisible scales of influence might be embedded in a situated activity, contributing to its coherence and meaning.

To return to Jihun's writing, I myself fell victim to the bias of 'presence' when I set up a video camera in his workspace to document Jihun's writing process. It soon became evident that resources for the text were coming from outside his lab. The text was being composed by many other parties beyond Jihun's lab, as we found earlier. Technological resources helped Jihun transcend space/time constraints in assembling the relevant resources for his writing. For example, while Jihun was composing, he made a phone call to a colleague in another lab to clarify some issues about his results. In another case, he consulted a colleague in Korea about a reference he needed using a text messaging service while he was traveling home from work by bus. This exchange was conducted through messages in Korean (with mixing of English for academic terms). The colleague provided information on a published English article and discussed relevant findings in Korean. The article is also shaped by the results of related experiments run by others beyond his own lab, and imaging of Jihun's own findings by those outside his lab. Such information was transferred to him electronically in the form of figures, images, and written reports and embedded directly into the evolving article. Therefore, the video camera set up in his work space could not capture the resources from diverse expansive space and time scales that constituted Jihun's text.

3.5 From Methodological Individualism to Distributed Practice

Scholars in language teaching and applied linguistics consider the individual as the locus of communicative competence, under the influence of structuralist cognitive epistemologies. In adopting this perspective, applied linguistics shares a methodological individualism that is common in other humanities and social sciences. The individual (or a collective of individuals) is treated as the reference for accounting for the generation of meaning and explaining the success of communication. However, in materializing communication, flat ontology treats meanings as emerging in activity in the interstices of people, objects, and the environment. From this point of view, the individual (or her or his mind) is not the repository of meanings, knowledge, or competence. They emerge in social, material, and semiotic networks. The locus of competence thus needs to be treated as a network of resources in interaction, and not the individual. Nigel Thrift (2007) states, "Intelligence is not the property of an organism but of the organism and its environment" (p. 154). By the same token, the individual is also decentered and embodied in networks. Consciousness and knowledge are treated as emerging in the interstices of mind, body, emotion, and affect. The mind is not the locus of knowledge or consciousness. Thrift (2007) further argues, "What we call 'thinking' in human beings does not occur just in the brain but at a series of sites in the body" (p. 166). In adopting this shift, we should be prepared to consider meaning and knowledge as always emergent, a process of becoming. The notion of distributed practice ensures that it is through interactions between diverse entities and agents that meanings can emerge. As we can see from Jihun's article, the ideas and its coherence, and 'competence', don't evolve from Jihun's mind alone. The article emerges in the interstices of the different material, social, and semiotic resources participating in the writing activity.

3.6 From Cognitive/Linguistic Shaping to Bricolage

The preceding perspective on meaning and knowledge also changes our orientation to the human/social activity in generating meanings and knowledge. Traditional understanding was that there was an originary or unitary foundation for the generation of meaning. It was theorized in different ways by different schools. Some humanist schools consider representations as emerging from each person's cognitive processes in the mind. More impersonal structuralist schools considered representations as emerging from a bounded and self-organizing structure, i.e. grammatical structure, culture, society, or knowledge paradigms. These structures gave coherence to meaning representations. However, the flat ontology perspective considers meanings as put together in non-synchronous and non-linear ways by different parties in relation to diverse material ecologies in disparate space and time. In this manner, the flat ontology perspective resembles the activity of bricolage. Bricolage is the ability to produce something spontaneously, making do with the resources available at hand to accomplish things in creative, unscripted, and dexterous ways. Similar to bricolage, communicating is a pragmatic and functional assembling of resources and texts. Though individuals may not always come ready with the words or ideas they need for communicating, they can draw from those available in the material ecology to assemble them for their purposes. The notion of distributed activity would specify that whatever meanings or knowledge we bring with us before a communicative activity may not be fully useful. I explain later the possibility that through repeated interactions and activity, there are possibilities for certain communicative norms, genre patterns, knowledge paradigms to emerge through sedimentation. But since they cannot be assumed to be universally shared or suitable for each specific situation, one has to still negotiate with the parties and resources in a setting for constructing meaning. This understanding also raises the possibility that the types of competence one brings before an interaction may not be relevant. Competence is the ability to fashion meanings pragmatically with the resources and networks coming from different places and times. This competence requires sensitivity to any established norms for typical communicative activities and the relevant expectations of the audience, which need to be judiciously negotiated.

Such activity resembles the work of a handyman (or bricoleur) who makes things happen with great dexterity and resourcefulness from whatever is available in the immediate setting, rather than the competence of an expert who comes ready with predefined skills and abilities, with very orthodox ways of accomplishing something. Considering the way Jihun's article was put together, we might consider that practice a bricolage. His activity through the successive drafts I studied was to assemble semiotic resources from different people at different places and times. His collaborators from other departments and universities sent him photographs, texts, and diagrams that he put together. Different parties at different points also commented on his drafts, both orally and through embedded comments. The process of writing was also not linear and controlled. Jihun's first draft constituted the introduction and a set of nine images demonstrating his findings. The rest of the article emerged through the assembling of the writing and texts by his collaborators at different times in relation to the requirements of the journal.

3.7 From Arboreal to Rhizomatic Development of Proficiency

Structuralism has conceived language acquisition as developing like a tree. This model is causal, cumulative, and linear. The foundation for language competence is the mastery of grammar. Grammar constitutes the deep structure in the subterranean, invisible, language acquisition device (Chomsky, 1965). The root works with the trunk, constituting surface structural features such as phonology or inflectional morphology, to build advanced proficiency in written genres, specialized registers, disciplinary discourses, or pragmatic rules for variable situations. The massive amount of research undertaken in the 1970s and 1980s to discover the 'natural' order of morphosyntactic features learned by students as indicative of universal grammar (see, for example, Dulay et al., 1982) treats deep structure as itself cumulatively developing. Resources such as body, emotions, setting, or objects are treated as part of environmental contexts that are extraneous or secondary to competence. They are not part of the language tree.

The rhizome complicates the causality, cumulativeness, and linearity of the arboreal metaphor in interesting ways. In botany, a rhizome is a plant stem that grows horizontally under or along the ground and often sends out lateral roots and shoots from its nodes. New plants develop from the shoots. Ginger, iris, and violets are *rhizomes*. In a rhizome, the root and the branch are not different. The same part can function as both. Secondly, the root can be subterraneous or above ground. Adopting the rhizome as a model, in the place of the arboreal model of structuralism, complicates the competence/performance or mind/environment distinction. More importantly, the nonlinearity of the rhizome allows for different trajectories of language development. It is possible in this model for someone to master literacy proficiency before oral proficiency or a specialized scientific register before mastery of casual English. The rhizome can also account for the possibility of someone shuttling between verbal resources identified as Korean, Mandarin, and English, without the need to have separate proficiencies symbolized by separate trees. The status of nonverbal resources in communication is also different. The rhizome accommodates the possibility of someone employing artefacts and nonverbal resources equally as verbal resources for successful communication. Note also that the 'individual' would be decentered in this model, with features such as the mind, body, and emotion occupying separate nodes in the network and playing an equal role in activities.

3.8 From Competence to Emplacement

The term *competence* connotes cognitive mastery and individual agency to capture the emerging orientation to language practice and development in the flat ontology perspective. A better alternative is the term *alignment*, as theorized by scholars in the socio-cognitive orientation, because it foregrounds the working together of diverse resources for meaning making. These scholars define alignment as "the means by which human actors dynamically adapt to – that is, flexibly depend on, integrate with, and construct – the ever-changing mind-body-world environments ... In other words, alignment takes place not just between human beings, but also between human beings and their social and physical environments" (Atkinson et al., 2007, p. 171).

Though the definition can capture one's ability to merge diverse resources in communication, it has been employed in a way that differs from the material orientation theorized previously. In studies on

English language learning, Atkinson and his co-authors have accounted for 'competence' in terms of English grammar alone. The other semiotic resources are treated as mediating the more important and separate development of grammatical proficiency in a single language. For example, languages evident in situated interactions (such as the Japanese verbal resources used by their subjects) are treated as mediating resources, not constituting a more inclusive translingual capacity for semiotic assemblages. Furthermore, while the body and world are given considerable significance in facilitating cognition, the mind is given more importance. Affect and perception are not given equal status as cognition. There is repeated emphasis that cognition is primary, for example, "SLA is in fact eminently cognitive – if the primary purpose of cognition is to help its users adapt to and function in the world" (Atkinson, 2011, p. 162). A material orientation would suggest that the purpose of the body is to keep the brain viable in some encounters (Nishino and Atkinson, 2015) and that the world generates the text as an assemblage, with the writer mediating other resources, and orchestrating their alignment for their proficiency development and communicative outcomes.

A term gaining currency in rhetoric studies to address a materialist orientation to language proficiency is 'emplacement' (Rickert, 2013; Pigg, 2014). This term has been used insightfully to describe how people attune to networks of social and material resources for writing. The somewhat passive formulation of the term allows for the more agentive work of bodies and objects beyond the cognitive orchestration of individuals. I define emplacement as the strategic and ongoing attunement to an assemblage of agents and resources in expansive spatiotemporal scales for the emergence of thinking and meaning in activity. Emplacement accommodates the possibility of nonrepresentational thinking, conceiving cognition and meaning as performative, embodied in activity and distributed across bodies and environments. All participants and resources in the network are treated as equally agentive, mediating each other for the emergence of meanings and outcomes. Furthermore, emplacement is not defined in terms of what individuals do, but what the networks in which they are emplaced achieve. In other words, emplacement compels us to consider meaning as generated collectively and equally by the ecological resources and social networks in an activity. However, emplacement doesn't treat the speaker/writer as fully determined by the network. Human agency is qualified as achieved in attunement with objects and networks. Human beings mediate these resources and networks strategically for their interests (Appadurai, 2015). In this sense, communication is treated as a qualified, responsive, negotiated, and ongoing activity in which people engage with rhizomatic networks for possible meaning outcomes.

4 Debates and Qualifications

Having outlined how a flat ontology will shift our orientation to communicative practice and the development of proficiency, we return to a consideration of traditional constructs, such as labelled languages, grammatical structures, and standardized norms. We don't have to do away with these constructs, but understand them differently from the angle of flat ontology.

Though the perspective of assemblages would treat verbal resources as mobile and fluid, to be used by speakers without restrictions as to which language they belong, there is still a place for labelled languages. Constructs such as English, German, or Spanish, with their own lexical features, can be explained as ideological. That is, these labels and the lexical corpus that constitutes them are defined by people's assumptions and attitudes. These language ideologies give shape to what constitutes their language. There is a need to understand these ideologies with sensitivity to people's aspirations for heritage, identity, territory, and ownership. Though these aspirations can take oppressive forms when a community excludes other people from its land or language based on their identity, there is also something empowering in people claiming and celebrating their heritage. Poststructuralist scholars, such as Gayatri Spivak (1993), would consider such claims as constituting a *strategic essentialism*. That is, while what constitutes 'English' is a very diverse corpus of lexical items from very divergent etymologies, treating them as forming a homogeneous corpus is strategic for a community's claims for identity, sovereignty, and territory. However, the understanding that labelling languages and claiming ownership is an ideological activity can in fact make everyone relaxed about their claims and implications. That they are ideological will prevent people from treating these claims as primordial and exclusive. This perspective can also make us open to how these labels can become expansive and inclusive in relation to social and historical changes. For example, the understanding now of English as a global language accommodates a more diverse corpus of verbal resources and speaker identities.

Can we still talk of a grammatical structure or other structured concepts such as registers, discourse conventions, and genre rules, which focus on language in isolation from other resources? It depends on what our scale of consideration is. If we narrow our scales of consideration to verbal resources, it is possible to understand how words pattern in particular ways for situated communication. A practice-based view of communication would suggest that patterns and structures evolve ground up, from a sedimentation of features that co-occur in repeated activity. Rather than assuming structures as *sui generis*, then, a materialist orientation would consider how structures evolve through sedimentation (see Eskildsen, this volume). Such an understanding will also have theoretical space for the revision and change of structures, allowing for human agency in resistance and creativity.

Beyond structures such as grammar, register, discourse, and genre, we can also go further and conceive of assemblages being structured as spatial repertoires. New materialist theoretician Karen Barad states, "What is needed is a method that enables genealogical analyses of how boundaries are produced rather than presuming sets of well-worn binaries in advance" (2007, pp. 29–30). Though she is not opposed to identifying "boundaries", these will emerge out of more expansive assemblage of resources and a conversation among diverse theoretical paradigms. The emerging structures will not claim to be universal or objective, but sensitive to the ideologies and inequalities that shape them, and the consequences of their use. This orientation to structures can also accommodate spatial repertoires.

Another construct that needs to be understood differently is the place of norms, as reflective of power, in communication. Flat ontology shouldn't be understood as flattening all status and power differences in communication. The notion of meaning as a process of becoming, through the synergies unleashed among assemblages in networks, does not mean that anything is possible in communication. That there are rules and norms for so-called 'proper' communication, and that there are strong beliefs about proper communication for specific contexts, is undeniable. There are many ways to explain them. In some cases, we can think of these norms as sedimented over a history of practice (cf. Harder, this volume). But there are also norms imposed by powerful and narrow interest groups. This is an ideological activity. However, such 'norms' can co-exist with the understanding of meanings as emerging from ground up through practice. Since such meaning-making activities shuttle across diverse space and time scales horizontally, they also traverse diverse scales vertically. At more macro-level institutional scales of gatekeeping, control, and surveillance, such norms and power effects have to be negotiated for meaning and successful communication. Negotiation is the key word here. Such processes of negotiation will lead to diverse levels of approximation and reconstruction of norms as possible in the communicative ecology. It is such negotiation strategies that also explain the possibility of resistant and transgressive communicative practices.

A consideration that makes such negotiation of norms and constructs necessary is the continued presence of "folk structuralist discourses" (Prior, 1987, pp. 273–274). What this means is that structuralism as an ideology is still with us. It provides some measure of control over the unpredictability and messy complexity of material life. In moving away from material context, and theorizing structures at a more abstract level, structuralism provides a neat, tidy, and convenient handle on everyday practice. Structuralist constructs therefore make life easier for teachers, researchers, and policy makers as they undertake their work. Furthermore, structuralism finds expression in policy formulations at various levels, as institutions regulate communicative life in terms of norms and rules. Therefore, grammatical structures, cognitive representations, and knowledge constructs have to be negotiated actively until more inclusive norms and ideologies are constructed. While scholars might adopt a flat ontology to understand translingual practice, they also have to contend with the possible monolingual, hierarchical, and structuralist understandings of others (cf. Hall, this volume, for some examples).

5 Pedagogical Implications

We move now to consider the pedagogical implications of a flat ontology for language and communication. How do we teach students to treat meaning as an assemblage emerging through material, social, and semiotic networks?

First, we have to understand the limitations of the traditional approaches to language teaching, based on structuralist principles. They have been influenced by representationalist constructs. That is, language teaching has largely focused on the knowledge of grammar needed to generate meanings. Secondarily, knowledge of culture, identities, and society has also been taught to facilitate performance in a language but as knowledge constructs needed to complement grammatical knowledge. Such pedagogical approaches might be considered product oriented. They focus on the 'what' rather than the 'how'. If they were of limited value earlier, they are even more irrelevant now. In the context of globalization, mobility, and technological changes, communication transcends community and language boundaries. Scholars like Blommaert (2010) treat diversity and unpredictability as the contemporary norm in social and communicative life. In such a context, normative structures cannot guarantee communicative success. We have to be always ready to negotiate different languages and communicative norms in every single interaction. Predefined representational constructs, such as the traditional word/knowledge/world pairings, are too fixed to facilitate intelligibility.

A non-representational approach, motivated by flat ontology, would focus on strategies and practices. It would focus on the 'how' more than the 'what'. The 'how' includes considerations such as the following: how to work with the ecological affordances in one's communicative setting; which strategies to use to negotiate meanings with the diverse people in a social network; how to get the best out of the resources in the material and semiotic networks available for one's purposes; how to leverage one's own assets and strengths in relation to the material constraints for one's voice and objectives. Such an orientation leads to a radically practice-based, or performative, pedagogy. Whereas traditional pedagogies treated such pragmatic and sociolinguistic consideration as an addendum to a grammar- or norms-based pedagogy, the new materialist perspective gives more importance to practice. Students would be taught to be sensitive to the grammars, meanings, and knowledge that emerge in and through activity in situated interactions. Even better, students should be sensitive to how activity and process are representations, not separate from meanings and knowledge.

An analogy can be borrowed from the way scholars have defined communicative competence. Canale and Swain (1980) divide it into four components: grammatical, sociolinguistic, discoursal, and strategic competence. The first three are largely representational. They have to do with a knowledge of norms and rules that shape communication, though the second and third relate to social practice. But the final construct, strategic competence, is non-representational. It relates to how language users manage breakdown and other unpredictable eventualities in communication. From a materialist perspective, it is strategic competence that should be primary in pedagogy. Being adept in managing practice in situated communicative interactions with the available resources would help one take care of grammatical, discoursal, and sociolinguistic diversity, leading to the emergence of co-constructed meanings. In the place of grammatical, sociolinguistic, and discoursal knowledge, one will find the dispositions for strategic competence more helpful for pedagogical development (see Canagarajah, 2013, for more on dispositions).

From this perspective, we should try to inculcate a different notion of human agency among our students. Whereas traditional pedagogies were based on a notion of self-sufficiency, i.e. each person developing the capacity to manage meanings by themselves for their own communicative objectives, flat ontology holds a qualified notion of human agency. One has to work with the available assemblages in relevant material, social, and semiotic networks for meaning. However, as mentioned earlier, just as objects mediate human agency, people also mediate objects (Appadurai, 2015). There are options and choices among semiotic resources and networks. One can be strategic in leveraging the resources and networks to nudge them towards one's objectives. This also means that there is no unqualified success in meaning making. Communicative objectives are always responsive, negotiated, and ongoing, with give and take. As we can appreciate, this will lead to a different ethic of communication, one based on collaboration rather than individuality; humility rather than pride; attunement rather than self-sufficiency.

References

Appadurai, A. (2015). Mediants, materiality, normativity. *Public Culture*, 27(2), 221–237.
Atkinson, D. (2011). A sociocognitive approach to Second Language Acquisition: How mind, body, and world work together in learning additional languages. In D. Atkinson, ed., *Alternative Approaches to Second Language Acquisition* (pp. 143–166). Oxford: Routledge.
Atkinson, D., Churchill, E., Nishino, T., and Okada, H. (2007). Alignment and interaction in a sociocognitive approach in second language acquisition. *Modern Language Journal*, 91, 169–188.
Barad, K. (2007). *Meeting the Universe Halfway: Quantum Physics and the Entanglement of Matter and Meaning*. Durham, NC: Duke University Press.
Blommaert, J. (2005). *Discourse: A Critical Introduction*. Cambridge: Cambridge University Press.
Blommaert, J. (2010). *The Sociolinguistics of Globalization*. Cambridge: Cambridge University Press.
Braidotti, R. (2013). *The Posthuman*. Cambridge: Polity.
Bullock, A. (1975). *A Language for Life: Report of the Committee of Inquiry Appointed by the Secretary of State for Education and Science under the Chairmanship of Sir Alan Bullock F.B.A.* London: Her Majesty's Stationery Office.
Canagarajah, S. (2013). *Translingual Practice: Global Englishes and Cosmopolitan Relations*. Abingdon: Routledge.
Canagarajah, S. (2018). Materializing competence: Perspectives from international STEM scholars. *Modern Language Journal*, 102, 1–24.
Canagarajah, A. S. and DeCosta, P. (2016). Introduction: Scales analysis, and its uses and prospects in educational linguistics. *Linguistics and Education*, 34, 1–10.
Canale, M. and Swain, M. (1980). Theoretical bases of communicative approaches to second language teaching and testing. *Applied Linguistics*, 1(1), 1–47.

Chomsky, N. (1965). *Aspects of the Theory of Syntax*. Cambridge: MIT Press.
Coole, D. and Frost, S. (2010). *New Materialisms: Ontology, Agency, and Politics*. Durham, NC: Duke University Press.
Deleuze, G. and Guattari, F. (1987). *A Thousand Plateaus*. Minneapolis: University of Minnesota Press.
Derrida, J. (1973) [1967]. *Speech and Phenomena and Other Essays on Husserl's Theory of Signs*. J. Allison, trans. Evanston, IL: Northwestern University Press.
Dulay, H., Burt, M., and Krashen, S. D. (1982). *Language Two*. New York: Oxford University Press.
Genesee, F., Lindholm-Leary, K., Saunders, W. M., and Christian, D., eds. (2006). *Educating English Language Learners: A Synthesis of Research Evidence*. Cambridge: Cambridge University Press.
Hymes, D. (1971). On linguistic theory, communicative competence, and the education of disadvantaged children. In M. L. Wax, S. A. Diamond, and F. Gearing, eds., *Anthropological Perspectives on Education* (pp. 51–66). New York: Basic Books.
Kendon, A. (2004). *Gesture: Visible Action as Utterance*. Cambridge: Cambridge University Press.
Kress, G. (2009). *Multimodality: A Social Semiotic Approach to Contemporary Communication*. London: Routledge.
Latour, B. (2005). *Reassembling the Social: An Introduction to Actor-Network-Theory*. Oxford: Oxford University Press.
Marston, S., Jones, J., and Woodward, K. (2005). Human geography without scale. *Transactions of the Institute of British Geographers, 30*(4), 416–432.
Massey, D. (2005). *For Space*. London: Sage.
Mondada, L. (2014). The local constitution of multimodal resources for social interaction. *Journal of Pragmatics, 65,* 137–156.
Nishino, T. and Atkinson, D. (2015). Second language writing as sociocognitive alignment. *Journal of Second Language Writing, 27,* 37–54.
Pennycook, A. (2017). Translanguaging and semiotic assemblages. *International Journal of Multilingualism, 14*(3), 269–282.
Pennycook, A. and Otsuji, E. (2015). *Metrolingualism: Language in the City*. Abingdon: Routledge.
Pigg, S. (2014). Emplacing mobile composing habits: A study of academic writing in networked social spaces. *College English, 66*(2), 250–275.
Prior, P. A. (1998). *Writing/Disciplinarity: A Sociohistoric Account of Writing in the Disciplines*. Mahwah, NJ: Erlbaum.
Rickert, T. (2013). *Ambient Rhetoric*. Pittsburgh, PA: University of Pittsburgh Press.
Rymes, B. (2014). *Communicating beyond Language: Everyday Encounters with Diversity*. Abingdon: Routledge.
Spivak, G. (1993). *Outside in the Teaching Machine*. New York: Routledge.
Thrift, N. (2007). *Non-representational Theory: Space, Politics, Affect*. Abingdon: Routledge.

16 Mobile Learners and 'English as an Additional Language'

Robert Sharples

1 Introduction

The number of pupils for whom English is an additional language (EAL) has grown steadily over the past twenty years, increasing by around 300 per cent in England since 1997 (Department for Education, 2018a; NALDIC, 2018a). This linear progression, however, masks wide disparities between groups of pupils and their experiences of education. The large majority are second- or third-generation British citizens born into multilingual homes (Strand and Demie, 2006; Strand, Malmberg and Hall, 2015). English is often their strongest language, so while officially classed as 'EAL', it may be more helpful to describe them as 'multiliterate' (New London Group, 1996; Datta, 2007) or 'advanced bilingual learners' (Conteh, 2012, pp. 12–14), as their different languages play distinct roles in their lives. Others will be new to the United Kingdom, perhaps also new to English and even to formal schooling, but with a set of contextually specific 'negotiation strategies and a repertoire of codes' (García, 2007, p. xiii) developed in different settings over time. These learners may have migrated with the intention of settling in the United Kingdom; they may be 'sojourners' whose parents are working or studying here for a period of time; or they may 'transmigrate', meaning that this is part of a longer migration or that they are regularly resident in a number of countries. Many 'EAL pupils' are therefore highly mobile, and such mobile learners are the focus of this chapter.

Pupil mobility is part of a global phenomenon – the increasing movement of people, resources, and ideas – that intersects with national education systems. Catalano (2016), for example, documents the narratives of a wide range of adult and child migrants, showing clearly that formal education is only one element in a complex set of decisions around how, when, and why to migrate. Likewise, Badwan's research into study abroad settings (this volume) shows that the "multiple identity investments" demanded of mobile learners are as much of a concern for adults as for young people. However, there is little scope for such complexity in the education system. Wallace's (2011) study of newly arrived young migrants in a West London school, for example, documents the tension between their desire to "belong, to become 'pupils' [and to assert] other identities and values as they respond to the school's curriculum regimes" (p. 98). Davies (2010, p. xv) likewise describes the ongoing challenge for both pupils and teachers of resisting the dominant monolingualism of the education system: "For [young migrants], encounters with new and different languages are a 'given', a natural consequence of growing global mobility. For all its naturalness, maintaining linguistic diversity in English-dominant societies requires conscious effort, and professional experience everywhere has shown that teaching and learning English is not just a common-sense enterprise." Mobility, multilingualism, and encounters with difference are thus intertwined, but the English education system is founded on assumptions of rootedness, monolingualism and homogeneity. Nowhere is this more clear than in the example of 'EAL' (English as an Additional Language), in which a single label must stand for such diversity of experience.

The terminology used in other Anglophone and Western education systems shows that migrant and multilingual learners are widely treated as a single category. In Australia, for example, the term EAL/D is used (adding 'dialect', which "intentionally include[s] students who speak a variety of Aboriginal English as their first language"; NSW Department of English and Communities, 2014, p. 4). In the United States, the terms ELL, LTEL, and LEP are common (for 'English language learner', 'long-term English learner', and 'limited English proficiency'; see Christian, 2006). Similar terms exist in non-Anglophone education systems, such as FLA (*français langue étrangère*) and DaZ (*Deutsch als Zweitsprache*). The categories are not fixed: in England, for example, EAL has largely replaced ESL, to "suggest that linguistic minority pupils already have other linguistic resources (sometimes more than one language) before learning English" (Leung, 2016, p. 159). Each categorisation represents an attempt to reconcile the complexity of migration and multilingualism with the relatively fixed curricula and assessments of public education systems. Each is informed by its own educational, social, cultural, and policy contexts; but I suggest that they all have two features in common.

The first is polysemy. 'EAL' (like its equivalents) represents both a category for multilingual pupils and a professional specialism. It can refer, for example, to both 'EAL learners' and 'EAL teachers' (e.g. in Department for Education, 2005, p. 5); to the needs of pupils learning

English as well as to a body of knowledge that incorporates research findings (e.g. Genesee et al., 2006) and pedagogical techniques (e.g. Pim, 2010). This polysemy extends within these domains: when applied to pupils, EAL conflates young people from a wide range of linguistic and cultural backgrounds, with widely varying experiences of migration and (formal and informal) education. When applied to teachers, it connotes a specialism in language pedagogy (the EAL teacher or assistant is the one who supports pupils to access the medium of instruction), whose work also involves detailed knowledge of subject curricula (because the language is not separable from the content; see Creese, 2005, on teaching partnerships). When applied to the content of many language-development lessons, the term 'EAL' is often used as an umbrella for work on academic language (with a particular focus on subject terminology), general English (often using generic EFL material), and work designed to make children feel secure and welcome (see Leung, 2016, for an overview).

The second common feature is the object of study: in essence, a set of linguistic patterns and a lexicon for each curriculum subject, as well as an overarching distinction between conversational and academic English (e.g. Cummins 1981, 2001; Gibbons, 2009). In this way, EAL is positioned as a 'cross-curriculum discipline' (National Association for Language Development in the Curriculum, 1999) and the task facing learners is to develop mastery of those patterns and lexicon so that they can engage in the mainstream curriculum. However, for migrant learners, the exigencies they face are much more complex, described as the "triple challenge" of "acquiring both colloquial and academic English"; developing "the knowledge, skills and understanding" required for curriculum success; and interpreting the (often hidden) "culturally-bound aspects of schooling" (National Association for Language Development in the Curriculum, 2009). As Goodwyn and Roberts (this volume) show, using the example of the secondary school subject 'English', curriculum subjects are dynamic, socially constructed bodies of knowledge that demand mastery of a range of spoken and written genres, and of space-dependent behavioural norms (see Canagarajah, this volume). What happens outside school is also significant: recent studies have emphasised the important role played by intergenerational learning (Ruby, 2017) and faith learning (Lytra et al., 2016), for example.

As a concept, therefore, EAL is neither simple to describe nor simple to integrate into the current system of formal schooling. In some senses it represents a curriculum-focused approach to additive bilingualism; in others, it is a "catch-all phrase to contrast a cohort of pupils whose home language(s) may be other than English with those whose first language is English" (Bracken et al., 2017, p. 7). The dichotomy itself may be unhelpful: where multilingual pupils account for some 20 per cent of the school population, as they do in England (Department for Education, 2018a), is a monolingual curriculum even still tenable? This chapter casts such questions in ontological terms and suggests that the idea of 'mobility' is a powerful tool for understanding the educational experiences of migrant learners. It begins by briefly reviewing the literature on EAL and its role as a de facto policy framing for young migrants. It then draws on critiques of Standard English and 'monolingualising' (Heller, 1995, p. 374) language policies to propose a 'mobile orientation': a set of meta-theoretical commitments and their instantiation in policy and practice. It closes by considering the implications for policy and practice, and the significance of mobility as a broader theoretical framing for public policy.

2 EAL Policy and Young Migrants

Although the number of young migrants in English schools has grown substantially over the past twenty years (Department for Education, 2018a), there has been no commensurate development in the policy response to migration and multilingualism. This section reviews the existing policy and links it to key developments in the research literature; as such, it describes a 'gap' between the diversity and complexity of young migrants' experiences and the relative homogeneity and rigidity of the available policy responses.

A lack of current and relevant education policy on migration (see Arnot et al., 2014; Schneider et al., 2016) means that pupil mobility is poorly distinguished from the larger category of 'EAL', and therefore that young migrants' needs are understood as primarily linguistic. This is problematic, especially at a time when the national policy framework for EAL has been largely abandoned by central government in England. Anderson et al. (2016, p. 1) express this in stark terms, as a "dismantling of EAL specialist provision and support across England", which they attribute to "the current political climate". It might more generously be seen as a side-effect of a broader set of reforms to the education system that have significantly reduced the role of local authorities in favour of a "school-led system" (Academies Act 2010; Education Act 2011; Gilbert et al., 2013), in which schools are responsible for identifying gaps in attainment and provision. In support of this, schools have been permitted to develop their own approaches to identifying, supporting, and assessing multilingual learners. Yet, they are often ill equipped to do so: specialist expertise was previously concentrated in local authorities, who have largely closed their EAL services under pressure from budget cuts, and the new 'middle-tier' actors (such as Regional Schools Commissioners and multi-academy trusts) have not inherited the same responsibilities to maintain specialist EAL support. Funding for EAL is no longer ring fenced, and all central government guidance has been discontinued, with the exception of a single document relating to out-of-class tuition (Department for Education, 2011). The limited data collection on language proficiency has also been halted (see Department for Education, 2018b, p. 13; National Association for Language Development in the Curriculum (NALDIC), 2018b). In sum, the provision of EAL support is 'at risk', according to one union that opposed the change (NASUWT, 2012, p. 5).

Where guidance for educating migrant pupils exists, it tends to focus only on refugee and asylum-seeking children. Here, responsibility is devolved to local authorities (which have a statutory duty to provide school places under the Education Act, 1996). Consequently, there is a large degree of regional variation in how, and to what extent, specialist support is offered to migrant learners. One exploratory study (Arnot and Pinson, 2009, focusing on young refugees and asylum seekers) suggests that local approaches are greatly influenced by the available funding and that authorities often seek to accommodate migrant learners within existing approaches, further conflating mobility with language, vulnerability, and ethnicity (pp. 5–6; cf. also Pinson et al., 2010). Much of the research base focuses on the early years and primary phases (Andrews, 2009; Murphy and Unthiah, 2015) where there may be a higher proportion of British-born advanced bilingual pupils, and in one influential study of EAL attainment (Strand et al., 2015) 'pupil mobility' is identified as a risk factor, particularly around the transition to secondary schooling. This suggests that new approaches, which disaggregate language, ethnicity, and mobility, in order to identify more clearly the experiences, needs, and achievements of migrant pupils, are urgently needed.

With no clearly articulated and widely shared policy framework available to schools, the most developed and most widespread option becomes the default. There are EAL specialists in many schools and (until recently) in almost all local authorities; many schools also employ bilingual teaching assistants to support multilingual children. This infrastructure, however, is not sufficient to offer a fine-grained response to migrant learners – especially not one that distinguishes their specific needs from the much larger number of British-born, advanced bilingual pupils. There is, for example, a significant shortage of specialist EAL staff and significant variation in whether a senior (or even trained) member of staff is responsible for EAL provision

(Mallows, 2009; Wallace et al., 2009; Wardman, 2012). Bilingual staff are often ineffectively deployed because of a widespread misconception that EAL is the sole responsibility of specialist teachers and teaching assistants (Martin-Jones and Saxena, 1996; Creese, 2005; Conteh, 2007). The limited funding now available to support young multilinguals is restricted to those who have been enrolled in English schools for a maximum of three years (Arnot et al., 2014, pp. 14–15) despite strong evidence that five to nine years of support is needed (Genesee 2015; Takanishi and Le Menestrel, 2017; Demie, 2018). As is widely noted in the literature, policy and practice often give too little support to multilingual learners. Migrant learners, whose experience of other education systems and ways of learning often go unrecognised, are doubly poorly served.

Underpinning this societal and educational complexity is an ontological stance that holds that language, along with many other aspects of social interaction, is essentially static and hierarchical. Badwan (this volume) describes this stance as the "standard ontology" in which language is essentially stable; Cunningham (this volume) calls it a 'shallow ontology' and associates it with a "lack of linguistic awareness". Canagarajah (this volume) contrasts "traditional constructs" (such as "labelled languages, grammatical structures, and standardised norms") with a "flat ontology", to recognise how interaction creates structure and categories in the social world. These varied critiques suggest an important area of study: the interaction between ontology, policy, and practice. This chapter has already argued that policy has struggled to reconcile the diversity of young migrants' experiences with the institutionally embedded social norms of the education system. In the following section, I outline an alternative.

3 Mobile Learners and Immobile Education Systems

In the previous section, I gave some reasons why EAL operates as a de facto policy framing for both multilingual and migrant learners. I argued that this risks marginalising migrant learners because their needs and experiences differ from those of pupils who have spent their school careers in a single education system. I also argued that this difference goes beyond language: most migrant pupils are also multilingual, but the experience of migration sets these pupils apart from the majority of EAL learners (who are better described as 'advanced bilingual', or 'multiliterate'). This section outlines an alternative perspective, based on an assumption that mobility and plurilingualism are the default state and that different languages and different types of learning can, and should, be part of mainstream public education.

I use the term 'mobile orientation' to describe this, echoing Canagarajah's (2013) 'translingual orientation' but with greater emphasis on contact between individuals and the institutions they interact with and within. It suggests both a characteristic of mobile young people and a need to re-orient institutional assumptions to include them.

In educational contexts, a useful distinction can be made between globally mobile learners and a 'settled' (or 'immobile') education system (Hamann, 2016 uses this term to include both the system itself and the "teachers, administrators and others who shape schools and school systems"; see also Hamann, 2001). A 'settled' orientation privileges the sociocultural, behavioural, and linguistic norms of a particular institutional setting (such as a school), because the majority of participants are familiar with those norms (whether as teachers, parents, pupils, or members of the wider community). Monolingualism becomes the norm, "a language in common" (Qualifications and Curriculum Authority, or QCA, 2000), and pupils are required to aspire to, and teachers are expected to demonstrate, 'good English' (though, as Cunningham, this volume, notes, there is a lack of consensus about what constitutes 'good English'). It is entirely reasonable, from a settled perspective, to support young multilinguals to access the mainstream curriculum by prioritising the majority language. The cost of this assumption is that different linguistic repertoires and behavioural norms become associated with non-conformity, for example, where non-standard language is associated with misbehaviour (e.g. Cameron, 1995) or when the behavioural norms of another education system are associated with a lack of education (e.g. Sharples, 2017). The settled-mobile distinction therefore entails ontological commitments, particularly in terms of language. These are then reflected in policy and in the expectations of young people in the classroom.

The 'settled' orientation also recognises the role of schools in reproducing social and linguistic norms. Like many other institutions, they are "both subject to, and producers of, apparently common-sense, everyday hegemonic discourses which privilege homogeneity above diversity, and monolingualism over multilingualism" (Blackledge, 2001, p. 304). Such 'common sense' discourses give rise to a number of assumptions, for example, that the mainstream curriculum should be monolingual; that there is a "universal L2 learner phenomenon" and that a multilingual learner can be "conceptualised as someone learning English as a social and linguistic outsider" (Leung et al., 1997, p. 546); and that the "journey to proficiency" is primarily cognitive, characterised by the "development of the interlanguage" and measurable in terms of the learner's mastery of predetermined lexis and grammatical structures (Creagh, 2017, p. 3). Many policy and pedagogical approaches to multilingual and migrant learners rest on such assumptions, for example, where EAL support is prioritised over participation in subject lessons.

A 'mobile orientation' operates from different assumptions. It recognises that migrant learners bring wide-ranging language, knowledge, skills and cultural assumptions with them to the classroom, and values these as legitimate and important aspects of mainstream education. It recasts the "triple challenge" (National Association for Language Development in the Curriculum, 1999) as a process of renegotiation: migrant learners are "shaped by different learning environments and their varying respective cultures" (Budach, 2014, p. 525). They bring wide-ranging language, knowledge, skills and cultural assumptions with them to the classroom, and must learn to adapt to the prevailing norms – but in doing so, they often contest and play with the 'settled' assumptions of the institution. This can be seen as a process of 'relocalising' (to adapt a term from Pennycook, 2010) the norms of other settings to their new classrooms. Classroom interaction, in this sense "is not only repeated social activity involving language, but is also, though its relocalization in space and time, the repetition of difference" (Pennycook, 2010, p. 43). In other words, the "triple challenge" is not simply a process of adapting to a mainstream norm, but also a series of encounters with those norms. Mobile learners' existing repertoires are inseparable from the norms they are adapting to, and their experiences of different languages and different ways of learning are in constant interplay. A 'mobile orientation' seeks to capture these overlapping social and linguistic processes.

Using Hall's typology (this volume), the distinction between 'settled' and 'mobile' can be framed as follows:

- 'Settled':
  = change in the cognitive domain to support norms in the social domain
  = *learners modify their I-English resources to correspond to N-English norms*
- 'Mobile':
  = change in the cognitive and social domains, in a dynamic relationship with norms in the social domain
  = *learners engage in languaging using their repertoire of linguisitic (I-language) and non-linguistic resources to engage with N-English (and 'N-culture') norms, leading to modification in their I-English (and 'I-culture') resources – and potentially in the local linguistic (and cultural) norms.*

This contrast can be seen in the broader shift towards plurality in the sociolinguistic literature: from "structural explanations of language [towards] ethnographic examinations of languaging" (May, 2014, p. 230). Migrant pupils arrive in their new school with their own histories of learning and schooling, with their own linguistic repertoires and funds of knowledge (Moll et al., 1992; González et al., 2005). They use these as a starting point to understand the norms of their new environment and, through repeated encounters with those norms, add to and adapt their existing resources.

Having sketched the key points of a 'mobile orientation', the remainder of this section will discuss two elements of a broader theoretical framework for analysing mobility in language education. It focuses first on the idea of migration trajectories, conceptualising the EAL classroom as one set of encounters among many, in different settings over time. This puts EAL provision in its broader context and emphasises that the school curriculum is not an end point of study but a way stage in life. It then examines Pratt's (1987, 1991) notion of sociolinguistic 'contact', in which powerful and less powerful groups encounter each other. While the dominant group's norms define the terms of the encounter, Pratt shows how subaltern voices can redefine those terms and be heard nevertheless. The implications for policy and practice are discussed in the final section of this chapter.

4 Migration Trajectories or Educational Journeys

This chapter has argued that migrant pupils differ from other multilingual pupils in important ways, particularly in that they bring experience of other education systems and other forms of learning into the classroom. A useful metaphor is 'trajectory': the series of learning encounters across the life course, which take place in a range of settings. It is important to distinguish this from the idea of a 'journey', which implies a destination and the possibility of arrival. The young migrants described in this chapter make complex transmigrations, in which the United Kingdom may be only an intermediate point. The term *trajectory* not only recognises the relevance of young people's pasts to the present moments captured in classroom interactions, but also emphasises the "nonlinearity" of "biographical ruptures and discontinuities" above the "assumed predictability of life cycles" (Hörschelmann, 2011, p. 378). Arriving at their new school should not be seen as a 'new start' or as an arrival after a long journey. It is better seen as a period of negotiation in which the young person's earlier experiences and hopes for the future are used to help make sense of the new environment.

Migration trajectories can be symbolic as much as geographical. Laursen and Mogensen (2016, pp. 13–15), for example, call attention to the ways that young migrants can manipulate "settled" assumptions about place, person, and language. They give the example of Ifrah, a young girl who was born in Denmark to Somali parents, whose retellings of her own experience are at odds with the knowledge held by her teachers. She points to Mogadishu on a map, for example, and describes it as her place of birth; she also describes getting "confused" in her Somali lessons over differences in vocabulary and tells a story of how her cousins correct her Somali after they return from a long trip to that country: "[w]ith her narrative about her cousins, Ifrah initiates a resignification of the myth of language competence which builds on an understanding of language as an unambiguous and nationally delimited linguistic entity that is linked to geographically defined language communities to which you can belong if you command the language" (p. 14). Using the categories of Hall's ontological framework (this volume), this can be recast as follows: through repeated encounters, retellings, and interactions (languaging), Ifrah modifies her repertoire of linguistic (I-language) and non-linguistic resources to engage with N-Danish and N-Somali (and 'N-culture') norms, leading to modification in her I-Danish and I-Somali (and 'I-culture') resources.

Contrast this with the notion of a young migrant's 'journey' through the education system. It is more limited in scope as it uses nominal start and end points (in both time and space); in this case, beginning with the young person's arrival in school and ending when the entitlement to compulsory or school-based further education is withdrawn (at ages 16 and 18 in the United Kingdom). The 'settled orientation' is clear in the way that key events (or milestones) are established at an institutional level and therefore set by others rather than defined by the young person. These key events might include sitting examinations or passing to the next year group or stage of the curriculum. These two conceptions of how young migrants move through schooling – migration trajectory and educational journey – exist in tension with each other. They represent different perspectives: the age groups, curriculum levels, and set milestones all emphasise the education system's role in defining the context and content of learning. The encounters, interactions, and personal histories shape what learning happens, and how.

5 The Classroom as Contact Zone

Pratt's (1991) concept of the 'contact zone' offers a useful way to think about how a mobile orientation might work in practice. First presented as an address to the Modern Languages Association in 1991, it describes "social spaces where cultures meet, clash, and grapple with each other, often in contexts of highly asymmetrical relations of power" (p. 34). Adopting the concept of 'contact zone' in the context of classroom interaction positions schools, teachers, and migrant pupils as equal participants: speakers in an institutional environment that they each uphold and contest in different measure, each with his or her own history of personal, professional, and educational experiences, and his or her own set of negotiation strategies and repertoire of codes. In the contact zone, texts and interactions are "heterogeneous on the reception end as well as the production end", in that they are understood "very differently [by] people in different positions in the contact zone" (pp. 36–37). Effective communication – and effective learning – therefore depends not on the pupils' ability to communicate in the majority language (or to adapt their 'EnEnglishments' to N-English norms in Hall's terms), but on the creative deployment of their mobile resources (Blommaert, 2010, p. 197) in the knowledge that their reception depends on the repertoires and norms of others.

A 'mobile orientation', similarly, does not privilege the social, behavioural, and linguistic norms of a particular setting (cf. Harder, this volume). Norms emerge locally, as speakers draw on their full repertoires to negotiate the differences between themselves and others. This is analogous to Pratt's (1987) critique of the "linguistics of community". "There is some irony", she argues, "in the thought of schoolrooms as stable, harmonious, smoothly-running discursive arenas in which teachers and pupils go on producing the same orderly cycles together day in and day out" (Pratt, 1987, p. 52).

The orderliness of classroom routines depends on taking an institutional, settled, monolingual perspective. Settled orderliness represents a status quo – a 'regime of truth', to use Foucault's (1977) term – from which migrant, multilingual learners are excluded until they have sufficiently adopted the behavioural and linguistic norms of that setting. A 'linguistics of contact' (using Pratt's, 1987, term) unsettles that status quo, repositioning the classroom as an interactional space in which speakers encounter each other and gain legitimacy through interaction.

Legitimacy is at the heart of Pratt's linguistics of contact. It has much in common with Miller's (2003, 2004) notion of 'audibility', "the degree to which speakers sound like, and are legitimised by, users of the dominant discourse" (Miller, 2004, p. 291). Traditional studies of classrooms, Pratt argues, are rooted in the ideals of 'orderliness', "single sets of shared rules and shared understandings", in which "'legitimate' is defined from the point of view of the party in authority. Teacher–pupil language, for instance, tends to be described almost entirely from the teacher's point of view" (Pratt, 1987, p. 51). That point of view, as several contributors to this volume make clear, privileges Standard English and a settled orientation. Multilingual pupils are not legitimate users of the dominant discourse (though they may be 'legitimate peripheral participants'; Lave and Wenger, 1991) until they have sufficiently mastered English to leave EAL support (as codified in the 'Fluent' proficiency descriptor; Department for Education, 2018b, p. 66). A mobile orientation offers a way of understanding young migrants as legitimate users of a range of discourses, of legitimising the presence of multiple discourses (or a repertoire of I-language resources deployed as both languaging/Englishing, with contextually appropriate – but not automatic – reference to N-English norms). In other words, it legitimises the young people's experiences of other languages, other education systems, and other ways of doing things. It challenges the "apparently common-sense, everyday hegemonic discourses which privilege homogeneity" (Blackledge, 2001, p. 304).

6 Implications for Policy and Practice

This chapter has discussed a distinction between 'settled' and 'mobile' orientations. It emphasised the value of learners' prior experiences, even when these came from other education systems or from informal learning, and their place in the classroom. This has a number of implications for policy and practice. In this chapter, there is scope to focus on just those points that would anchor a fuller response: language-rich curricula; mobility, trajectory, and contact; and programme design for late-adolescent migrant learners.

6.1 A Language-Rich Curriculum

Cunningham (this volume) notes that adherence to Standard English (N-English) norms can disadvantage many monolingual-English pupils as much as multilingual (EAL) learners. A curriculum that abandoned Standard English entirely would be greatly contested (see e.g. Snell, 2013; Canagarajah, this volume, Section 4) and would disadvantage learners in a number of ways. It is possible, however, to enrich classroom interaction without moving to either extreme. This could begin by recognising the linguistic repertoire of all pupils, with its idiolectal combination of standard and unstandardised forms, formulaic phrases, idioms, memes and more, which may superficially correspond to a number of N-languages (Hall, this volume). Pratt (1991, p. 33) lamented that, although she was "delighted to see schooling give Sam [her son] the tools with which to find" new experiences, she "found it unforgivable that schooling itself gave him nothing remotely as meaningful to do" with those tools. Young migrants bring knowledge of other places, languages, and ways of doing things into the classroom. Classroom strategies that employed them as part of a structured pedagogy, in which the pupils work towards producing N-ENGLISH discourse but can use all their resources to do so, would go some way to implementing a mobile orientation.

6.2 Rethinking Curricula for Global Mobility

The importance of welcoming young migrants' wider knowledge has been a point of discussion in the literature for decades. The Bullock Report (Bullock, 1975, p. 286), for example, made clear that young people should not be "expected to cast off the language and culture of the home as [they cross] the school threshold". The focus on 'trajectories' – life experiences, seen through the lens of migration – seeks to put this into practice. It allows teachers and researchers to emphasise what the young people bring to the school, rather than focusing on the implementation of the curriculum. The notion of classrooms as 'contact zones' – spaces where trajectories intersect – puts the young people and the institution on a more even footing. Like the adults in the school, they are seen as participants negotiating the difference between their own life experiences and those of others, using the full range of their communicative resources to do so.

This implies a need to rethink curricula for an era of global mobility. The current approach marginalises young migrants because it is rooted in two sets of assumptions that are not tenable under conditions of high mobility. The first is that the curriculum offers a necessary and sufficient context for learning, which implies that the curriculum need not change to accommodate learners from different backgrounds. The second is that difference from a monolingual, settled norm should be construed as a barrier to learning, with appropriate provision offered so that young migrants can access the curriculum. Far from expecting these young people to access the mainstream curriculum unproblematically, the emphasis should shift to understanding and drawing on the resources they bring to the classroom. Similarly, their difference from the putative mainstream norm need not be reified as either a cause for celebration or for concern: it can be a resource. Young people learn much about schooling from each other and from recognising the differences between what they know and what the curriculum expects of them. This is not a deficit to overcome, but a source of rich insights and potential learning.

6.3 Programme Design for Late-Adolescent New Arrivals

Young migrants are marginalised by education policy that conflates language, ethnicity and vulnerability. This is particularly problematic for young people who arrive in late adolescence, close to the end of compulsory education, with limited formal education or limited English proficiency. As a number of studies have noted, success in the school system depends on having enough time to master the complex registers and repertoires of academic English (see, for example: Strand et al., 2015; Demie, 2018). The principle of mainstreaming is widely asserted (see Andrews, 2009, for a review) so that all young people receive their statutory entitlement to a rich curriculum. However, a focus on mobility would entail considering a wider range of provision, available to all pupils. This might involve short-duration courses that give considerable flexibility within the broader structure of the school, allowing young people (and especially young migrants) to move through the programme at different speeds. It might also involve the use of alternative assessments to give access to valuable qualifications even over short periods.

7 Conclusion

In this chapter, I have also tried to outline a broader argument, showing that the fine grain of educational policy has significant ontological implications. I have proposed a 'mobile orientation' that better reflects the ways in which these young people bring their experiences of learning elsewhere into the classroom. Using Hall's typology (this volume), I have cast this as a distinction between an approach based on the norms of the institution and one based on the resources that the pupils bring from their migration trajectories. I have also sketched the beginnings of a theoretical framework to put this 'mobile orientation' into practice, based on the notions of 'trajectory' and 'contact'. In the closing discussion, I suggested three areas in which this analysis could be applied to practice: in supporting a language-rich curriculum for all pupils, in rethinking curricula for global mobility, and in designing programmes for young migrants who join a school system in late adolescence. In so doing, I hope to connect the discussion of ontology to public policy, giving theoretical support to broader discussions about how to support young multilingual migrants in mainstream education.

A single chapter can only serve to outline a complex agenda. There is a great deal of work to be done in developing theoretical responses to migration and multilingualism in schools (a challenge noted by Andrews, 2009, before a change of government led to the withdrawal of much funding and guidance). Moreover, the chapter focuses on a particular type of education system: primarily the English system (as policy changes have affected the devolved administrations of Wales, Scotland, and Northern Ireland differently; cf. Goodwyn and Goddard, this volume), but more generally a Western system, in a country with a dominant ideology of monolingualism. Further work needs to be done to connect this with other settings, for example in the global South, in officially and effectively multilingual countries, and in settings where there is a local/regional assumption of mobility and multilingualism. It also focuses on one institutional environment – a school – while arguing that young migrants move through different institutions and draw on their experience from them all. Further research will be needed to investigate different settings, such as faith groups, community schools, the legal and health care systems.

With those provisos in mind, the final words should perhaps recognise the individual impact of mobility. At the time of writing, the issue of migration fills newspaper pages, television reports, and online comments. In these debates, there often appears to be an assumption that migration will simply stop when the United Kingdom leaves the European Union, or when a wall is built in the United States, when fences are erected, or when accords are signed elsewhere in the world. This rests on further assumptions about why people migrate, and what national institutions can and should provide. These are perhaps the ultimate expression of a settled orientation that positions young migrants as "social and linguistic outsider[s]" (Leung et al., 1997, p. 546). A mobile orientation suggests instead that classrooms are spaces in which all participants are engaged in meaning making, that legitimacy can be gained both through use of the dominant discourse and by effective deployment of a multilingual repertoire, and that experience of learning in other places and at other times can be a valuable resource for the classroom here and now.

References

Academies Act. 2010 (ch. 32). London: The Stationary Office.
Anderson, C., Foley, Y., Sangster, P. et al. (2016). *Policy, Pedagogy and Pupil Perceptions: EAL in Scotland and England*. Cambridge: The Bell Foundation.
Andrews, R. (2009). *Review of Research in English as an Additional Language (EAL)*. London: The Stationary Office, Training and Development Agency for Schools.

Arnot, M. and Pinson, H. (2005). The Education of Asylum-Seeker and Refugee Children: A Study of LEA and School Values, Policies and Practices. Online. Accessed 14 July 2018 from www.educ.cam.ac.uk/people/staff/arnot/AsylumReportFinal.pdf

Arnot, M., Schneider, C., Evans, M. et al. (2014). *School Approaches to the Education of EAL Students: Language Development, Social Integration and Achievement*. London: The Bell Foundation, British Council.

Blackledge, A. (2001). Literacy, schooling and ideology in a multilingual state. *Curriculum Journal, 12*(3), 291–312.

Blommaert, J. (2010). *The Sociolinguistics of Globalization*. Cambridge: Cambridge University Press.

Bracken, S., Driver C., and Kadi-Hanifi, K. (2017). *Teaching English as an Additional Language in Secondary Schools: Theory and Practice*. Abingdon: Routledge/David Fulton.

Budach, G. (2014). Educational trajectories at the crossroads: The making and unmaking of multilingual communities of learners. *Multilingua, 33*(5–6), 525–549.

Bullock, A. (1975). *A Language for Life: Report of the Committee of Inquiry Appointed by the Secretary of State for Education and Science under the Chairmanship of Sir Alan Bullock F.B.A.* London: Her Majesty's Stationery Office.

Cameron, D. (1995). *Verbal Hygiene: The Politics of Language*. Abingdon: Routledge.

Canagarajah, S. (2013). *Translingual Practice: Global Englishes and Cosmopolitan Relations*. Abingdon: Routledge.

Catalano, T. (2016). *Talking about Global Migration: Implications for Language Teaching*. Bristol: Multilingual Matters.

Christian, D. (2006). Introduction. In F. Genesee, K. Lindholm-Leary, W. M. Saunders et al., eds., *Educating English Language Learners: A Synthesis of Research Evidence* (pp. 1–13). Cambridge: Cambridge University Press.

Conteh, J. (2007). Opening doors to success in multilingual classrooms: Bilingualism, codeswitching and the professional identities of ethnic minority primary teachers. *Language and Education, 21*(6), 457–472.

Conteh, J. (2012). *Teaching Bilingual and EAL Learners in Primary Schools*. Exeter: Learning Matters.

Creagh, S. (2017). Multiple ways of speaking back to the monolingual mindset. *Discourse: Studies in the Cultural Politics of Education, 38*(1), 146–156.

Creese, A. (2005). *Teacher Collaboration and Talk in Multilingual Classrooms*. Clevedon: Multilingual Matters.

Cummins, J. (1981). Age on arrival and immigrant second language learning in Canada: A reassessment. *Applied Linguistics, II*(2), 132–149.

Cummins, J. (2001). *Language, Power, and Pedagogy: Bilingual Children in the Crossfire*. Clevedon: Multilingual Matters.

Datta, M., ed. (2007). *Bilinguality and Literacy*. London: Continuum.

Davies, N. (2010). Preface. In C. Leung and A. Creese, eds. *English as an Additional Language: Approaches to Teaching Linguistic Minority Students* (p. xv). London: Sage.

Demie, F. (2018). English language proficiency and attainment of EAL (English as second language) pupils in England. *Journal of Multilingual and Multicultural Development*. Online first publication. doi: 10.1080/01434632.2017.1420658.

Department for Education. (2011). Developing Quality Tuition: Effective Practice in Schools (English as an Additional Language). Online. Accessed 16 May 2013 from www.gov.uk/government/uploads/system/uploads/attachment_data/file/183945/developing_quality_tuition_-_english_as_an_additional_language.pdf

Department for Education. (2018a). Schools, Pupils and Their Characteristics: Statistics on Pupils in Schools in England as Collected in the January 2018 School Census. Online. Accessed 3 July 2018 from www.gov.uk/government/statistics/schools-pupils-and-their-characteristics-january-2018

Department for Education. (2018b). School Census 2018 to 2019: Guide for Schools and LAs. Online. Accessed 14 July 2018 from www.gov.uk/government/publications/school-census-2018-to-2019-guide-for-schools-and-las

Department for Education and Skills. (2005). *Aiming High: Meeting the Needs of Newly Arrived Learners of English as an Additional Language (DfES-1381-2005)*. London: DfES.

Education Act. (1996). Ch. 56. London: The Stationary Office.

Education Act. (2011). Ch. 21. London: The Stationary Office.

Foucault, M. (1977) [1980]. Truth and power. In C. Gordon, ed. C. Gordon, L. Marshall, J. Mepham et al., trans., *Power/Knowledge: Selected Interviews and Other Writings, 1972–1977* (pp. 109–133). New York: Pantheon.

García, O. (2007). Foreword. In S. Makoni and A. Pennycook, eds. *Disinventing and Reconstituting Languages* (pp. xi–xv). Clevedon: Multilingual Matters.

Genesee, F. (2015). Myths about early childhood bilingualism. *Canadian Psychology, 56*(1), 6–15.

Genesee, F., Lindholm-Leary, K., Saunders, W. M. et al., eds. (2006). *Educating English Language Learners: A Synthesis of Research Evidence*. Cambridge: Cambridge University Press.

Gibbons, P. (2009). *English Learners, Academic Literacy, and Thinking: Learning in the Challenge Zone*. Portsmouth: Heinemann.

Gilbert, C., Husbands, C., Wigdortz, B. et al. (2013). *Unleashing Greatness: Getting the Best from an Academised System*. Online. London: The Academies Commission. Accessed 25 January 2013 from www.thersa.org/action-research-centre/education/reports-and-events/reports/unleashing-greatness

Gonzalez, N., Moll, L. C., and Amanti, C., eds. (2005). *Funds of Knowledge: Theorizing Practices in Households, Communities and Classrooms*. New York: Routledge.

Hamann, E. T. (2001). Theorizing the Sojourner Student (With a Sketch of Appropriate School Responsiveness). In M. Hopkins and N. Wellmeier, eds., *Negotiating Transnationalism: Selected Papers on Refugees and Immigrants*, vol. IX (pp. 32–71). Arlington, VA: American Anthropological Association.

Hamann, E. T. (2016). Front matter. In T. Catalano, ed., *Talking about Global Migration: Implications for Language Teaching*. Bristol: Multilingual Matters.

Heller, M. (1995). Language choice, social institutions, and symbolic domination. *Language in Society, 24*(3), 373–405.

Hörschelmann, K. (2011). Theorising life transitions: Geographical perspectives. *Area, 43*(4), 378–383.

Laursen, H. P. and Mogensen, N. D. (2016). Timespacing competence: Multilingual children's linguistic worlds. *Social Semiotics*, 1–19.

Lave, J. and Wenger, E. (1991). *Situated Learning: Legitimate Peripheral Participation.* Cambridge: Cambridge University Press.

Leung, C. (2016). English as an additional language – A genealogy of language-in-education policies and reflections on research trajectories. *Language and Education, 30*(2), 158–174.

Leung, C., Harris, R., and Rampton, B. (1997). The idealised native speaker, reified ethnicities, and classroom realities. *TESOL Quarterly, 31*(3), 543–560.

Lytra, V., Volk, D., and Gregory, E., eds. (2016). *Navigating Languages, Literacies and Identities: Religion in Young Lives.* Abingdon: Routledge.

Mallows, D. (2009). *Teaching EAL: Four Priorities for the Development of the English as an Additional Language (EAL) Workforce in Schools – Supporting Evidence.* London: Institute of Education.

Martin-Jones, M. and Saxena, M. (1996). Turn-taking, power asymmetries, and the positioning of bilingual participants in classroom discourse. *Linguistics and Education, 8*(1), 105–123.

May, S. (2014). Contesting metronormativity: Exploring indigenous language dynamism across the urban-rural divide. *Journal of Language, Identity & Education, 13*(4), 229–235.

Miller, J. (2003). *Audible Difference: ESL and Social Identity in Schools.* Bristol: Multilingual Matters.

Miller, J. (2004). Identity and language use: The politics of speaking ESL in schools. In A. Blackledge and A. Pavlenko, eds., *Negotiation of Identities in Multilingual Contexts* (pp. 290–315). Clevedon: Multilingual Matters.

Moll, L. C., Amanti, C., Neff, D. et al. (1992). *Funds of Knowledge for Teaching: Using a Qualitative Approach to Connect Homes and Classrooms.* Columbus: College of Education, The Ohio State University.

Murphy, V. and Unthiah, A. (2015). *A Systematic Review of Intervention Research Examining English Language and Literacy Development in Children with English as an Additional Language (EAL).* Oxford: University of Oxford.

National Association for Language Development in the Curriculum. (1999). *The Distinctiveness of English as an Additional Language: A Cross-Curriculum Discipline*, Working Paper 5. Luton: NALDIC.

National Association for Language Development in the Curriculum. (2009). Teaching and Learning of ICT to EAL Learners in the Primary Phase. Online. Accessed 13 July 2018 from www.naldic.org.uk/Resources/NALDIC/Initial%20Teacher%20Education/Documents/EALandICT.pdf

National Association for Language Development in the Curriculum. (2018a). EAL Pupils 1997–2013. Online. Accessed 3 July 2018 from https://naldic.org.uk/the-eal-learner/research-and-statistics/papers-posters-etc

National Association for Language Development in the Curriculum. (2018b). Withdrawal of English as an Additional Language (EAL) Proficiency Data from the Schools Census Returns. Online. Accessed 14 July 2018 from https://naldic.org.uk/about-naldic/campaigns-and-reports/position-statements/dfe-proficiency-data

NASUWT, The Teachers' Union. (2012). Ethnic Minority Achievement. Online. Accessed 13 December 2016 from www.nasuwt.org.uk/asset/B9E7ED3B%2DEA48%2D4086%2D951781 781D133F45

New London Group. (1996). A pedagogy of multiliteracies: Designing social futures. *Harvard Educational Review,* 66(1), 60–92.

NSW Department of Education and Communities. (2014). *English as an Additional Language or Dialect: Advice for Schools.* Online. Accessed 11 May 2018 from https://education.nsw.gov.au/policy-library/associated-documents/eald_advice.pdf

Pennycook, A. (2010). *Language as Local Practice.* Abingdon: Routledge.

Pim, C. (2010). *How to Support Children Learning English as an Additional Language.* Hyde: LDA.

Pinson, H., Arnot, M., and Candappa, M. (2010). *Education, Asylum and the 'Non-Citizen' Child: The Politics of Compassion and Belonging.* Basingstoke: Palgrave Macmillan.

Pratt, M. L. (1987). Linguistic utopias. In N. Fabb, D. Attridge, A. Durant et al., eds., *The Linguistics of Writing: Arguments between Language and Literature* (pp. 48–66). Manchester: Manchester University Press.

Pratt, M. L. (1991). Arts of the contact zone. *Profession,* 91, 33–40.

Qualifications and Curriculum Authority. (2000). *A Language in Common: Assessing EAL.* Department for Education and Skills. Accessed 16 May 2013 from http://media.education.gov.uk/assets/files/pdf/a/a language in common assessing eal.pdf

Ruby, M. (2017). *Family Jigsaws: Grandmothers as the Missing Piece Shaping Bilingual Children's Learner Identities.* London: Trentham.

Schneider, C., Hu, M., Evans, M. et al. (2016). *Language Development and School Achievement: Opportunities and Challenges in the Education of EAL Students.* Cambridge: The Bell Foundation.

Sharples, R. (2017). Local practice, translocal students: Conflicting identities in the multilingual classroom. *Language and Education,* 31(2), 169–183.

Snell, J. (2013). Dialect, interaction and class positioning at school: From deficit to difference to repertoire. *Language and Education,* 27(2), 110–128.

Strand, S., Malmberg, L., and Hall, J. (2015). *English as an Additional Language (EAL) and Educational Achievement in England: An Analysis of the National Pupil Database.* Oxford: University of Oxford.

Strand, S. and Demie, S. (2006). Pupil mobility, attainment and progress in primary school. *British Educational Research Journal,* 32(4), 551–568.

Takanishi, R. and Le Menestrel, S., eds. (2017). *Promoting the Educational Success of Children and Youth Learning English.* Washington, DC: National Academies Press.

Wallace, C. (2011). A school of immigrants: How new arrivals become pupils in a multilingual London school. *Language and Intercultural Communication*, *11*(2), 97–112.

Wallace, C., Mallows, D., Abbley, J. et al. (2009). *English as an Additional Language (EAL) Provision in Schools – 10 Case Studies*. London: Institute of Education.

Wardman, C. (2012). *Pulling the Threads Together: Current Theories and Current Practice Affecting UK Primary School Children Who Have English as an Additional Language*. London: British Council.

17 Mobility and English Language Education

How Does Mobility in Study Abroad Settings Produce New Conceptualisations of English?

Khawla Badwan

1 Introduction

The majority of English language learners around the world are introduced to English through formal education. This is the case either because English, for most of them, is a mandatory school subject or because they were advised to invest in learning an 'international language', or lingua franca, based on the belief that English opens doors for educational, professional, and social opportunities. In addition, learning English can also be associated with multiple identity investments that allow access to new social and cultural domains (cf. Norton Peirce, 1995, on Investment) or that enable learners to consume the language in settings where they are required or encouraged to practise what they have learnt (cf. Ros i Solé and Fenoulhet, 2010; Kubota, 2011). Irrespective of the motivational factors that underpin learners' engagement with and desire for learning English, there is one fundamental challenge that often goes unnoticed (unless triggered by a major destabilising event, as I discuss later): it is the challenge of how language learners conceptualise English in their minds, as well as the factors behind, and the implications of, such conceptualisations.

In what follows, I will look at 'English' as social practice to investigate how engagement in different social and academic domains can trigger multiple and sometimes conflicting conceptualisations of what 'English' is. The chapter draws a distinction between English *for* communication and English *as* communication, factoring in the impact of context on how learners perceive English.

To start, formal English language education plays a major role in shaping language learners' first, and probably most fundamental, conceptualisations of what English is, how it should be spoken, and what the ideal achievement level should be. What comes with formal education are syllabuses, textbooks, institutional and governmental requirements/standards, and proficiency tests, among many other requirements. Inevitably, such formalities bring along ontological commitments that could be viewed as facilitating the process of teaching and assessment. In other words, if an educational system is committed to a particular ontology of what English is, then textbooks can be adopted, performance can be assessed using one-size-fits-all criteria, and students' levels of English can be measured and quantified. Embracing a one-size-fits-all conceptualisation of English allows the use of words such as *competence* and *correctness* that, in turn, allow the measurement of students' English against a pre-determined level where boundaries are 'clearly' set and 'correct' use is 'easily' determined. In most cases, this ontological commitment is associated with 'Standard English', pinning the complex sociolinguistic system called 'English' down into one or two varieties: British English or American English; what Hall (2013) refers to as the 'monolithic view' of the language (see also Hall, this volume). This, of course, has considerable consequences for how language learners conceptualise English and its use in their life, as will be further discussed in this chapter.

There are multiple ideological, political, and practical reasons as to why most formal educational systems around the world are ontologically committed to the monolithic view of English, as will be further elaborated on in Section 4. However, there is a fundamental ontological challenge associated with embracing the monolithic view of English in educational settings. This is mainly because such a view does not clearly resonate with how language is actually used in everyday practices. English language learners are taught language *for* communication in predicted, homogeneous, imagined communities instead of being taught language *as* communication in unpredicted, real, and super-diverse communities (see also Canagarajah, this volume). The former implies that learners are trained to function in certain settings or social domains that are mainly academic. But what happens when language learners have to use English beyond these specialised domains, as is usually the case with study abroad students in English-speaking countries?

This chapter aims to first address and problematise the role of formal English language education in creating and perpetuating monolithic conceptualisations of English that are based on 'folk linguistic' views of how language is actually used in discursive practices. Next, I argue that mobility in study abroad settings can be a destabilising event that triggers participants to reconsider their ideas about English. In support of this argument, I present and discuss some of the common myths that language learners have about English that are challenged in study abroad settings. I conclude with a call to challenge current practices in formal language education in order to generate more pedagogically, and practically, honest conceptualisations of English.

2 English *for* Communication versus English *as* Communication

This section presents a fundamental ontological challenge facing English language education in the many situations worldwide in which learners are introduced to English as a 'foreign' language.

In such situations, the use of English is already restricted to certain domains because it is not used in the learners' immediate social environment. This means that learners encounter English in an imagined context and are taught what their textbooks and teachers present as Standard English grammar and pronunciation. This experience encourages the development of a belief that there are one or two kinds of English spoken in the world. Learners are taught formulaic expressions and short conversational phrases in which imagined interlocutors are friendly and cooperative. The topics they engage with are generally bland and superficial, and do not prepare them for the unpredictable and sometimes challenging communicative tasks in life outside the classroom. In other words, English learners are typically taught English *for* communication, not *as* communication. In this case, the English they learn is seen as an object with an imagined context that allows them to function in restricted domains. But is this how individuals use language as social practice?

Language, along with other semiotic systems such as colour, music, and signs, creates meaning (Halliday, 2009). The creation of meaning is subjective, individualised, contextualised, and often comes as a response to unpredictable stimuli. Language learners are already familiar with this complex task of 'languaging' as proficient speakers of their first language (see Canagarajah, this volume). In their first language, they are able to use language for local, everyday oral domains (Mahboob, 2017). With schooling they are then introduced to local, specialised, oral, and (often academic) written domains. With their ability to function in different domains and unpredictable situations, individuals use their L1 *as* communication.

Many of them are then introduced to English mandatorily as part of their formal education. The English that they learn in this setting is usually presented in a global, superficial context, mainly because local English language teaching (ELT) industries in many parts of the world do not have the recognition, authority, nor influence that global, 'native-speaker' dominated ELT industries have (see Wicaksono, this volume). Learners are taught English for use with an imagined, friendly audience and are trained to communicate in certain social settings. They are then tested on their ability to conform to 'native-speaker' grammar rules and vocabulary use. This, ultimately, creates a gap between their ability to use English *for* certain purposes and their ability to use English *as* communication in flexible ways that are not restricted to a limited range of domains. This is a fundamental ontological challenge that learners are usually unaware of until they experience geographical and social mobility in, for example, study abroad settings.

3 Formal English Language Education and the 'Standard' Ontology

The ontology of English as a school subject for language learners is influenced by the legacy of rationalism dating back to the seventeenth and eighteenth centuries (cf. Hall, this volume). It is a view that objectifies English as a linguistic system of forms and structures independent from its speakers and its context(s), as illustrated in the following quotation: "Language is a stable, immutable system of normatively identical linguistic forms that the individual consciousness finds ready-made and that is incontestable for that consciousness … Individual acts of speaking are, from the viewpoint of language, merely fortuitous refractions and variations or plain and simple distortions of normatively identical forms" (Voloshinov et al., 1973, p. 57). English, as a school subject for language learners, introduces a linguistic system with an associated set of beliefs about 'grammar rules' and 'standard pronunciation'. It is submitted to the same standardisation processes that other subjects such as maths or science are. The process entails studying from textbooks that are seen as main references, sitting for exams to measure achievements against pre-set goals, and being awarded scores that are believed to reflect learners' competence in this subject.

Language textbooks are still used for many reasons that we all understand and appreciate. However, as Duff (2016) argues, their use for educational purposes also has political, nationalistic, social, and cultural effects; meaning that teachers and students alike are constrained by what publishers and educational authorities believe is appropriate for the classroom. Usually this task involves presenting a particular variety of English, while marginalising or omitting mentions of other varieties. Commenting on this, Duff (2016, p. xiv) maintains that "presumably the textbook creators aim to romanticize particular linguistic and cultural ideals into which they aim to socialize newcomers or learners, on the one hand, and avoid delicate, controversial points within a particular region, on the other".

Such practices give rise to what Flores and Rosa (2015) call "prescriptive ideologies", which impose a particular way of using language, privileging particular practices, and stigmatising others. As a result, learners become driven by certain "ideological imaginings of language, culture, identity and political structure" (Blommaert, 2016, p. 244), meaning that language learners will inevitably view English through the lens of their textbooks, which mainly focus on Standard English and mainstream cultural and political values. These ideological imaginings can be very influential as they typically coincide with what learners accept as 'English'. Sadly, the legacy of structuralism and broader prescriptive ontologies of language are still prominent and prevalent in the English textbook industry, in spite of major paradigm shifts in sociolinguistic research that acknowledge linguistic complexity, variation, and linguistic rights. In this way, textbooks serve as ideological mechanisms that produce and perpetuate views about what should be determined as 'correct', 'standard', 'native-like', 'prestigious', and 'acceptable'.

In addition to the ideological challenge associated with textbooks, it is not uncommon to adopt one of what Gray (2002) calls "the global coursebooks", published by famous publishing houses in the United Kingdom or the United States. These textbooks are designed to be culturally 'neutral', with superficial content (a focus on generic communication skills, 'grammatical accuracy', and the ability to discuss generic themes), so that they can be adopted globally. This superficial focus does not even approximate how language is actually used in real life; presenting an ontological challenge for language learners who are encouraged by their textbooks to conceptualise English as merely the language of fun and friendship. This is an example what Kramsch (2015, p. 409) describes as "tourism discourse", obscuring the fact that English, like any language, is also used to communicate serious tasks and conduct challenging negotiations.

The argument presented here does not imply that language teachers are not aware of these ideological challenges. In fact, many of them are, but are also caught in a profound dilemma; torn between their professional inclinations (to talk about plurilithic Englishes in real life) and external pressures (related to exams or the fear of confusing their learners). Some pedagogical recommendations aimed at addressing this dilemma are presented in Section 6.

4 The 'Standard' Ontology: Reasons and Justifications

After discussing the manifestations of what I refer to here as the 'Standard' Ontology in formal language education, I would like to provide some context for why many educational systems around the world seem to be bound by the monolithic myth of English or the 'Standard' Ontology. To this end, I will discuss two main reasons before I move on to discuss some of the common ways of justifying the status quo.

First and foremost, the 'Standard' Ontology facilitates the commercialisation of English as a unique linguistic commodity with clear boundaries. Gray (2012) discusses three areas of commercialising English: commercial ELT, English language testing, and academic publishing. Gray (2002) indicates that accurate figures for ELT coursebook sales are difficult to obtain, although it has been estimated that the annual sales of British ELT coursebooks more than two decades ago were £70 to £170 million (Pennycook, 1994). The commercial ELT industry is based on the premise that English can be pinned down to a single variety, i.e. Standard English, and can be sold to customers worldwide. The complex sociolinguistic system underpinning language use in real life is barely represented in commercially produced textbooks, perhaps because capturing it would add layers of complexity, and would make English an amorphous commodity that is hard to describe and sell from a commercial perspective.

English language testing is also based on a similar ontological commitment. Pilcher and Richards (2017, p. 4) have criticised the ontology of English manifested in the International English Language Testing System (IELTS), arguing that "'English', rather than being an abstract and objective entity that can be removed from context for the purposes of testing anywhere, as IELTS assumes, is, in fact, individual and subjective, and uniquely intertwined with its subject content and context". Still, IELTS continues to be one of the most recognised tests and those responsible for the test are indeed well aware of the challenges and limitations associated with using it, as reflected in the following online official IELTS disclaimer: "The International English Language Testing System (IELTS) is designed to be but one of many factors used by schools, colleges, universities, and employers in determining whether a test taker has sufficient skills to successfully be admitted as a student or employed" (IELTS, n.d.). The 'Standard' Ontology allows the possibility of objectifying English so that tests can be designed, marking criteria can be devised according to degrees of conformity to 'standard native speaker' use, and results can be quantified for use in 'gate-keeping' decisions. Harsch (this volume) addresses these issues in more detail.

In addition to ELT books and proficiency tests, publishing houses offer another source of commodified English. Thompson (2005, cited in Gray, 2012) explains that these publishing houses have been successful mainly because young scholars who go to the United Kingdom and the United States for higher education get accustomed to British or American curricula and in turn embrace them when they return to their home countries. Therefore, even if certain curricula have not initially been designed for an international market, the business brought by Higher Education has made the dissemination of publications much more profitable.

We have seen how the 'Standard' Ontology plays a key role in the successful commodification of English and keeping this ontology alive is the basis for maintaining this enormously lucrative industry. However, there are other ideological and political reasons that underpin the commitment to the 'Standard' Ontology. Standard English as the teaching and learning target acts as an 'othering' mechanism that keeps learners in pursuit of Standard Native Speaker English (for more on the concept of 'Native Speaker', see Wicaksono, this volume). The idea of a Standard Native Speaker English encourages learners to think of English as something they need to gain, perhaps by copying an imaginary group of people, instead of something they already have, and that they have created for themselves. Widdowson (1994, p. 384) suggests, "[y]ou are proficient in a language to the extent you possess it, make it your own, bend it to your will, assert yourself through it rather than simply submit to the dictates of its form ... So in a way, proficiency only comes with non-conformity".

If learners were indeed able to own English, they would not be tested against Standard native speaker rules, nor would they be taught using textbooks published by international publishing houses. The top-down reality of English language teaching and testing around the world creates little room for non-conformity since, to succeed in this version of 'reality', learners are required to be competent, using what is assumed to be/marketed as the Standard variety of English. Furthermore, in many cases, learners of English are constantly required to prove that they can conform to these 'norms', as Heller and Duchêne (2010, p. 5) say: "If you have [learned the language of the nation], you still need to constantly prove yourself against the measures developed by the dominant group, who use the agencies of the state (schools, bureaucracies, language academies, the media) to describe what counts as linguistic competence and the means to identify it". A case in a point here is UK Higher Education admission requirements that not only dictate the type of language proficiency test that is deemed acceptable, but that also determine a minimum required score (however, anecdotal evidence suggests that very few staff in admissions departments are aware of what these scores mean in terms of *actual* language use).

As a result, many English language learners around the world are led to believe that English is a single monolithic entity, i.e. Standard English, a view embedded in most textbooks and proficiency tests. Even when learners go beyond the walls of classrooms and exam halls, many are still faced with institutional admission requirements (for jobs, study, or immigration purposes) that mainly measure their ability to conform to Standard English. It is, then, not surprising that the majority of English language learners fall for the monolithic myth of Standard English.

Nonetheless, there are various justifications for keeping the status quo. With reference to teaching, there are arguments that students need formal Standard repertoires to succeed in many specialised domains. Textbooks are needed because the majority of language teachers around the world are 'non-native' speakers of English and using international textbooks acts as a means of standardising language teaching (there are of course winners and losers in this situation). Some teachers, let alone learners, find it difficult to use English in different social domains. Some argue that it is impossible to commit the educational system to a flexible ontology of English that can be unnecessarily confusing for teachers and students. While acknowledging these concerns, it is important to help language learners develop a more accurate and inclusive conceptualisation of English, so that they appreciate that the English they learn inside the classroom is not necessarily the type of English they will use or encounter outside the classroom (see Sections 5 and 6).

5 Study Abroad and the Emergence of New Conceptualisations of English

Many study abroad students study in the United Kingdom, the United States and other 'Anglophone' nations having already studied English for years and met their host universities' entry requirements regarding English proficiency, among other criteria. For some of these students, a study abroad experience marks a major shift from using English *for* communication to using English *as* communication in a variety of social domains. This shift can be unsettling for some learners, as it may entail a major confrontation with long-held views about what 'English' is, for example, challenging an expectation that British English is a single variety, spoken throughout the United Kingdom. Indeed, the first ontological challenge that study abroad students are often faced with is that there is not always a one-to-one correspondence between the geographical location and the variety spoken in that location. This is particularly true in the linguistically super-diverse, larger cities that tend to attract more study abroad students. The discussion that follows focuses on the study abroad experience of students coming to the United Kingdom, though many of the experiences described are likely to be common in other Anglophone nations.

5.1 First Myth: There Is One Type of English Spoken in the United Kingdom

After years of being taught Standard English, many study abroad students who come to the United Kingdom find it difficult to cope with the diverse range of regional dialects, and the different World Englishes and ELF varieties spoken by the many multilingual speakers there. Super-diverse contexts and individuals with super-diverse repertoires defy the expectation that there is one type of English spoken in the United Kingdom and challenge the status of Standard English that learners may have expected, prior to their arrival. Many learners do not understand why these variations exist and may experience them as unexpected hurdles. Even though some learners come from linguistic backgrounds that include heteroglossic situations, many do not seem to expect that individual and regional differences are inherited features of any language, including English.

The different Englishes that study abroad students are exposed to in the United Kingdom are not reflected in classroom listening activities nor in listening tests, so these students often struggle in the early days of their sojourn and some of them resort to socialising with conationals to avoid second language anxiety associated with oral receptive skills. Pellegrino Aveni (2005) suggests that when the second language represents a threat to individuals' self-perception and security, feelings of anxiety and a reduced sense of one's self are produced. She explains that when individuals' self-presentation is under threat because of their inability to communicate in the second language, they make decisions as to whether speak or remain silent,

> learners may reduce the amount of L2 they produce in order to protect self-esteem; when self-esteem is not threatened in L2 use, learners may feel at ease to produce more L2 without fear of damaging their sense of status. A conflict arises between learners' intention to communicate in the L2 at any given moment and their desire to maintain their sense of status.
> (Pellegrino Aveni, 2005, p. 24)

To avoid embarrassment, individuals may employ "preventive practices" (Goffman, 1959, p. 13), which help them safeguard the impression they want to make or sustain. One manifestation of individuals' preventive practices can be seen through the prism of their socialisation preferences. Studies on the socialisation patterns of study abroad students (Bochner et al., 1977; Furnham and Alibhai, 1985; Hendrickson et al., 2010) have indicated that co-national bonds are important in supporting newcomers who struggle with second language anxiety. One of the main reasons behind this anxiety is that study abroad students expect to use the English repertoires they are familiar with in their new environment, but come to realise that very few of those they meet actually speak what they would identify as Standard English (Badwan, 2015).

Indeed, the myth that there is one English spoken in the United Kingdom creates false expectations and does not offer the necessary psychological preparation for many study abroad students, especially the ones who come from EFL contexts. For many of these students, study abroad is an unsettling experience that allows students to see English beyond being a school subject. The transition from being a language learner in a safe classroom space to a language user (and lifelong learner) in an unpredictable out-of-class space can be challenging and, as indicated previously, some students may resort to silence, controlled input, or co-national support as they go through this disquieting transition.

5.2 Second Myth: Meeting the Required IELTS Score Guarantees Academic Success

The pre-sojourn period is an important phase of investment in language learning. That is to say, students who aspire to study abroad see more value in their English classes and understand the gate-keeping powers of language proficiency tests such as IELTS. They invest time, money, and resources to attend English classes or test preparation courses in the hope of clearing the admission hurdles. Because many of these students were exposed to a neatly packaged variety of English, those with high scores are perhaps quite likely to believe that they are guaranteed academic success in the United Kingdom. In other words, they think that they have already gained sufficient linguistic resources to enable them to function in their new study abroad settings. Many students strive and succeed in their new environment in spite of this myth. However, it is not uncommon for some of them to go through a challenging transitional period during which they start to familiarise themselves with new English repertoires, forming new conceptualisations of English that are not so neatly packaged.

In a longitudinal, qualitative research project, involving eight study abroad students in UK Higher Education (UK HE), I found that some of my respondents, regardless of their IELTS writing scores, found it difficult to deal with their first essay assignments and were confused when their feedback suggested that they needed to use more 'academic' words (Badwan, 2015, 2017). Their first experience of academic genres and academic literacies triggered new conceptualisations of English. For instance, they became aware of a distinction between the types of English they needed to pass the IELTS test before arrival and the types of English they are expected to use at university after arrival. In addition, they became able to distinguish between IELTS English, academic English, daily life English, and other specialised English repertoires such as business- and engineering-related varieties. In other words, they started to conceptualise English differently.

5.3 Third Myth: Meeting the Required IELTS Score Guarantees Successful Social Communication

In addition to academic struggles, life outside university poses challenges that tend to be even more serious. As indicated in Section 3, many language learners learn English in their 'home' countries with an imagined community of co-operative interlocutors and predictable responses. The transition from an imagined homogeneous community to a real, super-diverse community is another destabilising factor that study abroad students may have to grapple with. The 'tourism discourse' (Kramsch, 2015) with which students are familiar does not resemble nor reflect many of their daily life encounters. I have argued in Section 3 that the ontological challenge of (dis-)associating English with friendly, fun contexts can have serious consequences for internationally mobile individuals. A direct consequence of not teaching English as communication in unpredictable situations is that many study abroad students lose voice and face when dealing with difficult situations that require negotiation or debate. Others feel unable to express feelings of sympathy, sadness, or solidarity beyond using 'I am sorry', because such feelings and the topics that come with them are commonly avoided in ELT materials in favour of 'neutral', superficially treated topics.

Intercultural communication in different social domains is another concern for language learners in study abroad settings. We are reminded by Jackson (2013, p. 183) that "students with an advanced level of proficiency in English, according to TOEFL or IELTS measures, did not necessarily have well-developed intercultural competence". This is true for two main reasons. The first reason is associated with the use of English as a global lingua franca and the challenge of determining the culture that comes with it due to constant tensions between individual, local, regional, and global contexts

(Baker, 2011; also this volume). Second, language teachers rarely discuss questions such as, 'whose cultural values are embedded in my language classroom?', 'how can I reflect local and global cultures in my classroom?', 'how can I help my students project regional/national/local identities in the classroom?' and 'how can I prepare my students to negotiate cultural difference?'. Similarly, language learners are typically left out of this conversation as they are subjected to top-down ELT policies and practices. This challenge is associated with the next myth.

5.4 Fourth Myth: English Is an Object Entity Independent of Individual Identity

After years of being exposed to English language input based on how to speak English 'grammatically' with 'standard' pronunciation, many study abroad students find themselves unable to answer the question of who they are as users/learners/speakers of English. In other words, the ontological commitment to English as a structural standard system overlooks a very important aspect of using any language: identity. Here I dwell on Norton's (2013, p. 4) definition of identity as "the way a person understands his or her relationship to the world, how that relationship is structured across time and space, and how the person understands possibilities for the future". Teaching English *for* communication means that learners view English instrumentally while detaching themselves from it. My research with study abroad students (Badwan, 2015) has confirmed this: most of my participants felt that they used English to function and to get by, but that it did not represent them. They did not feel they were used to using English to represent their identities. Responses such as "I don't taste English", and "I don't feel it represents me" are direct consequences of how it was introduced to them, i.e. *for* communication and not *as* communication.

Two of my participants reported that they felt that, initially, they projected a more serious identity in social situations because they did not know how to tell jokes in English or how to respond to them. Over time, however, their English, which was once objectified as a school subject, did become an individualised and contextualised means of communication and identity representation in study abroad settings. This was both a gain and a loss for my participants: while they adapted their English for use in social situations, their conceptualisation of English changed, making them wonder, "did we learn English or not?" (Badwan, 2017).

As Norton (2015) says, 'language' should not only be seen as a linguistic system of words and sentences, but should also be perceived as a social practice, "that engages the identities of learners in diverse and often contradictory ways" (p. 378). This means that instead of asking, 'can my learners speak correct English?' or 'can they pass the next test?', language educators should also ask 'can my learners express themselves in English?' and 'can they negotiate positions?'. Embracing this view would allow language teachers and learners alike to conceptualise English as communication and as a means of expressing themselves.

5.5 Fifth Myth: English Is an Object Entity, Independent of Context

This myth is concerned with treating English as an object entity whose value or status does not change according to the context. Like the other myths discussed earlier, it exists in the minds of most English language learners as a result of how English was introduced to them as part of their educational system. Sociolinguistic researchers looking into scalar approaches to language (Blommaert, 2007, 2010, 2015; Kell, 2011; Canagarajah and De Costa, 2015; Canagarajah, this volume) have indicated that as people move across geopolitical and national borders, the language and literacy practices that are valued in one part of the world are not necessarily valued in another place (Blommaert, 2010). Likewise, language ideologies or views linking language with issues of power, identity, and epistemology (Schieffelin et al., 1998) that are prevalent in certain parts of the world are not necessarily true in another part. So how does this affect study abroad students?

Since English is neatly packaged for commercial purposes, many learners invest in either what they (are encouraged to) think of as Standard British English or Standard American English. The choice is typically underpinned by ideological and political views of the world. The singular ontology of commercial English can lead language learners to believe that whatever English they have invested in is going to "travel well", to borrow Blommaert's (2005) term. Unfortunately, this is not always the case. Anecdotal evidence suggests that many study abroad students who come to the United Kingdom from different parts of the world such as the Middle East or China were taught a version of so-called 'American Standard English' and were exposed to the Hollywood film industry. These students arrive in the United Kingdom with the view that their English is going to maintain its value, only to be confronted with the reality that it does not. This is another destabilising realisation for language learners who were not taught to conceptualise English as an amorphous sociolinguistic system operating within complex contexts.

6 Towards Expansive Conceptualisations of 'English': Conscious Learning

I have presented the manifestations of and reasons and justifications for the 'Standard' Ontology in formal English language education and how this ontology creates myths about English. I have also discussed the implications of these myths for study abroad students who tend to grapple with multiple destabilising factors that challenge how they conceptualised what is called 'English' before they arrived in the United Kingdom. In this section, I argue for the need to offer a pedagogically honest English language education that allows learners to develop broader, more inclusive conceptualisations of English in order to help them see English as communication. I do not claim that there is an immediate recipe for success, but what I propose in this section is the need to embrace *'conscious learning'* to develop sociolinguistic awareness about English among language learners.

Cultivating 'conscious learning' in the language classroom helps students cope with the linguistic complexity outside the classroom. 'Conscious learning' is a term I borrowed from Holmes and Riddiford (2011) but have used in a more general sense to refer to raising ideological and sociolinguistic awareness about how language functions in heterogeneous, super-diverse communities. This is a major step towards effective preparation for study abroad learners. English language education needs to move away from an essentialist, monolithic conceptualisation of English in order to prepare learners to shift from being 'learners' of English in EFL contexts into 'users and lifelong learners' of English in the United Kingdom.

Language learners need to be given the option to choose the varieties they want to learn depending on where they want to be next, and language teachers need to be trained to help these learners become independent agents who can learn by themselves using various online and offline sources. My own proposal does not aim to add an extra burden onto language teachers who are already burdened with a long list of expectations. Rather, it stresses the importance of raising ideological and sociolinguistic awareness among language teachers and learners alike. This awareness offers teachers and learners more flexibility in their thinking about the outcomes of learning (Hall, 2013). Moreover, this awareness allows them to understand how English interacts with the who, what, where, and when of social interactions, discouraging perceptions of English as a decontextualised school subject and encouraging individualised ways of languaging and being in the world. With conscious learning, language learners become agentive individuals who are able to cope with the unpredictable affordances of social interaction; a step to help them develop their own voice, and express their being and becoming in the world inside and outside the classroom.

Conscious learning is also a way to introduce a 'repertoire pedagogy' that helps language learners to become aware of the different linguistic repertoires that they might need for communicative purposes. We are reminded by Blommaert and Backus (2013, p. 11) that a repertoire, in sociolinguistics, refers to "all the 'means of speaking', i.e. all those means that people know how to use and why while they communicate, and such means ... range from linguistic ones (language varieties) over cultural ones (genres, styles) and social ones (norms for the production and understanding of language)". A 'repertoire pedagogy', therefore, takes as its core mission the knowledge of the how and why of language use in different sociocultural domains. In other words, language learners are shown that, as part of languaging, individuals need to have diverse linguistic repertoires to enable them to function in academic, professional, business, formal, and informal domains. They also come to understand that the Standard English repertoires they have been taught are just one type of a range of repertoires they may need to acquire, depending on where they want to go and what they want to do next. A repertoire pedagogy as part of a conscious learning approach not only allows learners to make choices to invest in the repertoires they need in their lives, but also enables learners to conceptualise English as communication, a major step towards the psychological preparation of language learners who want to study abroad. Such an approach is also an attempt to generate more pedagogically and practically honest conceptualisations of English.

7 Conclusion

The discussion presented here offers a two-fold contribution: challenging the status quo in language education and proposing conscious learning in the language classroom. I am aware that any attempt to embrace the amorphous nature of English will come with challenges, in that it contradicts the premises on which established ELT industries are based. I also acknowledge the challenge of training language teachers (let alone learners, parents, and policy makers) to question their own long-held beliefs about what English is, but, as I have argued throughout this chapter, it is a route worth taking. I invite researchers and practitioners in the field to respond to this call for conscious learning and to open doors for future research on the implications of embracing conscious learning and repertoire pedagogy for the psychological preparation of study abroad students.

References

Badwan, K. (2015). *Negotiating rates of exchange: Arab academic sojourners' sociolinguistic trajectories in the UK*. Unpublished PhD thesis, University of Leeds.

Badwan, K. (2017). "Did we learn English or what?": A study abroad student in the UK carrying and crossing boundaries in out-of-class communication. *Studies in Second Language Learning and Teaching*, 7(2), 297–309.

Baker, W. (2011). Intercultural awareness: Modelling an understanding of cultures in intercultural communication through English as a lingua franca. *Language and Intercultural Communication*, 11(3), 197–214.

Blommaert, J. (2005). *Discourse: A Critical Introduction*. Cambridge: Cambridge University Press.

Blommaert, J. (2007). Sociolinguistic scales. *Intercultural Pragmatics*, 4(1), 1–19.

Blommaert, J. (2010). *A Sociolinguistics of Globalization*. Cambridge: Cambridge University Press.

Blommaert, J. (2015). Chronotopes, scales, and complexity in the study of language in society. *Annual Review of Anthropology*, 44, 105–116.

Blommaert, J. (2016). From mobility to complexity in sociolinguistic theory and method. In N. Coupland, ed., *Sociolinguistics: Theoretical Debates* (pp. 242–263). Cambridge: Cambridge University Press.

Blommaert, J. and Backus, A. (2013). Superdiverse repertoires and the individual. In I. de Saint-Georges, ed., *Multilingualism and Multimodality* (pp. 11–32). Rotterdam: SensePublishers,

Bochner, S., McLeod, B., and Lin, A. (1977). Friendship patterns of overseas students: A functional model. *International Journal of Psychology*, 12(4), 277–294.

Canagarajah, S. and De Costa, P. (2015). Introduction: Scales analysis, and its uses and prospects in educational linguistics. *Linguistics and Education*, 34, 1–10.

Duff, P. (2015). Forward of language, ideology and education. In X. L. Curdt-Christiansen and C. Weninger, eds., *Language, Ideology and Education: The Politics of Textbooks in Language Education* (Routledge Research in Language Education). Abingdon: Routledge.

Flores, N. and Rosa, J. (2015). Undoing appropriateness: Raciolinguistic ideologies and language diversity in education. *Harvard Educational Review*, 85(2), 149–171.

Furnham, A. and Alibhai, N. (1985). The friendship networks of foreign students: A replication and extension of the functional model. *International Journal of Psychology*. 20(3–4), 709–722.

Goffman, E. (1959). *The Presentation of Self in Everyday Life*. New York: Anchor Books.

Gray, J. (2002). The global coursebook in English language teaching. In D. Block and D. Cameron, eds., *Globalization and Language Teaching* (pp. 151–167). London: Routledge.

Gray, J. (2012). English the industry. In A. Hewings and C. Tagg, eds., *The Politics of English* (pp. 137–163). New York: Routledge.

Hall, C. (2013). Cognitive contributions to plurilithic views of English and other languages. *Applied Linguistics, 34*(2), 211–231.

Halliday, M. (2009). *Language and Society. Vol. 10, of the Collected Works of M.A.K. Halliday*. London: Continuum.

Heller, M. and Duchêne, A. (2012). Pride and profit: Changing discourses of language, capital and nation-state. In M. Heller and A. Duchêne, eds., *Language in Late Capitalism: Pride and Profit* (pp. 1–21). New York: Routledge.

Hendrickson, B., Rosen, D., and Aune, R. (2010). An analysis of friendship networks, social connectedness, homesickness and satisfaction levels of international students. *International Journal of Intercultural Relations, 35*(3), 281–295.

Holmes, J. and Riddiford, N. (2011). From classroom to workplace: Tracking socio-pragmatic development. *ELT Journal, 65*(4), 376–386.

IELTS (n.d.). Online. Accessed 24 August 2017 from www.ielts.org/policy/disclaimer

Jackson, J. (2013). The transformation of 'a frog in the well': A path to a more intercultural, global mindset. In C. Kinginger, ed., *Social and Cultural Aspects of Language Learning in Study Abroad* (pp. 179–204). Amsterdam: John Benjamins.

Kell, C. (2011). Inequalities and crossings: Literacy and the spaces-in-between. *International Journal of Educational Development, 31*, 606–613.

Kramsch, C. (2015). Language and culture in second language learning. In F. Sharifian, ed., *The Routledge Handbook of Language and Culture* (pp. 403–416). London: Routledge.

Kubota, R. (2011). Questioning linguistic instrumentalism: English, neoliberalism and language tests in Japan. *Linguistics and Education, 22*(3), 248–260.

Mahboob, A. (2017). Understanding language variation: Implications of the NNEST lens for TESOL teacher education programs. In M. Agudo and J. de Dios, eds., *Native and Non-Native Teachers in English Language Classrooms: Professional Challenges and Teacher Education* (pp. 13–32). Boston: De Gruyter Mouton.

Norton, B. (2013). *Identity and Language Learning: Extending the Conversation*, 2nd ed. Bristol: Multilingual Matters.

Norton, B. (2015). Identity, investment, and faces of English internationally. *Chinese Journal of Applied Linguistics, 38*(4), 375–391.

Norton Peirce, B. (1995). Social identity, investment, and language learning. *TESOL Quarterly, 29*(1), 9–31.

Pennycook, A. (1994). *The Cultural Politics of English as an International Language*. Essex: Longman Group Limited.

Pellegrino Aveni, V. (2005). *Study Abroad and Second Language Use*. Cambridge: Cambridge University Press.

Pilcher, N. and Richards, K. (2017). Challenging the power invested in the International English Language Testing System (IELTS): Why determining 'English' preparedness needs to be undertaken within the subject context. *Power and Education, 9*(1), 3–17.

Ros i Solé, C. and Fenoulhet, J. (2010). Language learning itineraries for the twenty first century. In J. Fenoulhet and C. Ros i Solé, eds., *Mobility and Localisation in Language Learning: A View from Languages of the Wider World* (pp. 3–27). Oxford: Peter Lang.

Schieffelin, B., Woolard, K., and Kroskrity, P. (1998). *Language Ideologies: Practice and Theory*. Oxford: Oxford University Press.

Voloshinov, V. N., Matejka, L., and Titunik, I. R. (1973). *Marxism and the Philosophy of Language*. New York: Seminar Press.

Widdowson, H. G. (1994). The ownership of English. *TESOL Quarterly*, 28(2), 377–389.

Part VII
Commentary and Conclusions

18 Pushing the Ontological Boundaries of English

Alastair Pennycook

1 Introduction

The questions of ontologies of English that this book poses come at a time of epistemological change in the fields of socio- and applied linguistics. The very fact that we can talk of 'socio- and applied linguistics' points to the coming together of these fields in ways that have usefully unsettled both. The *translingual turn* (García and Li Wei, 2014), for example, derives not so much from theoretical debates about language as from contexts of language education. Likewise, the ontological questions being asked in this book come from an applied linguistic orientation: most of the authors here are engaged in various aspects of English language education. This is a welcome move since it brings a theoretical debate about ontologies of English into a field often hampered by its pragmatism, while investigating these questions in the light of practical educational concerns (how does this matter for ELT practices?). There has been an unfortunate tendency to leave such questions to so-called 'theoretical' linguists, a serious oversight both because linguists have often failed in their task by assuming that the object of linguistic investigation – language or languages – is a known and settled entity (even if the epistemological questions of how it can be analysed have spawned a wide range of theoretical camps), and because applied linguists have failed as a result to ask the all-important questions that derive from a field of practice (Kramsch, 2015): what is it we're actually dealing with?

The multi- or trans-lingual turn has also reinvigorated many domains, not least studies of the global spread of English. A central problem with the way in which global English has been understood by the nations responsible for managing its export is that it is seen, paradoxically, as a monolingual enterprise, as a language that is learned and taught only in its own presence (Pennycook, 2008). Overlooked have been the ways in which English always needs to be seen in the context of other languages, as part of a more complex patterning of language use and learning in plurilingual classrooms (Lin, 2013). The more recent focus within studies of English as a Lingua Franca (ELF) has therefore been increasingly on its inherent multilingual and hybrid nature. This view of ELF as a set of resources within multilingual repertoires can be seen as part of the translingual shift towards thinking about languages as sociocultural artefacts that in real use are constantly mixed and blended together (Otheguy et al., 2018). From this perspective, we only need to posit one underlying linguistic repertoire from which language users draw, leaving the distinctions between languages to the social domain.

We of course still need to ask ideological questions about the global spread of English – Phillipson (2018) urging us yet again to consider English as an imperialist language – though these are generally not so much ontological questions (about what English is) as political concerns (about what English does). We need to understand the roles English plays in the world – as a playground bully in the Pacific (Barker, 2012), a destructive juggernaut among Aboriginal Australian communities (Ober and Bell, 2012), or a 'malchemy' that subjugates other language possibilities in Sri Lanka (Parakrama, 2012) – and thus to appreciate how English is enmeshed in complex local contexts of power and struggle (Pennycook, 2016). Unless we also pose ontological questions, however, asking not only searching political questions about the role of English in the world but also searching ontological questions about what English is in all these contexts (is imperial English the same thing as malchemical English?), we run the danger of assuming we know what English is for its users in such contexts. As Santos (2018) reminds us, we cannot change the world without also reinterpreting it. Before returning to look more seriously at what this may mean, I shall first look in greater depth at how ontologies of English are understood in this book.

2 Monolithic and Plurilithic English

Some of the chapters in this volume address ontological questions head on (Hall, Harder, Canagarajah, among others), while others let the ontological questions emerge, as it were, from more usage-based accounts of English learning (Eskildsen). The chapters on English in schools generally approach ontologies of English by looking at its instantiation as a school subject – School Subject English (SSE) – arguing that the ontology of English that is produced at the interface of competing policy, curriculum, teacher, and student interests is an ever-shifting object (Goodwyn, Roberts). Cunningham asks what the ontological status of 'good' English is in schools (a question related to, though also separable from, the all-pervasive 'Standard English' issue) as again we see how multiple actors constitute the ontological being of English. While other chapters – on ELF, mobility (Sharples), study abroad (Badwan), and so on – focus on popular (folk) discourses or broad discursive formations, these school-focused chapters shed light on how specific actors and interests produce images of English, pointing to the need to ask both ideological and locational questions when we seek to understand ontologies. These different approaches to ontologies of English therefore raise an important question: If ontologies of English, at least in the context of schooling, are produced by multiple actors (which, we might note, may be both human and nonhuman), how can we come to grips with this ontological diversity? Or when and how and under what circumstances and for which participants do curriculum documents, discussions about English, or popular discourses, become ontological statements?

For Hall (this volume), the question is how English is "conceived by applied and general linguists, language educators and laypeople", or what are "the ordinary understandings of English that underpin actual educational beliefs and practices?" From Hall's point of view, human languages are instantiations of the more fundamental language capacity (the ontological category that exists whether or not we have a name for the particular instantiations) that is reinterpreted through various collective identifications with nationhood (the second ontological category that is socially and ideologically driven), leading on to the 'folk ontology' of English as a manifestation of what he calls ENGLISHRY. This can in turn be connected to various idealisations about good, pure, or standard English. Hall's chapter grounds the discussion across the book, though some accounts (e.g. Wicaksono) draw on it much more than others (Eskildsen). While Hall's account aims to suggest plural ontologies of English (these are social instantiations of language), and to get beyond a basic single/plural account, it nonetheless sets up a core distinction that runs through most of the papers between monolithic and plurilithic versions of English (Pennycook, 2009; Hall, 2013). Different authors get at this in different ways: for Hall, there is an underlying language capacity that is then turned into various socially driven instantiations of English, while for others there are monolithic or plurilithic ways of thinking about English (either many Englishes or diverse English).

For many authors in this volume, then, there is a version of English – standard, static, rigid, monolithic – that needs to be opposed (an ideological as well as an ontological argument), with the focus on the ways 'standard' or 'good' English is constructed in contradistinction to the dynamics of 'real' English as it is used. Badwan describes the "standard ontology" as one in which language is essentially stable; Cunningham calls it a "shallow ontology" and associates it with a "lack of linguistic awareness". The way forward is to think in terms of a flexible, plural English. Across many chapters, therefore, the goal is to show that real English – whether as a lingua franca or something else – is a diverse and hybrid affair (Schaller-Schwaner and Kirkpatrick). In the area of language assessment, Harsch asks what varieties of English are taught and tested in EL2 contexts and how English is understood in its plurilingual ELF contexts; Nakatsuhara, Taylor, and Jaiyote examine the role of the L1 in relation to English. Goddard bridges the testing and SSE papers, looking at how English is tested in schools and arguing that analysis of types of assessment can afford equal insight into how English is taught and learned as studies of curriculum, and that this equally gives us insights into what English therefore is, even if this is never specifically articulated by a range of practitioners. As Goddard suggests, the many changes to the ways English is assessed have led to an array of "Englishes," not in the sense of world Englishes as varieties but of Englishes as ideological constructs.

For Wicaksono, the question of what constitutes a native speaker – or the native/non-native speaker divide itself – is an ontological one, based on whether we see English as monolithic or plurilithic. For Sharples, the ontological question is one that contrasts more static views of language with an emphasis on mobility. For Badwan, the problem is that the English that learners are taught and tested on does not match the English they will use and need in communicative settings. This is "a fundamental ontological challenge" of which "learners are usually unaware". Baker's related view, looking at ELF, is that "the current simplistic view of communication in ELT results in essentialised perspectives that fundamentally misrepresent the processes of intercultural and transcultural communication" and thus "serve as a poor model for English language learners and users". For Baker, like many of the other contributors, we need to reevaluate and expand core concepts such as communicative competence, in order to encompass a wider range of intercultural possibilities. As Schaller-Schwaner and Kirkpatrick put it, we can contrast more traditional ontologies of language that treat language as a fairly monolithic object or system with those that see language as a form of social practice, where system may either be seen as derived from usage or where system doesn't actually matter that much anyway. They suggest a way out of the dichotomy between singular and plural versions of English by means of that familiar applied linguistic strategy, the continuum, proposing a "spectrum of ontologies of English" on a "continuum of blurred understandings with language as a system at one end and language as social practice at the other."

Some chapters in this volume diverge from the general dualist position and the assumed values behind it (static standards bad; flexible multiplicities good). Harder generally accepts this distinction but unlike most authors here argues against the liberal consensus for plurality in teaching: "norms also have an essential role in the way the world (really) is" and "this in turn is essential to understanding what English (really) is." From this perspective, we have norms and diversity and need to be sensible about which we teach (the norms). Page seeks to outline more complex ontologies beyond the monolithic versus plurilithic framework that is implicitly or explicitly at the heart of much of this work. He also looks from the point of view of particular language users, which raises again the question of whose ontologies are at stake. From a usage-based linguistics (UBL) perspective, meanwhile, language use is the driving force for language development and language learning, and linguistic structures emerge as a function of human communicative needs and therefore correspond to the human perception and categorization of the world (Eskildsen). From this perspective, then, the only ontological discussion to be had is one between a usage-based approach that doesn't separate use and system (or prioritise the latter over the former) and the various dualist approaches (language as system vs. language in use) on display here. To understand what English is, we can look at people's linguistic repertoires in relation to social action.

Canagarajah takes us further into ontological debates, suggesting a much broader epistemological challenge through new materialist, posthumanist and object-oriented ontologies to arrive at a flat ontological position. This raises a very different set of questions to the other chapters since most take as givens the general playing field of language while opening up the monolithic/plurilithic divide for discussion. The issue for most chapters here is how English is constructed along narrow, deterministic lines by various named (school curricula, language tests) or unnamed (socially constructed, discursively produced) entities, and how we can instead think about English in more diverse terms. Canagarajah, however, is not operating between language capacity and manifestations, between idealised and real English, but asking different questions about what constitutes language to start with. He takes us from a representational to a performative view of language, from grammar, discourse, or genre structures to *spatial repertoires* (Pennycook and Otsuji, 2015), from methodological individualism to distributed practice. For Canagarajah, languages themselves – rather than singular or plural versions of languages – are ideological claims. They are claims made not against a backdrop of an assumed language capacity or state of languagehood, but rather from the context of a language ontology that includes much more than is usually taken to be part of language. This raises much broader ontological questions about language and it is these that I shall explore in the next section.

3 Pushing Ontological Questions Further

Ontological questions can be about both the *nature* of being – how things exist, what it means to say things exist – as well as the *existence* of things themselves. Ontological questions concern both the existence of the material world and of more abstract entities such as God, and have been a concern of Western philosophy since the Greeks through to the existentialists: Sartre's (1943) *L'être et le néant* – being and nothingness – concerns what he called 'phenomenological ontology'. For ontologies of English, there are several levels of question that can be asked. The central issue for most of the chapters in this volume concerns the nature(s) of this thing called English: What is the relation between its instantiation as a static, fixed, tested, and taught subject and its flexible, plural, diverse, and chaotic use? Is it one or many things? This we might call an internal ontological debate – how do we understand this thing called English? – focusing particularly on a discussion between monolithic and plurilithic accounts of English and opting in almost every case for the latter. This mirrors the argument elsewhere by Ortega (2018, p. 65) that the lack of dialogue between world Englishes and second language acquisition rests on the "different ontologies of language available in each discipline", on the one hand a pluralist and flexible view of diverse Englishes, on the other hand an essentialist and unquestioned view of language that adheres to received understandings within linguistics. Indeed, Ortega suggests that we have in applied and sociolinguistic fields a basic choice "between essentialist and non-essentialist ontologies of language". If this perhaps overstates the extent to which world Englishes exemplifies a non-essentialist position (it might be argued instead that it operates only with a pluralized vision of language), it nonetheless suggests the commonality of this two-way division between essentialist and non-essentialist approaches to language.

It's perhaps a shame that there is little discussion of World Englishes (WE) in these chapters, if only because the different ontologies proposed by WE and ELF approaches suggest two different ways of getting at diversity: a pluralizing strategy (many Englishes) or a complexifying strategy (diverse English). The WE position made its principal ontological intervention in its move to pluralisation: there are many varieties of English around the world (like national airlines, more or less one per country; Krishnaswamy and Burde, 1998).

Pluralization, however, arguably keeps basic ontologies of English intact, remaining tied epistemologically to linguistic approaches that the global spread of English calls into question (Bruthiaux, 2003; Pennycook, 2007a, b). Aside from those who object to the use of the term 'lingua franca' to describe English – on the interesting though oddly purist grounds that an already-existing language was not what the original term referred to (Kachru, 2005; Phillipson, 2018) – or those who object, more reasonably, to its inability to engage with questions of power and inequality (O'Regan, 2014; Phillipson, 2018), the recent trend has been to focus on ELF as one part of people's more complex multilingual repertoires. So the questions raised here are more complex than simple pluralization – many Englishes – and instead ask us to think about the different kind of thing English may be under different circumstances.

There are several other questions that need to be asked, however, if we are to push further with these ontological questions: the understanding of social construction, the relation between ontology, ideology, and standpoint, and the ontological status of language itself. Most of the chapters in this book operate with some form of binary opposition (even if some aspects are pluralized or placed on a continuum) between either an underlying general language capacity and socially constructed versions of language (English) or between a socially constructed ideal of standard language and real language use that is diverse and complex. There are several reasons for going beyond such observations. Let us consider first the question of social construction. We know that languages, like race and gender, are social constructs, though to say that something is socially constructed does not mean it is not real. For Haslanger (2012), it is crucial to avoid an "anti-realist approach to social categories such as race": race is socially constructed and we need to understand the "reality of social structures and the political importance of recognizing reality" (p. 30). At the same time, accepting the reality of social structures – language, race, or gender – by no means implies either that they have any other underlying biological reality or that they should be socially accepted. Indeed, quite the opposite: In this deeply unjust social world, "this reality must be resisted" (p. 30).

Looking at language from this perspective, and noting that the "fluidity of racial naming is paralleled by the indeterminacy of language naming" (Otheguy et al., 2018, p. 10) – the many disputes over what constitutes a language (internal versus external identification on *Ethnologue*, for example) – it is clear that these are social categorisations. This is not to downplay the importance of racial or linguistic terms – they are of huge consequence for people and how they identify themselves and others – but racial and linguistic terms establish social categorisations, not entities that pre-exist the naming (a *constitutive* rather than a *causal* claim). It is important, however, to turn this observation back onto some of the ways in which distinctions are made in these chapters between mythologised standardised language and real language use. What exactly is the epistemological framework that can draw such a distinction? Standard languages are social constructs but no less real because of this. This is not the realism of old-school sociolinguists, whereby standard English could be described simply as a dialect of English (Trudgill, 1999), nor the realism of realist social theory (Carter and Sealey, 2000), but rather a realism that holds that social constructions are real and that a distinction between unreal standard English and real language use cannot be sustained. While many of the questions about ontologies in this book derive from questions about classrooms and learners, and situate the ontological questions about English within a context of language education and multilingualism, it matters that we are able to take a clear stance not only from an ideological standpoint (we may indeed wish to take a political stand against various realities) but also from an ontological point of view.

This brings us to the second point that throughout almost all the chapters there is a clear ideological commitment to forms of diversity. This is, of course, not a problem in itself – unless one is not committed to diversity or sees in the emphasis on diversity a reluctance to engage with the real politics of difference (Kubota, 2016) – but it raises the question about how we understand ideologies in relation to ontologies. Ontological questions are commonly juxtaposed with epistemological ones – what things are and how we know them to be such. There are ways of being and ways of knowing and these two are related. The problem with the ontology-epistemology distinction in western philosophy is that like much of that history of thought, it views ideas in the abstract, as existing outside people, histories, locations and so on. The division between ideals and instantiations is an old trope of Western epistemology, one that has given us theory and practice, universals and particulars, and epistemology and ontology. To this classical Western framework of being and knowing, we need to add two important dimensions: ideology and standpoint.

By this I mean that we cannot talk about ways of being and knowing without including the ideological or discursive forces that constrain and produce thought or the locus of enunciation (or the question I raised earlier: ontologies for whom?) (Mignolo and Walsh, 2018). This points to the concern that both the standpoints and frameworks here are embedded in a set of philosophies that while claiming universality (or at least not specifying a locus of enunciation) in fact need to be seen in relation to a very particular set of Western or Northern epistemologies (Santos, 2018). This raises an important question about the scope of this volume – despite various excursions into domains outside the United Kingdom, it remains very English oriented. Hall's discussion of the construction of English in relation to nation (ENGLISHRY) obviously looks very different from other perspectives both within the United Kingdom (what does English mean for a girl of Punjabi background born in Birmingham?) and elsewhere (what does English mean for a fisherman from Papua New Guinea or a sex-worker in Thailand?). This is not just a question again of pluralization – the book would be better if it included a greater diversity of standpoints on English – but also an issue that we cannot talk about epistemology and ontology without also including questions of ideology and standpoint.

This brings us to the third, and potentially most important, issue. A number of chapters rely on a notion of language as a universal, species-specific category as a cornerstone to ground other ontologies (sociocultural beliefs). While for some the central question is a relation between different ontological claims to what English actually is, for others the relation is one between a general language capacity (which may or may not reflect external constructions of language) and the socially produced artefacts we call languages. According to Otheguy et al., "no one has denied that languages are ... ontological systems; the point has been all along that the dual ontology of the two separable named languages is anchored in sociocultural beliefs, not in psycholinguistic properties of the underlying system" (2018, p. 4). From this point of view, then, we can recognize that languages are both social constructions and ontological systems, and we can maintain a belief in an underlying system, but the psychological reality of separate languages in the brain is cast into doubt. But what if we push this one step further and ask whether there may not also be good reasons to question the status of an underlying linguistic system?

There are two related reasons for doing so. The first has to do with the questions Canagarajah raises about new materialism and distributed practice. Allied to a questioning of the boundaries between languages proposed from a translanguaging perspective is also a set of questions about the boundaries between language and other material and semiotic possibilities (Canagarajah, 2013; Pennycook, 2017). The point about spatial repertoires and distributed practice is that we move from methodological individualism (each individual is a repository of a shared universal language capacity) to ask what counts as language, what ontological distinctions we make between people and animals, language and the world, language and the body, language and things, and whether we give primacy to presumed universal categories or we see language in terms of distributed practice and therefore resolutely local (Pennycook, 2018). This is not only to follow the lead of usage-based and integrational inversions of the relation between language practices and language systems – languages are the products of social practices (systematicity emerges from social practice) and 'first-order' language use is the condition from which 'second-order' abstractions about languages as objects are derived (Love, 2009) – but also to ask whether there is any good reason to posit an underlying universal language capacity in the first place.

The second line of questions comes from the *ontological turn* in linguistic anthropology. Following the more general ontological turn in anthropology that proposes that we need to consider not only different epistemological positions on the world – different ways of knowing about the world – but also different ontologies – it is not just worldviews but also worlds that may in themselves vary (Viveiros do Castro, 2004; Haalbrad and Pedersen, 2017) – Hauck and Heurich (2018, p. 5) argue that the answer to the question "what is language?" must "remain plural". The "diverse phenomena" they describe across different Amerindian cultures "should not be understood as easily commensurable instances of a general phenomenon 'language'" since they "all may have different linguistic natures". As Course (2018, p. 5) likewise suggests, the idea of 'language' possibly "obscures a fundamental diversity of ultimately irreconcilable practices." From this point of view, the question is not whether two languages may be two different kinds of the same thing (two different instantiations of an underlying language capacity) but whether they may in fact be two different things altogether.

4 Conclusion: Beyond Mono- and Plurilithic Ontologies

To take ontological questions seriously in a way that does not merely reproduce western tropes of thought – ontology versus epistemology (English varies according to different ways of theorizing about it), universal versus particular (there is an underlying capacity with particular instantiations), sociality versus reality (the social constitution of categories can be distinguished from reality) – it is important that we push further with our ontological questions. The very globality of English demands such an ethical and political response to its spread. If language can mean different things to different people, we can no longer assume underlying systems and capacities as universal categories. If we question the ontologies that separate languages and other things, if we look at languages as fully and primarily social, if we ask whose perspectives count in understanding ontologies of English, then we are obliged to ask more than monolithic versus plurilithic questions. Ontological questions suggest we need to dig deeper, to ask whether questions about ontologies of English undermine common beliefs about language and languages in general.

References

Barker, X. (2012). English language as a bully in the Republic of Nauru. In V. Rapatahana and P. Bunce, eds., *English Language as Hydra: Its Impacts on Non-English Language Cultures* (pp. 18–36). Bristol: Multilingual Matters.

Bruthiaux, P. (2003). Squaring the circles: Issues in modeling English worldwide. *International Journal of Applied Linguistics*, 13(2), 159–177.

Canagarajah, S. (2013). *Translingual Practice: Global Englishes and Cosmopolitan Relations*. London: Routledge.

Carter, B. and Sealey, A. (2000). Language, structure and agency: What can realist social theory offer to sociolinguistics? *Journal of Sociolinguistics*, 4(1), 3–20.

Course, M. (2018). Words beyond Meaning in Mapuche Language Ideology. *Language & Communication*. https://doi.org/10.1016/j.langcom.2018.03.007

García, O. and Li Wei. (2014). *Translanguaging: Language, Bilingualism and Education*. Basingstoke: Palgrave Macmillan.

Hall, C. J. (2013). Cognitive contributions to plurilithic views of English and other languages. *Applied Linguistics*, 34, 211–231.

Haslanger, S. (2012). *Resisting Reality: Social Construction and Social Critique*. Oxford: Oxford University Press.

Hauck, J. D. and Heurich, G. O. (2018). Language in the Amerindian Imagination: An Inquiry into Linguistic Natures. *Language and Communication*, 1–8. https://doi.org/10.1016/j.langcom.2018.03.005

Holbraad, M. and Pedersen, M. (2017). *The Ontological Turn: An Anthropological Exposition*. Cambridge: Cambridge University Press.

Kachru, B. (2005). *Asian Englishes: Beyond the Canon*. Hong Kong: Hong Kong University Press.

Kramsch, C. (2015). Applied Linguistics: A theory of the practice. *Applied Linguistics*, 36(4), 454–465.

Krishnaswamy, N. and Burde, A. (1998). *The Politics of Indians' English: Linguistic Colonialism and the Expanding English Empire*. Delhi: Oxford University Press.

Kubota, R. (2016). The multi/plural turn, postcolonial theory, and neoliberal multiculturalism: Complicities and implications for Applied Linguistics. *Applied Linguistics, 37*(4), 474–494. doi: 10.1093/applin/amu045

Lin, A. (2013). Toward paradigmatic change in TESOL methodologies: Building plurilingual pedagogies from the ground up. *TESOL Quarterly, 47*(3), 521–545.

Love, N. (2009). Science, language and linguistic culture. *Language and Communication, 29*, 26–46.

Mignolo, W. and Walsh, C. (2018) *On Decoloniality: Concepts, Analytics, Praxis*. Durham, NC: Duke University Press.

Ober, R. and Bell, J. (2012) English language as juggernaut – Aboriginal English and indigenous languages in Australia. In V. Rapatahana and P. Bunce, eds., *English Language as Hydra: Its Impacts on Non-English Language Cultures* (pp. 60–75). Bristol: Multilingual Matters.

O'Regan, J. (2014). English as a Lingua Franca: An immanent critique. *Applied Linguistics, 35*(5), 533–552.

Ortega, L. (2018). Ontologies of language, second language acquisition and world Englishes. *World Englishes, 37*, 64–79.

Otheguy, R., García, O., and Reid, W. (2018). A Translanguaging View of the Linguistic System of Bilinguals. *Applied Linguistics Review*. doi: https://doi.org/10.1515/applirev-2018-0020

Parakrama, A. (2012). The *malchemy* of English in Sri Lanka: Reinforcing inequality though imposing extra-linguistic value. In V. Rapatahana and P. Bunce, eds., *English Language as Hydra: Its Impacts on Non-English Language Cultures* (pp. 107–132). Bristol: Multilingual Matters.

Pennycook, A. (2007a) *Global Englishes and Transcultural Flows*. London: Routledge.

Pennycook, A. (2007b). The myth of English as an international language. In S. Makoni and A. Pennycook, eds., *Disinventing and Reconstituting Languages* (pp. 90–115). Clevedon: Multilingual Matters.

Pennycook, A. (2008). English as a language always in translation. *European Journal of English Studies, 12*(1), 33–47.

Pennycook, A. (2009). Plurilithic Englishes: Towards a 3D model. In K. Murata and J. Jenkins, eds., *Global Englishes in Asian Contexts: Current and Future Debates* (pp. 194–207). Basingstoke: Palgrave Macmillan.

Pennycook, A. (2016). Politics, power relationships and ELT. In G. Hall, ed., *The Routledge Handbook of English Language Teaching* (pp. 26–37). New York: Routledge.

Pennycook, A. (2017). Translanguaging and semiotic assemblages. *International Journal of Multilingualism, 14*(3), 269–282.

Pennycook, A. (2018). *Posthumanist Applied Linguistics*. London: Routledge.

Pennycook, A. and Otsuji, E. (2015). *Metrolingualism: Language in the City*. London: Routledge.

Phillipson, R. (2018). English, the lingua nullius of global hegemony. In P. A. Kraus and F. Grin, eds., *The Politics of Multilingualism: Europeanisation, Globalisation and Linguistic Governance* (pp. 275–303). Amsterdam: John Benjamins.

Santos, B. de S. (2018). *The End of the Cognitive Empire: The Coming of Age of Epistemologies of the South*. Durham, NC: Duke University Press.

Sartre, J.-P. (1943). *L'être et le néant: essai d'ontologie phénoménologique*. Paris: Gallimard.

Trudgill, P. (1999). Standard English: What it isn't. In T. Bex and R. Watts, eds., *Standard English: The Widening Debate* (pp. 117–128). London: Routledge.

Viveiros de Castro, E. (2004). Exchanging perspectives: The transformation of objects into subjects in Amerindian ontologies. *Common Knowledge*, 10, 463–484.

19 *Using Ontologies of English*

Rachel Wicaksono and Christopher J. Hall

In our introductory chapter, we argued that applied linguistics must be more explicit about the ways in which English is conceptualised in and for the domains of language learning, teaching, and assessment. Now, after eighteen chapters that uncover, advocate, and contest beliefs about the nature of 'English' in a range of contexts and from a range of perspectives, we take stock of the project and consider its uses. We don't have the space here to reference all the arguments and evidence put forward by the authors of these chapters, but we will emphasise those points that we feel have helped to meet the aims of the book. Naturally, we give particular consideration to Pennycook's companion commentary in the previous chapter.

We start by reiterating the goals of the project. The seminar at York St John University that led to this book was not, of course, intended to 'settle' the ontological status of English, but rather to surface some of our existing conceptualisations, expose their similarities and differences, question the evidence on which our beliefs were based, and conceptualise anew. Given the choice to focus specifically on the entity we call 'the English language', and understandings of this entity in educational contexts, we sought to identify, interrogate, and ultimately shed light on these conceptualisations in ways that would potentially be useful to people working in relevant professional domains, especially teachers, materials writers, curriculum and test developers, and policy makers. The analysis was to be useful not in the sense of offering ready-made solutions to problems, but by providing prompts for reflection that could underpin actions in stakeholders' own educational contexts.

At the seminar, we proposed four key questions to guide the discussion, all of which were motivated by a desire to make theory *useful*:

1. How can an explicit focus and new thinking on ontologies of English challenge the monolithic assumptions pervading educational policy and practice?

2. What status and role should the concept of 'Standard English' have in language education?
3. To what extent are cognitively oriented and social-oriented plurilithic approaches compatible?
4. What can scholars of L1 and L2 Englishes learn from each other in making explicit their ontologies of English?

Additionally, two general objectives were identified by the assembled delegates in the final discussion session as crucial ones for Applied Linguistics, again reflecting an impulse to be useful, to *all* stakeholders:

5. To reflect on what different ontologies of English imply for, and how they are shaped by, educational policy and practice, multilingualism, marginalised and dominant groups, and economic/political ideologies.
6. To take a more activist stance to challenge dominant monolithic conceptualisations of English, chiefly by promoting awareness of users' actual knowledge and practices, and the alternative ontologies that these imply.

In what follows, our comments are framed by these original questions and objectives, and are made also in the light of the further project advocated by Pennycook in his chapter.

Pennycook (this volume) acknowledges the importance of thinking about ontological questions about English in the context of actual classrooms and learners. He argues that the separation of 'theoretical debate' from 'pragmatism' in the past has allowed ideas about 'what it is we are actually dealing with' to diverge in scholarly and professional contexts. This dangerous (and largely un-noticed) divergence of focus has, according to Pennycook, undermined the potential for useful collaboration between (scholarly) 'socio- and applied linguists' and (professional) classroom teachers. The theoretical linguists who traditionally engaged with ontological questions tended to conceptualise English and other named languages as abstract symbolic systems, independent of actual instantiations in minds and events, whereas teachers are surrounded by the actual speech, writing, or signs that reflect and create their environment and/but tend to think of named languages like English as single 'standard' linguistic codes that exclude 'non-standard' varieties and that are used best by their 'native speakers'. Hall (this volume) proposes a taxonomy of ways of thinking about 'the English language' that causally connects these different ideas, traces their history, and considers their consequences. Chapters in Parts II, III, and IV reflect on what different ontologies of English imply for, and how they are shaped by, educational policy and practice; and chapters in Parts V and VI focus on how new thinking might challenge traditional assumptions about 'English' in broader domains.

Pennycook's uses of the term *theoretical* in 'theoretical linguistics' and 'theoretical debate' highlight an enduring and important challenge for applied linguistics. The first use creates a contrast with applied linguistics, in which debates about language are rooted in the 'real world' context of English language education, as opposed to 'theoretical linguistics' that is characterised as being devoted to the description of an imagined abstraction. 'Theoretical debate', on the other hand, implies a critical discussion of ideas, assumptions, and beliefs in order to better understand why the 'real world' is (thought to be) as it is. As Pennycook suggests, and as this book demonstrates, 'theoretical debate' has (belatedly) commenced in applied linguistics, with practitioners, and scholars who work closely with them, asking themselves questions about the nature of the conceptual entity they are teaching and testing, and how this entity relates to the multilingual practices unfolding in the globalised world around them.

The collection and analysis of empirical data have demonstrated what many language teachers have always known: that learning and using 'English' in the classroom (inevitably for L2 and regularly also for L1) occurs as part of a multilingual environment, whether this is manifested only cognitively/internally or also socially/interactively. The complex plurilingual patterning of a typical language classroom challenges traditional boundaries between languages, and between language and other ways of communicating. In many cases, teachers have developed strategies to resist the use of other languages beyond the target one (demanding or pleading with their students to speak English only, for example) but have embraced the blurring of boundaries between language and other forms of semiosis (often using pictures, drawings, gestures, and facial expressions to convey meaning). Evidence of English language use outside the classroom has confirmed that what we are actually dealing with is communication via a multilingual/multimodal, hybrid blend of sociocultural artefacts. Chapters in Parts II and V of this book use evidence of actual language use in classroom and lingua franca contexts to help work out 'what it is we are actually dealing with' in these environments, and touch on the extent to which cognitively oriented and socially oriented plurilithic approaches are compatible.

Pennycook (this volume) rightly highlights the usefulness of ontological analysis for related questions about why we value some (varieties/uses of) language(s) more highly than others. These beliefs about language (language ideologies) help to explain why English is part of complex local contexts of power and struggle for power. Thus, careful consideration of what 'English' is can undermine assumptions about why (some versions and some uses of) 'it' is perceived as better than others. Thinking about ontologies, and then working our way towards thinking about ideologies, has the potential practical application of pointing to action, as chapters in Parts III and IV of this book show. In this way, we can create opportunities for a more activist stance to challenge dominant monolithic conceptualisations of English, in the learning and teaching contexts in which we work – an example of the potential practical use of 'theory'. So the two questions about what (people believe) English *is* (ontology) versus what English *does* (ideology) are indeed related, in that it helps to know what we mean by 'English' before we explore the consequences of our understanding(s) of it in practice. But the questions are (obviously) different: it is, we believe, legitimate to consider the ontological status of English as a separable component in the analysis of related ideologies (cf. Sharpe, 1974; Hall and Cunningham, in prep.).

Discussions of ideological, epistemological, and ontological issues in applied linguistics have frequently gone hand-in-hand with criticism of cognitive approaches to language (e.g. Firth and Wagner, 1997; Thorne and Lantolf, 2007; Pennycook, 2010, this volume; Canagarajah, 2013, this volume). It is argued that 'representational' views of language are antithetical to, rather than complementary with, those in which language is conceptualised as social practice. Languages as symbolic systems are seen as artefactual, only emerging from social practice, rather than as dynamic resources that also feed into it. Linguistic resources are seen as inseparable from other semiotic resources, rather than as ontologically distinct yet only meaningful when embedded in social practice. It is hard to reconcile such beliefs with the abundant evidence from cognitive neuropsychology for the systematic and perduring (but mutable) representation of language resources in individual long-term memory and their independent contribution to meaning- making in use. Take, for example, the consistent and compelling data from neuroimaging studies in recent decades. Measurements of neural activity such as event-related potentials (ERPs) have isolated patterns such as the so-called 'N400' peak, which is reliably observed in cases where individuals experience semantically inappropriate words in utterances (e.g. *bake* in *The cats won't eat/ bake the food Mary leaves them*), but not in the case of incongruities with non-linguistic input (e.g. music) or with grammatical or phonological incongruities (Kutas and Federmeier, 2000). A second and contrasting characteristic neural pattern is the P600 peak, which is triggered by grammatically (as opposed to semantically) anomalous words in utterances (e.g. *eating* in *The cats won't eat/eating the food Mary leaves them*; Osterhout and Holcomb, 1992). Studies of mental operations involving different kinds of resources (linguistic and non-linguistic) also demonstrate the involvement of neural substrates that are distinct for modality (e.g. Monti et al., 2012, on language vs. algebra). Such evidence is strongly suggestive of coordinated brain processes that are associated uniquely with linguistic, rather than other semiotic, resources.

To such 'double dissociations' in processing by unimpaired language users can be added cases of selective impairment or loss, in which one component or feature of language is affected and another spared. Examples include (1) people with aphasia who have impairments that selectively affect either verbs or nouns, but are not attributable to semantic features (Luzzatti et al., 2006); (2) dissociations in production between impaired access to the 'mental dictionary' in Alzheimer's disease, and to the 'mental grammar' in Parkinson's disease (Ullman et al., 1997); and (3) dissociations in ability to use recursion (embedding one thing in a thing of the same type) in language (e.g. sentence embedding like *My dog [chased the cat [which ate the cheese]]]*) but not in logical reasoning (e.g. perspective embedding like *To my surprise, she was happy*), and *vice versa* (e.g. in people with aphasia vs. people with Alzheimer's disease: Bánréti et al., 2016). Taken together, these abilities and disabilities strongly suggest that the basic constructs of theoretical linguistics (syntax, rules [as regularities], words, verbs, nouns, embedded clauses, etc.) have physical correlates in brains that can be distinguished from those that pertain to general systems of meaning, reasoning processes, or other semiotic processing domains. It is this set of cognitive resources that Hall (this volume) refers to as the LANGUAGE CAPACITY and, with other resources and processes, underpins LANGUAGING.

In her review of perceived incompatibilities between the fields of Second Language Acquisition and World Englishes, Ortega (2018, p. 69) points out that the former does not preclude a social–cultural understanding of English (or other languages learnt after the first). Furthermore, pointing to usage-based linguistics (cf. Eskildsen, this volume), she correctly observes that there is no need for a view of language as social practice to preclude simultaneous focus on its cognitive status in individuals. Indeed, we would argue that usage-based approaches provide a theoretical framework in which the two perspectives can be fruitfully combined – in other words, there is no need to choose between them. English is both social practice and (sedimented/entrenched) mental resource. Returning to the inevitable 'pragmatism' of applied linguistics, we recognise another reason why cognitively oriented perspectives, when formulated in usage-based terms, can be useful to practitioners involved in English learning, teaching, and testing. This is the reality that the linguistic resources of English tend to be developed (L2) or extended (L1) by learners in classroom contexts, and that the resources needed and/or expected will typically involve exonormative (effectively N-LANGUAGE) constraints (cf. Harder, this volume). To be able to contest the ideologies underpinning this orthodoxy, practitioners need ways of understanding learning that don't dismiss or marginalise the necessity of grammar (as regularity rather than regulation), and other linguistic resources, in LANGUAGING.

As we said at the beginning of this chapter, our aim in the York St John seminar and in this book was to identify and interrogate conceptualisations of English in ways that were potentially *useful* to people working in relevant professional domains, especially teachers, materials writers, curriculum and test developers, and policy makers. For actual solutions to specific problems to be successful, they need to be designed from the bottom up, by the people experiencing the problem (Widdowson, 1990). Hence, rather than offering solutions, we aimed to provide accessible and relevant prompts for reflection; reflection that could, and should, impel appropriate and timely actions in specific educational contexts (Pollard, 2002). While we agree that there are many interesting and useful questions about what English is thought to be, and thought to do, in other contexts (Pennycook, this volume), in order to maximise the usefulness of our discussion to teachers, materials writers, curriculum and test developers, and policy makers, we necessarily focused on educational contexts.

In a previous publication, we considered the usefulness of engaging in philosophical reflection for language professionals, specifically lexicographers dealing with the objective nature and existence of words, suggesting that (unlike theoretical linguists), "... *applied* linguists can't afford to be detained by ontological questions" (Hall et al., 2017, p. 249). Even in the very short space of time between writing that claim and this conclusion, our ideas about the usefulness of ontological questions for language professionals have changed – if not substantially, then at least in emphasis. While lexicographers, teachers, and other language professionals all have their day jobs to do, we think reflection on 'what it is we are actually dealing with' should also form part of what they regularly do. Of course, English teachers have to teach English, but there is no avoiding an idea of what 'English' is, whether or not they find time to identify and interrogate their corresponding ontological commitments. So on reflection, "detain" sounds too negative. In order to avoid the separation of 'theoretical debate' from 'pragmatism' that has allowed ideas about 'what it is we are actually dealing with' to diverge in scholarly and professional contexts (Pennycook, this volume), we now advocate that all language professionals should reflect on (versions of) the questions posed at the beginning of this chapter. Furthermore, we think that there is value for language professionals in working with stakeholders (students, test-takers, and individuals affected by English language policy making, for example), to surface *their* ontologies of English and explore areas of overlap, contradictions, and the practical implications of their theories.

How best to do this is the subject of another book.

References

Bánréti, Z., Hoffmann, I., and Vincze, V. (2016). Recursive subsystems in aphasia and Alzheimer's disease: Case studies in syntax and Theory of Mind. *Frontiers in Psychology*, 7, 405.

Canagarajah, S. (2013). *Translingual Practice: Global Englishes and Cosmopolitan Relations*. London: Routledge.

Firth, A. and Wagner, J. (1997). On discourse, communication, and (some) fundamental concepts in SLA research. *Modern Language Journal*, 81(3), 285–300.

Hall, C. J., Smith, P. H., and Wicaksono, R. (2017). *Mapping Applied Linguistics: A Guide for Students and Practitioners*. 2nd edn, London: Routledge.

Kutas, M. and Federmeier, K. D. (2000). Electrophysiology reveals semantic memory use in language comprehension. *Trends in Cognitive Sciences*, 4, 463–470.

Luzzatti, C., Aggujaro, S., and Crepaldi, D. (2006). Verb-noun double dissociation in aphasia: Theoretical and neuroanatomical foundations. *Cortex*, 42(6), 875–883.

Monti, M. M., Parsons, L. M., and Osherson, D. N. (2012). Thought beyond language: Neural dissociation of algebra and natural language. *Psychological Science*, 23(8), 914–922.

Ortega, L. (2018). Ontologies of language, second language acquisition and world Englishes. *World Englishes*, 37, 64–79.

Osterhout, L. and Holcomb, P. J. (1992). Event-related brain potentials elicited by syntactic anomaly. *Journal of Memory and Language*, 31(6), 785–806.

Pennycook, A. (2010). *Language as a Local Practice*. London: Routledge.

Pollard, A. (2002). *Reflective Teaching: Effective and Evidence-Informed Professional Practice*. London: Continuum.

Sharpe, R. A. (1974). Ideology and ontology. *Philosophy of the Social Sciences*, 4, 55–64.

Thorne, S. L. and Lantolf, J. P. (2007). A linguistics of communicative activity. In S. Makoni and A. Pennycook, eds., *Disinventing and Reconstituting Languages* (pp. 170–195). Clevedon: Multilingual Matters.

Ullman, M. T., Corkin, S., Coppola, M. et al. (1997). A neural dissociation within language: Evidence that the mental dictionary is part of declarative memory, and that grammatical rules are processed by the procedural system. *Journal of Cognitive Neuroscience*, 9(2), 266–276.

Widdowson, H. G. (1990). *Aspects of Language Teaching*. Oxford: Oxford University Press.

Index

A level, 98, 102, 117, 211, 221, 223–227
AAVE, 81, 154
accent, 47, 54, 88, 96, 98, 136, 145–149, 160, 214, 282
accommodation, xvi, 53, 55, 93, 174–175, 181, 193, 199, 258
accuracy, 14, 20, 27, 30–33, 144, 170, 200, 203, 274, 289, 339, *See also* correctness
actor network theory, 295, 297
adult needs, 101, 107–109, 113, 117–118
agency, 119, 123, 131, 242–243, 246, 267, 296, 307–308, 310, 312
alignment, 113–115, 117, 307–308
Alzheimer's Disease, 372
Aphasia, 372
applied linguistics, 4–7, 10, 13, 15, 101, 142–143, 253–254, 256–258, 274–276, 288, 290, 299, 304, 355, 368–372
appropriateness, 171, 182, 188
Aptis test, 205
ASEAN, 236–240, 248, 263
assemblage, 10, 217, 295, 297, 299, 307–311, 313
assessment, 92–93, 147, 150, 165–183, 187–206, 209–227, 254, 265–267, 278, 340–342, 358, 370, 373
Austin, J. L., 299–300

beliefs, 3, 5–6, 20, 32, 89–94, 113, 116, 118, 133, 142–143, 145–146, 154, 199, 254, 266, 310, 338, 349, 357, 363, 365, 368, 370–371
Blommaert, J., 300, 303, 311, 347, 349
Bloomfield, L., 45
Bourdieu, P., 44–45, 145
bricolage, 10, 217, 305–306
British Association of Applied Linguistics (BAAL), 7, 84
British Council, 205–206
Bullock, A., 114, 327
Byram, M., 181, 259–260

Cambridge Learner Corpus, 172
Cambridge School of English, 109
Canagarajah, S., 10, 14, 23–24, 29, 62, 69, 73, 87, 90–91, 169, 173–174, 204, 216, 257–261, 268, 295–313, 317, 320–321, 326, 336–337, 347, 356, 359, 363, 371
child language acquisition, 61
Chomsky, N., 5, 17–18, 46, 296, 306
clarification, 177, 181, 198, 258
code mixing, 234
code switching, 236, 241–243
Cognitive Grammar, 59, 61
collaborative word search, 65, 67
Common European Framework of Reference (CEFR), 9, 165, 168–178, 180, 182, 200, 205
communication
  cross-cultural, 50, 54, 255, *See also* transcultural communication
  intercultural, 169, 176, 181, 233, 253–254, 269, 345
  intercultural communication. *See also* intercultural awareness (ICA)
  strategies, 165, 180, 268
  transcultural, 253–255
community
  norms, 48, 50
  of practice, 68, 105, 113, 240, 243, 245, 248
competence, 10, 41, 43, 81, 84–86, 88, 90–93, 126, 165, 169, 181, 183, 205, 213, 236, 253–254, 296, 299, 301, 304–309, 324, 336, 338
  communicative, 10, 31, 150, 173–175, 181, 253–254, 258–262, 266–268, 300, 304, 312, 358
  discourse, 259
  interactional, 59, 64, 68, 74, 205
  intercultural, 174–175, 181, 253, 259, 263, 265, 268, 345
  linguistic, 86, 153, 258, 341
  performative, 259–261

377

378 Index

competence (cont.)
  strategic, 173–177
  symbolic, 259–261
comprehensibility, 43, 149–150
conscious learning, 10, 347–349
consciousness, 14, 22, 26, 147–148, 305, 338
constitutive norms. *See* norms
constructions, 8, 23, 30, 59–61, 64, 70, 73–74, 155, 219, 362–363
contact zone, 248, 324, 327
conversation analysis, 8, 41, 59, 61–66, 70, 196, 279
corpus, 9, 18, 23, 28, 41, 64, 88, 165, 171–172, 176, 179, 182, 301, 309
correctness, 14, 26–27, 32, 43–44, 92, 144, 173, 182, 282, 285, 336, *See also* accuracy
coursebooks. *See* textbooks
Cox, B., 106–108, 110–117, 126–129, 135, 222
creole, 51, 92, 156, 277
cultural analysis, 107, 110–111, 113–114, 117–119, 127, 130
cultural heritage, 8–10, 107–108, 110–113, 118–119, 127, 130, 222

deficit model, 142–144, 146, 148–149, 153
Dewey, J., 112, 123, 263, 267
diachronic perspective, 46
dialect, 20, 26, 92, 145–147, 150, 152–155, 204, 225, 240, 246, 275, 277, 316, 343, 362
dictionary, 25, 32, 80, 126, 372
discourse
  analysis, 9, 154, 171–173, 182, 217, 279
  competence, 259
  management, 194–197
  marker, 133, 282
distributed practice, 304–305, 359, 363–364
Dixon, J., 102, 105–107, 111–114, 127, 133
double dissociation, 45, 372

educational policy, 4, 10, 29, 119, 124, 144, 153, 328, 368–370
E-language, 17–20, 22, 24–25, 27, 173, 178
emplacement, 307–308
enenglishing, 24–25
English as a Lingua Franca (ELF), 5, 9, 29, 40, 49–54, 56, 80, 83, 94, 233–249, 253–269, 273, 356–358, 360

English as a Second Language (ESL), 148, 316
English as an Additional Language (EAL), 9–10, 142–156, 315–329
English for Specific Purposes (ESP), 9
English Language Teaching (ELT), 3, 5, 8, 10, 15, 80–95, 148, 236, 253–254, 273–290, 335–349, 355, 358
English literature, 8, 104, 108–111, 125, 130, 134, 211, 222–224, 226
Englishing, 23–26, 28–32, 88, 93, 95, 166–168, 174, 183, 326
entextualization, 301, 303
entrenchment, 22–24, 300, 305, 310, 372
epistemology, 6, 69, 122–124, 295–297, 347, 362–364
Ethnologue, 362
ethnomethodological conversation analysis (EMCA), 59, 61–62
event-related potentials (ERP), 371
Expanding Circle, 29, 83, 88

First Certificate in English (FCE), 192
flat ontology, 10, 295, 298–301, 303–305, 307, 309–313, 320
fluency, 200, 203, 284, 286
form-meaning pairing, 59–61
funds of knowledge, 153, 323

General Certificate of Secondary Education (GCSE), 102–103, 114, 131, 133–134, 210, 221–227
genre, 18, 128, 131, 133, 136, 172, 179, 215, 235, 240, 242–246, 248, 299–301, 305–306, 309–310, 317, 345, 349, 359
Global English, 8, 40, 48–53, 257, 263–266, 274, 355
globalization, 311
grammar, 25, 28, 88, 102, 117, 127, 130, 136, 194–196, 217–221, 226–227, 235, 266, 274, 279, 282–286, 296, 300, 306, 309, 311, 337–338, 373
Great Tradition, 110, 129, 131, 135

habitat factor, 243, 246–248
habitus, 145, 243, 246
Hall, C. J., 3–11, 13–32, 40–41, 46, 49, 52, 67, 80, 82–83, 87–88, 91–93, 142–144, 146, 166–167, 172–173, 178, 188, 190–191, 209, 212, 214, 218, 220,

233–235, 253–254, 258–259, 261–262, 265, 267, 273, 275–277, 284, 287–289, 311, 322, 324–325, 327–328, 336, 338, 348, 356–357, 363, 368–374

identity, 40, 44–45, 50, 52, 90, 122, 135–137, 152, 225, 235, 256, 275, 282, 309, 316, 335, 339, 346–348
  group, 19–20
  national, 6–7, 21–22, 24–27, 32, 80–84, 238–239
ideology, 5–6, 10, 53, 101–102, 123–124, 132, 137, 146, 150, 214, 295, 311, 329, 361–363, 371
idiolect, 17, 23, 142, 167, 326
I-English, 21–33, 142–143, 322
I-language, 16–19, 21–23, 27, 29–32, 87, 91, 144, 167–168, 174, 177, 182, 188, 191, 322, 324, 326
Inner Circle, 82, 84, 88–89
intelligibility, 10, 54, 87–90, 169, 181–182, 201–204, 247, 273–276, 278–279, 281–290, 312
interaction, 8, 31, 41, 59–74, 87, 89–91, 166–168, 170, 174–175, 179–181, 191, 194, 196, 199–200, 203–205, 239, 256–257, 261, 265, 279–283, 287–289, 301–302, 304–305, 308, 311–312, 320, 322–325, 348
intercultural awareness (ICA), 265, *See also* competence, intercultural
International English Language Testing System (IELTS), 179–180, 194, 266, 278, 340, 344–346
intersubjectivity, 62–63, 65

Jamaica, 277, 289
Japan, 10, 83, 148, 192, 199–202, 204, 273–275, 280, 283, 285, 287, 289, 308
Japan International Co-operation Agency (JICA), 273–274, 278–280, 282–290
Jenkins, J., 52, 55, 82–83, 88, 193, 199, 255, 258, 274

Kachru, B. B., 50, 52, 82, 88, 275, 278
Kenya, 29, 279–280, 282, 287, 289
Key Stage 1, 2, 3, 4, 5, 127–131, 134, 210–211, 217–227
Kingman, J., 116–117
Knowledge about Language (KAL), 117
Kramsch, C., 259, 339

Labov, W., 43–44
Language Acquisition Device, 306
language as system. *See* P-language
language attitudes, 144, 147–148, 154–155, 295
language capacity, 7, 13–18, 21–25, 32, 357–359, 361, 363–364, 372
Language in the National Curriculum (LINC), 117, 220
languaging, 19–25, 27, 30, 67, 88, 144, 166–169, 171–178, 181–183, 191, 196, 220, 237, 246, 249, 287, 323–324, 326, 337, 348, 372–373
langue, 19, 40, 43, 296, *See also* parole
Leavis, F. R., 109–113
L-English, 23, 25–27, 29–30, 32, 146
Limited English Proficiency (LEP), 143, 316
lingua franca, 5, 7, 9–10, 23–24, 29, 40, 49–50, 65, 80, 83, 88–89, 94, 142, 165, 169, 173–183, 191, 205, 233–243, 245, 248, 253, 255, 261–263, 267, 273–274, 278–280, 283, 335, 345, 356, 358, 361, 370
listening, 104, 109, 111–112, 114–115, 122, 126, 129–131, 150, 169–171, 179, 192–196, 199, 215, 222–224, 227, 287, 289, 343
literacy, 26, 103–104, 109–110, 112, 125–127, 136, 153, 211–213, 215, 218, 240, 307, 347
logical positivism, 39
London School, 104, 111, 114

Makoni, S., 14, 20
Malawi, 285
Marshall Islands, 284
mediated learning experience, 183
mediation scales, 170, 175
memory, 15, 371
  declarative, 29–31
  procedural, 29–31
metrolingualism, 257
middle class. *See* socio-economic status
migration, 81, 315–318, 320, 323–325, 327–329
miscommunication, 24, 198
mobility, 260, 309, 311, 335–349, 357–358
  mobile learners, 10, 315–329
  mobile orientation, 10, 315–329
  social mobility, 119, 152

monolingualism, 236, 240, 296, 315–317, 320–322, 329
monolithism, 14, 20, 26, 28–29, 32, 45, 47, 50, 53, 91–93, 115, 187, 254, 273, 276, 287, 301–303, 336, 340, 342, 348, 357–360, 365, 368, 371
moral panic, 147
multilingualism, 86, 150, 225, 233, 235–237, 253, 301, 315–318, 321, 329, 362, 369
multimodality, 222, 225, 298
multi-word expression, 61, 70

named language, 5, 10, 20, 248, 363, 369, *See also* N-language
naming practices, 92
nation, 14–15, 19–22, 24–27, 32, 49–50, 81, 102–104, 109, 119, 213, 255–256, 259, 264, 301, 341, 363, *See also* identity, national
National Curriculum for English, 106, 115–116, 131, 135, 210
National Literacy Strategy, 115, 117, 126
nativeness, 80–95, 266, *See also* N-language. *See also* N-ENGLISH
negotiation (of meaning), 174, 181–182, 205, 234, 256, 259–260, 262, 310, 315, 323, 325, 345
N-LANGUAGE, 25–33, 142–143, 145–146, 151, 155, 209, 322, 325–327, *See also* Standard English
neuropsychology, 371
new materialism, 295, 297–298, 363
N-ENGLISH, 19–21, 26–27, 31–32, 91, 166–168, 178, 214, 220, 235, 327, 373, *See* nativeness. *See also* N-ENGLISH. *See also* standardisation. *See also* Standard Language Ideology
non-nativeness. *See* nativeness
non-standardness, 3, 27–28, 32, 47–49, 143, 165, 167, 170, 177, 277, 282, 287, 289, 321, 369
norms. *See also* N-LANGUAGE
  constitutive, 22, 27, 44, 55
  regulative, 22, 27, 31

Ofqual (Office of Qualifications and Examinations Regulation), 209
Ofsted (Office for Standards in Education), 114–116, 134, 155, 221
Outer Circle, 29, 82, 88

parole, 40, 43, 296, *See also* langue
Pearson Test of English Academic (PTE Academic), 179–180
P-ENGLISH, 27–33, 212
Pennycook, A., 20, 23, 28, 49–50, 165, 257, 300, 322, 340, 355–365, 368–371, 374
performance, 33, 41, 43, 93, 115, 180, 188–196, 200, 260, 296, 307, 311, 336, *See also* competence
performative competence. *See* competence
performativity, 299
Personal Growth model, 106, 113
phonics, 211–214, 219
phonology, 17, 89, 148, 169, 202, 225, 262, 306
pidgins, 51, 156
P-language, 18–19, 26–32, 40, 166–167, 173, 178, 218, 220, *See also* system, language as
plurilingualism, 165, 169, 173–177, 181, 237, 253, 320, 356, 358, 370, *See also* multilingualism. *See also* translanguaging
plurilithism, 11, 14, 93, 234, 248, 267, 273, 276, 278, 339, 356–365, 369–370, *See also* monolithism
policy, 3–4, 6, 9–11, 13, 26, 84, 94, 105, 117, 119, 123, 125–128, 135–137, 142, 146, 152–154, 175, 211, 239, 248, 253–255, 268–269, 311, 316–321, 323, 326, 328, 349, 356, 368–370, 373–374
polysemy, 14, 26, 125, 316–317
posthumanism, 295
post-methods approach, 262
post-normative approach, 263, 267
pragmatics, 41
pragmatism, 355, 369, 372, 374
prestige, 43–45, 47–49, 55, 145, 240
proficiency, 85–86, 88, 90, 143, 173–177, 179, 181, 187, 193–194, 196, 199–201, 203, 274, 284, 300, 308–309, 316, 319, 321, 326, 328, 336, 340–345
pronunciation, 20, 54, 143, 149, 152, 168, 187, 193, 200, 202–204, 214, 236, 274, 337–338, 346

Quality Assurance Agency (QAA), 125, 131
Queen's English, 53, 55
Quine, W., 4–5

reading, 109–111, 114–115, 124–137, 211–216, 219, 222–224, 227, 301–303
realist social theory, 362
Received Pronunciation (RP), 214
register, 22–24, 28, 30, 170, 175, 235, 246, 306, 309–310, 328
reification, 258
repair, 62–67, 69, 72, 174–177, 181, 197–199
repertoire, 154, 174, 239, 241, 245–246, 301, 315, 322, 328, 342–344, 349
  cognitive, 8
  communicative, 10, 243
  linguistic, 10, 73, 87, 91, 155, 233–234, 236, 277, 321, 324–326, 349, 356, 359
  multilingual, 236, 242, 329, 356, 361
  semiotic, 74
  spatial, 300–301, 310, 359, 364
representationalism, 296, 300
rhizome, 10, 306–307

Saussure, F. de, 19, 295–296
scales, 9, 144–145, 169–171, 173, 175, 199–203, 257, 301, 303–304, 308–311
schema, 59–61, 64, 70, 74, 247
School Subject English (SSE), 8–9, 101–119, 122–138, 356, 358
Searle, J., 5, 21, 42
second language acquisition (SLA), 63–64, 69, 146, 150, 275, 308, 360
sedimentation. *See* entrenchment
Seidlhofer, B., 49–50, 52, 89, 233, 235–236, 246–247, 255, 274
semantics, 5, 60, 225
semiotic resource, 24, 64, 68, 260, 296–303, 305–306, 308, 313, 371–372
semiotics, 60, 63, 74, 217, 225, 304, 308, 311, 337, 364, 372
Shakespeare, W., 114, 123, 130, 136
Shelley, M., 122–124, 128, 137–138
Simple View of Reading (SVR), 212, 215–216, 219
social action, 8, 24, 59–60, 62, 64–65, 68, 73–74, 130, 359
social constructionism, 39
social justice, 119
social practice, English as, xvii, 7, 10, 23, 33, 39, 46, 69, 235, 247, 299, 312, 335, 337, 347, 358, 364, 371–372, *See also* languaging

socio-economic status, 62, 104, 111, 147, 152–153, 158, 258, 262
sociolinguistics, 41, 44, 48, 151, 279, 349
space. *See* spatiality
SPaG (spelling, punctuation and grammar), 218–221
spatiality, 62, 69, 295, 298, 300–303, 305, 310, 317, 322, 324–325, 329
speaking, 47, 52, 54, 64, 82, 89–90, 94, 104, 107, 109, 111–112, 114–115, 126, 129, 131, 146, 152, 170, 180–182, 187–188, 190–196, 199–201, 203–205, 212, 222–224, 227, 235, 238, 240–242, 245–246, 263, 282, 285–286, 336, 338, 349
speech event, 234, 240, 242–245, 248
spelling, 20, 54, 65, 102, 126, 136, 143, 152, 211, 213–214, 216–219
spoken language. *See* speaking
Standard Attainment Tests (SATs), 210, 218, 221
Standard English, 4–8, 14, 25–33, 45–48, 52, 54–55, 101, 109, 130, 142–156, 318, 326, 336–344, 347, 349, 357, 369, *See also* N-ENGLISH, standardisation, Standard Language Ideology
Standard Language Ideology, 6, 146, 154, *See also* N-LANGUAGE
standardisation, 6, 143, 338, *See also* N-LANGUAGE
Standards and Testing Agency, 209, 217, 219
strategic competence. *See* competence
strategic essentialism, 309
strategies, 312, 370
  classroom, 327
  communication, 24, 90, 165, 173–177
  language learning, 82
  negotiation, 315, 325
  spelling, 136
  task achievement, 93
structuralism, 295–297, 306–307, 311, 339
study abroad, 10, 315, 335–338, 342–349, 357
superdiversity, 257
symbolic competence. *See* competence
syntax, 60, 91, 262, 372

target language, 143, 165, 190, 200
teacher education, 8, 92–95, 115, 117, 146, 154, 263, 265, 267, 288–289

Index

teacher recruitment, 80, 84–85
teacher training. *See* teacher education
TEFL. *See* ELT
TESOL. *See* English Language Teaching (ELT)
Test of English as a Foreign Language (TOEFL), 179–180, 266, 345
Test of English for Academic Purposes (TEAP), 192, 199–201, 203–205
testing. *See* assessment
textbooks, 10, 87, 209, 286, 336–342
theorisation, 4
Tomasello, M., 42, 62
trajectory, 61, 323–326, 328
transcultural communication, 253–259, 262, 264–268, 358
translanguaging, 142, 165, 174–176, 178, 180–183, 254, 257, 363, *See also* translingual practice
translingual
  approach, 254, 257
  capacity, 308
  orientation, 299, 321
  practice, 311
  turn, 355–356
Trinity Integrated Skills in English (ISE), 179, 205

unstandardised English, 9
usage-based linguistics (UBL), 59–74, 359, 364, 372–373

validity (testing), 193, 200–201, 206
values, 44, 46, 103, 107, 126, 133, 203, 239, 276, 298, 300, 316, 322, 339, 346, 359
variation, linguistic, 28, 40, 44–49, 51–54, 64, 73, 87, 143, 148, 182, 214, 224, 234–235, 237, 239, 247–248, 253, 276–278, 339, 343
variety, language, 9, 20, 29, 32, 45, 47–49, 52–54, 89, 92, 143–144, 146–147, 154–155, 183, 188, 191–192, 198, 204–205, 264, 275, 287, 316, 338, 340–344
vocabulary, 30, 65–66, 129–130, 149, 153, 173–175, 194–196, 266, 281–283, 287, 324, 338
VOICE (Vienna Oxford International Corpus of English), 50, 89

Widdowson, H. G., 246, 259, 261, 275, 277, 288, 341, 373
word gap, 153
working class. *See* socio-economic status
World Englishes, 5, 29, 82, 88–90, 92, 142, 191, 204–206, 275, 343, 358, 360–361, 372
writing, 18, 24, 54, 66, 69, 81, 88, 101, 109, 112, 114–115, 125–137, 146, 152, 168, 215, 218–219, 222–225, 227, 240, 301–306, 308, 329, 344, 369, 373
written language. *See* writing